SARDINIA

ELEVATION

1800m
1500m
1200m
900m
600m
300m
0

CAGLIARI
Sardinia's only true city,
with its captivating mix of quarters,
imperious walls and great food

NORA
A well-preserved
Classical Roman port town

COSTA VERDE
Some of the island's best-preserved
and most stunning beaches

MEDITERRANEAN SEA

MARE DI SARDEGNA

Sardinia
1st edition – June 2003

Published by
Lonely Planet Publications Pty Ltd ABN 36 005 607 983
90 Maribyrnong St, Footscray, Victoria 3011, Australia

Lonely Planet Offices
Australia Locked Bag 1, Footscray, Victoria 3011
USA 150 Linden St, Oakland, CA 94607
UK 72 – 82 Rosebery Ave, London EC1R 4RW
France 1 rue du Dahomey, 75011 Paris

Photographs
Many of the images in this guide are available for licensing from
Lonely Planet Images.
w www.lonelyplanetimages.com

Front cover photograph
Costa Smeralda, Sardinia, Italy (Paolo Curto, The Image Bank)

ISBN 1 74059 033 3

text & maps © Lonely Planet Publications Pty Ltd 2003
photos © photographers as indicated 2003

Printed by The Bookmaker International Ltd
Printed in China

Although the authors and Lonely Planet try to make the information as accurate as possible, we accept no responsibility for any loss, injury or inconvenience sustained by anyone using this book.

Sardinia

Damien Simonis

LONELY PLANET PUBLICATIONS
Melbourne • Oakland • London • Paris

ARCIPELAGO DI LA MADDALENA
Seven magical islands strewn
across the deep blue sea

GOLFO DI OROSEI
Water of the most extraordinary
hues lapping the coves from
Cala Luna to Cala Goloritzé

CASTELSARDO
A proud fortress town clinging
to a high promontory which juts
proudly out into the sea

CAPO CACCIA
Dramatic cliffside stairs leading
to the Grotta di Nettuno caves

ALGHERO
A sandy coloured medieval town
that retains its Catalan identity

NURAGHE SANTU ANTINE
Along with the Nuraghe Su Nuraxi,
one of the finest of the
island's ancient nuraghes

BOSA
An atmospheric medieval town
huddled beneath castle ruins
and a short hop from a fine beach

Contents – Text

Contents – Maps

INTRODUCTION

SASSARI & THE NORTHWEST

OLBIA & THE GALLURA

NUORO & THE EAST

ORISTANO & THE WEST

SOUTHWEST SARDINIA

CAGLIARI & THE SOUTHEAST

MAP INDEX

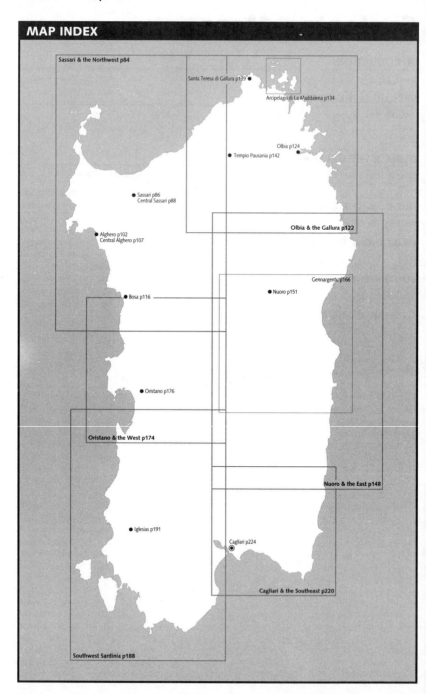

Sassari & the Northwest p84

Santa Teresa di Gallura p139 ●

Arcipelago di La Maddalena p134

Olbia p124 ●

● Tempio Pausania p142

● Sassari p86
Central Sassari p88

Olbia & the Gallura p122

● Alghero p102
Central Alghero p107

Gennargentu p166

● Nuoro p151

● Bosa p116

● Oristano p176

Oristano & the West p174

Nuoro & the East p148

● Iglesias p191

Cagliari p224
◉

Cagliari & the Southeast p220

Southwest Sardinia p188

The Author

Damien Simonis

With a degree in languages and several years' reporting and sub-editing on Australian newspapers (including *The Australian* and *The Age*), Sydney-born Damien left the country in 1989. He has since lived, worked and travelled extensively throughout Europe, the Middle East and North Africa. Since 1992, Lonely Planet has kept him busy in *Jordan & Syria, Egypt & the Sudan, Morocco, North Africa, Italy, Tuscany, Florence, Venice, Spain, The Canary Islands, Madrid, Barcelona* and *Catalunya & the Costa Brava*. He has also penned other guidebooks and written and snapped for publications in Australia, the UK and North America. When not on the road, Damien resides in splendid Stoke Newington, deep in the heart of north London.

From Damien

Special thanks to Andrea Branca, Gian Paolo Epifani for helping us find our feet in the first confusing weeks in the north of the island. Thanks also to Andrea's wife Anna and son Mario for their hospitality, and to all the friends from the lab, with whom we shared a memorable (and hormonally charged) meal.

Thanks also to Katya and Giacomina (Santa Teresa), and Signor Cocco (Santa Teresa) for the fine feast.

A heartfelt *grazie infinite* to Mattea Usai, the Scorpion Queen of Seneghe (Oristano). Mattea included us in her world, convincing us to trail down for a Sunday festivity and leading us to a string of wonderful people: the Salaris family who hosted us; Raimondo Cossa (whose knowledge of the region seems boundless) and Olga; Professor Mario Cubeddu, author of several works on Sardinia, and Carla; Francesco & Doloretta Cubeddu; William Gasparini and Cristina Vallin (the Padua contingent). Also thanks to Mattea's brother Bachisio and others for their warm welcome to Murra mania!

Stefano Meloni in Cagliari gave me a much needed hand with the musical side of Sardinia – thanks for the CD! Professore Salvatore Rubino helped me with some valuable information on the *tonnarotti*.

For their warm welcome, a big *abbraccio* goes to Marco, Lucia, Laura and all the other Marcos at The Monastery.

Gigi, Natale, Ignazio, Ireneo & Il Re rolled out a liquid welcome mat in Desulo, in the heart of the Barbagia, that even the following day's hangover could not erase from the memory.

Stefano Cavedoni, honorary Sardinian from Bologna but resident in Rome, was generous with his knowledge and contacts, not all of whom I could follow up – next time.

Finally, this book is for Janique, who shared with me the joy and burden of discovering this wonderful island. An enormous *merci* and several medals for bravery are due to her for enduring the rigours of guidebook travel and jangled authorial nerves with (mostly) a patient smile.

This Book

The 1st edition of *Sardinia* was written by Damien Simonis.

From the Publisher

The 1st edition of *Sardinia* was produced in Lonely Planet's Melbourne office. Editing was co-ordinated by Melanie Dankel with assistance from Helen Yeates, Barbara Delissen, Melissa Faulkner, Stefanie Di Trocchio and Craig Kilburn. Mapping was co-ordinated by Adrian Persoglia aided by Amanda Sierp, Chris Thomas, Tony Fankhauser, Anneka Imkamp, Jack Gavran, Natasha Velleley and Pablo Gastar. Indra Kilfoyle co-ordinated layout with Sally Morgan, Tamsin Wilson and Birgit Jordan (colour wraps). Thanks also to Quentin Frayne for the Language chapter, Csanad Csutoros for the climate charts and Annika Roojun for the cover. General thanks also go to Michala Green, Susan Rimerman, Ray Thomson, Mark Griffiths and Huw Fowles. *Tante grazie!*

Finally, thanks to Damien for all his hard work on the book.

Foreword

ABOUT LONELY PLANET GUIDEBOOKS

The story begins with a classic travel adventure: Tony and Maureen Wheeler's 1972 journey across Europe and Asia to Australia. There was no useful information about the overland trail then, so Tony and Maureen published the first Lonely Planet guidebook to meet a growing need.

From a kitchen table, Lonely Planet has grown to become the largest independent travel publisher in the world, with offices in Melbourne (Australia), Oakland (USA), London (UK) and Paris (France).

Today Lonely Planet guidebooks cover the globe. There is an ever-growing list of books and information in a variety of media. Some things haven't changed. The main aim is still to make it possible for adventurous travellers to get out there – to explore and better understand the world.

At Lonely Planet we believe travellers can make a positive contribution to the countries they visit – if they respect their host communities and spend their money wisely. Since 1986 a percentage of the income from each book has been donated to aid projects and human rights campaigns, and, more recently, to wildlife conservation.

Although inclusion in a guidebook usually implies a recommendation we cannot list every good place. Exclusion does not necessarily imply criticism. In fact there are a number of reasons why we might exclude a place – sometimes it is simply inappropriate to encourage an influx of travellers.

UPDATES & READER FEEDBACK

Things change – prices go up, schedules change, good places go bad and bad places go bankrupt. Nothing stays the same. So, if you find things better or worse, recently opened or long-since closed, please tell us and help make the next edition even more accurate and useful.

Lonely Planet thoroughly updates each guidebook as often as possible – usually every two years, although for some destinations the gap can be longer. Between editions, up-to-date information is available in our free, monthly email bulletin *Comet* (W www.lonelyplanet.com/newsletters). You can also check out the *Thorn Tree* bulletin board and *Postcards* section of our website, which carry unverified, but fascinating, reports from travellers.

Tell us about it! We genuinely value your feedback. A well-travelled team at Lonely Planet reads and acknowledges every email and letter we receive and ensures that every morsel of information finds its way to the relevant authors, editors and cartographers.

Everyone who writes to us will find their name listed in the next edition of the appropriate guidebook. The very best contributions will be rewarded with a free guidebook.

We may edit, reproduce and incorporate your comments in Lonely Planet products such as guidebooks, websites and digital products, so let us know if you don't want your comments reproduced or your name acknowledged.

How to contact Lonely Planet:
Online: e talk2us@lonelyplanet.com.au, W www.lonelyplanet.com
Australia: Locked Bag 1, Footscray, Victoria 3011
UK: 72-82 Rosebery Ave, London, EC1R 4RW
USA: 150 Linden St, Oakland, CA 94607

Introduction

The sea and Sardinia have always had a tricky rapport. From across the blue all sorts have arrived – from Phoenicians to Pisans and Piedmontese. They have all left their mark, often in blood, and the Sardinians have regarded them all with a mix of initial ingenuous hospitality and diffidence. Time and again they have fought oppression and more often than not lost, frequently retreating into the interior of their island and themselves in response.

In a sense little has changed. From across the sea growing waves of outsiders come in search of treasure. Once it was in the silver mines of the southwest; today it is the shimmering wonders of the coast. Like the Phoenician traders almost three millennia ago, most of the newcomers venture little beyond their chosen beaches. The second largest island in the Mediterranean is a wild, ancient and seemingly impenetrable place.

Around its coast Sardinia wears a necklace of translucent pearls: some of the most idyllic beaches in the Mediterranean. The English language doesn't have the adjectives to describe the varieties of blue, green and almost purple hues of Sardinia's waters. Thankfully, many spots remain ignored by mass tourism.

But there is much more to this minicontinent. Across its length and breadth singular monuments to its little known past are scattered. Some 7000 nuraghes, the stone towers of an ancient and unidentified people, dot the landscape. Curious temples and sacred wells, *domus de janas* (fairy house) tombs, the mass graves of the *tombe dei giganti* (giants' tombs), mysterious menhirs, remains of entire Bronze-Age villages and pretty Classical sites complete the picture.

The nuraghes were probably forts but the most forbidding fortress of all is the densely wooded Gennargentu massif that rises, snow-mantled in winter, in the heart of the island. Long considered inaccessible and peopled even now by a proud and defiant bunch who seem a race unto themselves, it is becoming an increasingly popular destination

for hikers. Spectacular gorges, rugged valleys and spare mountain summits all exert their untamed fascination on newcomer and repeat visitor alike.

Sardinia, long neglected by all and sundry, cannot boast the refined cities that one trips over incessantly in much of mainland Italy, but it is not without its prizes. The capital, Cagliari, has an alluring southern air laden with the many layers of its deep past. Catalan Alghero in the northwest is a briny taste of Spain, while proud Castelsardo juts high over the sea in the island's north.

The Pisans and Catalans in particular left behind a rich medieval heritage. The charming, bite-sized Romanesque churches in the Pisan style of Tuscany scattered about the countryside are especially evocative of a bygone era.

The Sardinians are no slouches at the dinner table. Seafood and many popular pasta dishes abound for the coastal crawlers, but the true essence of the island's cuisine lies in its hearty roast meats, suckling pig, kid and lamb. And they produce some excellent wines; the beefy Cannonau reds are by now widely known but the buff will soon unlock a treasure chest of fine dry whites, soft reds, sparkling rosés and gorgeous syrupy dessert wines – not to mention the local *filu e ferru* firewater!

More than anyone else in Italy, the Sardinians have, without pretence or fanfare, clung fiercely to their traditions. Year-round, colourful celebrations take place and even today in more remote villages you will occasionally espy folk in distinctive traditional dress. Nor has the Sardinian tongue, closer to Latin than Italian, been allowed to die.

This proud, rugged and beautiful island is one of the last great surprises of the Mediterranean.

Facts about Sardinia

The Roman temple of Antas, set in pretty country north of Iglesias in the southwest of Sardinia, had long before the Romans' arrival been the site of worship of a deity known as Sardus Pater, a heroic figure. Worship of this mysterious character was clearly significant as at some point the entire island was named after him, although nobody can put a date to it. Like so much about Sardinia, its very name remains shrouded in mystery.

HISTORY
The Mists of Time
Discoveries since the late 1970s have radically altered assumptions on how long humans have been living on Sardinia. For a long time it was thought that the earliest presence dated to the Neolithic period, perhaps no more than 6000 BC. The unearthing of the remnants of basic tools around the village of Perfugas, and subsequently elsewhere, now indicates a human presence in the Paleolithic era (Old Stone Age). Conservative guesses put it at 120,000 BC, but some experts believe primitive people may have lived here as long ago as 400,000 BC. As for their origins, it is believed the earliest settlers probably came from the Italian mainland, although it is possible other waves arrived from North Africa and the Iberian peninsula via the Balearic Islands.

Neolithic Settlements
Precious little is known about what Paleolithic people were up to in Sardinia, whether they had contact with people from elsewhere in the Mediterranean or simply evolved in parallel.

From about 5500 BC, the picture becomes a little clearer, as finds (mostly of ceramics and tools) tell more of the story of ancient Sardinians. It is clear that, here as elsewhere in the Mediterranean basin, people began to settle down, raise basic crops and develop animal husbandry. This set them apart from their hunter-gatherer ancestors.

Sardinia was rich in obsidian, a glassy black magma stone coveted all over the Mediterranean and ideal for the making of cutting tools and arrow tips. It seems Sardinian obsidian was exported as far as France. The variety of imported Neolithic-era ceramics found on the island also indicates outsiders came to Sardinia in search of the precious material and were in contact with locals.

While early Neolithic tribes lived in caves, by the 3rd millennium BC many had taken the fundamental step of creating small villages. Archaeologists talk of the Ozieri culture, after finds made around that town indicating the presence of such villages. Simple circular huts with stone foundations, wooden walls and thatched roofs were the standard shelter and, in these early days, no form of defensive perimeter was needed. The earliest signs of complex funerary rituals date to this period, which saw the excavation of the first *domus de janas* (fairy house) tombs built into living rock, sometimes decorated with simple, symbolic engravings.

The Age of Nuraghes
By 1800–1500 BC, in the early Bronze Age, things had changed radically. Sardinians began building the mysterious stone towers, or nuraghes , that have kept historians and archaeologists guessing until this day. Early nuraghes were simple free-standing towers (for more on how they were built see Architecture later) and may have played a military role. At the same time the use of metals to make tools and, significantly, weapons was by now widespread. It appears that Sardinian tribes, which perhaps before had lived in peace, had by now discovered the dark art of war.

During the period 1500–1300 BC, the Sardinians were making more complex structures of up to three storeys and adopting the *tholos* shape, akin to a conical beehive. Sardinian society appears to have undergone big changes at this time. Around the grand towers were raised defensive walls with outer towers. Much as happened in medieval villages huddled around castles two millennia later, Sardinians began to cluster their houses in and outside the protective walls of the main nuraghes. Other lone towers continued to go up and it is thought these marked tribal territory and frontiers, serving also as advance watchtowers.

Frustratingly, no written records of any kind have come down to us, leading most scholars to assume that the Sardinians never created a written version of their language. Rich if enigmatic testimony to their social and religious life has remained. While nuraghic villages were turning into complex structures with imposing forts, sacred sites were also growing in sophistication. Well temples *(pozzi sacri)* of extraordinary complexity (see Architecture) were built from around 1000 BC, and by this time folk had already developed the art of the *bronzetti*, or bronze figurines (see Painting & Sculpture).

Ceramics found all over the island and compared with finds elsewhere in the Mediterranean suggest there was a good deal of contact between ancient tribes as far as Italy, southern France and eastern Spain.

By the beginning of the 1st millennium BC, the tribes scattered across the island seem to have formed a fairly homogenous group. They could not have known it, but their demise was already in preparation.

The Phoenicians & Carthage

Traders from Greek Mycenae are believed to have been nosing around the island as early as 1200 BC. They weren't sufficiently interested to attempt settlement but they may have given the island one of its earliest names, Ichnusa (nowadays a local brand of beer). The name means footprint and according to the ancient tales god (we're not sure *which* god) supposedly took a (rather large) pile of stones and trod on it, thus creating the island's outline.

It is not known to what extent the Mycenaeans dominated the island's economic and cultural life, although their influence on local art, in particular ceramics, is clear.

As Mycenae faded, the Phoenicians (who came from present-day Lebanon) emerged as the prime force throughout the Mediterranean, dotting its coast with trade bases. Their commercial routes took them as far as the Atlantic, and Sardinia became an important element of their network. By at least 850 BC they had begun to establish settlements there. Indeed, semitic inscriptions suggest Spain-based Phoenicians may have set up at Nora, on the south coast, as early as 1100 BC.

Throughout the 8th and 7th centuries BC the Phoenicians established and strengthened their coastal trading settlements along the south and west coast: Karalis (Cagliari), Nora, Bithia (near modern Chia), Sulci

(modern Sant'Antioco), Tharros and Bosa. As they tightened their grip on the lead and silver mines of the southwest, they felt the need to protect themselves against an increasingly restless local populace, and so they built an inland fortress on Monte Sirai around 650 BC. They had reason to be concerned, as stroppy Sardinians united to attack several of the Phoenicians' bases in 509 BC.

Against the ropes, the Phoenicians appealed to Carthage (in North Africa), itself a former Phoenician settlement, for aid. This it did, and with greater gusto than could have been imagined. They soon had much of the island under their control, except the wild and mountainous regions of the Gennargentu and the Ogliastra coast, which came to be known as the Barbaria (later Barbagia, meaning foreign or beyond the pale). The conquest of Sardinia was just one episode in this emerging power's path to domination of the western Mediterranean.

During Phoenician rule the bulk of Sardinians living in the coastal areas came to assimilate the new culture, abandoning the nuraghes and gradually disappearing as a separate culture and race. The Carthaginians remained in control until they clashed with their expanding Mediterranean rival, Rome. Defeated by the Romans in the First Punic War (264–241 BC), the Carthaginians were obliged to evacuate the island in 238 BC.

Rome Takes Command

Roman control did not bring the immediate removal of Carthaginian civilisation and by some reckonings it was another five centuries before all traces of the Carthaginian language had been wiped out. Carthaginian religious customs were long maintained and many Carthaginians remained in the public administration.

But the arrival of the Romans brought profound change. With characteristic efficiency they expanded the Carthaginian cities and settlements, built a network of roads to facilitate communications and control of the island and even penetrated Le Barbagie.

The Campidano area, an important source of grain to the Carthaginians, became, along with Sicily and occupied North Africa, the granary of the entire Roman Empire. Later on farmers diversified producing wine, olives and fruit. Trade was active with the Italian mainland, Iberia and especially North Africa.

But controlling the island was no walk-over and the Romans found themselves frequently battling insurgents, especially in the untamed Barbagia. The initial campaign of conquest took seven years and the island was finally declared a province (with Corsica) in 227 BC. In 216 BC the Sardinians, led by Ampsicora, joined the Carthaginians in the Second Punic War and revolted against their Roman masters. The following year they were crushed in the second battle of Cornus but rebellions remained on the menu for the next 200 years. That of 177 BC was a drawn-out affair in which tens of thousands of Barbagia Sardinians died and as many as 50,000 were sent to Rome as slaves.

Throughout the centuries of Roman rule an uneasy equilibrium was maintained. The more Romanised cities, coast and farm country stood in opposition to the restless indigenous pastoralists of Le Barbagie. Although some cities and many noble families gained Roman citizen status and came to speak Latin, the island remained an underdeveloped and over-exploited subject territory throughout.

The Vandals Move in...
The collapse of Rome in the early 5th century left Sardinia in the lurch. Refugees arrived from the mainland and invaders were not far behind. The Vandals, who had established a kingdom in North Africa, disembarked in Sardinia in AD 456 and Corsica soon after.

Admittedly biased Byzantine chroniclers record the 80-odd years of Vandal rule as a time of raids and misery for the island's inhabitants. The Vandals also used the island as a place of exile for vexatious Christians, especially bishops and other notables, from North Africa. The scant reminders historians have of this time suggest that the chroniclers probably exaggerated. It appears Karalis and other port towns remained busy, especially with commerce between the island and North Africa. In any event, the Vandals did not have things their own way for long.

... And the Byzantine Empire Strikes Back
By the early 6th century all that remained of the Roman Empire was its eastern half, now known as Byzantium and with its capital in Constantinople (modern Istanbul). Its rulers had not forgotten the glory of better days and Emperor Justinian embarked on a campaign of conquest aimed at restoring the old empire. His most celebrated general, Belisarios, after retaking mainland Italy, went on to bring much of North Africa under Byzantine control. The Vandals, defeated in North Africa in 534, abandoned Sardinia, which joined Corsica and the Balearic Islands to form one of Byzantium's seven African provinces.

Civil administration of the island was in the hands of a *judex provinciae* (provincial judge) based in Karalis (Cagliari), while a *dux* commanded a military garrison from Forum Traiani (Fordongianus).

Christianity, whose appearance in Sardinia had come late in Roman times, now spread more rapidly, following the Eastern Orthodox rites of Byzantium. But Le Barbagie remained largely beyond its control and Pope Gregory lamented the area's paganism as late as the end of the 6th century. The new religion only began to gain a foothold after the pope orchestrated a peace treaty between the Byzantines and Le Barbagie's leader, Ospitone, in 594, but the rebellious region remained to all intents and purposes independent.

Arab Raids, Dark Times & the Giudicati
Constantinople didn't have the strength or reach to re-establish the Empire but did manage to hang on to its widespread territories until a new and wholly unexpected force exploded on to the scene in the late 7th century. From the deserts of Arabia burst forth the zealous Muslim armies of Mohammed. They quickly overran the Middle East and North Africa and in 711 made their first raid on the Sardinian coast.

With the Muslim conquest of North Africa and much of Spain, Sardinia found itself increasingly isolated. In the 8th and 9th centuries, trade across the Mediterranean fell, and Constantinople, threatened on several fronts, could no longer protect far-flung possessions like Sardinia.

The repeated raids by Arab corsairs, combined with the spread of malaria as coastal farm country was abandoned and left to turn into bog, obliged the Sardinians to leave coastal towns like Tharros and Nora.

In Cagliari, the *judex provinciae* assumed full control of the island but this soon proved an unwieldy solution and in the 10th century power was transferred to four provincial *judikes* (or *giudici*) whose territories *(giudicati)*, were called Gallura, Torres, Arborea and Cagliari. For the first time since the Carthaginian conquest, Sardinians were running their own affairs. The *giudicati* came to be ruled by kings whose power was, however, circumscribed by a council of nobles (the *corona de logu*).

The *giudicati* frequently fought one another and soon attracted outside attention. Already in the late 11th century, religious orders such as the Vittorini monks (connected with the powerful Italian city state of Pisa) were granted land and concessions in the Giudicato di Cagliari. In 1157 Barisone d'Arborea married into the ruling family of Barcelona, thus initiating the island's long relationship with the Spanish peninsula. Seven years later he had himself crowned king of all Sardinia, a move that failed singularly due to the lack of finances to buy the promised support of Pisa's rival, Genoa.

Pisa & Genoa Vie for Control

External meddling in the affairs of Sardinia accelerated during the course of the 13th century.

As early as 1187 the Giudicato di Cagliari had a non-Sardinian *giudice*, the Tuscan Guglielmo di Massa. Later Genoese influence would grow at the Cagliari court, as in the northern Giudicato di Torres (aka Giudicato di Logudoro).

But the Pisans weren't far behind and ultimately invested more effort in the island. Seeking to counter the Genoese and improve their own position in Sardinia, the Pisans first exercised pressure on the Giudicato di Cagliari, whose capital was not the by now long-abandoned Karalis but nearby Santa Igia. After building a fortress in what is now the Castello district of Cagliari, the Pisans sacked Santa Igia and took control of the *giudicato* in 1258.

Shortly afterwards, the Pisan Ugolino della Gherardesca moved in to the town of Villa di Chiesa (now Iglesias), using it as a base to crank the silver mines back into action.

In 1259, the Giudicato di Torres ceased to exist and was carved up by various powerful Genoese families and the Giudicato d'Arborea. Twenty-five years later the area's main city, Sassari, became an autonomous

commune along the lines of Tuscan city states, but soon found itself ruled by a Genoese *podestà* (governor). At the same time Pisan influence was growing in the Giudicato di Gallura, which moved in to take direct control in 1297. The policy of ruling Sardinian territory direct from Pisa was extended to what had been the Giudicato di Cagliari in the wake of the fall from grace of Ugolino della Gherardesca in 1288.

Only the Giudicato d'Arborea, albeit under heavy Pisan influence but also keeping close ties with the Crown of Aragon in Spain, remained independent. The Catalano-Aragonese kingdom, with its heart in the thriving port city of Barcelona, was more than a little interested in the island. Some Catalan noble families already had big stakes in Sardinia's northwest. This must have played more than a decisive role in the decision by Pope Boniface VIII in 1297 to create the theoretical Regnum Sardiniae et Corsicae (Sardinian and Corsican kingdom) and hand it over to the Catalano-Aragonese king, Jaume II.

The Crown of Aragon Muscles In

Jaume II never got around to making the Pope's declaration a reality. Only in 1323 did Catalano-Aragonese forces, transported by 300 warships, land on the southwest coast to begin the business of conquest. They never did take Corsica (definitively occupied by France in 1553).

Allied with Arborea, the newcomers quickly took Cagliari and Iglesias and established pacts of vassalage with other local nobles around the island. Relations between Barcelona and Arborea soon deteriorated when the latter realised their erstwhile allies were bent on assuming complete control. By 1353 Arborea had become an adversary and a long period of insurrection began. The northwestern port town of Alghero, retaken after a brief revolt, saw its entire population expelled and replaced by Catalan colonists. The same fate awaited the people of Castellaragonese (now Castelsardo).

King Pere III established a local administration, or Parlement, in 1355. This institution was maintained until the 18th century and at least gave Sardinians some voice in the running of their affairs.

Meantime, the insurgency continued. From 1356 to 1404, the kings of Arborea

(Mariano IV, Ugone III and then Queen Eleonora) continually harried the Catalano-Aragonese and at one point had ejected them from all but Cagliari and Alghero.

Eleonora d'Arborea (1340–1404) in particular has gone down in history as Sardinia's Boadicea or Joan of Arc. It was largely under her direction that the resistance continued for so long. She is also remembered for the advanced law code, or Carta de Logu, that she introduced in Arborea and which the Catalano-Aragonese later extended to the whole island.

Five years after Eleonora's death, the Sardinians were defeated at the Battle of Sanluri. Unrest continued to simmer and resulted in one final concerted uprising in the 1470s, quickly throttled in the Battle of Macomer in 1478.

The Spanish Mire

Meanwhile, things were about to change for the Crown of Aragon. In 1479 the principle Spanish kingdoms of Castile and Aragon were united. Spanish (ie, Castilian) officials started arriving to take over the running of the Crown of Aragon's possessions, including Sardinia. The two and a half centuries of Spanish rule that ensued were marked above all by lethargy and slow decline.

Emperor Carlos V dropped by on his way to raid Tunis (1535) and Algiers (1541) in an attempt to rid the western Mediterranean of piracy. The campaign failed and in the end the Spaniards found themselves obliged to accelerate the Catalano-Aragonese policy of building defensive watch towers around the Sardinian coast.

Under the Spaniards the feudal structures put into place by the Catalano-Aragonese were deepened, leaving the bulk of the mostly rural population to toil for the most meagre of livelihoods in a seemingly immutable life of unrelenting struggle and misery. Great tracts of the country wound up as possessions of powerful Spanish nobles who never so much as visited the island. Even a century after Spanish rule ended, much of the land taken over by Iberian nobility was still in their hands.

Sardinian farmers were burdened with barely sustainable taxes and the island's economy stagnated as Spain's fortunes declined during the 16th and 17th centuries. Ironically, traders from Genoa (whose bankers had become one of Madrid's prime sources of finance) gradually came to dominate the island's international trade, replacing the Catalans.

The centuries of Catalano-Aragonese and then Spanish rule left an indelible impression on the island. Many of the traditional festivals still celebrated across Sardinia date to this era and the Sardinian language is littered with Catalan and Spanish words.

As the 17th century came to a close it became apparent that the last of Spain's Habsburg rulers, Carlos II, would die without leaving a direct heir. In Sardinia, as in Spain, society was divided by pro-Habsburg and

The Mystery of the Four Moors

In 1999 it was finally official. The standard that for centuries had come to represent Sardinia in the eyes of the island's people was now the flag. It is a strange emblem by any reckoning. The heads of four Moors (*i quattro mori*), all looking right and with headbands wrapped around their foreheads, are divided by a red cross (some think of St George) on a white background.

For a flag so clearly laden with symbolism, the only element lacking is a convincing explanation of what the symbols might mean. The first reliable documentation of this bizarre coat of arms dates to the mid-15th century, at the time of Sardinia's incorporation into the Crown of Aragon. Some say the four Moors represent defeated Arab kings. Others have ventured to see in them the image of slaves.

Various versions, with the four heads facing in different directions and variously crowned, adorned with headbands or blindfolded, appeared over the years. By the 18th century the standard version had the heads blindfolded and looking left. In 1952 this became the region's official coat of arms, although increasingly the heads were facing right. By the late 1990s, many objected to the blindfolding and some town councils even produced their own version with the blindfolds converted back into headbands, giving them a rather swash-buckling, pirate look. The trend stuck and was finally enshrined in the 1999 decision.

pro-Bourbon factions. The death of Carlos in 1700 triggered the War of the Spanish Succession and in 1708 Austrian forces backed by English warships occupied Sardinia.

The French-backed Bourbon candidate to the Spanish throne, Felipe V, won the day but the cost to Spain was high. Madrid lost many of its territories, including Sardinia, awarded to Austria under the terms of the 1713 Treaty of Utrecht. Vienna was not too keen on its new possession, still known as the Kingdom of Sardinia, and did little to oppose a Spanish attempt to retake it in 1717. The rest of Europe was, however, not amused and obliged the Spaniards to pull out again a year later under the Treaty of London. This time Sardinia was assigned to the Duchy of Savoy. The dukes would have preferred the juicier morsel of Sicily to the much neglected, poverty-stricken rural backwater of Sardinia. But at least the dukes, whose territories encompassed modern-day Piedmont, could now call themselves kings.

Tale of Two Kingdoms

What the Savoy rulers found in 1720 exceeded their worst expectations. The lamentable state of the island's economy and agriculture and the lethargy of the feudal noble class came as a shock to the Piedmontese viceroys, but they were determined to make the best of a bad thing.

Many Spanish influences would prove resistant to efforts by the Savoys to expunge them, but already in 1726 administrators were told to promote the use of Italian on the island.

Attributing the low farm output to underpopulation (there were no more than 300,000 people in Sardinia at the time), the authorities encouraged colonisation. The only such experiment to really work was the transfer of Ligurians from Tabarqa in Tunisia to the island of San Pietro in 1738, where they founded the city of Carloforte. These primarily fishing folk, however, did little to alter the state of farming.

The 18th century was marked by a series of famines in between good years on the land. Although times were rarely easy, farm output generally stabilised and the population increased (reaching 436,000 in 1782). Attempts were made to modernise the current feudal system of land-holding to favour greater production. The Savoys also set about resurrecting the near moribund universities of Cagliari and Sassari.

Rocky times were never far away. The French Revolution cast its shadow over Sardinia like the rest of Europe. Sardinian militia repulsed attempted landings by French forces (including some under a young Napoleon in the Maddalena islands) in 1792. In return for this demonstration of loyalty, a delegation of Sardinians went to see King Vittorio Amedeo III in Turin to demand a relaxation of absolutist Savoy rule and a greater degree of self-rule. Virtually all their requests were turned down, a result that could only lead to unrest.

In 1795 senior Savoy administrators were killed by angry mobs in Cagliari and the whole island sank into a confused revolutionary ferment. The patriotic revolutionaries were most visibly represented by a radical judge, Giovanni Maria Angioi, who occupied Sassari but failed in his attempt to march on Cagliari. By the time the Savoy royal family moved to Cagliari from Turin in 1799, ejected from their mainland possessions by Napoleon, the revolutionary wave had been crushed.

The early decades of the 19th century brought a greater degree of calm. King Carlo Felice built the highway bearing his name between Cagliari and Porto Torres, ordered the establishment of basic schooling and promoted drastic change in land ownership to encourage greater production. The Enclosures Act of 1820, aimed at turning over all common land to private ownership, may have been motivated by laudable economic thinking but it excluded the poorest farmers, as well as pastoralists, from the use of land previously open to all. The more desperate turned to banditry, especially in the interior.

The abolition of feudal privileges in 1835 was also a big step forward but small farmers, who in the following years were able to get a hold of freed-up land, found themselves bearing crushing debt to the state, which in turn had to compensate the ejected former feudal owners. In all, the painful land reforms seemed to do little for the poorest farmers.

In 1847, the island's status as a separate entity ruled through a viceroy came to an end. Tempted by a series of reforms introduced in the Savoys' mainland territories, a delegation requested the 'perfect union' of the Kingdom of Sardinia with Piedmont, in the hope of acquiring more equitable rule. The request was granted with surprisingly little delay. From now on the island would be ruled directly from Turin.

At the same time events were moving quickly elsewhere on the Italian peninsula. In a series of military campaigns and diplomatic manoeuvring, the Savoys managed to create a united Kingdom of Italy in 1861 (a process completed in 1870), under the aegis of the Kingdom of Sardinia.

Rule from Rome was not substantially different from that of Turin. On the one hand slow improvements were made. The first railway lines opened in the 1870s and by 1913 Sardinia elected its first ever Socialist MP to the Italian parliament. But life remained tough for most Sardinians and the years leading to WWI were not empty of unrest. Miners' strikes (ruthlessly put down), rampant banditry and food riots all marked this uneasy period.

The World Wars

Italy's decision to enter WWI in 1915 on the Allied side was motivated mostly by a desire to grab what it considered Italian territories still in the hands of Austria. The country was utterly unprepared for conflict on such a scale and would pay a high human price for extremely modest territorial gain.

More than most units, the tough Sardinians of the Brigata Sassari distinguished themselves in the merciless slaughters of the northern Italian trenches. From the outset the men and officers of the brigade were praised in dispatches for their extraordinary valour. Per capita it is reckoned that Sardinia lost more young men on the front than any other Italian region.

When the survivors returned home after the war's end in 1918, they were changed men. They had departed as illiterate farmers and returned as a politically awakened force. Many joined the new Partito Sardo d'Azione (Sardinian Action Party) whose central policy resided in the demand for administrative autonomy for the island. The party formed the strongest opposition to Benito Mussolini's Fascists, until they completed their stranglehold on power in Rome in 1924.

The Fascist period was a strange one for Sardinia. Recognising that something had to be done to lift Sardinia out of its poverty, grand programmes were laid on but only partially or clumsily carried out. Land reclamation around the two new towns of Mussolinia (now Arborea) and Fertilia created new farming land, but only a fraction of that envisaged. Mining received a new impetus and the extraction of lignite (the poor quality 'Sulcis coal') was stimulated with the creation of yet another new grid-pattern town, Carbonia. Some progress was made in the effort to eradicate malaria. The cities also grew rapidly and increased their illiteracy.

In all, however, Sardinia suffered from the Fascist attempts to make Italy economically self-sufficient (thus cutting it out of international trade circuits). Joining Hitler in WWII only exacerbated matters. Thankfully Sardinia was not invaded but Allied bombing raids in the first half of 1943 destroyed three quarters of Cagliari. Perhaps worse still, war left the island virtually isolated. The ferry between the mainland and Olbia was not back in daily operation until 1947.

The end of the war brought a revolution in Italy's political structure. In a 1946 referendum the people voted to dump the monarchy and create a parliamentary republic. In 1948, along with four other regions, Sardinia was granted a special autonomy statute, granting the island its own parliament and a degree of local policy-making latitude – arguably the greatest degree of political 'independence' since the era of the Giudicati, although it fell short of many Sardinians' expectations.

DDT & the Demise of the Malarial Mosquito

More significant even than the creation of the Regione Autonoma della Sardegna in 1948 was the programme put in place to eradicate malaria. Since even Roman times much of the Sardinian coast and some of its plains had been under siege from malaria-carrying mosquitoes. The so-called Sardinia Project, run by the Rockefeller Foundation, had spectacular results. Swamps were drained and the mosquitoes disappeared. In the 1920s an average of 78,000 cases of malaria were registered each year (!); the figure dropped to 40,000 in 1947. In 1950, for the first time in possibly a couple of thousand years, not one single new case was reported.

Still, by the early 1950s, Sardinia was still one of the poorest and most backward of Italy's regions. Good news came with the creation of the national Cassa per il Mezzogiorno (1950), an instrument designed to channel funds into the country's poor south. It would pump millions into Sardinia in the coming decades, although it was not always terribly well spent.

With the coast liberated of the scourge of malaria, hopes were high for economic benefits, but they were slow in coming. Much previously idle land could now be farmed but the impact on the overall economy was limited. In the following years, however, two other side effects emerged. From the early 1960s much hope was placed in big, new industrial plants that proved of limited help to the island's economy. But coastal tourism, which began to take off in this period, may prove to be an economic lifesaver.

While the emergence of the Aga Khan's chic tourist resort of the Costa Smeralda in the 1960s signalled an avenue of hope for Sardinia, the creation of industrial complexes in Porto Torres, Portovesme and elsewhere soon revealed itself a false dawn. By the late 1970s output had fallen drastically and much of the workforce had been laid off. Rubbing salt into the wounds, the age-old mines of the southwest also went into decline (and finally shut down in the mid-1990s).

Agricultural reforms were also slow to take effect and in some cases ill-directed. The net result was that, although the quality of life in Sardinia gradually rose from the 1950s to the 1980s, serious problems remained. The most eloquent expression of this was the wave of emigration that hit the island from the late 1940s. The arrival of TV (the island was the last part of Italy to be hooked up to the network in 1956) and greater awareness that life *could* be better led increasing numbers of mostly young men to choose flight over futile fight. In the 1960s alone as much as 10% of the population left Sardinia for the Italian mainland or Western European countries like West Germany, Switzerland and France.

By the mid-1970s, which brought the international oil crisis and years of instability across Italy, Sardinia found itself in a strange situation. Swarms of fun-seeking mainland Italian summer holiday-makers brought new and startling ways of thinking and living to the attention of what had been until recently a highly archaic, conservative rural society. It came as a shock to the system. Even today,

the more liberal urban and coastal centres contrast remarkably with the doggedly traditional, and increasingly empty, rural heartland. The latest 'invasion' has had the effect of wrenching at least a part of the island's society from medieval torpor to 21st-century modernity with breakneck rapidity.

The 1980s brought a new wind in Sardinian politics, hitherto dominated by the main conservative DC party and the Communists. The Partito Sardo d'Azione, dormant since its foundation in the 1920s, made a remarkable comeback as Sardinians began to reflect more profoundly on their identity. Renewed interest in the Sardinian language, culture and history have outlived the party's short-lived electoral successes and opened a debate on the island's political status that continues today. While it is true that Sardinians have lost a lot of ground to Italians since the arrival of the Savoys in 1720, and that separatists' dreams of an independent Sardinia are about as likely as the vision of pigs taking to the air, the simple rediscovery of, and pride in, the islanders' *sardità* (Sardinianness) is a healthy sign for the future.

Sardinia Today

Most Sardinians would agree that the island has come a long way since the end of WWII. But much remains awry in this still comparatively isolated land. Sure, the place floods with tourists for about three months of the year, but otherwise it is left largely to its own devices.

Whenever a local politician makes it to a position of power in Rome, Sardinians can almost be heard to mutter prayers of intercession. The presence of Sassari's Beppe Pisanu, a key player in Silvio Berlusconi's right wing Forza Italia–led government, and perhaps the latter's predilection for the Costa Smeralda, has directed Rome's attention to the island more than might usually be the case.

There is much to attract that attention. Water shortages (see Ecology & Environment), poor roads and infrastructure, high unemployment and continued lawlessness in the more remote parts of the region are just some of the challenges facing the regional and national governments.

GEOGRAPHY

At 23,813 sq km (24,090 sq km if you count all the offshore islands), Sardinia is bigger than Tuscany, where many of its tourists come from. Curiously, Sardinia is closer to North Africa than to Italy, by just 10km!

People tell you strange things at times. Sardinia, some Italians who have holidayed there will tell you, is largely flat. Flatness, it would appear, is relative. True, the highest point (Punta La Marmora) is a rather modest 1834m. (Corsica, a spit away to the north, has mountains of nearly 3000m and capped with snow year-round.) But with less than 20% of plains country, Sardinia is anything but flat. The northeastern Gallura region is criss-crossed by hills spread out like moguls on a ski run and this is true across much of the north. Further inland the range around Monte Limbara, and hill country further west, creates a wall stretching from outside Olbia across to Sassari.

The coast around Porto Torres and a pocket between that port, Alghero and Sassari is relatively flat. And south of Oristano stretches the Campidano, the island's one-time granary and flat as a tack. But to its west rises up the difficult hill country of the Iglesiente and, to the east, the Gennargentu massif, Gerrei and Sarrabus.

All these hills and low mountains seem to have been chopped up into a labyrinth of deep, twisting valleys and gorges too. The lie of the land, until recently, left many towns and villages isolated and, driving around the island today, twisting and turning, climbing up hill and dropping down dale, you soon begin to feel swallowed up by this deceptively difficult terrain.

The coast is a mixed bag. In some places high cliff walls rise sheer out of the Mediterranean, most spectacularly along the southern stretch of the Golfo di Orosei (Nuoro province), the coast north of Bosa, the beautiful Costa del Sud, parts of the Costa Verde and southwest coast, and around Capo Falcone and Capo Caccia in the northwest. By contrast, other stretches of coast can be almost monotonous, with a regular parade of beach after beach. Such stretches include the line of strands east of Port Torres and the coast from Orosei north to Olbia.

The river Tirso, at 150km the longest on the island, rises in the northeast on the provincial frontier between Nuoro and Sassari and flows gradually southwest to empty into the Mediterranean just west of Oristano. The other main rivers are the Flumendosa,

which flows 127km from the heart of the Gennargentu massif and empties into the sea on the southeast coast around Muravera. The Coghinas flows 123km to the north coast, reaching the sea a little way east of Castelsardo. The Tirso and Coghinas each pass through the island's two largest artificial lakes, Lago Omodeo (22 sq km) and Lago Coghinas (13 sq km). The rivers and lakes are frequently well below par and in the summer of 2002 the lakes were nearly dry.

Other rivers of some small note include the Temo, which flows through Bosa, and the Cedrino, which courses from the high Lago Cedrino west of Dorgali to the coast at Orosei.

The main rivers take the Italian name *fiume* (river) while secondary watercourses have kept the Spanish *rio* or Catalan *riu*.

CLIMATE

Given the island's size, it enjoys a mixed climate, milder on the coast and with more extreme, continental tendencies inland.

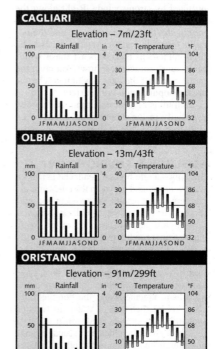

Summers tend to be long on the coast and even more so in the south. In a good year you can be already swimming in April and still taking the occasional dip in late October. Average daytime temperatures in coastal cities like Cagliari, Olbia and Alghero can range from around 10°C or a little less in winter to 25 to 30°C in July and August. In high summer the temperature can easily rise higher.

Inland, temperatures drop lower in winter and rise higher in summer. The broad Campidano plain can be a sauna in July, while the high villages in and around the Gennargentu massif frequently drop below 0°C in winter. Locals will tell you that, in the higher inland districts, autumn starts after 15 August – you soon start to feel a slight night in the evening air. There's no doubt that, in the heat of summer, the mountainous areas bring cool relief. It is not unheard of to encounter jolly cold days up around Punta La Marmora and other peaks even in August.

The island, especially the north, can be buffeted by strong winds. Right along the north coast the predominant winds are the *maestrale* (from the northwest) and the *ponente* (from the west). Around the Bocche di Bonifacio in the northeast these winds blow, and sometimes howl, on average more than half the year – which is why the area is popular with windsurfers.

Rainfall is highest in autumn and winter, especially in the mountainous areas of Le Barbagie. As a rule of thumb, it rains more in the north than the south.

ECOLOGY & ENVIRONMENT

Sardinia's single biggest headache is lack of water. As demand grows in the cities and expanding tourist resorts, the problem becomes more acute. Most of the capital, Cagliari, was down to four hours of running water a day in summertime rationing in 2002.

The problem is not just the drought that has afflicted the island for the past few years, leaving even the biggest artificial lake, Lago Omodeo, virtually empty. Equally important are mismanagement and the complete absence of maintenance of water distribution systems. Estimates of how much water is lost through leaky pipes and seepage range anything from 20% up. Although millions of euros were set aside by the EU for infrastructure projects in Sardinia in 2000 (and must be used by 2006), not one cent has been allocated to water supply projects (indeed no money has been allocated to anything as yet, leaving Sardinians worried that through sheer inertia their regional government will potter along, do nothing and allow the 2006 deadline to pass). Optimistic newspaper reports on visiting Israeli experts showing locals how to turn deserts into gardens with hi-tech water-management schemes are indeed mouth-watering, but few Sardinians believe any of it will ever apply to them. For decades the pros and cons of building expensive desalination plants have been discussed… and discussed.

Back in the 1960s petrochemical and other heavy industrial plants were established at various points around the island (notably Porto Torres, Portovesme, Sarroch, Arbatax and south of Oristano). This policy of creating industrial poles of attraction in deeply depressed rural regions (similar projects were implemented in the poor south of the Italian mainland) have contributed little to the island's economy but created local pockets of air and water pollution. Although they still operate today, the oil crisis of the 1970s and the end of mining in the Iglesiente have virtually doomed them to remain ugly white elephants.

On the subject of ugly, the other great white economic hope for Sardinia, tourism, has brought its own problems. Much of the island's coast remains refreshingly wild and beautiful but the spread of tourist resorts along the east coast, especially in the northeast from Santa Teresa di Gallura to Olbia (taking in the relatively benign Costa Smeralda) and around Villasimius in the south, has forever scarred the landscape. Pockets of development elsewhere around the island are growing and it appears developers could cook the goose that laid the golden egg.

Erosion has been a problem too. The prevailing westerly winds of the north, for instance, in 2001 swept away much of the fine white sand that made the Spiaggia della Pelosa in the Stintino peninsula so special. Nature's will can be difficult to fight.

On the up side, in spite of the isolated industrial plants, the water around the island is extraordinarily clean. Local fishermen still manage to eke out a living on the local catch, although there is nothing like the abundance of sea life there was even in the 1960s.

FLORA & FAUNA

Sardinia's 'savage, dark-bushed, sky-exposed land', as DH Lawrence put it, is studded with wild highlands split by beautiful gorges, stark plains, pockets of dense woodland, and kilometres of unspoiled coastline.

Hunting remains a common pastime in Sardinia, but plenty of wildlife remains, notably the wild boar, eagles, vultures, pink flamingos, the Sardinian deer and a colony of griffon vultures on the west coast. Miniature horses run wild on the high basalt plateau of the Giara di Gesturi.

Flora

To see the best of Sardinia's wild flowers you need to visit in spring. April tends to be a good month. If you leave it too late into May you'll miss the best as summer sets in.

In the higher woodland country of central and northeastern Sardinia, various types of oak, especially cork oak, dominate. The latter are easily identifiable as the bark is regularly stripped away from the trunk as high as the first branches. Cork has long been an important industry on the island and the area around Tempio Pausania is rich in this tree. The nearby town of Calangianus is one of the main centres for processing the material.

Highland flowers like the peony add a splash of colour to some of the more barren mountain areas, especially around Bruncu Spina and Punta La Marmora.

At lower altitudes typical Mediterranean scrub, *macchia*, predominates where land is uncultivated and there are no trees. The term covers a wide range of plants, including gorse, juniper, heather, broom and arbutus (aka strawberry trees). Orchids, gladioli and irises may flower beneath these shrubs, which are colourful in spring. Aromatic herbs like lavender, rosemary and thyme often thrive in these areas too. Perhaps the best known of *macchia* plants in Sardinia is the ubiquitous *mirto* (myrtle), from whose berries and leaves two fine sweet liqueurs, bearing the same name, are extracted.

Along some stretches of the coast (particularly along the east coast but also in parts of the Costa Verde and elsewhere), the *macchia* gives way to shady stands of pine. Many beaches on the east and south coasts are backed by lovely pine stands where locals choose to picnic and lie out the hottest hours of the day. Palm trees are not uncommon but most are imported. An exception are the so-called dwarf palms, whose leaves are used to make wicker baskets.

Fauna

On The Ground Several species in Sardinia are labelled 'minor', not because they are in some way inferior but because they are smaller than their mainland counterparts.

Take the case of the *cinghiale sardo* (Sardinian wild boar), a smallish animal with a particularly prominent snout. Hunting has reduced its numbers dangerously over the years, and so the much bigger wild boar from mainland Italy, especially Abruzzo, has been imported to boost numbers. Interbreeding is creating a newer, bigger breed – true Sardinian boars are becoming hard to find.

Another classic example are the wild *cavallini* or little horses that roam the strange high plateau of the Giara di Gesturi in the northern reaches of the Marmilla district. And weirder still are the white donkeys of the Isola Asinara in the northwest.

Mouflon, the wild sheep much coveted by locals for their remarkably curved horns (used to make handles for quality Sardinian knives), were on the verge of extinction but now roam less accessible parts of the interior in greater numbers. The *cervo sardo*, or Sardinian deer, is now a protected species and lives in a handful of reserves, including Monte Arcuenta in the Iglesiente and Monte Arcosu, a little way west of Cagliari.

You are unlikely to see them but turtles use some coastal spots, especially where there are dunes, as nesting places.

Happily, you won't see poisonous snakes or other nasties either, because there are none.

In The Air Thousands of flamingos visit Sardinia in the winter months and stop over especially in the lagoons (*stagni*) of Oristano province and around Cagliari.

In other months you still might see some, as several hundred older and younger ones, unable to undertake the long trips to/from Africa or the Camargue in France (according to the season), stay behind here. The flamingos are joined by a host of other wetland birds, including herons, crane, spoonbill, cormorants, terns, various kinds of duck and more.

Although in some ways emblematic of the island's birdlife, the flamingos are by no means alone. Golden and Bonelli's eagles patrol the high skies, as do the black vulture, bearded vulture (lammergeier), the Peregrine falcon and even occasionally the rare Eleonora's falcon. The griffon vulture maintains a colony in the west of the island, along the coast between Alghero and Bosa.

National Parks & Reserves

Sardinia boasts three national parks, two regional parks and a series of mostly marine reserves.

The most extensive of the national parks is the Parco Nazionale del Golfo di Orosei e del Gennargentu, which takes up a great swathe of central Nuoro province, including the Gennargentu massif (and the island's highest peaks), the magnificent gorges of the Gola Su Gorroppu and the matchless beauty of the Golfo di Orosei coast between Cala Gonone and Santa Maria Navarrese.

The Parco Nazionale dell'Arcipelago di La Maddalena encompasses all the islands of the archipelago, although clearly much of the main island and its port town, La Maddalena, do not quite fit the bill of park. Isola di Caprera, joined to Isola della Maddalena by a narrow causeway, has its own status as state natural reserve.

Finally, the most recent of the parks is the Parco Nazionale dell'Asinara, former prison island and home to the unique white donkey.

Areas with some degree of protection under their status as marine reserves include Capo Carbonara in the southeast, the Sinis peninsula and its offshore island, Isola Mal di Ventre, the Isola Tavolara and nearby Punta Coda Cavallo, and the Isola di Budelli, within the Parco Nazionale dell'Arcipelago di La Maddalena.

GOVERNMENT & POLITICS

Sardinians with a sense of irony like to tell you that it was Sardinia that absorbed all of Italy in the 19th-century campaign to unite the country. For the Savoy dukes, before becoming monarchs of the new unified Italy, had only attained regal status by becoming (almost unwillingly) kings of Sardinia in 1720. And thus, on paper at least, the kingdom of Sardinia presided over the liberation of the rest of Italy from foreign powers and its subsequent unification under one crown.

Wryness aside, Sardinia's fate, even after unification, has for the most part seemed

only barely connected with that of the rest of the country. After WWII and the national vote to make Italy a parliamentary republic in 1946, the many differences that set Sardinia apart from the rest of the country were at least recognised in the decision to grant the island (along with four others of Italy's 20 regions) a statute of semi-autonomy and its own regional government in 1948. The statute of autonomy, since modified to increase the region's revenue-raising powers, fell short of many Sardinians' hopes but has at least put a portion of the island's destiny back into its own people's hands.

The region is divided in four provinces: Sassari (the biggest in Italy), Nuoro, Oristano (created in 1974) and Cagliari. Each province is further broken down into *comuni* (the local government level), of which there are 377 across the island.

A national law permitting the creation of new provinces has all Sardinia in ferment. Some believe that carving out new provinces would bring government closer to the people, while others feel it would mean little more than a costly multiplication of bureaucracy. Candidates include: Gallura (with capital in Olbia), a province whose creation would largely be at the expense of Sassari; Ogliastra (which would comprise much of the Nuoro east coast – a considerable source of tourist euros); Medio Campidano and Sulcis (both of which would be carved out of Cagliari province). The national government in Rome views these proposed new divisions with less than lukewarm enthusiasm and has appealed to the Constitutional Court to block the changes. At the time of writing the issue remained very much up in the air.

The youthful right-wing Mauro Pili (born 1968) was elected regional president in 2001 but he soon found himself under siege, with the opposition calling both for his dismissal for incompetence and new elections in mid-2002. Even coalition partners, the far-right Alleanza Nazionale, suggested one of their own candidates might make a better fist of the job. Pili's own party, the Italian prime minister and media magnate Silvio Berlusconi's Forza Italia, has stuck by its young man, who at the time of writing was showing no signs of caving in.

Hovering on the sideline of politics is the Partito Sardo d'Azione, the descendant of the nationalist party formed after WWI and fervent exponent of the Sardinian national cause. Since the party congress of 1979 its stated policy aim has been Sardinian independence, although many *sardistas* envisage a loose federal association with the rest of Italy. In the mid-1980s the PSDA reached the apogee of its electoral power, winning more than 10% of the regional vote in regional and national elections and managing to take control of some local councils. Nowadays it has largely run out of steam and contents itself with the occasional vociferous independence demonstration and pushing of 'national' issues like the teaching and promotion of the Sardinian language.

ECONOMY

In some respects nothing much has changed over the centuries. Farming remains an important part of the local economy and until the 1970s accounted for the biggest slice of the workforce. The main products of the land are wheat, olives, wine and cork. Milk- and meat-producing cattle no longer figure highly but the raising of sheep and goats (for milk, cheese and meat) is big business. Indeed, Sardinia accounts for half of Italy's ewe's milk.

That said, since WWII the younger generations have been leaving the land. Small holdings and traditional methods mean that even today many farmers make a meagre living and up to two-thirds of the island's food needs are imported. Still, research on improving the sheep stock and artificial insemination is advancing rapidly and moves are afoot to widen export markets for products such as the island's *pecorino* cheese. Fishing also makes a small contribution to the economy.

Lead and zinc mining, as well as the extraction of low-grade coal, in southwestern Sardinia slowed in the 1970s. Metals (including silver) had been mined in the area since ancient times and prior to WWII Sardinia accounted for 90% of lead and 75% of zinc production in Italy. The last functioning mines were finally shut in the mid-1990s.

Ambitious plans to create poles of heavy industry (eg, petrochemical plants at Porto Torres and around Cagliari, and a thermo-electric power complex and aluminium smelter at Portovesme) in the 1960s have largely failed to propel the island into economic modernity. Tourism has until recently brought seasonal bonanzas in summer and some effort is being made to promote the island out of peak season too.

Big obstacles remain in the way of cranking up the island's economy. The road system, with few dual-carriage highways and no motorways, hampers communications and transport. The water issue affects farming and industry as well as day-to-day life. A certain lethargy seems to pervade the place. Why, Sardinians ask, have the millions of euros of EU funding designated for improving infrastructure and initiating other projects been left untouched by the region? Strangely, no-one seems to have found anything to spend the money on! At least it hasn't disappeared in a swamp of corruption, as might have happened elsewhere in Italy. Problem is, there is a time limit on when it can be used.

The Italian President, Carlo Ciampi, in 2002 called on the Sardinians to pull together to give the island a kick-start. He sees the future in hi-tech and small enterprises, a model that has worked well in several Italian regions.

Predictably, unemployment plagues Sardinia. Figures show it oscillating between 18.7% and 20.1% (the national figure is 9.5%), one of the worst figures in the EU. Youth (25 and under) unemployment stands at 52%. One lugubrious local newspaper report pointed out that, with the exception of two other Italian regions (Campania and Calabria), to find worse figures you had to look to Bulgaria (where in one region the figure is 75.5%). Of those working an alarming 20% work 'black', unregistered and without contract (and clearly not paying taxes).

POPULATION & PEOPLE

The Sardinians are a hardy and proud. There are, however, surprisingly few of them and the numbers are falling. Out of a total Italian population of around 58 million, only 1,648,044 live in Sardinia. The number of Sardinians is probably much greater, since over the decades (especially 1950–80) many have migrated to the mainland and abroad.

Almost half the present population is concentrated in the southern province of Cagliari (764,253). Next comes Sassari (459,149), followed by Nuoro (267,997) and Oristano (156,645).

Population density in Sardinia is just 69 per sq km, compared with the Italian average of 192 and 425 in Campania, the country's most densely populated region.

With a low birth rate, little inward migration and many young people opting to move to the Italian mainland, the island's population looks doomed to drop. The national statistics institute, Istat, predicts the population could fall to 1,230,000 by 2050. Local statistics published in 2002 said the population fell by 3% the previous year.

They may be small in numbers but the Sardinians are big in heart. True, centuries of foreign or distant and disinterested rule have left them reserved and the easy, casual contact often possible with Italians in other regions is more of an exception than the general rule in Sardinia. But once the initial diffidence is surmounted, most people find the Sardinians to be disarmingly friendly and generous.

In the interior, especially in the small towns of Nuoro province, attitudes to outsiders (even from other parts of the island) can still be prickly. These people are, more than other Sardinians, deeply attached to their land and traditions, and have long regarded outsiders (who have frequently brought bad news, more tax and harsh treatment) at best warily and at worst with hostility. Exchanges can at first be cordial but icy. But once that ice is broken, you may find yourself being wined and dined way past your capacity.

EDUCATION

The universities of Cagliari and Sassari both got started towards the end of the 16th century. They have since gone through ups and downs, at times plummeting to disastrous depths of neglect, but today are vibrant centres of learning.

Between them, the universities cover such areas as architecture, economics, political science, letters, pharmacy, law, medicine, engineering and general science. Some faculties have decentralised sites in the areas of Nuoro and Oristano. A grand total of 55,400 students are enrolled at the two universities.

The illiteracy level of around 4% is almost double the national average but lower than in many parts of southern Italy. In 1951, 22% of the population was illiterate.

ARTS

Little more than a footnote in the grand opus of the Italian arts, Sardinia nonetheless presents its own rich pallet. In architecture its treasures range from the mysterious nuraghes to the countryside Romanesque churches built mostly under the Tuscan influence of the Pisans. Some interesting material in painting and sculpture also awaits discovery. In the 20th century in particular Sardinian writers have left an indelible mark on Italian literature, while in music the past 20 or so years have seen an encouraging rediscovery and, on occasion, reinterpretation of traditional song, instruments and dance.

Architecture

Ancient Sardinia Excepting the mysterious ziggurat-style temple of Monte d'Accoddi, which dates to the third millennium BC, the most striking architectural testimony to this ancient island's distant past are the nuraghes. Some 7000 of these strange stone towers have been counted around the island, and the earliest may have gone up as far back as 1800 BC.

These Bronze Age structures, usually made of great slabs of dark basalt or trachyte, have defied explanation. The roughly hewn stones were piled up in circular fashion, diminishing in radius towards the top and held together by the gravity.

Nowadays some are little more than isolated and ruined circular trunks where before may have stood three-storey towers. The most remarkable complexes boast towers still largely intact, surrounded by defensive walls and smaller towers and often the remnants of an attendant village with its largely circular dwellings. The towers all follow similar patterns. They tend to have a rounded, conical or 'beehive' shape (also known as *tholos*-shaped), particularly noticeable inside the better-preserved ones. The more elaborate towers had what seems to have been a meeting room at their core, surrounded by a circular walkway from which stairs would lead to the higher floors.

Most believe the towers, at least later in their history when perimeter walls were raised, served as the heart of a defensive system – the ancient precursor to medieval castles, only frequently built in the plains rather than atop hills.

Before the first *nuraghe* was built, the ancient Sardinians, whoever they were, were already digging tombs into the rock all over the island. Later dubbed *domus de janas* (fairy houses) by Sardinian farmers, they were later joined (in the late-Neolithic period and early Bronze Age) by menhirs and betyls, vaguely anthropomorphic statues raised in burial grounds and sacred sites, and *tombe di giganti* (giants' tombs), so-called because the symbolic entrance area, or *exedra*, was marked by a tall, imposing, central stone slab with a sculpted, curved top. At the bottom of this slab, flanked on either side by a row of shorter slabs, is a little entrance leading to the long corridor-shaped communal grave behind.

Finally, from about 1100–1000 BC, the nuraghic peoples began constructing their elaborate *pozzi sacri* (sacred wells or well temples). Those discovered display many common traits. Including a keyhole shaped opening in the ground with a triangular stairwell leading down to the well. The wells always face the sun and are so oriented that at the solstices the sun shines directly down the stairs. The building techniques were more refined than those employed in the nuraghes and nowhere is this more evident than in the Santa Cristina site, near the grand Nuraghe Losa in the west of the island (see the Oristano & the West chapter), and the Su Tempiesu site northeast of Nuoro.

Classical Sardinia Precious little remains of Phoenician or even Carthaginian settlements in Sardinia, which have either disappeared or were so completely altered by their Roman successors that nothing was left for anyone but keen-eyed archaeologists. In Sant'Antioco and atop Monte Sirai, both in the southwest of the island, you can see modest remains of Carthaginian sites, notably their necropoli and *tophets* (long thought to have been a site of ritual human sacrifice but more recently considered as sacred sites where deceased infants and children were ritually cremated).

The Roman legacy is more obvious. The two outstanding towns are Nora (near Cagliari in the south) and Tharros (in the west). These ports started as Phoenician trading settlements but what you see today are Roman roads, columns, the remnants of

temples, public baths, theatres and patricians' houses. A grander Roman theatre survived in Cagliari too. In the southwest, the Tempio di Antas is a Roman construction but in front of it survives part of its Carthaginian predecessor. The ruins of Porto Torres (in the north) and the hot baths of Fordongianus are further evidence of the Roman presence on the island.

Romanesque to Baroque Most appealing of all are the charming Romanesque churches scattered about the Sardinian countryside. Most date to the 12th and 13th centuries. Equally noteworthy for the buff are a handful of more ancient churches, such as San Giovanni di Sinis, part of which dates to the 6th century.

The Romanesque gems are mostly concentrated in the northwest. The style first emerged in the Lombard plains of northern Italy. Adopting the classical Roman structure of the basilica, Romanesque churches were generally composed of a nave and two aisles, no transept and one, three or sometimes five apses. Initially they were bereft of sculptural ornament except for the semicircular arches above doorways and windows. The apses were semicircular too. Such churches were most commonly accompanied by a free-standing square-based bell tower, also adorned with layers of semicircular arched windows.

In Tuscany the style quickly became more ornate, especially in cities like Pisa and Lucca, with abundant local supplies of marble and other stone nearby. It was the Pisans who brought the style to Sardinia as they began to meddle in the island's affairs.

Although the churches vary a great deal, some common elements are easily traced. The typically Tuscan bent for two-colour banding with two types of stone in the facade and sometimes right around the building is a standard feature. Marble was in short supply and in the northwest the predominant stone, deep red trachyte, was used with whatever light-coloured stone (such as limestone) was handy to create the two-tone effect. Some churches are otherwise bereft of decoration, while some are rich in geometrical tracery and the sculpted heads of humans and beasts. One of the biggest and most curious Romanesque churches on this island is the sunny limestone Basilica di

San Gavino, with its strange apses on either end of the church, in Porto Torres.

The Pisans also left behind some startling examples of secular architecture, such as the grand defensive towers in Cagliari.

The Catalano-Aragonese, and subsequently Spaniards, who followed the Pisans left a mix of Gothic and later some baroque efforts behind them, often rolled into one as baroque baubles were added to nobler Gothic structures.

Sassari's two main churches, the Duomo and the Chiesa di Santa Maria di Betlem, are examples of this fusion. Indeed the latter displays a wonderful late-Romanesque richness in its facade, along with its Gothic and baroque features. The Duomo's facade, on the other hand, is a superb example of a baroque reminiscent of the sugary excesses of Lecce in southeastern Italy. Other fine examples of purely baroque buildings can be discovered in Cagliari.

Modern Times From the late-18th century until today, truly inspired architecture has been in short supply. The occasional neoclassical or neo-Gothic whim (such as Cagliari's town hall) awakens mild curiosity, but by and large inspiration has been conspicuous by its absence.

Gaetano Cima (1805–78), a native of Cagliari whose studies took him to Turin, presided over the island's architectural scene through much of the 19th century. Regarded by some as the island's greatest ever architect, he indulged in a neoclassical renewal of many buildings, including private mansions and Cagliari's Ospedale Civile. The facade of the Chiesa di San Francisco in Oristano also bares his signature.

Painting & Sculpture
Ancient Art As far back as the fourth millennium BC, ancient Sardinians were displaying the first signs of artistic awareness with simple, engraved decoration of their ceramics. By the third millennium BC and possibly before, the ancients were already etching symbols, frequently representing bulls, inside the rough walls of the *domus de janas* rock tombs. By the second millennium BC, menhirs (great stone blocks lightly sculpted to represent female and male human forms) were being erected in sacred sites (such as Pranu Mutteddu, near Goni).

Around the island (and indeed all over the Mediterranean) the ancients carved simple stone figures apparently representative of a female divinity.

Over the centuries the sophistication in ceramics decoration grew but the really startling development came in the Late Bronze Age (from about 1000 BC) with the emergence of the wonderful *bronzetti*, bronze figurines representing all manner of people, including chieftains, warriors and wrestlers, as well as bulls and other animals and little votive boats.

Ancient Greek and Mycenaean traders and then Phoenicians, who began to establish coastal settlements in the 9th century BC, brought the islands into closer contact with the art of Classical Greece and the Middle East. While not much remains of the settlements of the Phoenicians or their Carthaginian offshoots, they left behind plenty of artistic treasure. Assembled in the island's museums, items range from fine ceramics to jewellery, including some exquisite gold pieces, glassware and sculpture.

Much more of the Roman legacy has survived, including mosaics (some left *in situ* in places like Nora), ceramics, statuary, jewellery and so on. The best collections are in the archaeological museums of Cagliari and Sassari.

From the Middle Ages to the 18th Century If Sardinia's Romanesque churches followed the example of churches from the same period elsewhere in the Christian Mediterranean (eg, northern Spain and Italy) they may well have been richly decorated with frescoes and wooden sculpture. Nothing much has survived to this day however.

By the end of the 14th century a series of good, and in some cases outstanding, painters, influenced by trends in Catalonia and Spain, were at work in Sardinia. To the great annoyance of art historians many remain anonymous and something of an elaborate guessing game continues in the assigning of works to one or other *maestro*.

The Catalano-Aragonese brought not only soldiers and war, but also art, and in particular the *retablo* (*retaule* in Catalan) which are intricate, multi-panelled displays painted on wood and placed behind the altar. This very Iberian item was first imported from Barcelona. Then came artists, such as Joan

Mates (documented 1391–1431), one of whose *retablo* is displayed in Cagliari's Pinacoteca Nazionale, the island's most important collection of Sardinian masters.

It is unknown whether the Maestro di Castelsardo (documented at the end of the 15th and early 16th centuries) was one of those artists to come from Barcelona, or whether he had simply spent some time in the Catalan capital. A number of his works, all vivid colour on backgrounds either glittering with gold or intensely dark, still hang in the cathedral in Castelsardo. He also left a smattering of works elsewhere on the island.

Among his contemporaries were the Maestro di Sanluri (one of the earliest Sardinian artists to pick up on lessons from the Renaissance and move away from the stuffy rigidity of Gothic painting) and Maestro di Olzai, both named after locations where they left behind works, who were active towards the end of the 15th century.

If Sardinian art had a golden age, it was probably the 16th century, dominated by the so-called *scuola di Stampace* (Stampace School) at whose core was the Cavaro family. The star was Pietro (documented 1508–38), who was schooled in Barcelona and Naples and some of whose works, among them a remarkably expressive *SS Pietro e Paolo* (Sts Peter & Paul), hang in the Pinacoteca Nazionale. His father Lorenzo (documented 1500–18) and son Michele (documented 1538–84) are also represented in the same collection, along with colleague Antioco Mainas (documented 1537–71). Despite their undoubted talent, it is remarkable that painting in Sardinia still retained a somewhat stilted Gothic feel at a time when in the great cities of mainland Italy the Renaissance had already come and gone.

Little is known about the Maestro di Ozieri except that he worked in the latter half of the 16th century and that, along with Pietro Cavaro, he is considered one of the masters of Sardinian painting. He was imbued with the flowing Mannerism of Michelangelo and Rafael but also influenced by artists from as far afield as Naples and the Netherlands. Today one of his most important works, the *Deposizione di Cristo dalla Croce*, can be seen in the cathedral in Ozieri.

The 17th and 18th centuries in the island were largely dominated by the work of outsiders who came and went. A couple of exceptions early on were the Alghero-born Francesco Pinna (documented 1591–1616) and Bartolomeo Castagnola (documented 1598–1611). As elsewhere in Europe, the 18th century was dominated by baroque, evident in architecture as well as in the decorative frescoes that often came with church remakes – Cagliari's cathedral sports some good examples of the genre.

From the 19th Century to the Present

In Sardinia, Giovanni Marghinotti (1798–1865) hit the artistic stage much as Gaetano Cima dominated the architectural scene. His work ranged from altar pieces for churches all over the island to portraits of King Carlo Alberto and a series of romantic flights of fantasy depicting scenes of life in Roman and medieval Sardinia. Antonio Ballero (1864–1932), painter and writer, was strongly influenced by the French Impressionists.

The early 20th century belonged to Giuseppe Biasi (1885–1945), who adopted bold colours and forms in his approach to painting, producing a wide assortment of works from landscapes to portraiture.

Landscapes and rural scenes also dominated the oeuvre of some of his immediate successors, among them Stanis Dessy (1900–86), Giovanni Ciusa-Romagna (1907–58) and Cesare Cabras (1886–1965).

The 1970s inspired a popular art movement that spread from town to town across the island – *murales* (murals). Born of the student and workers' unrest of 1968, the murals were often a political statement. Those of Orgosolo, a rough and tumble village with a reputation for banditry, are perhaps the best known but the *murales* of San Sperate, outside Cagliari, are also worth checking out. Sculptor Pinuccio Sciola (born 1942) has added open-air statues to San Sperate. Times have moved on but the *murales* keep coming, not only here but in other towns as well.

Sardinia's most important sculptor of the first half of the 20th century, Francesco Ciusa (1883–1949), is best known for his *Madre dell'Ucciso*, now in Rome. It won the Venice Biennale prize in 1907.

Costantino Nivola (1911–88) took the baton from Ciusa. His works in bronze and menhir-inspired statues are best admired in the museum dedicated to his work in Orani. More is on show in Piazza Satta in Nuoro, as well as that city's MAN modern art museum.

Literature

Grazia Deledda (1871–1936), born in Nuoro, towers above the world of Sardinian literature and was one of Italy's most important realist writers of the early 20th century. Her best known novel is probably *Canne al Vento*, which recounts the slide into poverty of the aristocratic Pintor family, but all her works share a strong local flavour, following the lives and loves of local people. Her writings are tinged with a melancholy fatalism and a certain barely contained wildness. She moved to Rome in 1900 and in 1926 won the Nobel Prize.

Deledda said of her Sassari-born mentor, Enrico Costa (1841–1909), that he had written 'so many Sardinian novels, brimming with a warm love for his country and full of enthusiasm or sadness for the beauty and misery of the island'. One such novel, *La Bella di Cabras*, follows a tragic love story but is also laced with historical and folkloric tidbits shedding light on 19th-century Sardinian society.

Sebastiano Satta (1867–1914), lawyer, socialist and poet, was another son of Nuoro. In his working life he advocated a better deal for the island's poorer classes, while in his poetry (such as *Versi Ribelli* and *Canti Barbaricini*) he celebrated his country, especially Le Barbagie, in all its wildness and natural nobility.

Salvatore Satta (1902–75), yet another Nuoro boy, was foremost a lawyer and lecturer who ended up in Rome, but his posthumously published *Il Giorno del Giudizio* was a revelation. The book follows the decline of a well-off Nuoro family and has been compared with the Sicilian classic on roughly the same theme, Giuseppe Tomasi di Lampedusa's *Il Gattopardo*.

Satta's contemporary, Giuseppe Dessì (1909–77), who was raised in Villacidro but like so many Sardinians wound up in Rome, is best known for his novels and short stories, firmly bedded in an uncompromising realism, penned between 1939 and the early 1970s. *Il Disertore* recounts the story of a WWI deserter, caught between a sense of duty and his own moral code. Notable contemporaries of Dessì were Salvatore Cambosu (1895–1962) and eminent politician and intellectual Emilio Lussu (1890–1975).

Post-WWII writers include Calasetta-born Paride Rombi (1921–97), yet another scribbling lawyer whose prize-winning novel *Perdu* was also an act of solidarity with the Sulcis area's working classes, whose plight he describes in the book. Maria Giacobbe (born 1928) is a journalist and writer who has lived in Denmark since 1958 and is best known for her 1957 novel *Diario di una Maestrina*, about a small-town teacher.

Better known beyond Sardinia is Gavino Ledda (born 1938) who won few friends in the island with *Padre, Padrone*, a stark account of his own harsh life as a shepherd, battling the elements to stay alive under the tyranny of his father and nature. He only learned to read as an adult in the army, which was his ticket out of the cycle of poverty and ignorance that still afflicted many of his age in postwar Sardinia. The book was turned into an equally heart-rending film by the Taviani brothers in 1976.

Music

Many Sardinian youngsters prefer to listen to Italian pop, rock and rap, or the foreign equivalent. But the rise in interest in world music, at home and abroad, has probably saved the day for traditional Sardinian music.

The most obvious symbol of Sardinian folk music is the *launeddas*, or Sardinian reed pipes, which have added cheer to town feasts since at least the 18th century. In the standard version, this consists of three pipes of varying length. It is, in a sense, a simple version of the bagpipes, only with no bags. Instead the player uses his mouth and cheeks, almost constantly swollen with air, as a substitute for the bag. Although the instrument can be found all over the island, it is more common in the south. You can pick up several CDs with this kind of music, including Burranca's *Launeddas* and *Sonadas a Launeddas* by Sandro Flau.

In the northern half of the island folk have traditionally had a penchant for vocal music and traditional song has long been dominated by the *canto tenore*, four voices (usually male) unaccompanied by any sort of instrument. An example is the group from Bitti called Mialinu Pira.

Duos of singer and guitarist are a more recent phenomenon. A good one to look for is Duo Oliena, who play traditional folk music.

Choral music has deep roots in the island's musical history. They go back centuries and in the past might have sung

Bandits, Feuds & the Good Old Days

Even today inland country people can live by what may seem like harsh laws. Family *faide* (feuds) continue much as they have done down through the centuries. The code of the *vendetta* rules. If your family has done something to my family, you can be sure that sooner or later mine will retaliate. An eye for an eye.

Banditry, for which various parts of Nuoro province (eg, towns like Orgosolo) were long known (the island's Italian rulers declared much of the area a no-go zone throughout the 19th century), appears to have largely subsided but locals are still attached to their guns and a fiery liberty.

The phenomenon of banditry is largely linked to the historically precarious nature of the inland pastoralists' existence. Frequently driven to despair by crippling taxes, official disinterest and tough conditions on the land, the hardy men of the Barbagia have often turned to arms and frequently been regarded as Robin Hood–style heroes by their neighbours.

In the 1960s some bandits, among them the well-known Graziano Mesina, hit upon another money-making venture – kidnapping. Bandits would grab a member of a rich family, secrete them away in some inaccessible and mountainous corner of the province and demand healthy ransoms. Frequently the kidnap victims were killed, sometimes after torture. At a loss how to deal with the problem, Rome often opted for the iron fist approach to solving the problem, even sending in army units on occasion to flush out criminal bands. One of Italy's most prominent kidnap victims was the singer-songwriter Fabrizio de André, taken in 1979. He survived the event.

In the 1990s kidnappers adopted a new strategy. Rather than demand huge ransoms and embark on a protracted psychological game, some groups would try a blitz version, taking someone hostage and demanding a quick but relatively modest payment (such as the equivalent of €10,000) in return for immediate release. It seems that since the mid-1990s the kidnapping business has lost its lustre.

In their heyday, kidnappers could generally be sure of getting away with their crimes. Local people were too afraid of reprisals to help out the authorities. Indeed, given the complete absence of testimony and witnesses, it was not uncommon for known kidnappers to go about their normal lives completely undisturbed by the police.

---

anything from a traditional ode to the Savoy monarchs, *Cunservet Deus su Re*, to love songs such as the 19th-century classic, *Non Potho Reposare*. Several popular *coros* (choirs) sing their way around the island and have CDs out. Look out for Coro di Pozzomaggiore's *Sentimentos – Polyphonies Sardes*, Coro Ortobene's *Su Balu 'e S'Astore* and Coro Logudoro's *Melodias*.

One of the most intriguing vocal arts is the so-called *poesia cantata* (sung verses). At least as far back as the 19th century, villagers with a little talent would gather for some impromptu poetry duels, shooting improvised, sung verses at one another. Little of this was ever written down but you can find CDs with a classic duo from the mid-20th century, Remundo Piras and Peppe Sozu.

Contemporary Performers The last two decades of the 20th century saw a mushrooming of groups and individual artists in Sardinia, some indulging in a greater degree of *sardità* than others.

The most accomplished group is Cordas et Cannas. Their music, while based in folk tradition, has been given a modern polish lending it wide appeal.

Sardinia's most widely acclaimed musician is Paolo Fresu. One of Italy's best jazz trumpeters, there is nothing at all Sardinian about what he does, but Fresu has a habit of popping up as a guest on a lot of other Sardinian groups' CDs.

Franco Madau is a solid local *cantautore* (singer-songwriter) among whose better ballads can be found on CDs like *Animas Torran* and *Su Cantadore Malaitta*.

Elena Ledda, while perhaps a little too folksy for some, is the most accomplished female vocalist in Sardinia today. Mauro Palmas, who does wonderful things with the mandolin and laud, sometimes plays with Ledda's band.

More saccharine and in the vein of Italian light pop is Piero Marras, described by some as the Lucio Dalla of Sardinia (Dalla is *very* light Italian pop!). Marras has no shortage of albums: *Abbardente & Funtanafrisca*, *Tumbu*, *Stazzi Uniti* and *Fuori Campo* just to name a few.

A couple of groups that are rougher around the edges and whose material can be hard to come by include Tanit, a guitar ensemble, and Arcu de Chelu.

Dance

Various traditional folk dances still survive in Sardinia. Many are similar and generically referred to as *ballo sardo* (Sardinia dancing), or *su ballu tundu* (dancing in the round). They have much in common with Mediterranean folk dancing elsewhere. Sometimes people dance in a circle, on other occasions they pair off and scoot about with one arm held around the other's waist and facing the same way. Various combinations of quick steps backward and forward, followed by more lively movements, typify the dancing. For an idea of the music that typically accompanies the dancing you could try Lino Talloru's CD, *Balli Sardi a Chitarra*. There has been much speculation on the connections between *ballo sardo* and the similar *sardana* (circular folk dance) of Catalunya in northeastern Spain.

SOCIETY & CULTURE

The Sardinians can be a reserved lot. An understanding of the island's history provides part of the clue why. With the exception of the medieval Giudicati, the island has pretty much known only invasion and foreign masters. Since the days of the Catalano-Aragonese most of these masters (including the Italian government) have been at best largely indifferent to the island and its people and at worst exploited them. At least that's how many Sardinians see things.

In spite of that, the reserve is often no more than a surface defence. Break the ice and you will find the Sardinians a warm and sincerely

hospitable people. Sardinian reserve also has its advantages. Foreign women are less likely to encounter the cloying and ceaseless male attention that can occur elsewhere in Italy and the phenomenon of the fast-talking con artist is also rarer on the island.

You can still occasionally see older folk wandering about in traditional dress in the smaller inland towns, especially in Le Barbagie and some other hill areas (such as Logudoro). It was still a common sight until well into the 1950s.

RELIGION

Sardinia, like the rest of Italy, is predominantly Roman Catholic. While church attendance has fallen across Italy since the end of WWII, churches still tend to fill up regularly for Mass, even during the week, in many parts of Sardinia.

When the 1929 Lateran Treaty between the Vatican and the Italian state was modified in 1985, Catholicism was dropped as the state religion.

The Sardinian calendar is festooned with religious celebrations and some of them reflect the long centuries of Iberian domination. This is no more evident than in several towns' Easter celebrations. Places like Castelsardo, Iglesias and Tempio Pausania all put on solemn night processions dominated by the ominously hooded members of religious brotherhoods more readily associated with Spain.

Other customs seem more particular to the island. Across Sardinia are scattered *chiese novenari*, small countryside chapels that are the object one or more times through the year of nine-day pilgrimages. These churches are generally surrounded by *cumbessias* (also known as *muristenes*), simple lodgings to house the celebrating pilgrims who come to venerate the saint honoured in the church.

Facts for the Visitor

SUGGESTED ITINERARIES
Sardinia may be an island, but it's a big one. Even with your own transport, you may be surprised how long it can take to get from A to B. If time is limited you will need to plan ahead.

One Week
It is pointless trying to cover the island in such a short period. Choose an area and home in on it. You could explore the northwest, dedicating a day or two to Alghero and then following the coast north as far as Stintino. Another day each would be well spent in Sassari and Bosa and, if time and energy permit, you could head south for the ancient site of Tharros. With a car you could search out some of the many Romanesque churches and ancient nuraghic sites (especially Santu Antine) scattered about inland.

Similarly, you could base a week's trip on Cagliari (easily worth two days) and the south. You could head west from the capital to the ancient site of Nora and then the beaches around Chia. From there continue along the magic Costa del Sud and on to the islands of Sant'Antioco and San Pietro.

Another week-long option would see you based in the Golfo di Orosei. Three possible bases are Cala Gonone, Dorgali or Santa Maria Navarrese. From there plenty of excursions by boat, bus or car and on foot suggest themselves. Visit what are arguably the most beautiful beaches and coves (such as Cala Luna, Cala Mariolu and Cala Goloritzè) on the entire Sardinian coast and explore the caves of the Grotta del Bue Marino. Head up to the Altopiano del Golgo for horse riding, the extraordinary Golgo abyss and hearty country cooking. Trek the Gola Su Gorroppu gorge and make a side trip to the city of Nuoro.

You could throw a week at the northeast too, dealing the exclusive Costa Smeralda a glancing blow, exploring the Arcipelago di La Maddalena, and touring the broad open beaches west of Santa Teresa di Gallura en route to the striking hilltop coastal town of Castelsardo. Mix these in with some excursions inland to places like Tempio Pausania and the ancient sites around Arzachena and the time will sail past!

Two Weeks
The simplest answer is to join together two of the above suggestions. With the freedom of your own wheels, you could make a tour around the coast, touching on some of the highlights along the way.

One Month
You can move the length and breadth of the island. A circular route might start at any of the points of entry and take you not only along the coast but well inland. You will get a taste of the coast's variety: from the granite weirdness of Capo Testa to the grand cliffs of Capo Caccia west of the Alghero and from the beaches of Porto Ferro in the northwest to Spiaggia Scivu on the Costa Verde. In between swimming, you could seek out a range of ancient nuraghic sites and Romanesque churches across the island's interior, indulge in some trekking in the mountainous country of Nuoro province and explore the cities of Cagliari, Alghero and Sassari.

PLANNING
When to Go
Depending on your aims, you can visit Sardinia any time. Winter is out for sun lovers and midsummer for agoraphobes.

The best times are spring and autumn. In a good year, you could be happily stretched out on the beaches in April and as late as October. Touring the interior is best in spring (March to May and into June), when the wild flowers are in bloom and the countryside is at its greenest. Many towns celebrate their patron saints' festivals in spring. The months of September to October are also good.

From mid-July, all of Italy thunders to the sound of millions hitting the holiday roads – and Sardinia is one of their primary objectives. Hundreds of thousands pour in daily until towards the end of August, by which time the flood starts to flow in the opposite direction. It's a bad time to join in, as accommodation can be hard to find, prices reach for the sky and the summer heat can become unbearable.

You may wish to organise your trip or itinerary to coincide with one or more of the many festivals that litter the local calendar (see the Festivals special section).

31

i your time in Sardinia lounging around on beaches, sipping wine and eating great
    ;ht want to mix it up with some trekking, urban exploration and travelling back in
    d of the ancients. Some top picks include:

- Plunging / the impossibly blue-green-purple waters of the Golfo di Orosei
- Marvelling at the mysteries of the nuraghic sites, from Su Nuraxi to Santu Antine
- Tucking into a dish of *culurgiones*, followed by some succulent *porcetto*
- Poking around the nooks and crannies of the capital, Cagliari
- Sipping fine wines, from Cannonau reds through to Vermentino whites
- Searching out the Romanesque churches of the northwestern hinterland
- Hiking along the deep Gola Su Gorroppu gorge
- Exploring the classical seaside sites of Tharros and Nora
- Swimming on the beaches of the Costa Verde
- Scooting around the islands of the Arcipelago della Maddalena
- Diving into the web of alleys in the Catalan town of Alghero

The Worst
Not all is shimmering waters, curious sites and good food. You might think twice about:

- Getting caught in 20km traffic jams at the approach to Olbia port on an August weekend
- Wandering around many of the desolate villages of the interior, especially in Nuoro province
- Over-indulging in *filu e ferru*, the island's firewater
- Traipsing the streets of Carbonia, one of Mussolini's unhappier creations
- Acquiring a sandwich and a Coca Cola in Porto Cervo at astounding prices
- Travelling in the asphyxiating heat of mid-August

Maps

Island Maps The German publisher Marco Polo presents a clear map of the island (Map 9 of their *Italien* series), *Sardinien*, scaled at 1:200,000. The Touring Club d'Italia publishes a map on the same scale but it is not as up to date. Another Italian publisher is Istituto de Agostini. Look for Foglia 9 (Sheet 9) of their *Carta Generale d'Italia* series (scaled at 1:200,000).

A couple of publishers do area maps of certain parts of the island. Coedisar has a series that includes titles like *Carta del Sinis e del Montiferru, Carta del Iglesiente* and *Carta del Sulcis Occidentale*.

Walking Maps Various publishers put out hiking maps, especially covering the more popular areas around the Nuoro province. The best are the IGM series scaled at 1:25,000, which are, however, not easy to come by. The Florence-based **IGM** *(Istituto Geografico Militare; ☎ 055 273 27 60; W www .nettuno.it/fiera/igmi/igmit.htm; Viale Filippo Strozzi 10)* has a website with a list of shops where its maps are sold, or you can purchase them by mail.

What to Bring

Sardinia is hot in summer but variable in winter. Even in summer, you should bring a light pullover for the occasional evening when things cool down unexpectedly – especially in the hilly interior. Otherwise light clothing will generally be sufficient from June to September. In winter you should be prepared for cold weather at night, although you can often get surprisingly mild weather by day.

Italians like to dress well, so for dining out in the bigger towns or hanging around in cafés and bars you'll feel more comfortable with casually dressy clothes. A pair of hardy, comfortable walking shoes with rubber soles will come in handy too.

Unless you plan to spend large sums in dry-cleaners and laundries (self-service laundrettes are virtually non-existent in Sardinia), it's wise to pack a portable clothesline. Many hotels ask guests not to wash clothes in the room, but such rules are rarely enforced.

RESPONSIBLE TOURISM
In a nutshell, respect the monuments and works of art, the towns and their people as you would your own prized possessions. Tread softly and always with respect. At the many archaeological sites refrain from clambering over the monuments except where indicated (you can often follow paths to the top of nuraghic sites and wander around them).

TOURIST OFFICES
Local Tourist Offices
The region's tourist offices are broken down into provincial and local divisions. The regional directorate, or **Assessorato del Turismo** *(☎ 070 60 62 80; Viale Trieste 105)*, in Cagliari, is more of an administrative unit and unlikely to be of use to tourists.

Each provincial capital is home to an **Ente Provinciale per il Turismo** (ENIT), again largely administrative and promotion offices, although you can get information from them sometimes.

In the capitals and many other towns you will find an **Azienda Autonoma di Soggiorno e Turismo** (AAST) with information on the town and surrounding area. Some of these offices are more useful than others but it is always worth popping in.

The addresses and telephone numbers of local tourist offices as well as some useful provincial offices are listed throughout this book.

Tourist Offices Abroad
Information on Sardinia is available from the Italian State Tourist Office in the following countries:

Australia (☎ 02-9262 1666, |e| enitour@ihug.com.au) Level 26, 44 Market Street, Sydney 2000
Austria (☎ 00800 00482542, |e| delegation.wien@enit.at) Kaerntnerring 4, A-1010 Wien
Canada (☎ 416-925 4882, |e| enit.canada@on.aibn.com) Suite 907, South Tower, 175 Bloor Street East, Toronto, Ontario M4W3R8
France (☎ 01 42 66 03 96, |e| enit.parigi@wanadoo.fr) 23 Rue de La Paix, 75002 Paris
Germany *Berlin:* (☎ 030-247 83 98, |e| Enit-berlin@t-online.de) Kontorhaus Mitte, Friedrichstrasse 187, 10117
Munich: (☎ 089-531 317, |e| enit-muenchen@t-online.de) Goethestrasse 20, 80336

Frankfurt: (☎ 069-259 126, |e| enit.ffm@t-online.de) Kaiserstrasse 65, 60329
Netherlands (☎ 020-616 82 44, |e| enitams@wirehub.nl) Stadhouderskade 2, Amsterdam 1054 ES
Spain (☎ 91 559 97 50, |e| italiaturismo@retemail.es) Gran Via 84, Edificio España 1-1, Madrid 28013
Switzerland (☎ 01-2117917, |e| enit@bluewin.ch) Uraniastrasse 32, 8001 Zurich
UK (☎ 020-7355 1557, |e| italy@italiantourist board.co.uk) 1 Princess St, London W1B 2AY
USA *Chicago:* (☎ 312-644 0996, |e| enitch@italiantourism.com) 500 North Michigan Avenue, Suite 2240, Chicago, IL 60611
Los Angeles: (☎ 310-820 1898, |e| enitla@earthlink.net) 12400 Wilshire Blvd, Suite 550, Los Angeles, CA 90025
New York: (☎ 212-245 4822, |e| enitny@italiantourism.com) 630 Fifth Avenue, Suite 1565, New York, NY 10111

VISAS & DOCUMENTS
Passport
Citizens of European Union (EU) member states can travel to Italy with their national identity cards. People from countries that do not issue ID cards, such as the UK, must carry a valid passport. All non-EU nationals must have a full valid passport.

If you've had your passport for a while, you should check that the expiry date is at least some months off, otherwise you may not be granted a visa (if you need one). If your passport is stolen or lost while in Italy, notify the police and obtain a statement, and then contact your embassy or consulate as soon as possible.

The only time you are likely to have your passport stamped is when you arrive by air, but not if you are coming from another Schengen area country (see Visas, later). If you plan to stay for an extended period, you should insist on having the entry stamp. Without it you could encounter problems when trying to obtain a *permesso di soggiorno* – permission to remain in the country for a nominated period – which is essential for everything from enrolling at a language school to applying for residency in Italy (see Permesso di Soggiorno under Visas).

Visas
Italy is one of 15 member countries of the Schengen Convention, an agreement whereby

all EU member countries (except the UK and Ireland) plus Iceland and Norway abolished checks at internal borders in 2000.

EU, Norwegian and Icelandic nationals do not need a visa, regardless of the length or purpose of their visit to Italy.

Nationals of many other countries, including Australia, Canada, Israel, Japan, New Zealand, Switzerland and the USA, do not need to organise a visa for tourist visits of up to 90 days. If you wish to work or study in Sardinia you may need a specific visa, so contact an Italian consulate before you travel.

If you are a citizen of a country not mentioned in this section, check with an Italian consulate whether you need a visa.

Permesso di Soggiorno Visitors are technically obliged to report to the *questura* (police headquarters) and receive a *permesso di soggiorno* (permit allowing them to remain in the country) if they plan to stay at the same address for more than one week. Tourists staying in hotels and the like need not bother, as hotel owners register guests with the police.

A *permesso di soggiorno* only becomes a necessity if you plan to study, work (legally) or live in Italy. Obtaining one is generally a lengthy business. For details of what you need, approach the *questura* nearest to your accommodation.

Work Permits Non-EU citizens wishing to work in Sardinia need to obtain a *permesso di lavoro* (work permit). If you intend to work for an Italian company, the company must organise the *permesso* and forward it to the Italian consulate in your country – only then will you be issued an appropriate visa. In other cases, you must organise the permit through the Italian consulate in your country of residence.

Some foreigners don't bother with such formalities, preferring to work `black' in areas such as teaching English, bar work and seasonal jobs. In Sardinia however, the scope for such work is limited. See Work later in this chapter.

Study Visas Non-EU citizens who want to study at a university or language school in Sardinia must have a study visa. These visas can be obtained from your nearest Italian embassy or consulate. You will normally require confirmation of enrolment, proof of payment of fees and adequate funds to support yourself before a visa is issued. The visa will then cover only the period of the enrolment. This type of visa is renewable in Italy but, again, only with confirmation of ongoing enrolment and proof that you are able to support yourself – bank statements are preferred.

Travel Insurance
Don't leave home without it! It will cover you for medical expenses, luggage theft or loss, and for cancellation of and delays in travel. Cover depends on your insurance and type of ticket, so ask your insurer and ticket-issuing agency to explain where you stand. Ticket loss is also covered by travel insurance, but keep a separate record of your ticket details (see Copies, later).

Paying for your ticket with a credit card often provides limited travel accident insurance, and you may be able to reclaim the payment if the operator doesn't deliver. Ask your credit card company what it will cover.

Driving Licence & Permits
If you plan to drive while in Italy, take your driver's licence. Those driving their own vehicles will need to carry the vehicle's papers and insurance. See the Getting There & Away chapter for more details.

Hostel Card
With only three youth hostels on the island you may not consider it worth the effort of becoming a member of Hostelling International ([w] www.iyhf.org/mediterranean _italy_gb.html) just for a trip to the island. Should you decide when you get there that you want to use the hostels, you can become a member on the spot. You take out a card that requires six stamps, each costing €2.58 to be paid in addition to the accommodation cost. When you have the six stamps, you are considered a member of the association for the remainder of the calendar year.

Travel Discounts
An International Student Identity Card (ISIC) or similar card can get you discounted entry prices into some sights and help with cheap flights out of Italy and other travel discounts. Similar cards (ITIC)

are available to teachers. They also carry a travel insurance component. If you're aged under 26 but not a student you can apply for a Euro<26 card, which gives much the same discounts as ISIC.

These student cards are issued by student unions, hostelling organisations and some youth travel agencies. Their usefulness is a trifle limited in Sardinia, but on balance you are better off with one than without. You won't always be entitled to discounts, but you won't find out until you flash the card.

In Sardinia offices of the Centro Turistico Studentesco e Giovanile (CTS) issue ISIC, ITIC and Euro<26 cards.

Copies

All important documents (passport data page and visa page, credit cards, travel insurance policy, air/bus/train tickets, driving licence etc) should be photocopied. Leave one copy with someone at home and keep another with you, separate from the originals.

It's also a good idea to store details of your vital travel documents in Lonely Planet's free online Travel Vault in case you lose the photocopies. Your password-protected Travel Vault is accessible online – create it at W www.ekno.lonelyplanet.com.

EMBASSIES & CONSULATES
Your Own Embassy

Embassies can generally do little for their citizens if they get themselves into trouble with the law. They can assist with replacement passports and perhaps with arranging an English-speaking lawyer.

Italian Embassies & Consulates

The following is a selection of Italian diplomatic missions abroad. Italy maintains consulates in additional cities in many of the countries listed here:

Australia (☎ 02-6273 3333, fax 6273 4223, W www.ambitalia.org.au) 12 Grey St, Deakin, ACT 2600
    Consulates: (☎ 02-9392 7900) Sydney, (☎ 03-9867 5744) Melbourne
Austria (☎ 01-712 5121, fax 01-713 9719, e ambitalviepress@via.at) Metternichgasse 13, Vienna 1030
Canada (☎ 613-232 2401, fax 613-233 1484, W www.italyincanada.com) 21st floor, 275 Slater St, Ottawa, Ontario KIP 5H9
    Consulates: (☎ 514-849 8351) Montreal,

(☎ 416-977 1566) Toronto, (☎ 604-684 7288) Vancouver
France (☎ 01 49 54 03 00, fax 01 45 49 35 81, e ambasciata@amb-italie.fr) 47 rue de Varenne, Paris 75007
Germany (☎ 030 254400, fax 030 2544 0169, W www.ambasciata-italia.de) Dessauer Strasse 28/29, 10963 Berlin
Ireland (☎ 01-660 1744, fax 668 2759, W www .italianembassy.ie) 63–65 Northumberland Rd, Dublin
Netherlands (☎ 070-302 1030, fax 070-361 4932, W www.italy.nl) Alexanderstraat12, The Hague 2514 JL
New Zealand (☎ 04-473 53 39, fax 472 72 55, W www.italy-embassy.org.nz) 34 Grant Rd, Thorndon, Wellington
Switzerland (☎ 031 352 41 51, fax 031 351 1026, e ambital.berna@spectraweb.ch, W www3.itu.int/embassy/italy) Elfenstrasse 14, Bern 3006
UK (☎ 020-7312 2200, fax 7312 2230, W www .embitaly.org.uk) 14 Three Kings Yard, London W1Y 4EH
    Consulates: (☎ 0131-226 3631) Edinburgh, (☎ 0161-236 9024) Manchester
USA (☎ 202-612 4400, fax 518 2154, W www .italyemb.org) 3000 Whitehaven St, NW Washington DC 20008
    Consulates: (☎ 212-7737 9100) New York, (☎ 213-826 6207) Los Angeles

Embassies in Italy

Most countries have diplomatic representation in Rome. Some addresses follow:

Australia (☎ 06 85 27 22 93, W www.australian -embassy.it) Via Alessandria 215, 00198
Austria (☎ 06 844 01 41, W www.austria.it) Via Pergolesi 3, 00198
Canada (☎ 06 44 59 81, W www.canada.it) Via G B de Rossi 27, 00161
France (☎ 06 68 60 11, W www.france-italia.it) Piazza Farnese 67, 00186
Germany (☎ 06 49 21 31, W www.ambgermania .it) Via San Martino della Battaglia 4, 00185
Ireland (☎ 06 697 91 21) Piazza Campitelli 3, 00186
Netherlands (☎ 06 322 11 41, W www.olanda.it) Via Michele Mercati 8, 00197
New Zealand (☎ 06 440 29 28, e nzemb.rom@ flashnet.it) Via Zara 28, 00198
Switzerland (☎ 06 80 95 71, W www.eda.admin .ch/rome_emb/i/home) Via Barnarba Oriani 61, 00197
UK (☎ 06 422 00 00, W www.britain.it) Via XX Settembre 80a, 00187
USA (☎ 06 4 67 41, W www.usembassy.it) Via Vittorio Veneto 119a-121, 00187

Consulates in Sardinia

A handful of countries are represented by honorary consuls in Cagliari. Turn to the Cagliari & the South-East chapter for details.

CUSTOMS

People entering Italy from outside the EU are allowed to bring in one bottle of spirits, one bottle of wine, 50ml of perfume and 200 cigarettes duty-free.

Duty-free allowances for travel between EU countries were abolished in 1999. For *duty-paid* items bought at normal shops in one EU country and taken into another, the allowances are 90L of wine, 10L of spirits, unlimited quantities of perfume and 800 cigarettes. VAT-free shopping *is* available in the duty-free shops at airports for people travelling between EU countries.

MONEY

A combination of travellers cheques and credit or cash cards is the best way to carry your money.

Currency

On 1 January 2002, the euro (€) unseated the lira and became the new currency of Italy as well as 11 other EU nations.

The seven euro notes come in denominations of €500, €200, €100, €50, €20, €10 and €5, in different colours and sizes. The eight euro coins are in denominations of €2 and €1, then 50, 20, 10, five, two and one cents.

On the reverse side of the coins each participating state decorates the coins with its own designs, but all euro coins can be used anywhere that accepts euros.

Exchange Rates

country	unit		euros
Australia	A$1	=	€0.55
Canada	C$1	=	€0.62
Japan	¥100	=	€0.77
New Zealand	NZ$1	=	€0.50
UK	UK£1	=	€1.46
USA	US$1	=	€0.91

Exchanging Money

You can change money in banks, at the post office or in a *cambio* (exchange) booth. Banks are generally the most reliable and tend to offer the best rates. The post office is a good option too. However, you should look around and ask about commissions. These can fluctuate considerably and a lot depends on whether you are changing cash or cheques.

The post office charges a flat rate of €2.58 per cash transaction for amounts equivalent to up to €1032. Banks generally charge a similar rate and sometimes more. Travellers cheques attract higher fees and some places charge per-cheque fees. Exchange booths often advertise `no commission', but the rate of exchange can be inferior to that in the banks. Typical rates include a set transaction fee of €2.50 and 5% commission on cash or travellers cheques (generally a little less for euro travellers cheques). In some places the commission rate falls for larger amounts of money (say €500 and above).

At worst, exchange offices can charge like wounded bulls: up to 12.5% on foreign currency travellers cheques, 8% on euro travellers cheques and 6.5% on foreign cash.

Balanced against the desire to save on such fees by making occasional large transactions should be a healthy fear of pickpockets – you don't want to be robbed the day you've exchanged a huge hunk of money to last you weeks!

Cash There is little advantage in bringing foreign cash into Sardinia. True, exchange commissions are often lower than for travellers cheques, but the danger of losing the lot far outweighs such petty gains.

Travellers Cheques These are a safe way to carry money and are easily cashed at banks and exchange offices. Keep the bank receipt, listing the cheque numbers, separate from the cheques and keep a list of the numbers of those you have already cashed – this will reduce problems in the event of loss or theft. Check the conditions applying to such circumstances before buying the cheques.

Note that even cheques denominated in euros generally involve at least a transaction fee and frequently a percentage commission as well. Most hard currencies are widely accepted, although you may have occasional trouble with the New Zealand dollar. Get most of the cheques issued in largish denominations to save a bit on per-cheque exchange charges.

Travellers using the better-known cheques, such as Visa, American Express (AmEx) and

Thomas Cook, will have little trouble in Sardinia. If you lose your AmEx cheques, call its 24-hour toll-free number (☎ 800 87 20 00). For Thomas Cook or MasterCard cheques call ☎ 800 87 20 50 and for Visa cheques call ☎ 800 87 41 55.

Take along your passport when you go to cash travellers cheques.

Credit/Debit Cards & ATMs Carrying plastic (whether a credit or ATM card) is the simplest way to organise your holiday funds. You don't have large amounts of cash or cheques to lose, you can get money after hours and on weekends and the exchange rate is better than that offered for travellers cheques or cash exchanges. By arranging for payments to be made into your credit card account while you are travelling, you can avoid paying interest.

Major credit cards, such as Visa, Master-Card, Eurocard, Cirrus and Euro Cheques cards, are accepted in Sardinia. They can be used for many purchases (including in many supermarkets) and in hotels and restaurants (although cheaper hotels and smaller trattorie and pizzerie tend to accept cash only).

Credit/debit cards can also be used in a *bancomat* (ATMs) displaying the appropriate sign or (if you have no PIN number) to obtain cash advances over the counter in many banks – Visa and MasterCard are among the most widely recognised for such transactions. As a rule your bank will charge you 1.5% to 2% for using your cards abroad, but some banks have introduced sneakier added charges (that do not appear on statements) as well. You should make sure you understand all of the charges made before taking your cards abroad.

If your credit/debit card is lost, stolen or swallowed by an ATM, you can telephone toll-free to have an immediate stop put on it. For MasterCard the number in Italy is ☎ 800 86 80 86; for Visa, phone ☎ 800 87 72 32 in Italy; for AmEx cards call ☎ 800 86 40 46.

International Transfers One reliable way to send money to Sardinia is by TT or swift transfer through the foreign office of a large Italian bank, or through major banks in your own country, to a nominated bank in Sardinia. It is important to have an exact record of all details associated with the transfer, particularly the exact address of the Italian

bank to where the money has been sent. The money will always be held at the head office of the bank in the town to which it has been sent. Urgent telex transfers should take only a few days, while other means, such as telegraphic transfer or draft, can take weeks.

It is also possible to transfer money through AmEx and Thomas Cook. You will be required to produce identification, usually a passport, in order to collect the money. It is also a good idea to take along the details of the transaction.

One of the speedier options is to send money through Western Union. Call Italy's toll-free number (☎ 800 60 16 22) for the address of the outlet closest to you. The sender and receiver have to turn up at a Western Union outlet with their passport or other form of ID and the fees charged for the virtually immediate transfer depend on the amount sent. For instance, to send €65 to €130 you pay €14.50. To send €1000 the fee is €49.50. The Banca di Sassari acts as an agent for Western Union in Sardinia.

Security

Petty theft can be a problem in the cities and some of the more touristed beach resorts, so you need to keep an eye on your belongings.

Keep only a limited amount of your money as cash and the bulk in more easily replaceable forms, such as credit/debit cards or travellers cheques. If your accommodation has a safe, use it. If you must leave money and documents in your room, divide the former into several stashes and hide them in different places. Lockable luggage is a good deterrent.

Euro-Sting

Despite solemn declarations from the European Central Bank, no-one in Sardinia has any doubt that the euro has brought with it a sudden and unpleasant rise in the cost of living. In the summer of 2002, reports circulated that prices in Cagliari's fresh produce markets had as much as doubled over the previous year, and the cost of eating out had risen an average 25% across the island. Anyone visiting before and after the introduction of the euro could not fail to notice the difference, regardless of the official line on inflation remaining unchanged.

On the streets, keep as little on you as possible. The safest thing is a shoulder wallet or under-the-clothes money belt or pouch. External money belts tend to attract attention to your belongings rather than deflect it. If you eschew the use of any such device, keep money in your front pockets and watch out for people who seem to brush close to you.

Costs

Sardinia sits about mid-way on the scale of expense in Italy, although in summer it can edge closer to the top of the scale.

A prudent backpacker might get by on around €40 to €50 a day, but only by camping or staying in B&Bs and the cheapest of hotels. You'd have to keep to one simple meal a day and buy a sandwich or pizza slice for lunch.

You can get by more comfortably on €80 a day if you stay in the cheaper hotels. You could enjoy one good meal a day and a light lunch, and still have money left over for sights and a few drinks.

A traveller wanting to stay in comfortable mid-range hotels, eat two square meals a day and enjoy the odd drink and other minor indulgences should reckon on a minimum daily average of between €100 and €120 – more if you are driving.

A basic breakdown of costs per person during an average day for the budget to mid-range traveller could be: accommodation €13 (youth hostel) to €40 (single in a budget hotel or per person in a comfortable double), breakfast €3 (coffee and croissant), lunch €5 (sandwich/pizza slice and mineral water), bottle of mineral water €0.80, sit-down lunch/dinner €15 to €30. On top of that, you have to add transport around the island or petrol (expensive) if you are driving.

Tipping & Bargaining

You are not expected to tip on top of restaurant service charges, but it is common to leave a small amount, perhaps €1 per person. If there is no service charge, the customer might consider leaving a 10% tip, but this is by no means obligatory. In bars, Italians often leave small change as a tip. Tipping taxi drivers is not common practice, but you should tip the porter at top-end hotels.

Bargaining is common in flea markets, but not in shops. While bargaining in shops is not acceptable, you might find that the proprietor is disposed to give a discount if you are spending a reasonable amount of money.

It is quite acceptable (and advisable) to ask if there is a special price for a room in a hotel if you plan to stay for more than a few days.

Taxes & Refunds

A value-added tax of around 19%, known as IVA (Imposta di Valore Aggiunto), is slapped onto just about everything in Italy. If you are resident outside the EU and you spend more than €155 in the same shop on the same day, you can claim a refund on this tax when you leave the EU. The refund only applies to purchases from affiliated retail outlets that display a 'tax free for tourists' sign. You have to complete a form at the point of sale, then get it stamped by Italian customs as you leave. At major airports you can then get an immediate cash refund; otherwise it is supposed to be refunded to your credit card (in practice this seems to be a little hit and miss). For information, pick up a pamphlet on the scheme from participating stores.

Receipts

Tax laws lay the onus on the buyer to ask for and retain receipts for all goods and services. This applies to everything from a litre of milk to an Alfa Romeo. Although it rarely happens, you could be asked by an officer of the Guardia di Finanza (Fiscal Police) to produce the receipt immediately after you leave a shop. If you don't have it, you may be obliged to pay a hefty fine, the size of which seems to be largely at the discretion of the police – from €50 to €1000!

POST & COMMUNICATIONS
Post

Italy's postal system is not Europe's most reliable but it is improving.

Francobolli (stamps) are available at post offices and authorised tobacconists. Look for the official *tabacchi* sign: a big `T', usually white on black. Since letters often need to be weighed, what you get at the tobacconist's for international airmail will occasionally be an approximation of the proper rate. Tobacconists keep regular shopping hours.

Information about postal services can be obtained on ☎ 160 or you can visit the online site: W www.poste.it.

Sending Mail The cost of sending a letter *via aerea* (airmail) depends on its weight, destination and method of postage. For regular post, letters up to 20g cost €0.41 within Europe and €0.52 to Africa, Asia, the Americas, Australia and New Zealand. Postcards cost the same.

Few people use the regular post, preferring the slightly more expensive *posta prioritaria* (priority mail service), guaranteed to deliver letters to Europe within three days and to the rest of the world within four to eight days. Letters up to 20g sent *posta prioritaria* cost €0.62 within Europe and €0.77 to the Americas, Africa, Asia, Australia and New Zealand. Letters weighing 21g to 100g cost €0.77/1.24 (standard/priority) within Europe and €1.03/1.55 to Africa, Asia, the Americas, Australia and New Zealand.

For more important items use *raccomandato* (registered mail). This costs €2.58/2.69 for Europe/the rest of the world on top of the cost of the standard 20g letter. For letters of 21g to 100g the cost is €2.94/3.20. Or you could send *assicurato* (insured mail), the cost of which depends on the value of the object being sent (€5.16 for a standard 20g letter in Europe and €5.27 to the rest of the world). Insured mail is not available to the USA.

An air-mail letter can take up to two weeks to reach the UK or the USA, while a letter to Australia will take between two and three weeks. Postcards take even longer because they are classed as low-priority mail. Put them in an envelope and send them as letters.

Receiving Mail Poste restante is known as *fermo posta* in Italy. Letters marked thus will be held at the counter of the same name in the main post office in the relevant town. Poste restante mail to Cagliari, for example, should be addressed as follows:

John SMITH,
Fermo Posta,
09100 Cagliari
Italy

Postcodes are provided throughout this guide. You will need to pick up your letters in person and you must present your passport as ID.

Telephone

The international country code for Italy is ☎ 39. You must always include the initial 0 in area codes.

Direct international calls from Sardinia can easily be made from public telephones using a phonecard. Dial ☎ 00 to get out of Italy, then the relevant country and area codes, followed by the telephone number.

The state-run Telecom Italia is the largest telecommunications organisation in Italy, and its orange public pay phones are liberally scattered throughout Sardinia. The most common accept only *carte/schede telefoniche* (telephone cards), although some accept cards and coins. Some card phones also accept ordinary credit cards.

Telephone area codes all begin with 0 and consist of up to four digits. The area code is followed by a number of anything from four to eight digits.

Area codes are an integral part of all telephone numbers in Italy, even if you are calling within a single zone. If you are in Cagliari and are calling another fixed line in Cagliari the first three digits of the phone number will be ☎ 070.

Mobile phone numbers begin with a three-digit prefix such as ☎ 330, 335, 347, 368 etc. Free-phone or toll-free numbers are known as *numeri verdi* and start with ☎ 800. The national-rate phone numbers start with ☎ 848 and ☎ 199.

For directory inquires, dial ☎ 12. For international directory inquires call ☎ 176.

Phonecards You can buy phonecards (€2.50 or €5) at post offices, tobacconists and newspaper stands, and from vending machines in Telecom offices. You must break the top left-hand corner of the card before you can use it. Alternatively, some tobacconists sell international cheap-rate phone cards. Check out the relative costs for the destinations you want to call before purchasing. Unfortunately, there is always a small element of risk as some cards can be duds.

Lonely Planet's ekno global communication service provides low-cost international calls – for local calls you're better off with a local phonecard. ekno also offers free messaging services, email, travel information and an online travel vault, where you can securely store all your important

documents. You can join online at ⓦ www
.ekno.lonelyplanet.com.

Costs Call rates have been greatly simpli-
fied in Italy. A *comunicazione urbana* (local
call) from a public phone costs €0.10 every
minute and 21 seconds. For a *comunicazione
interurbana* (long-distance call within Italy)
you pay €0.10 when the call is answered and
the same for every 57 seconds.

The cost of calling abroad has fallen
greatly. A three-minute phone call from a
pay phone to most European countries and
North America will cost about €1.90. Aus-
tralasia is a different proposition: three minutes chew up €4.10; calling from a private
phone is cheaper. Calling foreign mobile
phones is more expensive to Europe and
North America, but the same to Australia
and New Zealand.

For information on costs (in Italian) call
☎ 800 66 63 33.

Travellers from countries that offer direct
dialling services paid for at home country
rates (such as AT&T in the USA and Telstra
in Australia) should think seriously about
taking advantage of them.

Mobile Phones You can buy SIM cards in
Italy for your own national mobile phone
(provided you own a GSM, dual- or tri-
band cellular phone) and buy prepaid time.
This only works if your national phone
hasn't been blocked, something you might
want to find out before leaving home. If
you buy a SIM card and find your phone *is*
blocked you won't be able to take it back.
You won't want to consider a full contract
unless you plan to live in Italy for a good
while, and even then the benefits are not always tangible. You need your passport to
open any kind of mobile phone account,
prepaid or otherwise.

Both TIM (Telecom Italia Mobile) and
Vodaphone-Omnitel offer *prepagato* (prepaid) accounts for GSM phones (frequency
900 mHz). The card can cost €50 to €60,
which includes some prepaid phone time.
You can then top up in their shops or by
buying cards in outlets like tobacconists and
newsstands.

TIM and Vodaphone-Omnitel retail outlets operate in virtually every Italian town.
Call rates vary according to an infinite variety of call plans.

Wind and Blu are two smaller mobile
phone operators with consequently fewer
outlets around the country.

US mobile phones generally work on a
frequency of 1900 mHz, so for use in Italy,
your US handset will have to be tri-band.

Fax
You can send faxes from post offices, some
tobacconists, copy centres and stationers.
Faxes can also be sent from some Telecom
public phones. To send a fax within Italy,
expect to pay €1.30 per page. International
faxes vary. To the UK for instance you pay
€2.46 for the first page and €2.15 per page
thereafter.

Email & Internet Access
If you bring your laptop, be aware that the
big international servers like AOL (ⓦ www
.aol.com) and its subsidiary CompuServe
(ⓦ www.compuserve.com) have only unreli-
able slow access dial-in numbers in Sardinia.
You may find yourself making long-distance
calls to faster nodes in Rome and Milan.

Several Italian ISPs offer free Internet connections. Some of ones worthwhile checking
out are: **Tiscalinet** (ⓦ *www.tiscalinet.it*), **Vir-
gilio** (ⓦ *www.virgilio.it*) **Kataweb** (ⓦ *www
.kata web.it*) and **Libero** (ⓦ *www.libero.it*).

Most people take the simpler route of relying on Internet cafés and other public access points to collect mail. For this you'll
need to carry three pieces of information
with you to enable you to access your Internet mail account: your incoming (POP or
IMAP) mail server name, your account name
and your password. Your ISP or network
supervisor will be able to give you these.

The bad news is that access points are not
abundant on the island. You will be lucky to
find more than one or two such centres in any
given location (often with only two or three
computers), and then only in major centres.

It is also an expensive affair, frequently
costing €4 to €5 an hour (although in some
places it can come down to about €2.50 an
hour). Clearly there is no great demand for
Internet-access centres in Sardinia!

DIGITAL RESOURCES
The World Wide Web is a rich resource for
travellers. You can research your trip, hunt
down bargain air fares, book hotels, check
on weather conditions or chat with locals

and other travellers about the best places to visit (or avoid!).

Start at the Lonely Planet website (**w** www .lonelyplanet.com), where you'll find succinct summaries on travelling to most places on earth, postcards from other travellers and the Thorn Tree bulletin board, where you can ask questions before you go or dispense advice when you get back. You can also find travel news and updates to many of our most popular guidebooks, and the subwwway section links you to the most useful travel resources elsewhere on the Web. Other useful sites include:

AlgheroNet For a more detailed look at what's going on in this delightful town, tune in to this website. It will link you to sister sites on Sassari, Olbia and Nuoro. (**w** www.algheronet.it)

CTS This is the site of Italy's main student travel organisation. (**w** www.cts.it, Italian only)

InfoSardegna Here you will find tips on everything from hotels through to beaches, restaurants, monuments and island traditions. (**w** www .infosardegna.com)

In Sardinia For those who read Italian, this is a handy introductory site to all things Sardinian, with history, gastronomy, latest news and views and stories from the Sardinian diaspora. (**w** www .webinsardinia.com, Italian only)

Regione Autonoma della Sardegna The island region's official site provides a wealth of general information on Sardinia in several languages. (**w** www.regione.sardegna.it)

SardegnaNet In Italian, English and German, these pages offer tips on sporting activities in Sardinia, including mountain biking, sailing, diving and trekking. You can also find information on accommodation and dining out. (**w** www .sardegna.net)

Sardegna On Line Magazine This site has all sorts of nuggets of practical information, ranging from villas for rent to ambulance phone numbers. Check the day's weather or get acquainted with local gastronomy. (**w** www.sardegna.com)

Sardinia on the Web This is a kind of Web hub, with a long list of links on all things Sardinian. (**w** www.crs4.it/Sardinia.html)

Sardinia Point Here you will find oodles of information on most conceivable aspects of the island, from music to *seadas* (sweet pastries). Some of the information is in English. (**w** www .sardiniapoint.it)

BOOKS

Most books are published in different editions by different publishers in different countries. Therefore we have not always given publishers' names in the following listings.

For information on Sardinian literature, see Literature under Arts in the Facts about Sardinia chapter. Books on Sardinia in English are in short supply.

Lonely Planet

If your time in Sardinia only serves to whet your appetite further for all things Italian, you can choose from a range of companion guides, including: *Rome, Rome Condensed, Florence, Venice, Venice Condensed, Turin, Genoa & Milan, Tuscany* and *Sicily*. *Italy* covers the entire country and *Walking in Italy* is a useful guide for experienced and not-so-experienced walkers who want to explore Italy's great outdoors.

The *Italian phrasebook* lists all the words and phrases you're likely to need in Italy.

Lonely Planet's *World Food Italy* by Australia's leading food writer, Matthew Evans, is a full-colour book with information on the whole range of Italian food and drink.

Guidebooks

If you read Italian the Touring Club Italiano's thick red volume *Sardegna* is doubtless the most detailed single-volume guidebook to the island, with more than 700 pages (somewhat heavy going at times) of detailed information on the island and its various sights, but nothing much on the beaches and countryside.

Carlo Delfino Editore publishes a long series of booklets on specific sights in Sardinia in its Sardegna Archeologica series. They cover several museums and places, ranging from Classical Nora and Tharros through to the Nuraghe di Santu Antine. They cost €5 to €6 and are useful tools for better understanding the island's outstanding ancient sites and museums. Some are in English too.

Walking & Mountain Biking

Maurizio Oviglia's *Sardegna*, published by the Club Alpino Italiano and Touring Club Italiano, is an exhaustive guide to mountain hikes across the island.

Gennargentu in Mountain Bike, by Francesco Pintore and Carlo Deidda (in Italian), offers a wealth of tips on getting about this mountainous national park region on two wheels.

Travel

D H Lawrence included the island on his meanderings through Italy and the result was *Sea and Sardinia*, an occasionally caustic but never tedious appraisal of the place.

French poet Paul Valéry was sufficiently moved by his time on the island to pen *Images d'Un Voyage de la Sardaigne*.

History & Politics

For a general overview of Italy you could try *Italy: A Short History* by Harry Hearder, *History of the Italian People* by Giuliano Procacci and *A History of Contemporary Italy: Society and Politics 1943–1988* by Paul Ginsborg. The latter is an absorbing account of post-war Italian society.

For an introduction to Sardinian history, *Storia della Sardegna* (edited by Manilo Brigalia) is not a bad first choice in Italian.

Food & Drink

A useful introduction to Sardinian cooking (translated from Italian) is *The Cooking of the Sardinians* by Paolo Prada and Vanda Ricciuti.

Another useful introduction is Gian Paolo Caredda's *Gastronomia in Sardegna*.

VIDEOS

A handful of videos on Sardinian themes can be dug up in a few bookshops around the island.

La Storia di Sardegna gives a brief run-down on the island's history (available in several languages).

Coasts of Sardinia (Videosar, €15.50) takes you around the coast, and possibly to some spots you won't have made it to.

SardegnArcheologia has a series of videos on important sites including *Tharros, La Regina del Sinis* and *Nora, La Città Risorta dal Mare* (in Italian; €10 each).

Alghero (€10), on the city of the same name, comes in a Catalan version (*L'Alguer*) as well as Italian. It can be found in bookshops in that city.

FILMS

The 2002 remake of Lina Wertmüller's 1970s classic, *Swept Away*, starring Madonna as the billionaire wife stranded on an island with an unkempt sailor, was shot partly in Sardinia; Carla Cartoe was a prominent figure.

NEWSPAPERS & MAGAZINES
English Language

The *International Herald Tribune* is available from Monday to Saturday. It has a daily four-page supplement, *Italy Daily*, covering specifically Italian news. British daily papers, including the *Guardian*, the *Times*, the *Daily Telegraph*, the *Independent* and the *Financial Times*, as well as various tabloids, are sent from London.

These papers are available from newspaper stands in Via Roma, Cagliari, and in a few of the coastal resorts but can be as much as two days late. The same goes for press from other European countries.

National Press

The Italian press is labyrinthine and not always satisfying. Foreign coverage tends to be spotty.

Several important dailies based in Rome, Milan and Turin get nationwide distribution. Milan's *Corriere della Sera* is the country's leading daily and its national and foreign coverage is about the best you will find. Rome's *Il Messaggero* and *La Repubblica* are widely distributed and Turin's *La Stampa* is also reasonable.

Sardinian Press

The island has two regional papers. In business since the late-19th century, *L'Unione Sarda* gives some scant attention to national and international affairs, as well as Sardinian regional topics. A series of pages then covers the provinces. There is even an English-language page (in summer at least).

The Cagliari-based paper (which often attracts a sneer in the north) gets its only serious competition from Sassari's *La Nuova Sardegna*, a bright tabloid equally devoid of foreign news. A handful of local papers also appear around the island.

RADIO & TV
Radio

You can pick up the BBC World Service on medium wave at 648kHz, on short wave at 6.195MHz, 9.410MHz, 12.095MHz and 15.575MHz, and on long wave at 198kHz, depending on where you are and the time of day. Voice of America (VOA) can usually be found on short wave at 15.205MHz.

There are three state-owned stations: RAI-1, RAI-2 and RAI-3. They combine classical and light music with news broadcasts and discussion programmes.

Commercial radio stations are a better bet if you're after contemporary music. National ones include Radio Capital, Italia Radio and Radio Deejay. Popular local stations include Radio Sardegna and the more boisterous Radiolina. Frequencies change depending on where you are on the island.

TV
Italian television is so bad it is compelling. An inordinate number of quiz shows and variety programmes with troupes of scantily clad women compete with local and foreign soaps and vociferous discussion programmes. An occasional credible documentary or film slips through the net.

The state-run channels are RAI 1, RAI 2 and RAI 3. The main commercial stations are Canale 5, Italia 1, Rete 4 and La 7. Local stations include Sardegna 1, Sardegna 2 and Videolina.

PHOTOGRAPHY & VIDEO
Film & Equipment
You'll find no shortage of film processing outlets in the main towns. A *rullino* (roll) of film is called a *pellicola*, but you will be understood if you ask for `film'. A 100 ASA colour film will cost €4.20 to €5 for 36 exposures, depending on the brand and the store. Developing costs around €10 to €12 for 36 exposures in standard format. A roll of 36 *diapositive* (slides) costs €5 to €5.60 to buy and €4 to €5 to develop.

Tapes for video cameras, including V8, are often available at the same outlets or can be found at stores selling cameras, videos and electrical goods.

Restrictions
Photography is not allowed in some churches, museums and galleries. Look for signs as you go in. These restrictions do not normally apply to archaeological sites.

Photography of military buildings (barracks and so on) is prohibited.

Photographing People
The standard rules about photographing people apply in Sardinia. It is appropriate to ask, at least by gesture, if you may snap someone. Children normally love it but adults may not (just as you may not!). In the interior of the island, you may well be advised to put your cameras away, especially in the rough and ready towns of the Barbagia region in Nuoro province. The reaction to unsolicited snapping is rarely one of contentment, and scowls of disapproval have been known to transform into rifle shots.

Airport Security
Italian airports are equipped with modern inspection systems that do not damage film or other photographic material carried in hand luggage.

TIME
Italy is one hour ahead of GMT/UTC.

Daylight-saving time starts on the last Sunday in March, when clocks are moved forward one hour. Clocks are put back one hour on the last Sunday in October. When telephoning home, remember to make allowances for daylight saving.

ELECTRICITY
Voltages & Cycles
The electric current in Italy is 220V, 50Hz, but check with the hotel management because some places, especially older buildings, may still use 125V.

Plugs & Sockets
Power points have two or three holes and do not have their own switches, while plugs have two or three round pins. Some power points have larger holes than others. Italian homes are usually full of plug adaptors to cope with this anomaly.

Make sure you bring international plug adaptors for your appliances. It is a good idea to buy these *before* leaving home, as they are virtually impossible to get in Sardinia. Travellers from North America need a voltage converter (although many of the more expensive hotels have provided for 110V appliances such as electric razors).

WEIGHTS & MEASURES
Italy uses the metric system. Basic terms for weight include *un etto* (100g) and *un chilo* (1kg). A standard metric-Imperial measures conversion table can be found on the inside back cover of this book.

Note that for numbers, Italians indicate decimals with commas and thousands with points.

LAUNDRY

Coin-operated laundrettes are virtually non-existent in Sardinia, although we found one in Cagliari. At a traditional *lavanderia*, which you will find in most towns, you pay to have things washed and pressed but the cost can be exorbitant. *Lavasecco* (dry-cleaning) is another option. In either case charges can range from around €3 for a shirt to €7.50 for a jacket. You usually have to wait a day to pick up.

TOILETS

Public toilets are not widespread and most people use the toilets in bars and cafés, although it is polite to buy a coffee first. Keep some loo paper with you, as café and bar loos are frequently bereft of this item.

HEALTH
Medical Services

If you need an ambulance anywhere in Sardinia call ☎ 118.

The quality of medical treatment in public hospitals is acceptable but not always top notch. Private hospitals and clinics generally provide better services but are expensive for those without medical insurance. Certain treatments in public hospitals may also have to be paid for, and in such cases can be equally costly.

The public health system is administered along provincial lines by centres generally known as Unità Sanitarie Locali (USL) or Aziende Sanitarie Locali (ASL). Through them you find out where your nearest hospital, clinics and other services are. Look under 'U' or 'A' in the telephone book (sometimes the USL is under 'A' too, as Azienda USL).

Under these headings look for Poliambulatorio (Polyclinic) and the telephone number for Accetazione Sanitaria. You need to call this number to make an appointment: just rolling up will often not work. Clinic opening hours vary widely, with the minimum generally being about 8am to 12.30pm Monday to Friday. Some open for a couple of hours in the afternoon and on Saturday mornings too.

Each ASL/USL area has its own Consultorio Familiare (Family Planning Centre) where you can go for contraceptives, pregnancy tests and information about abortion (legal up to the 12th week of pregnancy).

For emergency treatment, go straight to the *pronto soccorso* (casualty) section of a public hospital, where you can also get emergency dental treatment. Sometimes hospitals are listed in the phone book under Aziende Ospedaliere.

Medical Cover

All foreigners have the same right as Italians to free emergency medical treatment in a public hospital. EU citizens are entitled to the full range of health care services in public hospitals free of charge, but you will need to present your E111 form (inquire at your national health service before leaving home). Australia has a reciprocal arrangement with Italy that entitles Australian citizens to free public health care – carry your Medicare card.

Citizens of New Zealand, the US, Canada and other countries have to pay for anything other than emergency treatment. Most travel insurance policies include medical cover (see Travel Insurance earlier in this chapter).

General Preparations

Make sure you are healthy before you leave home. If you are embarking on a long trip, make sure your teeth are OK, because dental treatment is particularly expensive in Italy.

Medical Kit Check List

The following is a list of items you should consider including in your medical kit – consult your pharmacist for brands available in your country.

- **Aspirin** or **paracetamol** (acetaminophen in the USA) – for pain or fever
- **Antihistamine** – for allergies, to ease the itch from insect bites or stings and to prevent motion sickness
- **Loperamide** or **diphenoxylate** – 'blockers' for diarrhoea
- **Insect repellent, sunscreen, lip balm** and **eye drops**
- **Calamine lotion, sting-relief spray** or **aloe vera** – to ease irritation from sunburn and insect bites or stings
- **Antiseptic** (such as povidone-iodine) – for cuts and grazes
- **Bandages, Band-Aids (plasters)** and other wound dressings
- **Scissors, tweezers** and a **thermometer** (note that mercury thermometers are prohibited by airlines)

If you wear glasses, take a spare pair and your prescription. If you lose your glasses, you will be able to have them replaced within a few days (sometimes within a few hours) by an *ottico* (optician).

Travellers who require a particular medication should take an adequate supply as well as the prescription, with the generic rather than the brand name, as this will make getting replacements easier. Basic drugs are widely available and many items requiring prescriptions in countries such as the USA can be obtained over the counter in Italy.

No vaccinations are required for entry into Italy unless you have been travelling through a part of the world where yellow fever or cholera is prevalent. Tampons and condoms are freely available in pharmacies and supermarkets.

Basic Rules

Stomach upsets are the most likely travel health problem, but in Sardinia the majority of these will be relatively minor and probably due to overindulgence in the local food. Some people take a while to adjust to the regular use of olive oil in the food.

Water Tap water is generally drinkable, but the sign *acqua non potabile* tells you when it is not. Water from drinking fountains is safe unless there is a sign telling you otherwise but locals tend to drink the bottled stuff.

Environmental Hazards

Heatstroke This serious, occasionally fatal, condition can occur if the body's heat-regulating mechanism breaks down and the body temperature rises to dangerous levels. Long, continuous periods of exposure to high temperatures and insufficient fluids can leave you vulnerable to heatstroke.

The symptoms are feeling unwell, not sweating very much (or at all) and a high body temperature (39° to 41°C or 102° to 106°F). Where sweating has ceased, the skin becomes flushed and red. Severe, throbbing headaches and lack of coordination will also occur, and the sufferer may be confused or aggressive. Eventually the victim will become delirious or convulse. Hospitalisation is essential, but in the interim get victims out of the sun, remove their clothing, cover them with a wet sheet or towel and then fan continually. Give fluids if they are conscious.

Prickly Heat An itchy rash caused by excessive perspiration trapped under the skin, prickly heat usually strikes people who have just arrived in a hot climate. Keeping cool by bathing often, using a mild talcum powder or even resorting to spending time in air-conditioning may help.

Sunburn You can get sunburnt surprisingly quickly, even through cloud. Use a sunscreen, a hat and some barrier cream for your nose and lips. Calamine lotion is good for soothing mild sunburn. Don't forget to protect your eyes with good-quality sunglasses.

Infectious Diseases

Diarrhoea Despite all your precautions, you may still have a bout of mild travellers' diarrhoea. Dehydration is the main danger with diarrhoea, particularly for children and the elderly, so fluid replenishment is the number-one treatment. Weak black tea with a little sugar, soda water or soft drinks allowed to go flat and diluted 50% with water are all good. With severe diarrhoea, a rehydrating solution is necessary to replace minerals and salts and you should see a doctor. Stick to a bland diet as you recover.

Hepatitis This is a general term for inflammation of the liver. The symptoms are fever, chills, headache, fatigue, feelings of weakness and aches and pains, followed by loss of appetite, nausea, vomiting, abdominal pain, dark urine, light-coloured faeces, jaundiced (yellow) skin and the whites of the eyes may turn yellow.

Hepatitis A is transmitted by contaminated food and drinking water. You should seek medical advice but there is not much you can do apart from resting, drinking lots of fluids, eating lightly and avoiding fatty foods. Those who have had hepatitis should avoid alcohol for some time after the illness as the liver needs time to recover. Hepatitis E is transmitted in the same way as hepatitis A; it can be particularly serious in pregnant women.

Hepatitis B is spread through contact with infected blood, blood products or body fluids – for example, through sexual contact, unsterilised needles, blood transfusions or contact with blood via small breaks in the skin. Other risk situations include having a shave, tattoo or body piercing with contaminated equipment. The symptoms of hepatitis B may be more severe than type A and the disease can lead to long term problems such as chronic liver damage, liver cancer or a long-term carrier state. Hepatitis C and D are spread in the same way as hepatitis B and can also lead to long-term complications.

There are vaccines against hepatitis A and B, but not against the other types of hepatitis. Following the basic rules about food and water (hepatitis A and E) and avoiding risk situations (hepatitis B, C and D) are important preventative measures.

HIV & AIDS Infection with the human immunodeficiency virus (HIV) may lead to acquired immune deficiency syndrome (AIDS), which is a fatal disease. Any exposure to blood, blood products or body fluids may put the individual at risk. The disease is often transmitted through sexual contact or dirty needles – vaccinations, acupuncture, tattooing and body piercing can be potentially as dangerous as intravenous drug use.

Sexually Transmitted Diseases HIV/AIDS and hepatitis B can be transmitted through sexual contact – see the relevant sections earlier. Other STDs include gonorrhoea, herpes and syphilis; sores, blisters or rashes around the genitals and discharges or pain when urinating are common symptoms. In some STDs, such as wart virus or chlamydia, symptoms may be less marked or not observed at all, especially in women. Chlamydia infection can cause infertility in men and women before any symptoms have been noticed. Syphilis symptoms eventually disappear completely but the disease continues and can cause severe problems in later years. While abstinence from sexual contact is the only 100% effective prevention, using condoms is also effective. Gonorrhoea and syphilis are treated with antibiotics.

Insect-Borne Diseases

Leishmaniasis This is a group of parasitic diseases transmitted by sandflies and found in coastal parts of Sardinia. Cutaneous leishmaniasis affects the skin tissue, and causes ulceration and disfigurement; visceral leishmaniasis affects the internal organs. Avoiding sandfly bites by covering up and using repellent is the best precaution against this disease.

Lyme Disease An infection transmitted by ticks, Lyme disease usually begins with a spreading rash at the site of the tick bite and is accompanied by fever, headache, extreme fatigue, aching joints and muscles and mild neck stiffness. If untreated, these symptoms usually resolve over several weeks but, over subsequent weeks or months, disorders of the nervous system, heart and joints may develop. Treatment works best early in the illness. Medical help should be sought.

Bites & Stings

Jellyfish Beaches are occasionally inundated with jellyfish. Their stings are painful but not dangerous. Dousing in vinegar will de-activate any stingers that have not fired. Calamine lotion, antihistamines and analgesics may reduce the reaction and relieve pain. If in doubt about swimming, ask locals if any jellyfish are in the water.

Ticks Always check your body if you have been walking through a tick-infested area. In recent years there have been several reported deaths on Sardinia related to tick bites. Health authorities have yet to pinpoint the cause.

SOCIAL GRACES
Dos & Don'ts

In the interior regions of Nuoro province especially, be circumspect about the use of cameras on people. Locals do not take kindly to being photographed, especially if not asked beforehand. It is not completely unheard of in more remote places for camera shots to meet with grapeshot.

You may be denied entry to many of Sardinia's churches if it is deemed you are inappropriately clothed. This basically means covering up shoulders and, on occasion, wearing long trousers.

The standard greeting is the handshake. Kissing on both cheeks is generally reserved for people who already know one another.

WOMEN TRAVELLERS

Women travelling alone can on occasion find themselves plagued by the unwanted attentions of men. This usually involves cat-calls, hisses and whistles and, as such, is more annoying than anything else. Get used to being stared at – because it's likely to happen often.

Lone women may find it difficult to re-main alone. You can find yourself in un-wanted company as you walk along the street, drink a coffee in a bar or try to read a book in a park. Usually the best response is to ignore them, but if that doesn't work, po-litely tell them that you are waiting for your *marito* (husband) or *fidanzato* (boyfriend) and, if necessary, walk away. Avoid becom-ing aggressive as this almost always results in an unpleasant confrontation. If all else fails, approach the nearest member of the po-lice or *carabinieri*.

Basically, most of the attention falls into the nuisance/harassment category. However, women on their own should use their com-mon sense. Avoid walking alone in deserted and dark streets and look for hotels that are central and within easy walking distance of places where you can eat at night. Women should also avoid hitchhiking alone.

It is wise to dress more conservatively in the towns of inland Sardinia than you would on the beaches. Skimpy clothing is a sure attention-earner – you should take your cue from the Italian women on this one.

GAY & LESBIAN TRAVELLERS

Homosexuality is legal in Italy and the age of consent is 16, but there is little in the line of an open gay scene in Sardinia. Overt displays of affection by homosexual couples, espe-cially away from the coastal resorts, could attract unpleasant responses in many places.

Organisations

The national Italian organisations for gay men and lesbians are **ArciGay** and **ArciLes-bica** (☎ 051 644 70 54, fax 051 644 67 22; *Piazza di Porta Saragozza 2, 40123 Bologna)*.

Associazione di Cultura Omosessuale – Kaleidos (☎ 349 263 9791, fax 178 223 96 00; *Via Leopardi 3, c/o Sinistra Giovanile, Cagliari)* is the only local gay organisation operating on the island.

You'll find any number of Italian gay sites on the Internet, but some are all but useless. ArciGay's website (**w** www.arcigay.it) has general information on the gay and lesbian scene in Italy, while the companion Gay. It's

site (**w** www.gay.it, Italian only) provides listings information for everything from bars and discos to gay beaches and beauty cen-tres. The pickings in Sardinia, however, are slim indeed.

DISABLED TRAVELLERS

Not a great deal has been done in Sardinia to ease the way for disabled travellers. Get-ting around can be a problem for the wheel-chair bound and few buildings have been modified for disabled access.

The Italian State Tourist Office in your country may be able to provide advice on Italian associations for the disabled and in-formation on what help is available in the country.

Organisations

The UK-based Royal Association for Dis-ability and Rehabilitation (RADAR) pub-lishes a guide called *European Holidays & Travel Abroad: A Guide for Disabled Peo-ple*. It is dated but can be a useful general guide. Contact **RADAR** (☎ 020-7250 3222; **w** *www.radar.org.uk; Unit 12, City Forum, 250 City Rd, London EC1V 8AS)*, or look at their website. You can also find accommo-dation listings on the Disability World web-site (**w** www.disabilityworld.com).

Another organisation worth calling is **Holiday Care** (☎ 01293-774535; 2nd floor, *Imperial Buildings, Victoria Rd, Horley, Surrey RH6 7PZ)*. It produces an information pack on Italy for disabled people and others with special needs. Tips range from hotels with disabled access through to where you can hire equipment and tour operators dealing with the disabled.

Accessible Travel & Leisure (☎ 08702-416127; **w** *www.atlholidays.com; Avionics House, Quedgeley Enterprise Centre, Naas Lane, Gloucester GL2 4SN)* claims to be the biggest UK travel agent dealing with travel for the disabled. The company lays a lot of emphasis on accessibility rather than dis-ability and encourages the disabled to travel independently.

The **Associazione Italiana Assistenza Spastici** (**w** *www.aiasnazionale.it; Via Cipro 4/h 00136 Rome • ☎ 070 379 10 10; Viale Poetto 312, 09126 Cagliari)* operates an in-formation service for disabled travellers called the Sportello Vacanze Disabili. They have a branch in Sardinia.

SENIOR TRAVELLERS

Senior citizens will find they are not entitled to too many discounts around Sardinia, although admission to some of the sites is reduced for those 65 (sometimes 60) and over.

You should also seek information in your own country on travel packages and discounts for senior travellers, through senior citizens' organisations and travel agents. Consider booking accommodation in advance to avoid inconvenience.

TRAVEL WITH CHILDREN

Don't try to overdo things by packing too much into the time available, and make sure activities include the kids as well. Remember that visits to museums and galleries can be tiring, even for adults.

Allow time for the kids to play, either in a park or in the hotel room; taking a toddler to a playground for an hour or so can make an amazing difference to their tolerance for sightseeing in the afternoon. Kids generally love the beach so indulging in slothful seaside activities will rarely meet with disapproval from the wee ones.

When travelling long distances by car or public transport, take plenty of books and other activities, such as colouring pencils and paper. Include older children in the planning of the trip – if they have helped to work out where they will be going, they are likely to be much more interested when they get there.

Discounts are available for children (usually aged under 12) on public transport and for admission to museums, galleries and other sites.

You can buy baby formula in powder or liquid form, as well as sterilising solutions such as Milton, at *farmacie* (chemists). Disposable nappies (diapers) are widely available at supermarkets and *farmacie* (where they are also more expensive). Fresh cow's milk is sold in cartons in some bars and in supermarkets. If it is essential that you have milk, you should carry an emergency carton of UHT milk, since most bars usually close at 8pm.

You can hire car seats for infants and children from most car-rental firms, but you should always book them in advance.

For more information, see Lonely Planet's *Travel with Children*.

DANGERS & ANNOYANCES
Theft

Theft in bigger towns and tourist resorts is not as prevalent as in some mainland Italian areas. Still, you should use common sense. Wear a money belt under your clothing and keep important items, such as money, passport and tickets, there at all times. If you are carrying a bag, wear the strap across your body and have the bag on the side away from the road to deter snatchers, who sometimes operate from motorcycles. Don't leave valuables lying around your hotel room.

Parked cars are prime targets, particularly those with foreign number plates or rental-company stickers. Leave a local newspaper on the seat so it looks like a local car. *Never* leave valuables in your car – in fact, try not to leave anything in the car and certainly not overnight. It is a good idea to pay extra to leave your car in supervised car parks.

In case of theft or loss, always report the incident at the *questura* within 24 hours and ask for a statement, otherwise your travel insurance company won't pay out.

Traffic

Traffic can be pain in Sardinia, especially in summer when some roads are choked. In the bigger towns, you need to keep a keen eye on what is going on around you. It's not as crazy as in big mainland cities and drivers tend to respect street lights, although pedestrian crossings are another matter.

LEGAL MATTERS

The average tourist would probably only have a brush with the law if robbed.

Drugs

Italy's drug laws are relatively lenient on drug users and heavy on pushers. If you're caught with drugs that the police determine are for your personal use, you'll be let off with a warning. If it is determined that you intend to sell the drugs in your possession, you could find yourself in prison. The police determine whether or not you're a pusher, since the law is not specific about quantities.

Drink Driving

The legal limit for blood alcohol level is 0.08% and random breath tests do occur.

[Continued on page 55]

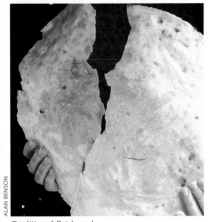
Traditional flat bread

Fresh *pecorino* cheese

Sardinian sweets and cakes

Antipasto platter with prosciutto

Minestrone with pesto

Even frequenters of Italian restaurants or the Italian mainland will be perplexed by some aspects of Sardinian menus. Sure, you'll find pizzas and many familiar dishes common across all of Italy, but the island offers its own rich contribution to the Italian table. And the deeper you dig, the more surprises you are likely to unearth.

Although plenty of seafood is available on the coast, true Sardinian cuisine is hearty inland fare, with meat and animal innards taking pride of place. Still, some local seafood specialities excel and the overall result is a surprising variety. Add into the mix some wonderful wines and foodies should be able to keep their mandibles happily engaged. Things are more limited on the dessert front, although a few excellent local items are worth seeking out.

It's a good thing the local food is scrummy because you can count the number of restaurants offering cuisine from other countries on two hands. Even regional cooking from other parts of Italy is noticeably absent.

Those looking for fancy haute cuisine may be disappointed in Sardinia. Relatively few places offer the kind of inventive international cooking you might find in London, New York or Paris. Here the cooking is hearty and largely traditional.

Staples

Bread When you sit down to eat you will likely be presented with a bread basket even before you have ordered. Sardinians wouldn't consider a meal without bread. Already you have discoveries to make – they say every Sardinian village has its own kind of bread!

A common thick circular loaf from the Campidano region but now found everywhere is the *civraxiu* (siv-**ra**-ksyu), with a crispy crust and soft white interior. Similar is the *tundu*.

In the north another type of bread reigns: *pane carasau*, also know as *carta da musica* (music paper), is a wafer-thin, long-lasting crispy bread traditionally made for shepherds. It is vaguely reminiscent of Indian poppadams, salty and quite addictive. It predominates in the Gallura, Logudoro and Nuoro regions.

Bathed in olive oil and added salt, *pane carasau* becomes a moreish snack known as *pane guttiau*. A fancier version often served as a first course is *pane frattau*, from the Barbagia area. The *pane carasau* is bathed in tomato sauce, grated *pecorino* cheese and *uovo in camicia* (soft-boiled egg).

Another common bread is the *spianata* or *spianada* from the Logudoro region. It's a little like Middle Eastern pitta. In Sassari snack bars you'll discover *fainé*, the chickpea flour-based *farinata* (pizza-style flat bread) imported centuries ago by Ligurians from northwestern Italy and used for making pizza-like snacks.

The Spaniards made a fine contribution with *panadas*, scrumptious little pies that can be filled with anything from lamb or pork to eel. The town of Oschiri is especially well known for them.

Cheese The bulk of cheese production in Sardinia comes from ewe's milk. By far the most common is *pecorino*, and the island produces

Title page:
Balls of coloured pasta, Vilasimius
(Photograph by Dallas Stribley)

Lot of Rot

Want a nice cream cheese in Sardinia? Ask around for *formaggio marcio* or *casu marzu*, literally 'rotten cheese'. You won't find it in shops but farmers have a tried and tested method for making it. They take a block of cheese, make a hole in it and insert a drop of oil to attract the cheese fly *(Piophila casei)*. The fly leaves behind its larvae (a less polite word would be maggots) that happily start chomping away at the cheese. As they squirm around, they turn the cheese nice and creamy! Hmm!

about 80% of all Italy's output. *Pecorino romano*, originally from the Lazio region around Rome, is made in wheels of around 20kg. It is dense and pale with a pale crust and is the cheese of choice for accompanying pasta. The *pecorino sardo*, also pale, can be matured for six months or more, giving it a tangier flavour than the *pecorino romano*. Ricotta, similar to cottage cheese, is made from the whey of ewe's and goat's milk and comes in various types. It also comes in a more pungent aged version.

Fiore sardo ('Sardinian flower') is a centuries-old cheese recipe and is eaten fresh, smoked or roasted and packs a fair punch.

Fresa and *peretta* are the two main cow's milk cheeses, produced on the island in far smaller quantities than those made from ewe's milk.

Starters & First Courses

Antipasti (Starters) Although traditionally Sardinian meals largely did without starters, cross-pollination with other Italian cuisines has influenced local habits. You'll find many Italy-wide favourites like olives, melon and prosciutto, little seafood tasters and the like. Be aware that with a first and second course your hunger will usually be well satisfied and *antipasti* can add significantly to the bill.

Pasta & Other First Courses According to some theories, spaghetti was invented in Sardinia. There's not a lot of proof of this but the islanders have cooked up their own styles of pasta.

Among the most tempting are *culurgiones* (spelled in various ways). A kind of ravioli, *culurgiones* come in several different shapes and with various fillings. Typically they come with ricotta or *pecorino* cheese fillings and are generously bathed in a tomato and herb sauce. *Culurgiones de l'Ogliastra*, a version made in the central eastern part of Nuoro province, are stuffed with potato puree and sometimes meat and onions. A little *pecorino*, olive oil, garlic and mint are added. Again a tomato sauce is the usual accompaniment.

Also common are *mallodoreddus*, a dense seashell-shaped pasta usually served with *salsa alla campidanese* (a sausage and tomato sauce) They sometimes go by the name of *gnocchetti sardi*.

Maccarones furriaos are strips of pasta folded over and topped with a sauce (often tomato-based) and melted cheese. *Maccarones de busa*, or just plain *busa*, are shaped by wrapping the pasta around knitting needles. Thus 'pierced', the pasta soaks up as much sauce as possible.

Others you may come across are *pillus*, a small ribbon pasta, and *filindeu*, a thread-like noodle usually served in soups.

Some typical Sardinian pasta toppings include:

alla sarda or *alla Campidanese* – sausage and tomato sauce often served with *mallodoreddus*
bottarga – olive oil and mullet roe (also known as Sardinian caviar)
alla dorgalese – meat (usually lamb) sauce
sugo di aragostelle – shrimp sauce
alle arselle – clam sauce, also known as *all'algherese*
ai ricci – sea urchins
mazzafrissa – a sauce made (in the north) with flour and cream

Of course you will also encounter plenty of pasta dishes from other parts of the country (see also the Food Glossary in the Language chapter at the end of this book).

You don't have to stick with pasta. Soups and broths are often on the menu. *Minestra* or *minestrone* (broths) can range from chicken (*gallina*) through to *piselli con ricotta* (peas and ricotta), *ceci* (chickpeas) or *lenticchie* (lentils). Other soups might be fennel- or endive-based.

In Gallura, *suppa quatta* is a favoured opener. Layers of bread and cheese are drowned in broth and then is oven-baked to create a thin golden crust.

Main Courses

Sardinians point out that they are by tradition *pastori, non pescatori* (shepherds, not fishermen). Nowadays you will be regaled with lobster and every other kind of imaginable seafood on dining tables up and down the coast. There is some tradition of seafood in Cagliari, Alghero and other coastal towns but elsewhere the phenomenon has arrived from beyond Sardinia. Real Sardinians eat meat! So if you want to explore traditional Sardinian cooking, you'll need to search out more traditional eateries on the coast or head inland.

Ask around for good *agriturismi* (farm holiday stays). The good ones serve great local food. In Gallura, especially farmhouses are known as *stazzus* and sometimes operate as country restaurants.

Fish & Seafood Lobster is *the* local speciality and is featured on the menus of most of Alghero's restaurants, and pasta dishes in seafood sauces also predominate. No doubt the city's long Catalan occupation had an influence over local eating habits. How many of the lobsters are caught locally is a moot point and the price you pay for the privilege may make you think twice. At around €10 for every 100g of the sea critter, you will need a reasonably well-lined wallet.

Muggine (mullet) is popular on the Oristano coast and *tonno* (tuna) dishes abound. *Cassola* is a tasty fish soup while *zuppa alla Castellanese*, a Castelsardo speciality, is similar but with a distinctly tomato edge. *Burrida*, found in Cagliari, is a dish of *gattucci di mare* ('little sea cats', actually dogfish) marinated in a sauce of nuts, parsley and garlic.

Meat While it is possible to get such generic dishes as veal, entrecote, steak and the like, the hearts of Sardinian carnivores beat to a different drum.

Three specialities dominate: *porceddu*, *porcetto* or *porchetto* (suckling pig); *capretto* (kid meat); and *agnello* (lamb). Perhaps surprisingly *porceddu* is often easier to come across than the other two although quality can be uneven.

When it's good, *porceddu* is very good but the primary product is often of indifferent quality and frequently imported from as far off as Eastern Europe to meet demand. Well-prepared animals should provide copious, succulent meat. Inferior products will consist mostly of skin and gristle. In summer especially, demand way outstrips the availability of good meat. (You may be surprised to learn that the most sought after porcine delicacy is pig's ear!)

Much the same can be said of *capretto*, although it is harder to find it on menus. The meat, especially if it is *capra* (adult goat meat), can be a little tough and gristly. When the meat is more tender, it is particularly tasty if prepared in a thyme sauce.

Agnello is particularly popular around December but can be more difficult to find at other times. They say the best lamb doesn't weigh more than 6kg when selected for sacrifice. If cooked outdoors over an open fire the lamb is slowly roasted on a spit and doused in lard. A country classic that you are unlikely to come across is *carne a carrarglu* ('meat in a hole') – the meat is compressed between two layers of hot stones and covered in myrtle in a hole dug in the ground. Sardinians say you can still come across country folk who will prepare this but it is a rarity.

Other common meats that wind up on the dinner table include rabbit, partridge, wild boar and chicken.

A wonderful local sauce for any meat dish is *al mirto*. The red myrtle makes for a lightly fruity, slightly tangy addition.

Sardinians like their entrails. Few restaurants are likely to serve them up to outsiders but you'd be surprised how good some of them can be.

A favourite is *zimino*. The word usually refers to a roast fish feast, but in traditional inland cooking it is a host of entrails, for instance of calf. *Zimino rosso* is heart, diaphragm, liver, kidney and other red innards – the heart and diaphragm are especially appreciated. Sardinians will tell you that *zimino bianco* is better – white intestinal meats apparently difficult to get a hold of now because of the BSE ('mad cow disease') scare.

Tataliu or *trattalia* is a mix of kidney, liver and other intestines cooked up together in kind of stew or on skewers. It is done with veal, lamb, kid or suckling pig meat. *Cordula* is similar but commonly prepared in a broth of peas.

Horses for Courses

Sardinians have a thing about horses. They raise them, ride them, have a strange breed of 'miniature' ones, export them... But equines don't enjoy, as it were, sacred cow status as a result. Quite the opposite. There's nothing a traditionally minded Sardinian likes better than sitting down to a slab of horsemeat. And we're not horsing around here. Indeed donkey meat is another favourite. While not enjoying the exalted status of *porceddu*, *capretto* or even *agnello*, horsemeat is much sought after by red-blooded Sardinians.

Another favourite is *granelle*, calf's testicles sliced, covered in batter and lightly fried.

Sweets & Desserts

A good meal wouldn't be the same without some local desserts, and Sardinians have a handful of tasty sweets up their sleeves.

A common one is the *seadas* (or *sebadas*), a delightfully light pastry (vaguely like a turnover) filled with ricotta or sour cheese and drenched in honey.

A wonderful speciality of the Oristano area are the cinnamon-flavoured *mustazzolus*, vaguely reminiscent of German *Lebkuchen*. When home-made they're delightful – the best ones are allowed to rise as long as a month. Less complicated are the almond biscuits known as *gueffus*, best dipped in the deep yellow sweet Vernaccia wine (see later).

As if in homage to the days when the island owed its allegiance to Catalan (commonly referred to as Aragonese) and later Spanish masters, Sardinians still eat *crema catalana*. Mind you the local version, a kind of thick crème caramel, bears little resemblance to what you find in Barcelona these days (distinguished above all by its burned, caramelised crust and a more custardy centre).

Wine & Spirits

Sardinia is home to almost two dozen DOC wines and produces some strong reds and sweet dessert whites. Increasingly vintners are trying to please a broader market with light dry whites and more sophisticated reds. A few rosés are also worth trying.

Many Sardinian families still make their own stuff. It is not always a refined treat for the palate but if offered some it will give you an idea of how traditional wines used to be.

You can pick up a bottle of perfectly good dinner wine for about €4 to €6 in supermarkets.

Among the best dry whites are the Vermentino, produced in much of the north of the island. The Vermentino di Gallura is the only wine type in Sardinia to have been awarded the coveted DOCG status (in 1996). It is a dry, refreshing drop.

Right: Produce from Alghero

Show Your Metal

Filu e ferru is made from a distillate of grape skins in much the same way as grappa and roars down your throat. It got its odd name from moonshine days. To avoid taxes (the Italian state has long held a monopoly control over the production of hard liquor, which it taxes accordingly), people would make their own and bury bottles of the stuff. To be able to find it, they'd mark the spot with a thin iron strip (the *filu e ferru*). When a guest came around for a tipple, the host would call out for the *filu e ferru*, a barely disguised code that has long since become the name for the drink itself. Moonshine versions can reach 60% alcohol, while the legal stuff hovers around 40%.

Another Vermentino worth seeking out is the Canayli, which since 1998 has won several prestigious Italian wine industry awards. You'll see vineyards turning out the Vermentino grapes all over the northeast of Sardinia, such as around Tempio Pausania and Berdiccha.

The best known vintner on the island is the Sella & Mosca group just outside Alghero who make all sorts of wines. Their Torbato Terre Bianche is a nice champagne-style drop.

Among Sella & Mosca's best reds are Tanca Farrà and the prize-winning Marchese di Villamarina. In general the island's best-known reds are made from the Cannonau grape variety. There are many to choose from around the island, although there is a special concentration in and around Nuoro province. Look out for those from Dorgali, Oliena and Jerzu. Also worth tasting are wines using the Nebbiolo wine grape, introduced by the Piedmontese in the 18th century.

Among the island's dessert wines one of the best known is Vernaccia (15% to 18% alcohol), a heavy amber drop made mostly around Oristano and taken as an aperitif or to accompany such sweets as *mustazzolus*. The best Vernaccia is Perra from Narbiola in Oristano province.

Malvasia (malmsey) is another dessert wine made mostly in the Bosa area. Sella & Mosca produces a good sweet drop, the Torbato Passito, and the Anghelu Ruiu fortified wine.

Liqueurs & Hard Liquor You can get many of the classic Italian postprandial digestive drinks, such as **grappa** (like Sella & Mosca's Grappa Anghelu Ruiu) and **amaretto** in Sardinia, but some local products provide some strong competition.

Limoncino is a sweet, lemon-based drink that is virtually same as the better known *limoncello* found all over the Amalfi coast south of Naples.

Also vaguely sweet is the ubiquitous *mirto*, made from the red fruit of the myrtle bush. At its best it is a deliciously smooth drop. A less common white version is made from myrtle leaves and goes by the same name.

The island's transparent firewater is *filu e ferru*. For more on this see the boxed aside 'Show Your Metal'. Zedda Piras is a reliable brand of *mirto* and *filu e ferru*.

[Continued from page 48]

See Road Rules in the Getting Around chapter for more information.

Police

If you run into trouble in Italy, you're likely to end up dealing with the *polizia nazionale* (national police) or the *carabinieri*. The former are a civil force and take their orders from the Ministry of the Interior, while the *carabinieri* fall under the Ministry of Defence. There is a considerable duplication of their roles, despite a 1981 reform of the police forces. Both forces are responsible for public order and security, which means that you can visit either in the event of a robbery or attack.

The *carabinieri* wear a black uniform with a red stripe and drive dark-blue cars with a red stripe. They are well trained and tend to be helpful. Their police station is called a *caserma* (barracks), a reflection of their military status.

The *polizia* wear powder-blue trousers with a fuchsia stripe and a navy-blue jacket, and drive light-blue cars with a white stripe. People wanting a residence permit will have to deal with them. Their headquarters is the *questura*.

In Sardinia, the presence of both forces is unusually high, in part due to the island's history of problems with banditry. Road blocks on highways and sometimes in cities are common and sooner or later you will probably be pulled over for a routine check of passport and car papers. Smile, because getting surly does not cut the mustard with these guys.

Vigili urbani are the local traffic police. You will have to deal with them if you get a parking ticket or your car is towed away. The *guardia di finanza* are responsible for fighting tax evasion and drug smuggling. It's

unlikely, but you could be stopped by one of them if you leave a shop without a receipt for your purchase.

Your Rights

Italy has anti-terrorism laws that could make life difficult if you are detained by the police. A suspected terrorist can be held for 48 hours without a magistrate being informed and can be interrogated without the presence of a lawyer. It is difficult to obtain bail and you can be held legally for up to three years without being brought to trial.

BUSINESS HOURS

Business hours vary but generally shops open from 9am to 1pm and 4pm to 8pm Monday to Saturday. In summer, in many of the more touristy areas (such as Alghero, Bosa, Olbia, the Costa Smeralda, Santa Teresa and many of the southern resorts), shops tend to open until 11pm. The length of the midday break can range from three hours from 1pm to as much as five (in Bosa for instance).

Bigger department stores (like Coin and Rinascente), which you will only find in Cagliari and Sassari, and some supermarkets have continuous opening from 9am to 8.30pm Monday to Saturday. A few open on Sunday too.

Banks tend to open from 8.30am to 1.30pm and 3pm to 4.30pm (hours vary from bank to bank however) Monday to Friday. They close at weekends, when in most places you will have difficulty changing money. Most banks have ATMs that accept foreign credit/debit cards (see Money).

Major post offices open from 8.15am to 5pm or 6pm Monday to Friday, and also from 8.30am to midday or 1pm on Saturday. Smaller post offices generally open from 8.15am to 1.15pm Monday to Friday, and 8.30am to midday on Saturday. All post offices close at least two hours earlier than normal on the last business day of each month (not including Saturday).

Pharmacies open 9am to 12.30pm and 3.30pm to 7.30pm. Most close on Sunday and Saturday afternoon. In any given area there will be at least one pharmacy rostered on to do extra hours, usually until 10pm. When closed, pharmacies are required to display a list of nearby pharmacies rostered on.

Many bars and cafés (the kind where people drop in for a sandwich, coffee or

Emergency Numbers	
In an emergency call the following nationwide numbers:	
Military Police (Carabinieri)	☎ 112
Police (Polizia Nazionale)	☎ 113
Fire Brigade (Vigili del Fuoco)	☎ 115
Highway Rescue (Soccorso Stradale)	☎ 116
Ambulance (Ambulanza)	☎ 118

quick heart-starter) generally open from 7.30am to 8pm. Those with a nocturnal vocation open until about 1am during the week but as late as 3am on Fridays and Saturdays. Clubs and discos might open from around 10pm to 5am (sometimes later), but often there'll be no-one there until after midnight.

Restaurants open from about noon to 3pm and 7.30pm to 11pm. Few kitchens remain open beyond this time. In summer most restaurants tend to open seven days for lunch and dinner. In the coastal resorts many restaurants shut for several months in off-season. Those that stay open all year (in the cities and areas less dependent on summer tourists) usually close one day a week (although most open daily from June to September).

The opening hours of museums, galleries and archaeological sites vary enormously. As a rule, museums close on Monday but from June to September many sights open daily. Outside the high season, hours tend to reduce drastically and more out of the way sights frequently close altogether.

PUBLIC HOLIDAYS

Most Italians take their annual holiday in July/August, deserting the cities for the cooler coastal or mountain resorts. What this means for Sardinia is that a good deal of Italy's vacation populace heads *for* Sardinia, along with a healthy contingent of foreigners. But the Sardinians have to go on holiday too – many leave the big towns for holiday apartments and quite a few businesses and shops close in mid-summer, particularly during the week around Ferragosto (Feast of the Assumption) on 15 August. Settimana Santa (Easter Week) is another busy holiday period for Italians.

National public holidays include the following dates:

New Year's Day 1 January
Epiphany 6 January
Easter Monday March/April
Liberation Day 25 April
Labour Day 1 May
Feast of the Assumption 15 August
All Saints' Day 1 November
Feast of the Immaculate Conception
8 December
Christmas Day 25 December
Feast of Santo Stefano 26 December

Individual towns also have public holidays to celebrate the feasts of their patron saints. See the Festivals chapter for details of such special days in Sardinia.

ACTIVITIES

Sardinia is not overburdened with major museums and important art galleries. So, aside from modest sight-seeing and the popular activities of eating, drinking, plonking yourself on a beach or touring around (all popular and recommended pursuits!), you could indulge in a little more physical activity.

Cycling

If you're into mountain-biking, check out the information on trails at **SardegnaNet** (**W** www.sardegna.net), in English, German and Italian. A few places around the island hire out mountain bikes, but if you are at all serious about it you may want to bring your own. Touring bikes can be put to good use too, with plenty of options for long coastal rides or inland exploration. Bear in mind that, in summer especially, traffic on coastal roads can be hairy.

Diving

Although the Mediterranean is not one of the world's greatest locations for diving, there are plenty of interesting spots around the island. If you're into wrecks, the coast around Cagliari is littered with vessels sunk in WWII and a German ship sunk by a British submarine in 1943 lies in the Golfo di Orosei.

Other classic spots include: Arcipelago di La Maddalena and the granite seabed of Capo Testa; the sea caves of Capo Caccia in the northwest; the Isola di San Pietro, with its abundant fish life; the submarine calcareous spires around Isola Tavolara; and the colour seabed off Capo Carbonara near Villasimius.

Sailing

Sailing is predictably popular around the coast. Exclusive yachts from around the world call in at Costa Smeralda and the area around Alghero is always alive with the sails of locals' boats. It's a nice way to come to Sardinia and there are anchorages around the island.

Walking

The best walking can be done in Nuoro province, the most mountainous on the island. Increasingly popular are the classic gorges of the Gola Su Gorroppu and the wild Supramonte. Hikers can also reach the magical inlets and beaches of the Golfo di Orosei on foot (otherwise only accessible by sea) and all sorts of less challenging options present themselves. There is little in the way of properly marked and signposted trails in the Supramonte and other mountain areas so it is recommended you go with local guides rather than attempting anything too challenging on your own. Foreign hikers can and do get lost frequently.

Windsurfing

Windsurfers have several good options around the island. In the southeast around Villasimius there are some good spots, but the most popular are around Santa Teresa di Gallura and Palau in the northeast.

COURSES

Although not many of Sardinia's visitors come to study Italian, there is no reason why you can't. Indeed, steering clear of such traditional centres of learning Italian, like Florence and Perugia, ensures you will have greater local contact and make quicker linguistic progress.

The Istituto Italiano di Cultura (IIC), which has branches all over the world, is a government-sponsored organisation aimed at promoting Italian culture and language. It puts on classes in Italian and provides library and information services. This is a good place to start your search for places to study in Italy. Try the IIC's websites at ⓦ www.iicmelau.org (Melbourne, Australia), ⓦ www.iicsyd.org (Sydney), ⓦ www .italcultur-qc.org, Italian and French only (Montreal, Canada), ⓦ www.iicto-ca.org/ istituto.htm (Toronto), ⓦ www.iicparis.org, Italian and French only (Paris), ⓦ www.ital cultur.org.uk (London) and ⓦ www.italcult ny.org (USA).

WORK

It is illegal for non-EU citizens to work in Italy without a *permesso di lavoro* and Silvio Berlusconi's right-wing national government is pushing through increasingly tough immigration laws.

Getting a work permit is a tiresome exercise. Arm yourself with much patience. EU and Swiss citizens are allowed to work in Italy, but they still need to obtain a *permesso di soggiorno* (residence permit) from the main *questura* in the town in which they intend to reside, ideally before they look for employment. See Work Permits and Permesso di Soggiorno under Visas & Documents earlier in this chapter for more information.

Immigration laws require foreign workers to be 'legalised' through their employers, which can apply even to cleaners and babysitters. The employers then pay pension and health-insurance contributions. This doesn't mean, however, that there aren't employers willing to take people without the right papers.

Work options in Sardinia are pretty limited. English teaching is an option, and seasonal work in bars or with some water sports outfits may be possible – generally you will need at least some command of Italian. If you have sailing experience you might get lucky with the yachts calling in places like Porto Cervo and Porto Rotondo in the Costa Smeralda area.

Teaching English

The most obvious source of work for foreigners is teaching English, but even with full qualifications an American, Australian, Canadian or New Zealander might find it difficult to secure a permanent position. Most of the larger, more reputable language schools will hire only people with a work permit, but their attitude can become more flexible if demand for teachers is high and they come across someone with good qualifications. The more professional schools will require a TEFL (Teaching English as a Foreign Language) certificate. You need to look at the beginning of the academic year (around early September) and can get lucky in January too.

In Sardinia even qualified teachers cannot hope to earn much more than €15 an hour. Some schools will hire teachers without papers and pay under the table, but at still lower rates.

ACCOMMODATION

Prices quoted in this book are intended as a guide only. They reflect high season prices, which means that in other periods you may be pleasantly surprised by the drop in rates – sometimes approaching half the August prices.

The four provincial tourist offices (EPT) publish annual guides to hotels, camping grounds and various other accommodation options for their provinces. These are generally pretty complete. They should be available from about March each year and tourist office staff can generally be persuaded to send them on request.

Three categories of accommodation not well covered in these guides are rental apartments, *agriturismo* (farm stays) and the growing phenomenon of B&B (bed & breakfast) – basically rooms in private homes. Another similar category, where breakfast is not included, are *affittacamere* (rooms for rent in private houses).

A couple of agencies for rental apartments are listed below; otherwise you can ask in tourist offices as you go. They are most commonly found in the northeast of the island in an arc from Olbia to Santa Teresa di Gallura and around Alghero in the northwest.

Seasons & Reservations

It is a good idea to book a room if you're planning to travel during peak tourist times, which means Easter and July to August.

Many places, particularly on the coast, shut in the winter months (generally November to Easter). In the cities and larger towns accommodation tends to remain open all year. The relative lack of visitors to the island in these down periods means you should have little trouble getting a room in those places that do stay open.

The better hotels usually require confirmation by fax, email or letter, as well as a deposit.

It is also possible to book ahead for *agriturismi* and B&Bs although rarely necessary outside of August. The simplest option while travelling around is to inquire in tourist offices as you go or contact the organisations mentioned below.

Camping

Most camping facilities in Sardinia are serious complexes with swimming pools, restaurants and supermarkets. They tend to offer camping space as well as a variety of other accommodation options, such as bungalows. With hotels at a premium and expensive in many parts of the island in July and August, camping grounds can be an important option, especially given that quite a few have enviable seaside locations.

Prices at even the most basic camping grounds can be surprisingly expensive during the peak months of July and especially August. That said, given what many hotels charge in the same period, camping or even a bungalow may be an attractive option.

. Generally at most grounds there is no need to book for camping space or to park a caravan. If you want a bungalow, treat them like hotel rooms and book in advance in July and August.

Most camping grounds operate only in season, which means roughly April to October (in some cases June to September only).

In addition to per person camping rates, which oscillate between about €8 and €15 in high season, you need to calculate that car space is usually €2 to €3 extra, as is a hook-up for electricity. Tent space is often (but not always) free, and all sorts of other options may affect price too. Showers, for instance, are often free but sometimes involve a charge of €0.50 to €0.80.

In the course of the guide, per person prices in high season are given, occasionally with bungalow prices. The latter can easily reach €100 for two at the fancier camping grounds in the peak middle weeks of August.

Independent camping is prohibited in many parts of the island, especially parks and along much of the coast. Out of the main tourist season, independent campers who choose spots not visible from the road, who don't light fires and try to be inconspicuous shouldn't have too much trouble. Always get permission from the landowner if you want to camp on private property.

Full lists of camping grounds in and near cities and towns are usually available from local tourist offices. Each province's accommodation guide (updated annually) provides lists of camping grounds.

Hostels

Ostelli per la gioventù (youth hostels) are run by the **Associazione Italiana Alberghi per la Gioventù** *(AIG;* w *www.ostellion line.com)*, which is affiliated to Hostelling International (HI). You need to have an HI card to stay at these hostels, but given that there are only three on the island (spread around the northwest), it may not be worth your while becoming a member just for a trip to Sardinia.

Accommodation is in segregated dormitories, although two of the three hostels in Sardinia offer family rooms (at a higher price per person). Hostels usually have a lock-out period between 9am and 3.30pm. Check-in is from 6pm to 10.30pm, although some hostels will allow you a morning check-in before they close for the day.

Hotels

Hotels (which can go by the name of pensione or *albergo*) in Sardinia are generally unexciting. Until the 1960s there were not too many around, so the chances of staying in a charming old hotel are few and far between. The grand majority are unimaginative modern buildings, whose main attributes turn more on position (near the sea, views and so on) and services such as swimming pools and space. As a rule, most places are kept clean and tidy. Serious dives are as rare as the glittering jewels.

At the bottom end, you can find a few places in Cagliari and the interior where you might not pay more than about €20 a person but as a rule of thumb bank on about €40/60 per single/double for a decent budget hotel. From there the prices can reach the sky at five-star resorts.

Agriturismo, B&Bs & Rental

Agriturismi, originally conceived of as farm stays where guests could get a taste of rural life, have undergone a transformation since the first ones began operating in the 1970s. Most have largely become country-style restaurants, perhaps with a few rooms available to respect the norms. Still, if you are touring around without bookings they can be worth following up (you'll see signs pointing the way to them as you go).

B&Bs are a recent phenomenon, governed by a different set of norms (Italy is the paradise of labyrinthine legislation). There is no island-wide umbrella group for these (but a couple of more localised organisations are emerging), so again you need to keep your eyes open as you go. They are popping up even in small villages and on occasion give you the chance to stay in characterful old homes. Some are listed in the provincial hotel guides but the best advice is to ask in local tourist offices (pro

locos) as you go. On average they cost €18 to €25 per person a night.

As a rule the only way to find out whether there are any *affittacamere* in the town you are visiting is by asking at the tourist office. A handful are listed in the provincial hotel guides.

For detailed information on all *agriturismo* facilities in Sardinia you can order a list at the Agriturismo in Sardegna website: W www.sardinia.net/agritur/. You can also find a handful listed by Agriturismoitaly at W www.agriturismoitaly.it/sardegna.htm.

You can also contact **Agriturist** (☎ 06 68 52 33 37; W *www.agriturist.it, Italian only; Corso Vittorio Emanuele 101, 00186 Rome)*. It publishes a book with agriturismo listings for the whole country (€14), available at the office, in selected bookshops and online.

You can find out more about some B&B options through a Sassari-based centralised service, **Sardegna Ospitale** (☎ 079 259 50 61, 259 50 69, fax 079 259 22 41; W *www.bbsardegna.com, Italian only; Via Cedrino 3)*. English-speakers can try the mobile phone number (☎ 347 724 23 31, fax 079 200 50 18).

Specific to Oristano province is **La Mia Casa** (☎/fax 0783 41 16 60; W *www.lamiacasa.sardegna.it; Posidonia Tourist Services, Via Umberto I 64, 09070 Riola Sardo)*, with more than 20 B&Bs on the books throughout seven villages in the province.

Another potentially useful port of call is the Oristano-based **Sardinian Way** (☎ 0783 751 72, fax 0783 777750 W *www.sardinianway.it; Via Carmine 14)*, which lists B&Bs and seaside houses for rent.

About the only way to locate *affittacamere* (local rooms for rent) is through tourist offices, although a handful are listed in provincial hotel guides. They are more common in the north than elsewhere.

Tourist offices can help with lists of apartments and villas for rent in popular parts of the coast.

GULP (☎ 0789 75 56 89, fax 0789 75 56 98; W *www.gulpimmobiliare.it; Via Nazionale 58)*, in Santa Teresa di Gallura, deals with apartments and villas for rent in the northeast of the island.

FOOD

The Sardinians share the general Italian delight in food and the convivial meal. Be adventurous and don't ever be intimidated by eccentric waiters or indecipherable menus and you will be doing your tastebuds a favour for which they will be eternally grateful.

See the Out to Lunch & Dinner in Sardinia special section for a rundown on the local delights for the palate. For a general glossary of food and culinary terms, see the Language chapter at the end of this book.

Restaurants

A *tavola calda* (literally 'hot table') usually offers cheap, pre-prepared meat, pasta and vegetable dishes in a self-service style. A pizzeria will of course serve pizza, but often has a full menu too. An *osteria* is in principle a wine bar or tavern offering a small selection of dishes. A trattoria is a down-to-earth family style eatery while the term *ristorante* (restaurant) is as broad in Italian as it is in English – anything from a divey diner to an exclusive five-star spot.

The problem is that increasingly the terms are used indiscriminately. A fine restaurant might wish to make itself sound more cosy or traditional by calling itself a trattoria or osteria. Likewise a cheap and nasty trattoria might try to put on airs by elevating itself to *ristorante*! At least you know the theory. In any event, always scan the menu, usually posted by the door, for dishes and prices.

Don't judge the quality of an eatery by its appearance. You are likely to eat your most memorable meal at a place with plastic tablecloths in a tiny back street or on a country lane. And don't panic if there is no printed menu: often this is a sign of fresh, authentic food. Just hope that the waiter will patiently explain the dishes and cost.

Most eating establishments have a cover charge (usually €1 to €3) and a service charge of 10% to 15%. Restaurants usually open for lunch from 12.30pm to 3pm, but many are not keen to take orders after 2pm. In the evening, opening hours vary but a rule of thumb is to look for dinner from about 8pm to 11pm. In coastal resorts in summer you can eat considerably later but otherwise you can be hard pressed to find a kitchen still serving beyond 11pm.

Bars & Ice-Cream Parlours

Round off the meal with a *gelato* (ice cream) from a gelateria or a *digestivo* (digestive

liqueur) or *caffè* at a bar. Most bars serve *cornetti* (croissants), *panini* (rolls) as well as sweets and chocolate.

Fast Food & Takeaways

In most towns and resorts you will find plenty of outlets for pizza *al taglio* (by the slice). You could also try one of the *alimentari* (grocery stores) and ask them to make a *panino* (sandwich roll) with the filling of your choice.

Vegetarian

Sardinian cooking is very meat-oriented but vegetarians shouldn't have too many problems. Few restaurants are devoted to them but vegetables are a staple of the Italian diet. Most places serve a good selection of *antipasti* (starters) and *contorni* (vegetables prepared in a variety of ways). Vegans will doubtless find the going rougher.

Self-Catering

If you have access to cooking facilities, buy fruit and vegetables at markets (usually open in the mornings only), and salami, cheese and wine at *alimentari* (a cross between a grocery store and a delicatessen) or *salumerie* (dedicated usually to sausages, meats and sometimes cheeses too). Fresh bread is available at a *forno* or *panetteria* (bakeries that sell bread, pastries and sometimes groceries) and usually at *alimentari*. At a *pasticceria* you can buy pastries, cakes and biscuits. A *rosticceria* sells cooked meats. There are also supermarkets in most towns.

Meals

Sardinians rarely eat a sit-down *colazione* (breakfast). They tend to drink a *cappuccino*, usually *tiepido* (warm), and eat a *cornetto* or other type of pastry while standing at a bar.

Pranzo (lunch) is traditionally the main meal of the day and many shops and businesses close for three to four hours every afternoon to accommodate the meal and siesta that traditionally is supposed to follow. A full meal will consist of an *antipasto* (starter), a *primo piatto* (say a broth, pasta or risotto) and a *secondo piatto* of meat or fish. Italians often then eat an *insalata* (salad) or *contorno* (vegetable side dish), and round off the meal with fruit, or occasionally with a *dolce* (dessert), and *caffè*, often at a bar on the way back to work.

Cena (the evening meal) was traditionally a simpler affair, but in recent years habits have begun to change due to the inconvenience of travelling home for lunch every day.

DRINKS
Nonalcoholic Drinks

Tea Sardinians aren't big tea (*té*) drinkers. You can order tea in bars, although it will usually arrive in the form of a cup of warm water with an accompanying tea bag. If this doesn't suit your taste, ask for the water *molto caldo* (very hot) or *bollente* (boiling).

Granita Mainly a summer drink, Granita is made of crushed ice with fresh lemon or other fruit juices, or with coffee topped with whipped cream.

Soft Drinks All the main international brands of soft drink are available, along with a surprising variety of local variants. *Aranciata* is the local generic name for orange Fanta-style fizzy drinks. A 1.5L bottle

Caffè Society

An *espresso* (also known as *un caffè*) is a small amount of strong black coffee. A *doppio espresso* is double the amount while a *caffè lungo* can be the same thing or a diluted espresso. If you want a long black coffee (as in a weaker, watered-down version), ask for a *caffè Americano*.

A *caffè corretto* is an espresso 'corrected' with a dash of *grappa* or some other spirit and a *macchiato* ('stained' coffee) is espresso with a dash of milk (*latte*), which can come *caldo* (hot) or *freddo* (cold). *Caffè freddo* is a long glass of cold, black, sweetened coffee. If you want it without sugar, ask for *caffè freddo amaro*.

The *cappuccino* (coffee with hot, frothy milk), which can also be had with the froth scraped off (*senza schiuma*), is a morning-only drink for Italians. You will find it difficult to convince bartenders to make your cappuccino hot rather than lukewarm. Ask for it *ben caldo* or *molto caldo*.

The milk in a *caffè latte* comes straight from the packet rather than being frothed up in the coffee-making machine.

of such drinks costs around €1.30 when you purchase it in supermarkets.

Water Although tap water is drinkable throughout the island, most locals prefer to drink bottled *acqua minerale* (mineral water). This is available *frizzante* (sparkling) or *naturale* (still) and you will be asked in restaurants and bars which you prefer. If you just want a glass of tap water, ask for *acqua dal rubinetto* or *acqua naturale*. A 1.5L bottle costs about €0.80 in an average supermarket.

Alcoholic Drinks

Wine & Spirits *Vino* (wine) is an essential accompaniment to any meal, and *digestivi* (liqueurs) are a popular way to end one. Sardinia boasts a surprising array of local wines that, while not nearly as well known as their more famous cousins from mainland regions like Tuscany and Piedmont, can be very pleasing to the palate.

Wine is reasonably priced and you will rarely need to pay more than €8 for a good bottle of wine, although prices go up to more than €15 for really good quality. Prices escalate seriously in some restaurants. In supermarkets you can get a perfectly drinkable Vermentino or Sella & Mosca red for around €3 to €4. Big 5l tubs of cheap table wine can cost around €5 to €6, although you have a hard time lugging one around without a car!

You will often see many wines from other Italian regions on sale, but only rarely from beyond Italy.

Since the 1960s, Italian wine has been graded according to four main classifications. *Vino da tavola* (table wine) indicates no specific classification; IGT *(indicazione geografica tipica)* means that the wine is typical of a certain area; DOC *(denominazione di origine controllata)* wines are produced subject to certain specifications (regarding grape types, method and so on); and DOCG *(denominazione di origine controllata e garantita)* shows that the wine is subject to the same requirements as normal DOC but that it is also tested by government inspectors. These indications appear on labels.

A DOC label can refer to wine from a single vineyard or an area. DOC wines can be elevated to DOCG after five years' consistent excellence; they can also be demoted.

Further hints come with indications such as *superiore*, which can denote DOC wines above the general standard (perhaps with greater alcohol content or longer ageing). 'Riserva' is applied only to DOC or DOCG wines that have aged for a specified time.

The average trattoria will stock only a limited selection of bottled wines and generally only cheaper varieties. Most people tend to order the *vino della casa* (house wine) or the *vino locale* (local wine) when they go out to dinner.

Before dinner, Italians might drink a Campari and soda or a fruit cocktail, usually pre-prepared and often without alcohol. After dinner, try a shot of *grappa*, a very strong, clear brew (either an acquired taste or a relative of paint stripper, depending on your viewpoint), or an *amaro*, a dark liqueur prepared from herbs. If you prefer a sweeter liqueur, try the almond-flavoured *amaretto* or the sweet aniseed *sambuca*.

For more on wine areas and specific island tipples, see the Out to Lunch & Dinner in Sardinia section.

Beer Although they have some wonderful wines, Sardinians are Italy's biggest beer-drinkers. The main Italian labels are Peroni, Nastro Azzuro, Dreher and Moretti, all very drinkable and cheaper than the imported varieties. Dreher is actually a Sardinian beer. There is another local drop, Ichnusa (a company owned by Heineken), which you won't find outside Sardinia. Beers come either bottled or *alla spina* (on tap).

ENTERTAINMENT
Bars & Pubs
Sardinians, like other Italians, are generally rather civilised about their drinking. The idea of cramming into a crowded pub and sending oneself into alcoholic oblivion is not nearly as widespread as in more northern European climes.

You will find plenty of bars all over the island, especially located in the bigger towns and coastal resorts. You can get a beer, wine or anything else at practically any bar, where you might be just as likely to have a cup of coffee.

They range from workaday grungy through to chic places to be seen in. Those operating first and foremost as nocturnal drinking establishments can be expected to stay open until about 1am, sometimes as late as 3am on Friday and Saturday.

In summer many bars have outdoor terraces spilling out onto the pavement or into the piazza. Irish-style pubs have yet to make much of an impression in Sardinia, although one or two can be found in the bigger centres.

Clubs
Italians call clubs *discoteche* and sometimes pay a high price to gain entry. Admission ranges from around €15 up to €50 or more for hotspots on the Costa Smeralda during the summer. This usually covers the cost of the first drink; after that you could be paying anything from €6 for a beer to €10 or more for a mixed drink. Venues are usually enormous, with big dance floors, and the music ranges from mainstream Top 40 fare to hip-hop, trip-hop and so on.

Elsewhere around the island, you'll find clubs in and around Cagliari, Alghero and some of the seaside resorts like Villasimius, San Teodoro and dotted along the Oristano coast.

Live Music
Big rock concerts sometimes take place, especially in summer, in Cagliari's Anfiteatro Romano or at the Fiera Campionaria fairgrounds in the east of the city. Some big acts also play at Sassari's football stadium. Various Italian singers and the occasional foreign act play to the VIPs in bars scattered about the Costa Smeralda in summer. Some of the bars listed for Cagliari, Alghero and Sassari occasionally get live acts.

Cinemas
Italy has a proud dubbing tradition and the chances of seeing a foreign film in the original language are close to zero in Sardinia. If you don't mind your flicks in Italian, a cinema ticket costs up to €6.70. This can come down to €3.10 on cheap days (often Wednesday).

Theatre & Opera
In summer special theatre, opera and dance performances are sporadically put on at the Roman sites of Tharros and Nora. Similarly, various shows take place at Cagliari's Anfiteatro Romano. Otherwise, Cagliari and Sassari are the main centres for theatre, mostly in Italian. Works can range from Italian classics to contemporary works by Italian

and foreign playwrights, but almost exclusively in Italian.

SPECTATOR SPORTS
Football
Cagliari, one of the leading Serie B (2nd Division) clubs is the most important side in Sardinia. For details on how to see them at a home game, see the Cagliari & the Southeast chapter.

Sardinian Wrestling
The wild Barbagia region of Nuoro province is home to a local version of wrestling known as *'S'Istrumpa'*. Once practised at festivals, weddings and on other more impromptu occasions, this simple form of unarmed combat has been practised for thousands of years. See the Nuoro & the East chapter for more information.

SHOPPING
Isola (Istituto Sardo Organizzazione Lavoro Artigiano) is the official island-wide promoter of traditional crafts. It has shops in several cities and towns (some are indicated in the course of the guide) and can be a good first stop for those interested in picking up some gifts with local colour.

Basketware
Since ancient times the Sardinians have been making baskets and other containers of asphodel, rush, dwarf palm leaves and willow. You can still see women making them in the narrow streets of Castelsardo, which is as good a place as any to buy these items – increasingly aimed at visitors rather than local housewives.

Carpets & Rugs
Sardinian wool is used in the production of all sorts of carpets and rugs. In places like Aggius, near Tempio Pausania in the north of the island, the traditional cottage industry has been revived for tourists and you can get such items in stores all over the island. Colours tend to be muted and designs simple and geometric.

Ceramics
Pottery is a popular if fairly touristy item. All sorts of pretty ceramics can be found in souvenir and specialist shops in the coastal resorts and towns, especially in the north

(like the Costa Smeralda, Santa Teresa di Gallura and Alghero). The island has a long history of ceramics production but traditionally it was simple stuff for everyday use, with none of the elegance of material produced in other parts of Italy and Europe. Nowadays, however, you can find some beautiful work.

Clothing & Accessories
In Cagliari and to a lesser extent in centres like Sassari and Alghero you can shop for Italian fashion at reasonable prices. The Rinascente department store on Via Roma in Cagliari is a good starting point. The chichi towns along the Costa Smeralda are another option, although you can expect prices frequently higher than you'd pay in boutiques in Milan, Florence or Rome!

Coral
A (tightly controlled) speciality of the island, and more precisely of Alghero, is jewellery made from coral. The coast around Alghero, nowadays known as the Riviera del Corallo, has long been a source of this prized material. The seabed gives up mainly a crimson red coral but in jewellery stores around Alghero and elsewhere on the island you will also find items in a turquoise coral. You could pick up anything from modest earrings to gaudy, heavy necklaces combining red coral with gold.

Cork
One of the island's main industries is cork production. A drive around the countryside, especially in the north of the island around the cork town of Calangianus, reveals thick stands of cork trees, the bark stripped from the base of the trunk to the lowest branches. A common souvenir item are bottles of local drinks (like *mirto*) wrapped in cork.

Jewellery
The most delicate of gold and silver jewellery found in Sardinia is that made *a filigrana* (filigree). If you get a chance to glimpse the traditional baubles that were once part of the most colourful of traditional women's dresses, you will see that this is an art form with a long history. Ultrafine strings are made in the precious metals and intertwined much like lace to make fanciful jewels.

Knives

For many visitors, the single greatest items of interest are the fine pocket knives produced in several places around the island. Those from the non-descript northern village of Pattada, known as *sa pattadesa*, are the most celebrated but many other fine blades of different shapes and sizes can be found. Another important centre is Arbus, in the southwest. A good *s'arburesa* is worth every cent invested.

For more on these and other knives, how they are made and what to look for when buying, see the boxed text 'Sardinia's Cutting Edge' in the Sassari & the Northwest chapter.

Bastioni di San Marco, old Alghero

Woven handicrafts, Castelsardo

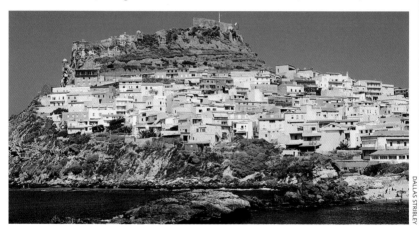
Castelsardo, Sassari

Cattedrale, Alghero

Grotta di Nettuno, Capo Caccia

Mural in Fonni, Le Barbagie

Cork trees stripped of their bark

Yacht off the Golfo di Orosei

Porto Cervo on the Costa Smeralda, the Gallura

Getting There & Away

A limited number of direct flights from various points in Europe, summer ferry services from France and year-round services from neighbouring Corsica combine to link Sardinia with the wider world. The bulk of travel options, however, involve actually passing through mainland Italy (if only to change flights). By sea, a host of vessels ply the waters between a series of mainland Italian locations and half a dozen Sardinian ports.

AIR
Airports
Sardinia is served by three well-distributed airports: Aeroporto Elmas at the capital, Cagliari, in the south of the island; Aeroporto di Costa Smeralda at Olbia in the northeast; and Fertilia (for Alghero and Sassari) in the northwest.

All three are served by Italian domestic flights and some scheduled and charter flights from around Europe. The airports are all well connected to their respective cities by local transport and are equipped with tourist offices, banks and the usual airport shops. Long distance buses also link the Fertilia and Olbia airports to more distant destinations.

The tiny Arbatax-Tortolì airstrip, 1½km south of Tortolì on the southern Nuoro coast, opens in summer for some regular flights and, above all, charter flights from the Italian mainland.

Departure Tax
Airport taxes are factored into ticket prices in Italy.

Other Parts of Italy
As a rule, flying is not a cheap option within Italy, but if you are coming from a far-flung corner like Venice or the deep south, it can be an attractive choice where time rather than money is the object. Deals to reduce the cost of flying between the mainland and Sardinia have helped keep the lid on prices.

Meridiana (☎ 199 11 13 33; ⓦ www.meridiana.it) is the main airline with flights from the Italian mainland to Sardinia. **Alitalia** (toll-free ☎ 848 86 56 41; ⓦ www.alitalia.it)

seems to have been largely knocked out of the game now, preserving only a regular series of flights to Cagliari departing from Rome (through which connections can be made for other cities). Traffic to Alghero's Fertilia airport is dominated by **Air One** (☎ 848 84 88 80; ⓦ www.flyairone.it). Other minor airlines, including **Air Dolomiti** (☎ 800 01 33 66; ⓦ airdolomiti.lufthansa.com), **Alpi Eagles** (☎ 041 599 77 88; ⓦ www.alpieagles.com) and **Minerva Air Lines** (☎ 848 86 56 41; ⓦ www.minerva-airlines.it, Italian only), operate a few flights travelling into Cagliari and Alghero.

One-way fares are expensive. If you get a return, purchasing an Apex (or even better a Super Apex) fare will bring the price down considerably (often down to about the cost of a normal one-way trip and sometimes less) in exchange for respecting certain conditions. Residents of Sardinia get special reductions.

The one-way sample fares, listed in the table 'One-way Airfares' on the next page, should only be taken as a rough guide. Frequencies take into account all airlines. With a couple of exceptions these are all direct flights. Greater possibilities open up, especially with Alitalia to Cagliari, if you are prepared to make a change of flight somewhere en route.

One-way Airfares

Cagliari

from	frequency (daily)	fare (€)	duration (min)
Bologna	up to 3	179	75
Genoa	up to 3	178	85
Naples	up to 1	161	65
Pisa	up to 6	166	65
Rome	up to 13	85	60
Turin	up to 1	190	80
Venice	up to 2	143	80
Verona	up to 3	179	80

Olbia

from	frequency (daily)	fare (€)	duration (min)
Bergamo	up to 1	166	65
Bologna	up to 4	166	60
Florence	up to 1	150	60
Milan	up to 10	166	75
Naples	3 weekly	158	120
Palermo (via Rome)	up to 2	197	210
Pisa	up to 2	130	50
Rome	up to 12	117	45
Turin	up to 1	190	65
Venice	up to 1	166	70
Verona	up to 6	179	65

Fertilia (Alghero)

from	frequency (daily)	fare (€)	duration (min)
Catania (via Rome)	up to 2	174	360
Genoa	up to 1	154	60
Milan	up to 3	111	55
Palermo (via Rome)	up to 5	154	165
Rome	up to 5	85	60
Turin (via Rome)	up to 1	194	60
Venice	up to 3	169	60

The UK & Ireland

Discount air travel is big business in London. Most British travel agencies are registered with ABTA (Association of British Travel Agents). If you have paid for your flight with an ABTA-registered agency that then goes bust, ABTA will guarantee a refund or an alternative. Unregistered travel agencies and bucket shops are riskier, but sometimes cheaper. Advertisements for tickets appear in the travel pages of the weekend broadsheets

and – in London – in *Time Out*, the *Evening Standard* and the free magazine *TNT*.

Travellers are increasingly using the Internet to search for good fares and some airlines, particularly the budget ones, encourage you to book online. Among sites you might like to search for competitive fares are: W www.planesimple.co.uk, W www.opodo .co.uk and W www.expedia.co.uk.

One of the more reliable, but not necessarily cheapest, agencies is **STA** (☎ 0870 160 0599; W *www.statravel.co.uk*), with several offices in London, and branches on many university campuses and in cities such as Bristol, Cambridge, Manchester and Oxford.

A similar agency is **Trailfinders** (☎ 020-7937 1234 for European flights; W *www.trail finder.com*). It has a short-haul **booking centre** (*215 Kensington High St, London W8 6BD*), and there are also offices in Belfast, Birmingham, Bristol, Cambridge, Glasgow, Manchester and Newcastle.

Other popular travel agencies include **ebookers** (☎ 0870 010 7000; W *www.ebook ers.com; 177-178 Tottenham Court Rd, London W1P 0LX*) and **Bridge the World** (☎ 0870 444 7474; W *www.b-t-w.co.uk; 4 Regent Place, London W1B 5EA*).

The two flag airlines linking the UK and Italy are **British Airways** (*BA;* ☎ 0845 773 3377; W *www.british-airways.com; 156 Regent St, London W1B 5LB*), and Italy's **Alitalia** (☎ 0870 544 8259, *www.alitalia.it; 4 Portman Square, London W1H 6LD*). Of the two, BA is more likely to have special deals. In either case flights, which can cost around UK£200 return, will often be routed through Rome.

The no-frills Irish airline **Ryanair** (☎ 0871 246 0000 in the UK, ☎ 899 88 99 73 in Italy; W *www.ryanair.ie*) flies to Alghero from London Stansted, with flights up to three times daily in summer (April to September). Fares vary wildly according to demand and season. For instance in early September you might be looking at UK£110 to UK£140 each way, while in November (one flight a day) you could pay as little as UK£14 to UK£18 each way.

Italy's **Meridiana** (☎ 020-7839 2222; W *www.meridiana.it; 15 Charles II St, London SW1*) has a couple of direct flights a week from April to mid-October from London Gatwick to Olbia. Flight time is two hours 20 minutes. Tickets cost around UK£500 return.

Finally, you could consider a flight to Genoa and catch a ferry from there, or even to Rome (and take a ferry from Civitavecchia). The latter option probably won't work out more cheaply, but might offer greater flexibility and the chance to make a stopover in the eternal city.

If you're coming from Ireland, you will almost definitely have to consider a flight via Rome. It might be worth going to London first and proceeding from there (say with Ryanair).

Continental Europe

Sardinia has long been a holiday destination for mainland Italians but is gaining favour among other Europeans. Flying there from elsewhere in Europe can often be costly, although as the island catches on, this may change.

France The student travel agency **OTU Voyages** (☎ 0 820 817 817, 01 44 41 38 50; W www.otu.fr, French only; 39 ave Georges Bernanos, Paris) has a central Paris office and another 30 offices around the country. You can books flights on the Web too.

Meridiana (☎ 01 44 61 61 50; W www.meridiana.it; 9 Blvd de la Madeleine, Paris) has a couple of flights a week from Paris to Olbia and a daily flight to Cagliari. These can both cost €226 return. Otherwise, flights involving a change of flight en route (eg, in Rome) with Alitalia and Lufthansa to either of these destinations can cost up to €533 return.

Germany In Berlin you could try **STA Travel** (☎ 030-310 00 40; W www.statravel.de, German only; Hardenbergstrasse 9). There are also offices in Frankfurt am Main (☎ 069-44 30 27; Bergerstrasse 109) and in 18 other cities across the country.

Air One (W www.flyairone.it) flies from Frankfurt to Fertilia (Alghero) for around €400 return. A return trip from Frankfurt to Cagliari with Alitalia can cost €430.

LTU (☎ 0211-941 88 88; W www.ltu.de, German only) has direct flights to Cagliari and Olbia from Düsseldorf and Nordrhein Westfalen airports. **Aerolloyd** (W www.aerolloyd.de, German only) flies to Olbia from Düsseldorf. Offers can come in around €330 return. The national carrier **Lufthansa** (☎ 01803-803803; W www.lufthansa.com)

also has direct flights travelling to Cagliari from Munich.

Netherlands Amsterdam is a popular departure point and a good budget flight centre. Try the bucket shops along Rokin. Return fares with Alitalia and KLM from Amsterdam to Cagliari (via Rome) tend to cost around €490.

Spain Getting cheap flights between Spain and Italy is difficult. Frequently the best-value flights are routed through another European city (such as Germany's Munich) and involve changing flights.

The Italian airline Meridiana sometimes has direct flights from Barcelona to Cagliari and Olbia. Inquire at travel agents.

One Madrid agency with a reputation for getting the best available deals is **Viajes Zeppelin** (☎ 91 542 51 54; Plaza de Santo Domingo 2). A youth and student specialist agency is **Asatej** (☎ 91 522 96 93; W www.asatej.com, Spanish only; Carrera de San Jerónimo 18, Madrid).

Return flights from either Madrid or Barcelona, almost always requiring a stop in mainland Italy, can easily cost €400 or more and will involve at least one change of flight in Rome.

The USA

The North Atlantic is the world's busiest long-haul air corridor and the flight options are bewildering. There are no direct flights from the USA to Sardinia. Depending on which airline you choose, you will have to make a change in Rome or Milan and possibly another European city en route too.

Standard fares can be expensive but you can generally find cheaper fares by shopping around. Charters are sometimes an option, although you are unlikely to find anything direct to Sardinia. Most airlines and many travel agencies operate interactive websites allowing you to search for and purchase tickets, although this is not always the cheapest way to go about things.

Reliable travel agencies include **STA** (☎ 1-800-781 4040; W www.statravel.com) and **Council Travel** (☎ 1-800-226 8624; W www.counciltravel.com). Both have offices in major cities. Discount travel agencies, known as consolidators, can be found in the weekly travel sections of the *New*

York Times, *Los Angeles Times*, *Chicago Tribune* and *San Francisco Examiner*.

Stand-by fares are often sold at 60% of the normal price for one-way tickets. **Airhitch** *(toll-free ☎ 1-800-605 44824;* **W** *www.airhitch.org)* is an online specialist. You will need to give a general idea of where and when you need to go, and a few days before your departure you will be presented with a choice of two or three flights. A one-way flight from the USA to Europe costs from US$180 (east coast) to US$250 (west coast), plus taxes. This won't necessarily get you to Sardinia, but it could get you a cheap flight to somewhere close.

From New York a return fare to Cagliari via Paris or London *and* Rome or Milan costs US$660/860 in low/high season. Something similar from Los Angeles will set you back US$880/1020.

If you can't find a good deal, consider a cheap transatlantic hop to London and stalk the bucket shops there.

Canada

Scan the travel agencies' advertisements in the *Toronto Globe & Mail*, *Toronto Star* and *Vancouver Sun*. **Travel CUTS** *(☎ 1-866-832 7564;* **W** *www.travelcuts.com)*, called Voyages Campus in Quebec, has offices in all major cities in Canada.

From Toronto a return fare to Cagliari via Paris or London *and* Rome or Milan costs C$1220/1490 in low/high season. From Vancouver you are looking at C$1420/1670.

Australia

Major dealers in cheap airfares are **STA Travel** *(☎ 1300 733 035;* **W** *www.statravel.com.au)* and **Flight Centre** *(☎ 133133;* **W** *www.flightcentre.com.au)*, although heavily discounted fares can often be found at your local travel agent. Look at the travel ads in the Saturday editions of Melbourne's the *Age* and the *Sydney Morning Herald*.

Flights to Sardinia from Australia will almost invariably involve a change of flight (and probably airline) in Rome or Milan. It will cost you A$1856 return to Cagliari from Sydney or Melbourne in low season. In high season it is more like A$2590.

New Zealand

Popular agencies are **STA Travel** *(☎ 0508 782872;* **W** *www.statravel.co.nz)* and **Flight Centre** *(☎ 0800 243544;* **W** *www.flightcentre.co.nz)*, with branches throughout the country. The *New Zealand Herald* has a travel section in which travel agencies advertise fares.

As from Australia, you will need to change flights at least once in Rome or Milan. Return fares can range from NZ$2400 to NZ$2800.

Asia

Although most Asian countries are now able to offer fairly competitive fare deals, Bangkok, Hong Kong and Singapore are still the best places to shop around for discount tickets.

STA Travel has branches in Bangkok, Hong Kong, Kuala Lumpur, Singapore and Tokyo. A plethora of flights from these cities converge on Rome, from where you will have to connect to fly on to Cagliari or other Sardinian airports.

LAND

Clearly you cannot drive or catch a train to Sardinia – that's the curious nature of islands. For details of sea approaches see below. The combination of overland travel from elsewhere in Europe and the boat trip make for a long voyage (necessary for those taking their own vehicles – an option worth considering) but may be the only option if you find air tickets too expensive.

Bus

Eurolines *(***W** *www.eurolines.com)*, in conjunction with local bus companies across Europe, is the main international carrier. You can contact them in your own country. Note that in summer (generally interpreted as July to August but sometimes including September depending on where you are travelling from) the prices increase as much as 10%.

Other Parts of Italy As a general rule, long-distance bus travel is not a wonderful option in Italy, unless you are coming from the south, in which case buses can be faster. From places like Bari, Brindisi and so on, you need to get to the ports of Naples or Civitavecchia (outside Rome). The former offers few departures to Sardinia, so it is better if you can make it up to Rome. For northern ports take the train (see later).

The UK If you want to do the bus and boat combination, you need to choose a port of departure. This is most likely going to be Genoa, although a few boats per month sail to Sardinia from Toulon and Marseille in France.

Eurolines *(☎ 0870 580 8080; 4 Cardiff Rd, Luton LU1 1PP)*, with the London terminal at Victoria Coach Station on Buckingham Palace Rd, runs buses to Genoa (via Paris and Milan) three times a week (leaving at 8am on Monday, Wednesday and Friday). The whole trip takes 26½ hours. Up to five services run in summer. The lowest youth (under 26)/senior (60 and over) fares from London to Genoa cost around UK£66 one way and UK£101 return. The full adult fares cost around UK£73/109 one way/return.

Eurolines buses also run to Marseille (20 hours; three to five times a week) and Toulon (21 hours; three to five times a week) via Lyon. Prices for both are UK£64/97 one way/return (UK£56/88 youth and senior).

France Eurolines *(☎ 0836 695252; 28 ave du Général de Gaulle, Paris • ☎ 01 43 54 11 99; 55 rue St Jacques, Paris)* has offices in several French cities. From Paris, you pay €69/125 (€63/113 for those under 26) one way/return to Genoa (15½ hours). If you wish to get the boat from French ports, take the train.

Germany & Switzerland Eurolines is represented by **Deutsche Touring GmbH** *(☎ 069-79 03 50; Am Römerhof 17, 60486 Frankfurt a/M)* and has numerous offices all over Germany.

Eurolines coaches leave three or four times a week from 10 German cities for Genoa. From Frankfurt am Main, for instance, the fare is €62/105 (€56/95 for those aged under 26) one way/return. The trip takes 15 hours.

For many, the train will be a more attractive option – see later in this chapter. There are no Eurolines bus services from Switzerland so you will have no real choice but to take the train to Genoa.

Spain Madrid and Barcelona are connected with Genoa (and beyond) through **Eurolines** *(☎ 902 40 50 40)* three to five times a week. The trip from Barcelona (13 hours) costs €71/128 (€64/115 for those aged under 26) one way/return. From Madrid (22¼ hours) you travel to Barcelona and change there for the Genoa bus. Fares are €101/182

(€90/164 for those aged under 26) one-way/ return. The office in **Madrid** *(☎ 91 528 11 05; Calle de Méndez Alvaro 83)* is at the Estación Sur de Autobuses (the main bus station). In **Barcelona** *(☎ 93 265 65 08; Carrer d'Alí Bei 80)* it's at the Estació del Nord.

Train
Although more expensive than the bus, travel by rail is infinitely more comfortable and can be quicker too. As with the bus, your options will be determined by your choice of embarkation point, which for most will mean Genoa.

On overnight hauls you can book a couchette for around €15 to €23 on most international trains. In 1st class there are four bunks per cabin and in 2nd class there are six bunks. It is always advisable, and sometimes compulsory, to book seats on international trains to and from Italy. Some of the main international services include transport for private cars – an option worth examining to save wear and tear on your vehicle before it arrives in Italy.

Other Parts of Italy If coming from elsewhere in Italy, it will almost always be easiest to get a train to the nearest convenient port.

Types of Train A wide variety of trains runs on the **Trenitalia** *(☎ 89 20 21; ⒲ www .trenitalia.it)* network. They start with slow all-stops *locali*, which generally don't travel much beyond their main city of origin or province. Next come the *regionali*, which also tend to be slow, but cover greater distances, sometimes going beyond their region of origin. *Interregionali* cover greater distances still and don't necessarily stop at every station.

From this level, there is a qualitative leap upwards to InterCity (IC) trains: faster, long-distance trains operating between major cities, for which you have to pay a *supplemento* on top of the normal cost of a ticket. EuroCity (EC) trains are the international version. They can reach a top speed of 200km/h (but rarely get the chance!).

Comfort and speed on the most important lines are provided by the *pendolino* trains, so-called because they 'lean' up to 8° into curves to increase standard InterCity speeds by up to 35%.

Pendolini and other top-of-the-range services, which on high-speed tracks can zip along at more than 300km/h, are collectively known as Eurostar Italia (ES).

InterCity Notte (ICN) trains provide most overnight services. You generally have the option of *cuccette* (couchettes) – four or six fold-down bunk beds in a compartment – or a proper bed (more expensive) in a *vagone letto* (sleeping car). The international version is the EuroNight (EN).

Tickets Apart from the standard division between 1st and 2nd class *(prima classe* and *seconda classe)* on faster trains (you can only get 2nd-class seats on *locali* and *regionali)*, you pay a supplement for being on a fast train, calculated according to the length of the journey. You can pay the supplement separately from the ticket. Thus, if you have a 2nd-class return ticket from Milan to Genoa, you might decide to avoid the supplement one way and take a slower train, but pay it on the way back to speed things up a little. You need to pay the supplement before boarding the train.

You can buy rail tickets at stations (often crowded) and from most travel agents. Automatic machines at most stations accept credit cards and cash. It is also possible to order tickets over the phone with credit card (☎ 89 20 21) or on the Web and pick them up at a special counter at the station or from one of the ticket machines. You need to book 24 hours in advance.

It is advisable, and in some cases obligatory, to book long-distance tickets in advance, whether international or domestic. In 1st class, booking is often mandatory (and free). Where it is optional (which is more often, but not always, the case in 2nd class), you may pay a €2 booking fee.

The following prices are approximate standard 2nd-class one-way fares (plus supplement) on InterCity trains. Pendolino and Eurostar Italia fares are higher.

from	to	fare (€)	duration (min)
Florence	Livorno	5.70	80
Milan	Genoa	12.86	90
Naples	Livorno	32.95	315
Rome	Livorno	21.69	180
Venice	Genoa	28.15	280*

* direct (many trains involve a change at Milan)

Validate your ticket by stamping it in one of the yellow machines scattered about stations (usually with a *convalida* sign on them). Failure to do so will be rewarded with an on-the-spot fine (which varies according to the distance of your intended journey). Return tickets must be stamped each way (each end of the ticket).

The ticket you buy is valid for two months until stamped. Once stamped it is valid for 24 hours if the distance of the journey (one way) is greater than 200km, six hours if it is less. The time calculated is for each one-way journey (so on a short return trip, you get six hours from the time of stamping on the way out and the same on the way back).

Seats on ES trains on Friday and Sunday must be booked. On other days wagons for unbooked seats are set aside. If you board an ES train on Friday or Sunday without a booking, you pay a €5 fine.

Passes & Discounts Eurail, InterRail, Europass and Flexipass tickets are valid on the national rail network. Possible local passes include the Railpass, Flexipass and Euro-Domino pass, all of which can be bought in Italy and abroad. They allow you unlimited rail travel for varying periods of time. None of these passes is much use unless you plan to travel extensively in Italy.

One discount option that could be worth looking into if you plan to travel a lot in mainland Italy as well as Sardinia is the *biglietto chilometrico*, valid for up to five people. This gives 3000km of rail travel in up to 20 journeys. It costs €116.72. You have to pay supplements on faster trains.

Children aged under four travel free and those between four and 12 pay half price.

People aged between 12 and 26 can acquire the *Carta Verde* and people aged 60 and over the *Carta d'Argento*. Both cost €25.82, are valid for a year and entitle holders to 20% off ticket price.

The *Carta Amicotreno* (€50) gives you (and a friend who travels with you) 10% off on tickets (except on Eurostar Italia trains), but only in 1st class on Fridays and Sundays. The card is valid for a year.

See also the Getting Around chapter for a Sardinia-specific pass.

The UK The days when people caught a combination of train and ferry to cross the channel are largely over for all those wanting to get beyond northern France. The easiest way to get a through ticket to your final destination (in this case probably Genoa) is to take the Eurostar through the Channel Tunnel to Paris and change there for your onward journey. The cheapest adult return fare to Genoa (changing in Paris and Milan) is UK£234 (including couchette for the Paris–Milan run). People under 26 pay UK£195.

For information and bookings contact the **Rail Europe Travel Centre** (☎ *0870 584 8848;* W| *www.raileurope.co.uk; 178 Piccadilly, London W1V 0BA).* Another source of rail information for all of Europe is **RailChoice** (☎ *020-8659 7300;* W| *www.railchoice.co.uk).*

France There is only one overnight train from Paris to Genoa via Turin. It leaves at 10.20pm from Gare de Lyon and costs €100.80 each way (including a couchette from Paris to Turin). You must change in Turin.

A little more expensive, but giving you greater leeway, is to get a TGV high-speed train to Turin or Milan and make a connection there. This generally involves making a change en route (in Lyon or Chambéry). The trip to Milan takes about six hours and costs €101 each way.

Services also connect other French cities with Genoa via the Mediterranean coast and Ventimiglia.

If you decide to leave for Sardinia from Marseille or Toulon, train is always the easiest bet for reaching those ports from other parts of France.

You can buy tickets at stations and online (W| www.sncf.com).

Germany & Switzerland The train is generally a more costly but more effective means of reaching Genoa (or Livorno if you so choose) from Germany than the bus. Numerous possibilities present themselves but generally involve at least two changes of train along the way. From Frankfurt am Main, for instance, the quickest trains take about 11 hours and involve two changes en route. You're looking at about €120 to €130 each way.

From Switzerland you must take a train to Milan and from there jump on to the first train south to Genoa. The cost as far as Milan

is up to Sfr81/153 one way/return from Geneva (add Sfr14 each way if you catch the more comfortable and slightly faster Cisalpino). The trip takes at least 3¾ hours. From Zürich (4½ hours) you pay Sfr72/135 one way/return (plus Sfr14 for the Cisalpino).

Spain From Spain, the only direct service to Italy is an overnight Barcelona–Milan train that runs from three to seven nights a week depending on the season (12¾ hours). A reclining seat costs €168 return (up to €526 in top class sleeping cars) to Milan. To that you must add the price of the Milan–Genoa stretch (see earlier).

Car & Motorcycle

Those choosing to travel overland to Sardinia are most likely to be those taking their own wheels. This is a perfectly sensible idea as the island's public transport network leaves a little to be desired and car hire is prohibitively expensive for anything other than a short spell.

As with bus or train, you need to make your way to the most convenient port. For many this will be Genoa, although if you choose you could add a few hours driving time and continue down as far as Livorno, from where the sea crossing is shorter.

Drivers coming from the UK, Spain or France may prefer to time their trip with vessels leaving from Marseille or Toulon (see following).

The UK To get your vehicle across the Channel you can use the **Eurotunnel** (☎ *0870 535 3535;* W| *www.eurotunnel.com),* the Channel Tunnel car train connecting Folkestone with Calais. It runs around the clock, with up to four crossings (35 minutes) an hour in high season. You pay for the vehicle only and fares vary according to the time of day and season. A standard return fare for a car and passengers can hover around UK£300. You can book in advance by phone or online, but the service is designed to let you just roll up.

Otherwise you can transport your car by Hoverspeed or ferry to France. **Hoverspeed** (☎ *0870 240 8070;* W| *www.hoverspeed.com)* fast boats take about two hours to cross from Dover to Calais and the standard return trip for a car with one or two passengers will cost about UK£250 to UK£270. **P&O Stena Line** (☎ *0870 600 0600;* W| *ww2.posl.com)* has frequent car ferries from Dover to Calais (1¼ hours). A typical advance-purchase return fare for a car and one passenger is UK£274. With both companies it is generally cheaper to travel before 7am and after 8pm.

From then on you stick your foot to the floor and charge across France's expensive toll-road system to your port of choice.

Paperwork & Preparations Proof of ownership of a private vehicle should always be carried (Vehicle Registration Document for UK-registered cars) in Europe. All EU member states' driving licences (pink or pink and green) are recognised.

Other foreign licences are supposed to be accompanied by an International Driving Permit (although in practice, for renting cars or dealing with traffic police, your national licence will suffice). The International Driving Permit is available from automobile clubs in your country and is valid for 12 months.

Third-party motor insurance is a minimum requirement and it is compulsory to have a Green Card, an internationally recognised proof of insurance, which can be obtained from your insurer. Also ask your insurer for a European accident statement form, which can simplify matters in the event of an accident. Never sign statements you can't read or understand: insist on a translation and sign that only if it's acceptable.

A European breakdown assistance policy such as the AA Five Star Service or RAC Eurocover Motoring Assistance is a good investment. In Italy, assistance can be obtained through the Automobile Club Italiano (ACI). See also Car & Motorcycle in the Getting Around chapter.

Every vehicle travelling across an international border should display a nationality plate of its country of registration. Two warning triangles (to be used in the event of a breakdown) are compulsory in Italy. Recommended accessories are a first-aid kit, a spare-bulb kit and a fire extinguisher. If the car is from the UK or Ireland, remember to have the headlights adjusted for driving in continental Europe.

In the UK, get more information from the **RAC** (☎ 0870 572 2722; Ⓦ www.rac.co.uk) or the **AA** (☎ 0870 600 0371; Ⓦ www.theaa.com).

Rental Car rental does not come cheap in Italy, although for stays of a week or so it works out cheaper and less stressful (on you and your own car) than bringing your own.

Prebooking a car through a multinational agency – such as Hertz, Avis, Budget Car or Europe's largest rental agency, Europcar – before leaving home will enable you to find cheaper deals than booking with the same agencies direct in Sardinia.

If you only decide once in Sardinia that you wish to hire, rental with the international agencies works out best if you call home and book there (as though you were yet to arrive in Italy) or online.

Look into fly-drive combinations and other programmes. You simply pick up the vehicle on arrival and return it to a nominated point at the end of the rental period. Ask your travel agent for information or contact one of the major car-rental agencies.

Holiday Autos (☎ 0870 400 0099, 0870 400 4447; Ⓦ www.holidayautos.co.uk) sometimes has good rates for Europe, for which you need to pre-book; its main office is in the UK. At the time of writing, they were charging UK£140 (all inclusive) for a small car (such as a three-door Fiat Punto) for one week (pick up at Cagliari airport), with the option of one-way rental.

No matter where you rent, make sure you understand what is included in the price (unlimited kilometres, tax, insurance, collision damage waiver etc) and what your liabilities are. The minimum rental age in Italy is 21 years. A credit card is usually required.

An alternative to standard rental is to take out a short-term lease on a new Renault. There are pick-up points in Rome and Milan (Malpensa) airports. For details of how this operates check out Renault's Eurodrive website at Ⓦ www.eurodrive.renault.com.

For more details of rental rates and options once in Sardinia, see Car & Motorcycle in the Getting Around chapter.

Purchase It is illegal for nonresidents to purchase vehicles in Italy. The UK is probably the best place to buy second-hand cars (prices are not competitive for new cars). You will be getting a left-hand-drive car (with the steering wheel on the right).

If you want a right-hand-drive car and can afford to buy new, prices are relatively low in Belgium, the Netherlands and Luxembourg. Paperwork can be tricky wherever you buy.

Motorcycle Sardinia is a great place for motorcycle touring. Given the state of some roads and summertime traffic, you will often find yourself zipping by hot and sweaty car drivers caught in slow or unmoving entanglements. Motorcycles are also easier to squeeze around city traffic and park and you will rarely need to book ahead to get a bike onto a ferry.

SEA

Apart from the big birds, the only way you'll get to Sardinia is by boat (swimming is not an option).

In addition to the crossings from more than half a dozen Italian ports, you can reach Sardinia by sea from France (Corsica, Marseille and Toulon) and from Tunisia.

Italy

Several companies run ferries of varying types and speeds from various Italian ports to Sardinia. For company contact details, see the 'Finding a Ferry' boxed text. Fare prices and frequency depend on season and company and can change several times in the course of the year. The 'Ferry Fares to Sardinia' table, below, gives standard high-season one-way fares (in *poltrona*, or reclining seat) for people (children aged four to 12 generally pay around half; those under four go free) and small cars. Depending on the service, you can

Ferry Fares to Sardinia

from	to	company	frequency	duration (hrs)	fare (€)	small car (€)
Civitavecchia	Arbatax	Tirrenia	2 weekly	10½	34.09	69.72
Civitavecchia	Cagliari	Sardinia F	2-3 weekly	13	54	82
Civitavecchia	Cagliari	Tirrenia	2-5 weekly	14½	40.28	77.98
Civitavecchia	Olbia	Moby	3-7 weekly	4¾	55	114
Civitavecchia	Olbia	Tirrenia	1-2 daily	8	24.53	85.47
Civitavecchia	G. Aranci	Sardinia F	6 weekly	6¾	42	82
Civitavecchia	G. Aranci+	Sardinia F	1-2 daily	3½	52	115
Civitavecchia	Olbia*+	Tirrenia	2-4 daily	4	46.99	98.59
Fiumicino	Arbatax*+	Tirrenia	2 weekly	4½	47.77	72.56
Fiumicino	G. Aranci*+	Tirrenia	1-2 daily	4	46.99	98.59
Genoa	Arbatax	Tirrenia	2 weekly	19	47.25	90.84
Genoa	Olbia*	Grimaldi	1 daily	8-10	73	113
Genoa	Olbia*	Moby	1 daily	9½	63	109
Genoa	Olbia	Tirrenia	1 daily	13¼	45.19	90.84
Genoa	Olbia*+	Tirrenia	1 daily	6	77.98	98.38
Genoa	Palau	Tris	3-7 weekly	11	57	89
Genoa	Palau*+	Tris	1 daily	6	89	97
Genoa	P. Torres	Grimaldi	1-2 daily	11	67	113
Genoa	P. Torres	Tirrenia	1 daily	8-9	45.19	90.84
Genoa	P. Torres	Tris	1 daily (night)	8-9	63.13	98.38
La Spezia	Palau	Tirrenia	1 weekly	12	57	89
Livorno	G. Aranci	Sardinia F	5-8 weekly	10	57	109
Livorno	G. Aranci+	Sardinia F	4-14 weekly	6	63	109
Livorno	Olbia	Moby	1-3 daily	7-11	56	109
Livorno	Olbia*	Linea Golfi	4-16 weekly	8	35	77
Naples	Cagliari	Tirrenia	1-2 weekly	16¼	40.80	77.98
Naples	Palau*	L. Lauro	1-2 weekly	14	70	120
Palermo	Cagliari	Tirrenia	1 weekly	13½	38.21	77.98
Piombino	Olbia*	Linea Golfi	4-16 weekly	8	35	77
Savona	Palau	Tris	1 weekly	14	57	89
Trapani	Cagliari	Tirrenia	1 weekly	11	38.21	77.98

* indicates the service runs in summer only (June to September); + shows a high-speed service also get cabins, whose price varies according to the number of occupants (generally one to four) and location (with or without window). Most companies offer discounts on return trips and other deals – always ask. You might want to consider a sleeping berth for overnight trips, which will cost as much as double.

Note that only Grimaldi, Moby Lines and Tirrenia have year-round services. The rest tend to operate from March/April to October.

Mainland France

SNCM (☎ 08 91 70 18 01 in France, ☎ 079 51 44 77 in Sardinia; W www.sncm.fr) and **CMN La Méridionale** (☎ 08 10 20 13 20) together operate ferries from Marseille to Porto Torres (via Corsica) from April to October. There are nine to 16 sailings each month, but in July and August some leave from Toulon instead. Crossing time is 15 to 17 hours (12½ hours from Toulon) depending on the vessel. A seat costs €72 in high season (July to August) and a small car €104. A basic cabin for two costs €173. You need to calculate a few euros extra for port taxes (which are added on when you purchase the tickets). Ask about special return-trip offers.

For tickets and information in Porto Torres, go to **Agenzia Paglietti** (☎ 079 51 44 77, fax 079 51 40 63; Corso Vittorio Emanuele 19).

Finding a Ferry

Here follows a rundown of Italian ports from which there are departures to Sardinia, with a list of company details and destinations.

Civitavecchia

Moby Lines (☎ 0586 82 68 23/4/5, W www.mobylines.it) Services to Olbia

Sardinia Ferries (☎ 019 21 55 11, W www.sardiniaferries.com) Runs ferries to Golfo Aranci and Cagliari

Tirrenia (☎ 199 12 31 99, W www.tirrenia.it) Has ferries to Olbia, Arbatax and Cagliari; fast boats also run to Olbia in summer only

Fiumicino

Tirrenia (☎ 199 12 31 99, W www.tirrenia.it) Has fast ferries to Golfo Aranci, and a few times a week to Arbatax, in summer only

Genoa

Grandi Navi Veloci (Grimaldi, ☎ 010 2 54 65, W www.grimaldi.it) Luxury ferries to Porto Torres and Olbia

Moby Lines (☎ 010 254 15 13, W www.mobylines.it) Ferries year-round to/from Olbia (and Bastia in Corsica)

Tirrenia (☎ 199 12 31 99, W www.tirrenia.it) Ferries and high-speed boats to Porto Torres, Olbia, Cagliari and Arbatax

Tris Traghetti (☎ 010 576 24 11, W www.tris.it, Italian only) Ferries and high-speed boats to Palau

La Spezia

Tris Traghetti (☎ 010 576 24 11, W www.tris.it, Italian only) Boats to Palau (en route to Porto Vecchio in Corsica)

Livorno

Linea dei Golfi (☎ 0565 22 23 00, W www.lineadeigolfi.it) Has ferries to Olbia (and a weekly service to Cagliari) from April to September

Moby Lines (☎ 0586 82 68 23/4/5, W www.mobylines.it) Services are available travelling to Olbia

Sardinia Ferries (☎ 019 21 55 11, W www.sardiniaferries.com) Regular services to Golfo Aranci

Naples

Linee Lauro (☎ 081 551 33 52, W www.lineelauro.it, Italian only) Has services once or twice a week to Palau (en route to Porto Vecchio in Corsica) from mid-June to mid-September

Tirrenia (☎ 199 12 31 99, W www.tirrenia.it) Once or twice weekly run to Cagliari

Palermo

Tirrenia (☎ 199 12 31 99, W www.tirrenia.it) Operates a service to Cagliari (at least once a week)

Piombino

Linea dei Golfi (☎ 0565 22 23 00, W www.lineadeigolfi.it) Has ferries to Olbia from April to September

Savona

Tris Traghetti (☎ 010 576 24 11, W www.tris.it) Boats to Palau (en route to Porto Vecchio in Corsica)

Trapani

Tirrenia (☎ 199 12 31 99, W www.tirrenia.it) Operates a weekly service to Cagliari (en route from Tunisia)

Corsica

There are regular links between Sardinia (Santa Teresa di Gallura) and Bonifaccio across the straits in Corsica. **Saremar** (☎ 0789 75 41 56) has four to eight daily departures each way depending on the season. Adult one-way fares range up to €8.52, depending on the season. A small car costs up to €27.89. Those landing in Bonifaccio pay a €3.10 port tax per person and €1.29 per vehicle. The trip takes 50 minutes. **Mobyline** (☎ 0789 75 14 49) has 10 daily crossings in July and August and four during the rest of the year. Prices are virtually the same.

Linee Lauro (☎ 081 551 33 52; W www .lineelauro.it), which runs a summer ferry from Naples to Palau in Sardinia also sails to Porto Vecchio in Corsica. You can catch the boat for the Palau–Porto Vecchio ride. It costs €10 per person, €20 per car and the crossing takes 1½ to two hours. It leaves twice a week.

Tris Traghetti (☎ 010 576 24 11; W www .tris.it) offers a similar service on its runs from La Spezia and Savona. Again departures to/from Palau are twice a week, with similar crossing times. Adults pay €13 and €29 for a car.

SNCM and CMN vessels running between Porto Torres and the French mainland (see earlier) call at Propriano or, less frequently, Ajaccio on the way. Usually the trip between Propriano and Porto Torres takes 3½ hours (3¾ hours to/from Ajaccio). The adult one-way fare in either case is €21 and €49 for a small car. Special return fares apply (eg, €93 for a car and two adults).

Tunisia

Once a week a Tirrenia vessel from Tunis arrives in Cagliari (stopping in Trapani, Sicily, en route). The trip takes around 36 hours and costs €57.48 on the deck in high season. Sleeping berths start at €73.08. A small car costs €93.73.

ORGANISED TOURS

You can get flight/accommodation packages aplenty, but relatively few companies offer organised tours of Sardinia.

Port Taxes

Some ports charge a small fee per person that is added to your ticket price. The per person fees include: Cagliari (€1.70), Civitavecchia (€1.70), Genoa (€1.87), Naples (€0.83), Olbia (€1.65) and Palermo (€1.70). Taxes are also applied to vehicles and easily reach €4.

The UK

A big specialist in Italy in general is Alitalia's subsidiary, **Italiatour** (☎ 01883 621900; W www.italiatour.com; 9 Whyteleafe Business Village, Whyteleafe Hill, Whyteleafe, Surrey CR3 0AT).

Headwater (☎ 01606 720033, fax 01606 720034; W www.headwater.com) has a week-long walking and boat-trip holiday to the Maddalena islands, and a walking tour of the main island, in which you are offered hiking on the Golfo di Orosei coast, up to Punta La Marmora and other parts of Sardinia.

ATG (☎ 01865 315678, fax 01865 315697; W www.atg-oxford.co.uk; 69-71 Banbury Rd, Oxford) runs an eight-day trip to eastern parts of the island, taking in the Golfo di Orosei, the Su Gorroppu gorge, Tiscali and other sites and walks in the area. The trip costs £1395 all inclusive.

Design Holidays (☎ 0870 727 3755; W www.designholidays.co.uk) is an upmarket holiday outfit that will ease you into a top-end holiday in Sardinia.

The USA

In the USA, **Breakaway Adventures** (☎ 1-800 -567 6286, fax 202-293 0483; W www.break away-adventures.com; 1312 18th Street, NW, Suite 401, Washington, DC 20036) operates trips to Italy. A week-long walking tour of the Maddalena islands costs up to US$1400.

Australia

A company with specialist knowledge of Italy is **ATI Tours** (☎ 02-9798 0588, toll-free ☎ 1800 069 985, fax 02-9716 0891; W www .atitours.com.au; 125 Ramsay St, Haberfield NSW 2045). They have a one-week general tour of Sardinia for A$1523.

Getting Around

AIR
Meridiana (see the Getting There & Away chapter) runs one or two daily flights between Cagliari and Olbia – which is admittedly a long grind overland. The flight takes 40 minutes and generally costs €60, although return trips can cost €73 to €82 if you book in advance. It leaves Cagliari at 9.30pm and Olbia at 7.20am.

BUS
Those without their own shiny steeds to carry them about will have to rely on buses (*pullman* or *autobus*) to get to most places. The rail system (see Train later) is useful for some major destinations but the network is limited. Buses get around just about everywhere but are often slow and infrequent.

Various bus companies operate services across the island.

The main one, **Azienda Regionale Sarda Trasporti – ARST** (☎ 800 86 50 42; W *www.arst.sardegna.it, Italian only*), runs local and long-distance services across most of the island.

PANI (☎ 070 65 23 26, 079 23 69 83) runs fast, limited-stops buses between the island's main centres (ie, Cagliari, Oristano, Nuoro, Sassari and Porto Torres).

Ferrovie della Sardegna – FdS (☎ 079 24 13 01, 079 25 26 01; W *www.ferroviesardegna.it*) operates extensive bus services in connection with its limited network of narrow-gauge railways.

In the southwest, **Ferrovie Meridionali della Sardegna – FMS** (☎ 800 04 45 53; W *www.ferroviemeridionalisarde.it, Italian only; Via Crocefisso 72, Iglesias*) buses dominate the roads and link up with ARST services. Despite the company name, FMS no longer operates trains as its lines have come under the control of the national Trenitalia railways.

Otherwise, smaller companies operate limited services, frequently in summer only. **Turmo Travel** (☎ 078 92 14 87; W *www.bus.it/turmotravel/olbia.htm, Italian only*) runs express buses from Cagliari up the east coast to Olbia (airport and port) and on to Santa Teresa di Gallura. Others you may come across include the Nuoro-based **Deplano** (☎ 0784 29 50 30), **Nuragica Tour** (☎ 079 51 04 94) and **Loguduro Tours** (☎ 079 28 17 28).

Each of the provincial capitals has an ARST *autostazione* (bus station), centrally located except in Nuoro. Other companies sometimes also use these bus stations, but by no means always. Pani, for instance, has

Bus Times

The following table of sample one-way trips provides an idea of the cost and time involved in making bus journeys around Sardinia. Frequencies given are for weekdays in summer. Further information appears in the individual destination chapters.

from	to	frequency (daily)	fare (€)	duration (hrs)
Alghero	Olbia	1	7.64	2
Cagliari	Olbia	1	14.93	5
Cagliari	Oristano	up to 7	5.84	1½
Cagliari	Santa Teresa di Gallura	1	17.50	6¼
Cagliari	Sassari	up to 7	13.43	3¼–3 hrs 40 mins
Olbia	Golfo Aranci	up to 8	1.19	20–30 mins
Olbia	Sassari	up to 3	5.84	1½
Porto Torres	Castelsardo	3–5	2.01	40–50 mins
Santa Teresa di Gallura	Castelsardo	up to 5	4.44	1½
Santa Teresa di Gallura	Olbia	up to 7	3.72	1 hr 50 mins
Sassari	Castelsardo	up to 5	2.01	1
Sassari	Oristano	4	7.18	2¼
Sassari	Santa Teresa di Gallura	up to 5	5.85	2½

its own separate *fermata* (stop) except in Sassari. Otherwise, bus companies merely have a stop (and sometimes a ticket office) elsewhere around town. Often you have to buy tickets from a nearby bar.

In smaller towns and villages there will simply be a *fermata* for interurban buses, not always in an immediately apparent location.

PANI, ARST and FdS tickets must generally be bought prior to boarding at either stations or designated bars, *tabacchi* (tobacconists) and newspaper stands near the stop. With other companies you generally buy the ticket on board. Timetables are sometimes posted, but don't hold your breath. Tourist offices in bigger towns occasionally have incomplete timetable information for their area. In smaller locations you would do well to ask in advance wherever you buy tickets. As services are often infrequent in out of the way locations, you need to plan ahead.

Services can be frequent on weekdays but reduce considerably on Sundays and holidays – runs between smaller towns often fall to one or none. Keep this in mind if you depend on buses as it is easy to get stuck in smaller places, especially on weekends.

TRAIN
State Railways
The Italian state railways, **Trenitalia** (☎ 89 20 21; ⓦ www.trenitalia.it), runs the bulk of the limited rail network in Sardinia.

At the stations you will find the *orario* (timetable) posted on notice boards. *Partenze* (departures) and *arrivi* (arrivals) are clearly indicated. You can get information on the phone and Web too.

A full timetable, *In Treno Sardegna*, is published every six months (winter and summer timetables) and is intermittently available (€1) at some newsagents and stations. The timetable also includes the limited FdS lines (see following). Note that there are all sorts of permutations on schedules – read the fine print to be sure that the train you want actually operates on the day you want. Some handy indicators are *feriale* (Monday to Saturday) and *festivo* (Sunday and holidays only); on occasion certain dates or periods when the service runs are specified.

Unlike on mainland Italy, there is only one class of service in Sardinia, the basic *Regionale*. Most of these trains are all-stops

jobs and there you won't find any fancy high-speed variations.

Some trains offer 1st and 2nd class, although the essential difference between them is the fact that few people opt to pay extra for the former.

Some sample one-way, 2nd class fares and times follow. Frequency is for direct trains. Those travelling from Cagliari to Olbia, for instance, have only one direct train. Otherwise they have to alight at Ozieri-Chilivani and wait for a connection. The same can be said for those travelling between Cagliari and Sassari or Porto Torres, with only two direct trains. To increase your options you have to change at Oristano or Ozieri-Chilivani. Macomer is also a busy stop, as you can pick up FdS trains from there for Nuoro and Bosa (see following).

Ferrovie della Sardegna (FdS)
This private railway offers a limited number of services. The trains are not the most recent models and often consist of no more than a handful of clunky carriages. These local lines are Sassari–Alghero, Sassari–Nulvi, Sassari–Sorso, Macomer–Nuoro and Cagliari–Isili (via Mandas).

In summer FdS puts on limited scenic services known as the *Trenino Verde* (Little Green Train). These lines are for tourists (although Sardinian residents sometimes use them and pay reduced fares) and some are particularly pretty, especially the Arbatax–Mandas line. The others are Palau–Tempio Pausania, Tempio Pausania–Nulvi (from where you can connect with a regular service to Sassari), Bosa–Macomer (which links with the Macomer–Nuoro line), Isili–Sorgono and the already mentioned Arbatax–Mandas line (which connects with the Mandas–Cagliari regular service).

More destinations are listed in Train under the Getting There and Away sections in Sassari and the Northwest, Nuoro, Cagliari and the Southwest chapters.

Tickets
See the Train section in the Getting There & Away chapter for general rules on ticket purchase and validation. Always remember to validate your ticket before boarding the train. If there are no machines or they are not working, inform the train conductors and they will validate the ticket. If the machines

Train Times

from	to	frequency (daily)	fare (€)	duration (hrs)
Cagliari	Olbia	1	12.95	4
Cagliari	Oristano	up to 17	4.55	1½–2
Cagliari	Sassari	2	12.10	4¼
Cagliari	Porto Torres	2	12.95	4½
Olbia	Golfo Aranci	up to 7	1.75	½
Olbia	Oristano	1	8.80	2 hrs 40 mins
Olbia	Sassari	3	5.60	1 hr 50 mins
Sassari	Oristano	4	7.75	2½
Sassari	Porto Torres	up to 10	1.25	15–20 mins

are working and you do not validate your ticket, you may be obliged to pay a €5 fine.

Rail Passes & Discounts
It is not worth buying a Eurail or InterRail pass if you are going to travel only in Sardinia (or even Italy). For some general information on Italian passes, valid on Trenitalia trains around the country, see the Train section in the Getting There & Away chapter. None is worth bothering about if you intend to travel in Sardinia only. One local pass that just might be worth a thought if you intend to quickly move around a lot is the weeklong Treno e Sardegna pass (€50), valid for all trains and buses run by Trenitalia and FdS.

CAR & MOTORCYCLE
You will find the only way to cover significant ground in Sardinia is by road. Remember that the distances can be deceptive for drivers – the going can get slow on the island's sinuous tarmac trails. If bringing your own car, remember to have your insurance and other papers in order.

If you want to hire a car or motorcycle, you will need to produce your driving licence. Certainly you will need to produce it if you are pulled over by the police or *carabinieri*, who, if it's a non-EU licence, may well want to see an International Driving Permit (IDP). Road blocks are common in Sardinia and the chances are high that you will pulled over sooner or later. Smile and comply with requests!

To drive your own vehicle in Italy you need an International Insurance Certificate, also known as a Carta Verde (Green Card). Your car-insurance company will issue this. For further details see Paperwork &

Preparations under Car & Motorcycle in the Getting There & Away chapter.

Roads
Ask Sardinians what their biggest gripes are, and roads will be close to the top of the list. (DH Lawrence found the same thing when he visited in the 1920s!) The mostly dual carriageway SS131 Carlo Felice highway from Cagliari to Sassari (and on to Porto Torres) and a similar stretch (SS131 DCN) from Olbia via Nuoro to Abbasanta (where it links with the Carlo Felice) are the main motorway-style highways on the island. Another strip (the SS130) runs west from the Carlo Felice to Iglesias and new dual carriageway stretches reach from Sassari part of the way to Alghero and from Porto Torres to that Sassari–Alghero road.

Other minor concessions to speedy motoring include improved runs like the *via di scorrimento veloce* (inland road) to bypass Castelsardo between Santa Teresa di Gallura and Sassari/Porto Torres.

If you move around the island a lot, you will come to know other key arteries. One of the most important is the SS125, or Orientale Sarda, which runs down the eastern side of the island from Palau in the north to Cagliari in the south.

These and many roads in the more touristed coastal areas are fairly well maintained, but in general narrow and curvy. In summer, when the island fills with visitors, it is virtually impossible not to get caught in long tailbacks along many of them. The area between Olbia and Santa Teresa di Gallura is particularly bad. You may find your patience thin in the midsummer heat and you won't be the only one executing dodgy overtaking manoeuvres at one point or another. Further inland, the quality of roads is uneven. Main arteries are mostly good but narrow and winding, while many secondary routes are potholed and in pretty poor shape.

Getting into and out of the cities, notably Cagliari and Sassari, can be a test of nerves as traffic chokes approaches and exits.

Road Rules

In Italy, as in the rest of Continental Europe, drive on the right side of the road and overtake on the left. Unless otherwise indicated, you must always give way to cars coming from the right. It is compulsory to wear seat belts if fitted to the car. If you are caught not wearing a seat belt, you will be required to pay an on-the-spot fine (around €30), although this doesn't seem to deter most Italians.

Random breath tests occasionally take place. If you're involved in an accident while under the influence of alcohol, the penalties can be severe. The blood-alcohol limit is 0.05%.

Speed limits, unless otherwise indicated by local signs, are as follows: on main highways (there are no *autostrade* in Sardinia) 110km/h, secondary highways 90km/h and in built-up areas 50km/h. Speeding fines follow EU standards and are: up to €130 for up to 10km/h over the limit, as much as €530 for up to 40km/h, and €1320 for more than 40km/h over the limit (along with suspension of licence for three months). Drivers of foreign cars are obliged to pay fines (with a reduction) on the spot. Failure to do so or at least make part payment with the obligation to pay the remainder later can lead to loss of your licence and/or the impounding of your vehicle for up to two months.

Since 2002 drivers are obliged to keep headlights switched on day and night on all dual carriageway highways.

You don't need a licence to ride a moped under 50cc, but you should be aged 14 or over; a helmet is compulsory. The speed limit for a moped is 40km/h. To ride a motorcycle or scooter up to 125cc, you must be aged 16 or over and have a licence (a car licence will do). Helmets are compulsory for everyone riding a motorcycle bigger than 50cc. For motorcycles over 125cc you will need a motorcycle licence.

On a motorcycle, you will be able to enter restricted traffic areas in cities and towns without any problems, and traffic police generally turn a blind eye to motorcycles or scooters parked on footpaths.

Motoring in Europe, published in the UK by the RAC, gives an excellent summary of road regulations in each European country, including parking rules. The motoring organisations in other countries have similar publications.

Road Distances (km)

	Alghero	Bosa	Cagliari	Iglesias	Nuoro	Olbia	Oristano	Porto Torres	Santa Teresa di Gallura	Sant'Antioco	Sassari	Tempio Pausania
Alghero	---											
Bosa	47	---										
Cagliari	195	148	---									
Iglesias	199	152	57	---								
Nuoro	133	86	186	190	---							
Olbia	138	143	287	291	115	---						
Oristano	143	56	92	96	94	195	---					
Porto Torres	35	82	235	239	143	122	138	---				
Santa Teresa di Gallura	136	208	314	321	204	62	222	104	---			
Sant'Antioco	238	191	96	39	229	330	135	278	360	---		
Sassari	35	82	216	220	124	103	124	19	101	259	---	
Tempio Pausania	103	150	256	260	146	46	164	87	58	299	68	---

City Driving

Driving in Italian towns and cities is quite an experience and may well present the unprepared with headaches. The Italian attitude to driving bears little similarity to the English concept of traffic in ordered lanes (a normal two-lane road can easily accommodate three). Remain calm and keep your eyes on the car in front and you should be OK. Once you arrive in a city, follow the *centro* (city centre) signs. Traffic signs, complex one-way street systems and a forest of rules on who may and may not use certain priority lanes and so on can make life interesting for the newbie.

Parking

Be careful where you park your car, especially in the cities. If you leave it in an area marked with a sign reading *Zona Rimozione* (Removal Zone) and featuring a tow truck, it will almost certainly be towed away and you'll have to pay a heavy fine.

Parking in city centres can be a pain and is generally restricted or meter parking. As a rule you pay around €0.60 to €1 per hour in marked parking zones (usually indicated in blue), sometimes as much as €2.07. Frequently, as in Sassari, you must pay an attendant. In some towns you must go to a bar and buy a ticket (on which you must scratch out the date and arrival time), which you leave on the dash.

Increasingly parking restrictions are now being introduced at some of the more crowded beaches. In the northeast of the island especially you will often be looking at €1 an hour (paid to parking attendants) and in some cases you are no longer allowed to park close to the beach.

Petrol

The cost of petrol in Italy is quite high. You'll pay around €1.10 per litre for the standard octane 95 *benzina senza piombo* (unleaded petrol) and €0.91 for *gasolio* (diesel).

If you are driving a car that uses LPG (liquid petroleum gas), you will need to buy a special guide to service stations that have *gasauto* or GPL (they are few and far between in Sardinia). By law these must be in non-residential areas and are usually in the country or on town outskirts. GPL costs around €0.55 per litre.

Rental

Some local rental agencies are listed under the major centres in this book. Most tourist offices and hotels can provide information about car or motorcycle rental.

Car It is cheaper to arrange car rental before leaving your own country, for instance through some sort of fly/drive deal. Most of the major car-hire firms, including Hertz, Avis and Budget, can arrange this for you. All you have to do is pick up the vehicle at a nominated point when you arrive in Italy. See the Car and Motorcycle section in the Getting There & Away chapter for suggestions on organising a rental car before arriving in Sardinia.

You have to be aged 21 or over (23 or over for some companies) to hire a car in Italy and you have to have a credit card.

If you decide to rent after arrival, shop around. You will find the main international outfits represented at the island's three main airports. In various towns and coastal resorts you'll find international and local rental outlets. At best, you will be looking at around €35 to €40 a day for a Fiat Panda or Punto, including insurance and limited kilometres. Frequently costs will be higher – as much as €55 a day for a Fiat Panda! Three-day and longer deals bring the daily cost down.

Motorcycle In some popular tourist centres (like Santa Teresa di Gallura and Alghero) you will find a few rental outlets offering motorcycles and scooters. The former can easily cost €60 to €75 a day for, say, a Honda 600. Scooters come in at around €25 to €30.

Most agencies will not rent motorcycles to people aged under 18. Note that many places require a sizeable deposit and that you could be responsible for reimbursing part of the cost of the bike if it is stolen. Always check the fine print in the contract. See Road Rules earlier in this section for more details about age, licence and helmet requirements.

Purchase

Car You cannot buy a vehicle in Italy unless you are legally resident, as the law requires that you be a resident to own and register one. You could get round this by having a friend who is a resident buy one for you.

It is possible to buy a cheap, small 10-year-old car for as little as €750, though you'll pay up to around €4000 for a reasonable five-year-old Fiat Uno and up to €5500 for a two-year-old Fiat Uno. Look in the classified section of local newspapers to find cars for sale.

Motorcycle The same laws apply if you are looking to own and register a motorcycle. The cost of a second-hand Vespa ranges from €300 to €1000, and a moped from €200 to €600. Prices for more powerful bikes start at around €800, depending on their condition.

Roadside Assistance

The Automobile Club Italiano (ACI) will provide free emergency roadside assistance once only to members of foreign automobile associations – but only to get you and the car to the nearest ACI-registered mechanic (which is not always convenient). If you are not a member of a foreign automobile association, you will pay a minimum fee of €82.70, but again this only gets you and the vehicle to the nearest garage. If you want your car to go to a specialist mechanic or to a more distant destination, you will have to shell out the towing costs – which are both there and back to the pick-up point. If you need roadside assistance call ☎ 116.

A European breakdown assistance policy, such as the AA Five Star Service or the RAC Eurocover Motoring Assistance, is a good investment.

Warning Although theft from cars is not a particularly big problem in Sardinia, it does occur. Rental vehicles and those with foreign plates are always more likely targets. Leave nothing visible in parked cars and where possible leave no valuables, even out of sight in the boot (trunk).

BICYCLE

Bicycle rental is not widespread but is possible in some of the more popular coastal areas, like Alghero and around the northeast coast (such as Santa Teresa di Gallura, La Maddalena, Palau and Olbia). Rental starts at around €8 a day to as much as €15 for mountain bikes.

If you plan to fly your own bike in, check with the airline about hidden costs. It will have to be disassembled and packed for the journey.

You should travel light on a cycle tour, but bring tools and some spare parts, including a puncture repair kit and a spare inner tube. Panniers are essential to balance your possessions on either side of the bike frame. A bike helmet is a good idea, as are a solid bike lock and chain to prevent theft.

Cycle touring across Sardinia is quite possible, although in summer the heat can make it an exhausting exercise. Although Sardinia has no mountains above 1850m, it is surprisingly hilly and often a challenge. You should be fit and also prudent, as roads are frequently narrow and local drivers not greatly accustomed to cyclists.

One organisation that can help you plan your bike tour is the **Cyclists' Touring Club** (☎ 0870 873 0060; w www.ctc.org.uk; Cotterell House, 69 Meadrow, Godalming, Surrey GU7 3HS UK). It can supply information to members on cycling conditions, itineraries and cheap insurance. Membership costs UK£27 per annum (UK£10 for under 26s).

Bikes can be taken on almost all trains in Sardinia. They are placed in a separate wagon and the cost (€3.50) is the same regardless of your destination. Bikes can also be transported for free on ferries to Sardinia.

HITCHING

Hitching is never entirely safe and we don't recommend it. Travellers who decide to hitch should understand that they are taking a small but potentially serious risk.

Sardinians themselves don't do it much and can be wary of picking up strangers, which can make getting around this way a frustrating business.

BOAT

Local ferries connect Palau (in the north) with Isola della Maddalena and Portovesme (in the southwest) with Carloforte on Isola di San Pietro. Ferries also link Carloforte with Calasetta, in the northwest corner of Isola di Sant'Antioco. All these ferries transport vehicles.

Services are more frequent in summer. Even so, car drivers should turn up a while before intended departure as boats fill quickly. For more details turn to the relevant sections in the Olbia & the Gallura and Southwest Sardinia chapters, respectively.

LOCAL TRANSPORT

All cities and major towns have a reasonable local bus service. Generally you won't need to use them, as the towns are compact, with sights, hotels, restaurants and long-distance transport stations within walking distance of each other. Tickets (generally €0.57 per ride) must be purchased in advance from newspaper stands or *tabacchi* outlets and stamped on the bus.

All three airports are linked by local bus to their respective town centres.

ORGANISED TOURS

In summer it is possible to join boat tours from various points around the coast. The most popular include trips out of Cala Gonone and Santa Maria Navarrese along the majestic Golfo di Orosei coast. A close second is a trip around the islands of the Maddalena archipelago. Boats frequently head out of Porto San Paolo, south of Olbia, for trips around Tavolara Island and the nearby coast. Others do trips out of Alghero and from the Sinis Peninsula. Most trips are done by motorboats or small tour ferries but a handful of sailing vessels are on hand (and more costly too). More details are provided in the relevant destination chapters.

Treks of all levels and durations are organised by a plethora of outlets in the province of Nuoro, especially in the towns around the Golfo di Orosei.

Tours of the bigger archaeological sites are organised out of some of the main holiday centres, such as Alghero.

Sassari & the Northwest

The province of Sassari is the largest in all Italy (which partly explains why we deal with half of it in the Olbia & the Gallura chapter!) and the most visited on the island. The northwest is packed with interest, from the taste of Spain in the Catalan enclave of Alghero, to grand ancient sites like the Santu Antine and Palmavera nuraghes. The area is also studded with jewels of Tuscan Romanesque architecture, beautiful churches dotted about the countryside.

The coastline is as magnificent as it is varied. On a wild day powerful rollers crash onto the Porto Ferro beach, while impossibly clear waters gently lap the sands of Spiaggia della Pelosa on the Stintino peninsula. Charming coastal towns like Bosa (just outside the province) and Castelsardo invite a detour.

SASSARI
postcode 07100 • pop 121,500

Sardinia's second city and rival to the capital, Cagliari, Sassari has a proud history as a centre of culture (its university opened in the 16th century) and as a breeding ground for rebellion as well as some of the nation's senior politicians.

The central squares and boulevards that spread north of the old quarter exude a somnolent grandeur. But as is often the case with provincial also-rans, the Sassaresi harbour a barely disguised antipathy for their cousins in the capital. 'Down there,' you will frequently hear, you are 'almost in Africa'. 'You'll see the difference,' they pronounce knowingly, as if no further explanation were required.

Sadly, little of the medieval city remains. Rather than spreading beyond its 13th-century walls, the city instead shed its old layers and slowly regenerated itself over the centuries, eliminating the old to make way for the new. Some jewels do remain intact and Sassari's two grand churches, the Duomo and Santa Maria di Betlem, are impressive. Coupled with its important archaeological museum, the city's sights alone warrant time. Sticking around for lunch and dinner should also be a priority – the choice is ample and the old city hides some wonderful traditional locales.

Highlights

- Submerge yourself in the turquoise waters of Spiaggia della Pelosa
- Marvel at the ancient nuraghes of Santu Antine and Palmavera
- Meander through the lanes and along the sea walls of the medieval Catalan town of Alghero
- Follow the spectacular coast road from Alghero to Bosa
- Treat the palate to some fine Sella & Mosca wines
- Explore the charming Romanesque churches scattered about the countryside
- Lounge around on the wild beach of Porto Ferro

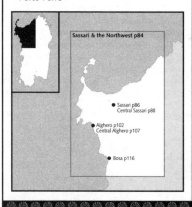

Sassari & the Northwest p84

● Sassari p86
Central Sassari p88

● Alghero p102
Central Alghero p107

● Bosa p116

History

Like many Sardinian inland towns, Sassari (Tatari in the local dialect) owes its medieval rise to prominence to the decline of its coastal counterparts. As the ancient Roman colony of Turris Libisonis (modern Porto Torres) succumbed to the hammer blows inflicted by malaria and repeated pirate raids, people gradually retreated to Sassari. Porto Torres (and at one point the town of Ardara) remained capital of the Giudicato di Torres (or Logudoro) but Sassari's increasing importance led it to break away from the *giudicato* and, with support from Genoa, declare

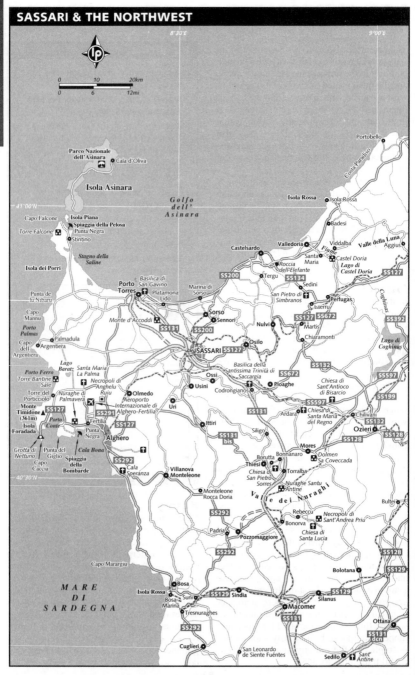

itself an autonomous city state, along the lines of the Tuscan cities, in 1294.

The city was coruled by a *Consiglio degli Anziani* (Council of Elders) and a Genoese *podestà* (governor) but the Sassaresi soon tired of Genoese meddling and in 1321 called on the Crown of Aragon to help rid them of the north Italians. The Catalano-Aragonese arrived in 1323 but Sassari soon discovered it had leaped from the frying pan into the fire. The first of many revolts against the city's new masters came two years later. It would take another century for the Iberian interlopers to fully control Sassari.

For a while the city prospered, but waves of plague and the growing menace from Ottoman Turkey sidelined Sardinia, leaving Sassari to slide into slow decline in the 16th century. One bright light was the establishment of a school by the Jesuits that early in the following century would become an important university.

The arrival of the Piedmontese in 1718 eased pressure but it was not until the mid-19th century that Sassari began to take off again. Commerce was resuscitated with the modernisation of Porto Torres and the laying of the Carlo Felice highway between the port, Sassari and Cagliari.

WWI and WWII did not directly affect Sassari, which since 1945 has been able to maintain a steady if slow pace of economic growth. It has also been a prodigious producer of national politicians. The biggest names are former presidents Antonio Segni (1891–1972), Francesco Cossiga (born 1928) and the charismatic communist leader Enrico Berlinguer (1922–84). Segni's son, Mario (born 1939), is an active left-of-centre leader in Rome and another local, Beppe Pisanu, became Prime Minister Berlusconi's interior minister in mid-2002.

Orientation

The main lines of the city run roughly east to west. The western end of town is closed off by the train station. Corso Vittorio Emanuele II runs east through the largely neglected old quarter to Piazza Castello, from where much of the 19th and early 20th century additions to the city continue eastward through the grand Piazza Italia and along Via Roma. Around here you will find offices of interest, the archaeological museum, some hotels and a fistful of mid- and upper-range restaurants.

Information
Tourist Offices The main city tourist office is the **AAST** (☎ 079 23 13 31, fax 079 23 75 85; W www.regione.sardegna.it/azstss; Via Roma 62; open 9am-1.30pm & 4pm-6pm Mon-Thur, 9am-1.30pm Fri). The information available here is patchy.

The provincial **EPT** (☎ 079 29 95 44, fax 079 29 94 15; Viale Caprera 36) is open limited and erratic hours and, while accommodating, has little material.

Money Banks abound in central Sassari. The **Banca Comerciale Italiana** (Piazza Italia 23) is one of several around the square with an ATM. The **Banca di Sassari** (Piazza Castello 8) is the rep for Western Union.

Post & Communications The main **post office** (Via Brigata di Sassari; open 8.15am-6.15pm Mon-Fri, 8.15am-1pm Sat) is central.

Email & Internet Access There's a handful of computers at **Phonecar** (Via Roma 33; open 9am-1pm & 5pm-8pm Mon-Fri). You pay €5 an hour.

Travel Agencies The national youth travel agent, **CTS** (☎ 079 20 04 00; Via Manno 35), has a branch in Sassari.

Bookshops A decent bookshop, **Libreria Gulliver** (☎ 079 23 44 75; Portici Bargone e Crispo 8) has a minuscule offering of novels in English, French and German.

Medical Services The **Nuovo Ospedale Civile** (☎ 079 206 10 00; Viale Italia) is south of the centre. In a medical emergency call ☎ 118 or ☎ 079 206 16 21. **Farmacia Simon** (Piazza Castello) often does a night shift.

Emergency The **questura** (☎ 079 283 55 00, Via Angioi 16) is the main police headquarters.

Dangers & Annoyances Sassari is a fairly orderly provincial town. You should take the normal precautions in the old centre, especially in the more run-down streets towards the station.

Museo Nazionale Sanna

The Museo Nazionale Sanna (☎ 079 27 22 03; Via Roma 64; over/under 25 €2/1, EU citizens

SASSARI

PLACES TO STAY & EAT
5 Hotel Giusy
6 Trattoria Da Peppina
19 Hotel Leonardo da Vinci
20 Da Gesuino
21 Frank Hotel
22 Hotel Grazie Deledda
23 Giamaranto

OTHER
1 Fontana di Rosello
2 Remains of Medieval Walls
3 Chiesa di Sant'Antonio Abate
4 Teatro Il Ferroviario
7 Sardinya Autonoleggio
8 EPT
9 PANI Tickets
10 Bus Station
11 Bar for ARST, FdS & ATP tickets
13 Avis
14 Caffè Italia
15 Palazzo della Giustizia
16 Chiesa di Santa Maria di Betlem
17 Museo Nazionale Sanna
18 AAST Tourist Office
18 Sergeant Pepper Disco Bar

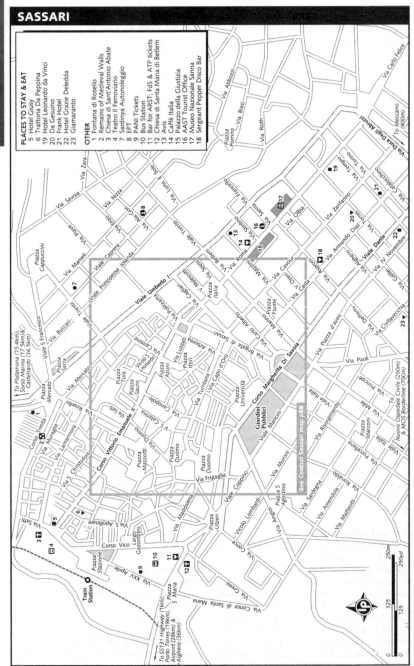

under 18 & over 65 free; open 9am-8pm Tues-Sun) holds one of the island's most important archaeological collections, covering the nuraghic period in depth.

On your right just after the ticket counter is a room filled with Sardinian traditional costumes, some dating to as recently as the 1940s.

After this the archaeological collection begins with displays of Stone-Age finds ranging from simple stone tools to ceramics. Rooms VII and VIII are given over to finds from ancient megalithic tombs and domus de janas (fairy tombs). Obsidian arrow heads, stone idols and a great variety of ceramics characterise the display.

All this serves as a prelude to Room IX (upstairs), where some fine nuraghic artefacts are gathered. The most intriguing window cases are those numbered 23 and 29 to 33. The bronzetti (bronze figurines) in No 23 are exquisite. Among the ceramics (pots, pans, stoves and so on) in the other window cases, it is the bronze ware that stands out. They include axeheads and similar tools, weapons, bracelets, votive boats and the like. The bronzetti in No 30, which include the figure of a bull, are intriguing.

Back downstairs Room X is dedicated to Phoenician and Carthaginian objects. Some exquisite pottery is mixed in with gold jewellery (window case 41) and masks (No 42). No 43 contains a stunning collection of jewellery, gold ornaments and ivory amulets. Rooms XI and XII contain Roman finds, mostly ceramics and oil burners but also some statuary and a sprinkling of coins, jewellery and objects like bronze belt buckles. Off to one side lies a stash of heavy Roman anchors.

Before exiting, have a quick look at the modest display of medieval objects in a separate hall that leads off Room VIII.

Piazza Italia & Around

As you head down Via Roma towards Piazza Italia, the brooding dark reddish brown hulk of the **Palazzo della Giustizia** (courts) looms on the south side of the boulevard. With its Doric columns and handy prison out the back, it is a typical inheritance from Fascist Italy's pre-war 'glory' days.

You soon emerge in the spacious Piazza Italia, a grand square dominated on one side by the equally imposing neoclassical **Palazzo**

della Provincia, an unequivocal expression of Sassari's comparative well-being towards the end of the 19th century. Across the square a rather different note is struck by the neo-Gothic **Palazzo Giordano**, the Banco di Napoli's Sassari HQ (under restoration). A statue of King Vittorio Emanuele II presides over it all in the middle of the square.

Museo della Brigata Sassari

The museum (Piazza Castello; admission free; open 9am-12.30pm & 2.30pm-4pm Mon-Fri, 9am-12.30pm Sat) honours the gallantry of this brigade, thrown into the thick of the trench fighting against the Austrians in northern Italy during WWI. Uniforms, photos, documents and other memorabilia evoke the period. In spite of the officially posted opening hours, we had trouble ascertaining just when it really is open. The square marks the spot where the Catalano-Aragonese raised a castle in 1330 on the edge of the then-medieval city to keep an eye on the restless townsfolk. It was gleefully demolished in 1877.

Corso Vittorio Emanuele II & Around

From Piazza Castello head down Corso Vittorio Emanuele II into the heart of the old town. Now a busy shopping promenade, it was once where the city's notables lived. Surprisingly few reminders of the city's medieval past are left.

Casa Farris (Corso Vittorio Emanuele 25) is in a lamentable state, but the Gothic windows are a clear indication that the building has managed, barely, to survive down the centuries. More interesting is **Casa di Re Enzo** (Corso Vittorio Emanuele 42), a remarkable 15th-century Catalan Gothic setting for what is now a stocking store. It is fronted by thick-set double arches and heavy hanging lamps. Wander inside to get a closer look at the vibrant frescos and ceiling paintwork.

The **Teatro Civico**, opposite Casa di Re Enzo, was built in 1826 on the site of the Palazzo della Città as a theatre. It has since been completely renovated.

From Corso Vittorio Emanuele, Via Cesare Battisti leads into the leafy Piazza Tola (long known as the Carra Manna, meaning public weighing machine). Several outstanding buildings look proudly onto this market square, among them is the massive

Palazzo d'Usini (1577), a rare example of 16th-century civil architecture in Sardinia.

Following Via Lamarmora west off the square, make for the Porta Rossello and then west along Corso Trinità, where you can admire the only substantial remnant of the city's medieval walls. The nearby early-17th-century **Fontana di Rosello** is a late-Renaissance effort by Genoese masters.

Duomo di San Nicola & Around

In the heart of the medieval quarter the extraordinary baroque facade of Sassari's cathedral *(Piazza del Duomo)* seems to emanate its own radiant light. Busy with bulging sculptural caprice, it bears an uncanny resemblance to the ebullient baroque style of Apulia, in southeastern Italy.

The 18th-century facade was added to a 15th-century Catalan Gothic body, which itself replaced a Romanesque church. The bare interior is a little disappointing after the frills and spills outside. Worth looking out for are the frescoes in the left transept and the Gothic fresco in the first chapel on the right as you enter. In the second chapel is fine painting of the *Martirio dei SS Cosma e Damiano* (Martyrdom of Saints Cosimo and Damien). A small **museum** *(admission free)* of valuable religious bits and bobs is out the back in the sacristy.

The narrow streets around here are much neglected but full of life – a tableau that takes you far from the suntan lotion–soaked tourist spots on the coast! You will no doubt arrive in the huge Piazza Mazzotti at some

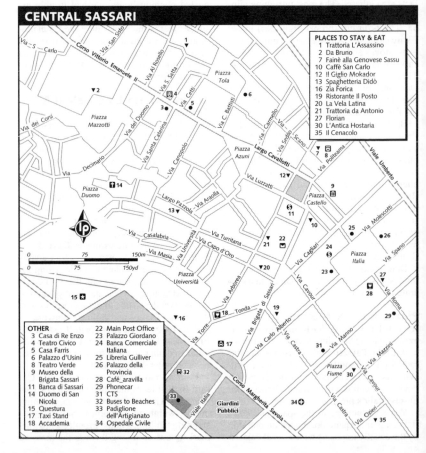

CENTRAL SASSARI

PLACES TO STAY & EAT
1 Trattoria L'Assassino
2 Da Bruno
7 Fainè alla Genovese Sassu
10 Caffè San Carlo
12 Il Giglio Mokador
13 Spaghetteria Didò
16 Zia Forica
19 Ristorante Il Posto
20 La Vela Latina
21 Trattoria da Antonio
27 Florian
30 L'Antica Hostaria
35 Il Cenacolo

OTHER
3 Casa di Re Enzo
4 Teatro Civico
5 Casa Farris
6 Palazzo d'Usini
8 Teatro Verde
9 Museo della Brigata Sassari
11 Banca di Sassari
14 Duomo di San Nicola
15 Questura
17 Taxi Stand
18 Accademia
22 Main Post Office
23 Palazzo Giordano
24 Banca Comerciale Italiana
25 Libreria Gulliver
26 Palazzo della Provincia
28 Café_aravilla
29 Phonecar
31 CTS
32 Buses to Beaches
33 Padiglione dell'Artigianato
34 Ospedale Civile

point. Demolition here has led to the ad-hoc creation of a fine carpark! Oh dear.

Chiesa di Santa Maria di Betlem
Just beyond what were the city walls stands the proud Romanesque facade of this eclectic church (*Piazza di Santa Maria*). The facade betrays Gothic and even vaguely Oriental admixtures. Inside, the Catalan Gothic vaulting has been preserved, but much baroque silliness has crept in to obscure the original lines of the building. Lining each aisle in chapels stand some of the giant 'candles' that the city guilds parade about town for the 14 August festivities.

Special Events
On the second-last Sunday of May hundreds of people from villages and towns around the island gather for the **Cavalcata Sarda**, or Sardinian Procession, a costume parade that was inaugurated in the 1950s. It is similar to the parade held in Nuoro for the Festa del Redentore in August.

Sassari's big traditional feast is, however, **I Candelieri**, held on 14 August where town representatives (teams represent various guilds from the 16th century) in medieval costume bear huge wooden columns (the 'candlesticks') through the town. The celebrations are held to honour a vow made in 1652 for deliverance from a plague but are also connected with the Feast of the Assumption (15 August).

In 2002 a scandal broke out as three new teams were refused entry. They claimed they represented three other guilds whose existence in medieval times they could prove. The governing committee refused to admit them. In addition, it decided to change the preliminaries to the day (rather than during the lead up as is traditional), having all the *Candelieri* line up in Piazza Italia – 'for the tourists' muttered disgruntled Sassaresi, who take the feast day very seriously. For more information on this festival, see the special section 'Viva la Festa!'.

Places to Stay
Sassari isn't overwhelmed with accommodation – eight hotels are on the books.

Hotel Giusy (☎ 079 23 33 27, fax 079 23 84 90; Piazza Sant'Antonio 21; singles/doubles €31/60) has the dual advantage of being cheap and handy for the train station. The modern brick building is anything but inspiring and rooms are a little clinical. Still they are perfectly acceptable and have balconies.

Frank Hotel (☎ 079 27 64 56, fax 079 26 25 18; Via Armando Diaz 20; singles/doubles €49/67) is a reasonable compromise on comfort and price in the new end of town. Rooms are of a good size, with TV, phone, air-con and heating.

Hotel Leonardo da Vinci (☎ 079 28 07 44, fax 079 285 72 33; W www.leonardodavinci hotel.it; Via Roma 79; singles/doubles €70/ 96) looks like it's had a spring clean and rooms are spick and span. The hotel has parking. Skip the breakfast, which is rich in fiscal terms.

Hotel Grazia Deledda (☎ 079 27 12 35, fax 079 28 08 84; W www.hotelgraziadeledda.it; Viale Dante 47; singles/doubles €82.60/ 108.50) is one of the town's top establishments, although it doesn't offer a great deal more than the Leonardo da Vinci. It's a comfortable if somewhat dowdy choice.

Places to Eat
Eating is a pleasure and all tastes and budgets are catered for. A local curiosity is *fainè*, a sort of poor man's pizza made of chickpea flour. It was introduced by the Genoese and is similar to their *farinata*.

Places to Eat – Budget A good place to stop for great lunchtime *panini* (€3) and gelato is **Caffè San Carlo** (*Portici Bargone e Crispo*), on the corner with Piazza Castello. It'll also do fine for a breakfast coffee over the paper.

Fainè alla Genovese Sassu (*Via Usai 17; open Mon-Sat*) is Sassari's original purveyor of fine *fainè*. Students and lunchtime snackers pile in for one or two (€4 a throw), washed down with a beer. Via Usai is crowded with other eateries.

Trattoria L'Assassino (☎ 079 23 50 41; Via Ospizio Cappuccini 1a; set dinner €18; open Mon-Sat) is hidden away in a back alley off Piazza Tola. The more adventurous will step beyond the set meal and try a selection of six starters (€13). These can include classics like *zimino rosso* (everything from braised calf's heart to diaphragm) and *lumaconi* (big snails). If you get really lucky you may find calf's testicles on the menu too.

Trattoria Da Peppina (☎ 079 23 61 46; Vicolo Pigozzi 1; meals €22; open Mon-Sat), tucked into a messy side alley off the lower end of Corso Vittorio Emanuele, is another classic of local cuisine. Here the emphasis is on horse and donkey meat *(asinello)*.

Zia Forica *(Corso Margherita Savoia 39; meals €15-20; closed evenings Aug)* is another good spot for a lunchtime helping of donkey. Locals treat it almost as a fast food place.

Trattoria da Antonio *(☎ 079 23 42 97; Via Arborea 2/b; meals €20; open Mon-Sat)*, affectionately known as Lu Panzone (the Big Belly), is a boisterous, no-nonsense establishment for trad Sardinian fare.

Had enough of the local stuff and want to return to more familiar ground?

Spaghetteria Didò *(Argo Pazzola 8; meals €18-22; open Mon-Sat)* is a guaranteed hit. Apart from the pasta, you can eat abundant, straightforward fish and meat courses.

Da Bruno *(☎ 079 23 55 73; Piazza Mazzotti 12; pizzas up to €5; open Thur-Tues)* offers an ugly location and cheap pizza. It's also one of the few places to open on a Sunday night.

Places to Eat – Mid-range The restaurant **La Vela Latina** *(☎ 079 23 37 37; Largo Sisini 8; meals €30; open Mon-Sat)* counts a handful of tables in a nicely restored building and on the pleasant veranda. The menu changes with the seasons: lots of seafood (good swordfish) in summer and meats and mushrooms from autumn into winter.

Ristorante Il Posto *(☎ 079 23 72 96; Via Costa 16; meals €25; open Mon-Sat)* offers good pizza (€4.50 to €6) but you might like to try something more substantial. The *filetto al mirto* (beef prepared in mirto liqueur) is a delicious main.

Da Gesuino *(☎ 079 27 33 92; Via Torres 17g; meals €25-30; open Mon-Sat)* is one of the few spots well beyond the old centre that also serves up some local classics at reasonable prices. The ravioli is good and you may find they offer snails, donkey meat and *porceddu* (suckling pig).

Places to Eat – Top End In an atmosphere vaguely reminiscent of a French bistro, **Il Giglio Mokador** *(☎ 079 23 57 36; Largo Cavallotti 2; meals €35; open Mon-Sat)* moves upscale, with some good seafood options (such as the grilled fish) and a fine wine list.

Florian *(☎ 079 20 80 56; Via Capitano Bellieni 27; meals €35-40; open Mon-Sat)* is a classic, with the elegant dining area stretching back behind the café of the same name that gives on to Via Roma. For those on a budget, it has a reasonable set menu for €20.

L'Antica Hostaria *(☎ 079 20 00 60; Via Mazzini 27; meals €40-45; open Mon-Sat)* enjoys a reputation as one of Sassari's top addresses. In intimate surroundings you are treated to inventive cuisine rooted in local tradition. Meat lovers should try the *tagliata di manzo* (beef).

Il Cenacolo *(☎ 079 23 62 51; Via Ozieri 2; meals €35; open Mon-Sat)* is one of several good spots in unlikely locations away from the centre of town. Behind the modest entrance lies an opulent interior perhaps more in keeping with its previous life as a luxury gym. The emphasis here is on fish and seafood.

Giamaranto *(☎ 079 27 45 98; Via Alghero 69; meals €35-40; closed Sun Aug)* is a bit of a hike but worth the effort. Flower boxes reveal its presence in the improbable setting of a rather ugly block of flats. The ambience is cheerfully bustling and the cooking mostly Sardinian.

Entertainment

Bars The cafés of Via Roma and around Piazza Castello undergo an almost imperceptible transformation as the evening sets in and coffee is shunted aside for cocktails. A couple of good ones are **Caffè Italia** *(Via Roma 42)* and **Café_aravilla** *(Via Roma 1)*, on the corner of Piazza Italia.

Accademia *(Via Torre Tonda)* is a lively, agreeable spot for a drink night or day. The shady terrace is popular and at night you may well be treated to a little live music.

Several bars are secreted away nearby in the lanes around Via Arborea.

MOS Borderline *(☎ 079 21 90 24; Via Rockefeller 16/c)* is about the only gay bar in town – and it's well out of the centre.

Clubs (Discoteche) The dance options in Sassari are not overly inspiring and young Sassaresi say the scene in Alghero is better.

If you're in town outside the summer you could try **Sergeant Pepper Disco Bar** *(☎ 079 282 80 55; Via Asproni 20)*. Otherwise, what action there is takes place well beyond the city centre – you'll need wheels or a taxi. **Meccano** *(☎ 079 27 04 05; Via Carlo Felice 33)* is probably the most popular. Another option is **Club Milano** *(Via Milano 26)*. Entry oscillates between €5 and €15.

Stella del Mediterraneo *(☎ 079 39 06 04; SS131 at fork for Bancali)* is a big holiday complex that winds up with the El Jem disco on summer nights.

Otherwise you can try a couple of spots on the beaches north of Sassari, such as **Iceberg** (see Platamona later).

Theatre The town's theatres tend not to move into gear until September to October, after the sting has gone out of the summer heat.

Teatro Il Ferroviario *(☎ 079 63 30 49; Corso Vico 14)* tends to put on more experimental pieces while **Teatro Verdi** *(☎ 079 23 94 79; Via Politeama)* is relatively mainstream.

The 19th-century **Teatro Civico** *(Corso Vittorio Emanuele II 39)* did not seem to be in action in 2002 but keep an eye out.

Shopping

Set in the town's central green lung, the leafy Giardini Pubblici, the Padiglione dell'Artigianato is a wonderful showcase for handicrafts produced by **Isola** *(☎ 079 23 01 01; open 9am-1pm & 4.30pm-8pm Mon-Sat)*.

Getting There & Away

Air Sassari shares **Fertilia airport** *(☎ 079 93 50 39)* with Alghero. It is about 28km west of the city centre. You will find money changing and car-rental facilities at the airport.

For information on flights and airfares into Fertilia, see the Air section in the Getting There & Away chapter.

Bus The main intercity *autostazione* (bus station) is on Via XXV Aprile near the train station. ARST, FdS, PANI and some ATP local buses travelling beyond the city leave from here.

Tickets for all but PANI can be bought at the bar next to the AGIP petrol station. PANI has a separate booth at the other end of the bus station. For other smaller companies (such as Nuragica Tour to Olbia airport) buy tickets on the bus.

PANI has up to seven services to/from Cagliari (€12.60, up to 3¼ hours). Three of them are direct and take 3¼ hours (€13.43). As many as six buses run to Nuoro (€6.77, 2½ hours) and seven to Oristano (€7.18, 2¼ hours).

Plenty of ARST and FdS buses run to Alghero (€2.32 to €2.58, 50 to 60 minutes), Porto Torres (€1.45, 20 to 30 minutes), Castelsardo (€2.01, one hour) and other destinations around Sassari province.

Train The main Trenitalia train station is just beyond the western end of the old town on Piazza Stazione. Two direct trains link the city with Cagliari (€12.10, 4¼ hours). Otherwise you have to change along the way, say in Oristano (€7.75, 2½ hours).

Several daily FdS trains connect with Nulvi, 35 km to the east. From there you can link up with the **Trenino Verde** *(☎ 079 24 57 40; W www.treninoverde.com, Italian only)* for the slow panoramic ride to Tempio Pausania. It runs on Thursdays and Fridays from late June to the end of August and the whole trip (€15 return from Sassari) takes two hours 40 minutes.

Car & Motorcycle Sassari is on the SS131 Carlo Felice highway linking Porto Torres in the north and Cagliari in the south. From Alghero, take the road north towards Porto Torres and then the SS291 east to Sassari (follow the signs for the new four-lane, *corsie*, highway). You take the same route from Fertilia airport.

A host of car-rental outlets are based at Fertilia airport. In Sassari itself **Avis** *(☎ 079 23 55 47; Via Mazzini 2)* is handy. **Sardinya Autonoleggio** *(☎ 079 29 11 13; Viale Caprera 8/a)* offers a Ford Fiesta or Citroën Saxo for €134 for three days all inclusive.

Getting Around

Sassari is planning to make itself a gift of a tram system with the train station as main terminus. The only outward signs of this in 2002 were an unusual degree of roadworks-induced traffic chaos and the controversy surrounding the viability and cost of the project.

To/From the Airport Up to seven ARST buses run daily from the main bus depot off Via XXV Aprile to Fertilia airport (€1.45, 30 minutes). **Autolinee Logudoro** *(☎ 079 28 17 28)* runs a special service to/from the same terminal to meet Ryanair flights from London (€2, 30 minutes). Buy tickets on the bus.

Nuragico Tour *(☎ 0789 2 14 87)* runs three daily buses from Porto Torres via Sassari direct to Olbia airport. To/from Sassari (€5.84) the trip takes 1½ hours.

Bus ATP local (orange) buses run along most city routes but you probably won't need one. ATP buses also run to the beaches north of Sassari.

Car & Motorcycle Parking is free in some of the streets southeast of Via Asproni and around the train station. Around busy Piazza Italia you must pay an attendant to park in blue zones – up to €2.07 for the first two hours and the same for each hour thereafter.

Taxi You can catch a taxi (☎ 079 25 39 39) from ranks on Emiciclo Garibaldi or along Viale Italia and Via Matteotti.

AROUND SASSARI
Sennori & Sorso
From a sightseeing point of view there's not a great deal to either Sennori or Sorso, although it's a nice drive through thick green vegetation to reach them – and the most likely route you will take from Sassari to head to Castelsardo.

Your palate might tempt you to stop in Sennori. Eat at **Da Vito** (☎ 079 36 02 45; Via Napoli 14; meals €30-40), where the fish, antipasti, in fact everything, is mouth-watering. It does a great *zuppa di faggiole e cozze* (mussels and bean soup). The owners will try to tempt you with all manner of delicious items. Trust them.

LOGUDORO & MEILOGU
Southeast of Sassari spreads the territory of Logudoro, a deformation of the vague original name that meant 'place of Torres' but that has also come to mean 'place of gold' for its golden summer plains of wheat and other crops. The naturally well-irrigated farm land is among the richest in Sardinia and, although never defined by strict boundaries, the Logudoro was an important part of the Giudicato di Torres. They say the *logudorese* dialect is the purest form of Sardinian. To the south stretch the Meilogu plains.

The territory is dotted with some of the finest Romanesque churches on the island, important ancient sites including the outstanding Nuraghe Santu Antine and, at its extreme eastern end, the knife-making town of Pattada.

Although it is possible to reach many of these places by public transport, especially in individual trips from Sassari, to do them in the kind of circuit that follows you need your own wheels.

Basilica della Santissima Trinità di Saccargia
You cannot miss the towering *campanile* (bell tower) of this church as you pass by on the SS597 road from Sassari to Olbia. Even before you have topped the last rise, the belltower emerges ahead on the horizon.

Easily the best known of Sardinia's Pisan Romanesque churches, the late-12th-century structure impresses with its basalt and limestone striped facade and graceful tower despite heavy-handed restoration in the early 1900s. The porch is embellished with all sorts of animal and geometric figures but the interior is bare. Remains of the adjacent monastery are in poor shape.

One legend says the church was built on the miraculous spot where a cow had been seen kneeling in prayer and offering its milk to the brothers of a nearby monastery. This would presumably explain the cow figures in the porch! Believe it or not.

Ploaghe
Three kilometres beyond the Santissima Trinità, a turn-off leads to this run of the mill farming town, notable only for its July festival (on the second Sunday of the month) in honour of Sant'Antonio Abate, the patron saint of people in the carrying trade and their beasts. In Ploaghe they stretch the meaning and after Mass the parish priest blesses a procession of cars! Up to seven buses run here from Sassari (€1.19, 20 minutes).

Ardara
Little remains to remind one of the importance of this town as early capital of the Giudicato di Torres (aka Giudicato di Logudoro). A quick turn to the left as you enter the town proper brings you face to face with the dark brooding mass of the **Chiesa di Santa Maria del Regno**, made of deep rust-red basalt. One of its oddest features is the squat belltower, hurriedly finished off in rough-and-ready manner after the church was completed and not at all typical of the style.

Chiesa di Sant'Antioco di Bisarcio

Head further east along the SS597 Sassari–Olbia road and you'll soon see a turn-off for this majestically ruined 11th- to 12th-century church *(open 9am-1pm & 3.30pm-7.30pm daily)*, 2km north of the highway.

The belltower was decapitated by a burst of lightning and much of the facade's decoration has been lost. But the uniquely French-inspired porch and interior, even if rather empty, convey the impression of its onetime grandeur, perhaps even more so in its forlorn state of abandonment in the middle of the countryside.

Ozieri

postcode 07014 • pop 11,526 • elev 375m

Ozieri is a substantial town, its tight web of lanes and houses cut into the slopes like farming terraces. Follow the signs for the *centro* and you will wind up in Via Vittoria Veneto, where the town's only hotel stands opposite the police station and intercity buses gather (adjacent to Piazza Garibaldi).

Behind and above this square, the **Museo Archeologico** *(Piazza San Francesco; admission with Grotta di San Michele €4.13; open 9am-1pm & 3.30pm-7.30pm Tues-Sun)*, housed in the former convent of the Chiesa di San Francesco, contains ancient finds, especially ceramic fragments, left behind by the Ozieri people (see History in the Facts about Sardinia chapter) in the Grotta di San Michele.

The 56m of caves that make up the **Grotta di San Michele** *(admission €2.50, with Museo Archeologico €4.13; open 9am-1pm & 3.30pm-7.30pm Tues-Sun)*, where many of the finds were made, are not overly thrilling and are inconveniently located on the edge of town on the road to Pattada.

From Piazza Garibaldi take Via Umberto I, which climbs to Piazza Carlo Alberto, a noble semi-circular space fronted by sober 19th-century mansions. From there Via Vittorio Emanuele III leads up to a little square capped by the **Fonte Grixoni**, a marble caprice erected by a noble on the site of what for centuries had been the town's main fountain. From there, swing around to the left and follow Via Grixoni up to the **Cattedrale dell'Immacolata** *(Piazza Duomo)*, which displays more bombast than the modest square before it can fairly contain. A grand, bright neoclassical facade was applied in the 19th century to what remained of the original Gothic structure. Inside is an important *Deposizione di Cristo dalla Croce* (the taking down of Christ from the Cross) by the enigmatic Maestro di Ozieri.

Places to Stay & Eat The only hotel in town, **Hotel Il Mastino** *(☎ 079 78 70 41, fax 079 78 70 59; Via Vittorio Veneto 13; singles/doubles €42/62)* is a fairly characterless no-nonsense affair. Rooms here are generally clean and tidy.

Il Sipario *(☎ 079 78 75 97; Piazza Garibaldi; meals €25)*, a former theatre and cinema (the name means 'the curtain', which remains closed up on the stage) upstairs from the porticoes, specialises in grilled meats.

Getting There & Away Buses stop just off Piazza Garibaldi. Up to eight ARST services run here from Sassari (€2.58, 50 minutes). Three or four FAB buses head west to Olbia (€4.44, up to 1½ hours). Regular buses run to Chilivani station, 7km northwest, to meet trains and return to town.

Pattada

The SS128bis snakes its way through farming country east of Ozieri 18km to Pattada, home of the island's most celebrated jack knives but otherwise hardly oozing fascination. Good knives are hand-crafted with mouflon horn handles. Shops are scattered about the village. One or two buses run here from Sassari via Ozieri.

Torralba & Nuraghe Santu Antine

Heading west from Ozieri, you pass through **Mores**, to the south of which lies the majestic **Dolmen Sa Coveccada**. Take the exit just before you enter Mores from the east and it's a couple of kilometres down the road. The dolmen, raised at the end of the third millennium BC, consists of three massive slabs of stone roofed over by a fourth. They were cut and chiselled to measure, although erosion has masked that fact.

From Mores proceed to Torralba, the village at the head of the so-called Valle dei Nuraghi (Valley of the Nuraghes). Driving around here you will see several of the ancient structures, but top priority goes to the Nuraghe Santu Antine *(☎ 079 84 72 96; admission including Museo Archeologico di Torralba €3; open 8.30am-sunset daily)*, 4km

Sardinia's Cutting Edge

Of all the fine knives made in Sardinia, the most prized is *sa pattadesa* (Pattada knife). The classic Pattada knife, first made in the mid-19th century, is the *resolza* with its so-called myrtle leaf–shaped blade that folds into the handle. Now that's a knife. Craftsmen in Pattada and around the island lovingly create all sorts of other high-quality cutters and slicers. The classic *s'arburesa* (from Arbus), for instance, has a fat, rounded blade and is used for skinning animals, while the *lametta* of Tempio Pausania is a rectangular job good for stripping the bark from cork oaks. Of the *pattadesa* knives the best known 'brand' is the *fogarizzu*. The best *arburesa* to look for is the *pusceddu*.

Knives are flogged to tourists all over the island, but the real thing is not always easy to find. The blades of quality knives are tempered by a handful of artisans who also create the handles. Whether a jack knife or not, the handle should be carved from a single piece of mouflon or goat horn (goat horns are largely imported from Corsica). A good knife will cost at least €10 a centimetre.

If the handles are made of two parts screwed together, you are not looking at a quality piece. Fakes abound too. Many knives are made with synthetic materials that look like horn but which wear out after a few years.

---

south of the town. The site of Santu Antine is a unique blast from the past – at least 1600 years BC! Set in fields and surrounded in the distance by the distinctive conical forms of ancient volcanoes, it is an extraordinary sight. If you only see one *nuraghe* in Sardinia, this one rivals Su Nuraxi at Barumini.

The complex was built over a succession of stages. The three-storey central tower (originally 21m high) was the first to be completed. It was followed by the three shorter towers and linking walls, forming a triangular compound. Outside the walls, the remains of other circular walls probably belonged to a settlement that existed in the shadow of the *nuraghe's* walls. The remnants of rectangular based structures are a reminder of the arrival of the Romans, who it seems were responsible for the partial destruction of the ancient building. The removal of the top (3rd) floor of the central tower was, however, the work of a 19th-century mayor from a nearby village who decided the stone would do nicely for a fountain.

Theories abound on the uses of the *nuraghe*. In origin it almost certainly had a defensive vocation but it seems the compound was also an important meeting place, perhaps for religious ceremonies.

You enter the compound from the south side and can walk through the three towers, connected through the walls by rough parabolic archways. Stairs lead to the top of these towers and the upper perimeter. The entrance to the main tower is separate. Inside you find a central chamber surrounded by a walkway. Four openings lead from this internal, circular hall into the chamber. Stairs lead up from the hall to the next floor, where a similar but smaller pattern is reproduced. Finally, you ascend another set of steps to reach the floor of what was the final, third chamber. Nowadays you can contemplate the open farmland all around.

Back in Torralba is the **Museo Archeologico** *(admission including Nuraghe Santu Antine €3; open 9am-8pm daily May-Oct, 9am-6pm daily Oct-May)*. The first item is a scale model of the Nuraghe Santu Antine, followed by an ethnographic display on customs of the local countryside (closed at the time of writing). Upstairs, one room holds a limited collection of archaeological finds from the Santu Antine site, while Roman remnants dominate the rest of the display. In the garden is a series of Roman milestones with some fascinating explanations (in Italian only) of the evolution of Rome's highway system.

Up to 10 buses from Sassari run to Torralba (€2.32). To get to the *nuraghe* from there you will have to walk (about an hour).

Borutta & Siligo

As the crow flies, the hamlet of Borutta is only a few kilometres from Torralba, but the circular road will make it about a 10km trip. The object, the fine Romanesque **Chiesa di San Pietro Sorres**, lies on a lane just southwest of the town.

Long abandoned, the church and neighbouring abbey had life breathed into them by a small Benedictine community invited to install themselves here in 1955. The abbey had to be rebuilt from scratch but the church was in better shape, and has been much improved over the years. The white-and-grey banded facade, with three levels of blind arches and patterned decoration all hark to its Pisan origins. Inside, the heavy stone Gothic pulpit resting on four legs is an intriguing item.

About 10km north of Borutta, the unprepossessing farming town of **Siligo** was home to Sardinian writer Gavino Ledda. In the opening of his classic *Padre, Padrone* (see Literature in the Facts about Sardinia chapter), Ledda describes how his father took him out of school in Siligo to send him into the fields to learn to be a shepherd. He only took up schooling again as an adult in the army!

Bonorva & Around

About 14km south of Torralba along the SS131 highway (exit to the east), this ridgetop farming town is home to yet another **Museo Archeologico** (☎ 079 86 78 94; admission €2, with Necropoli di Sant'Andrea di Priu €4; open 4pm-7pm Tues-Sat, 10am-1pm & 4pm-7pm Sun June-Sept, by appointment other months) just off Piazza Sant'Antonio. Housed in former convent buildings adjacent to the Chiesa di Sant'Antonio, the display starts in the Middle Ages and proceeds back in time through vaulted rooms to the Neolithic era.

More interesting is the excursion east of the town to the **Necropoli di Sant'Andrea di Priu** (☎ 079 86 78 94; admission €3; open 9.30am-7.30pm June-Sept, in other months call ahead). The road drops down from the heights that cradle Bonorva into farming country and the way is signposted. Before reaching the necropolis, take the turn-off for **Rebeccu**, a wind-swept and largely abandoned medieval hamlet with tiny lanes and tinier houses.

Back on the main road, you push on a couple of kilometres eastward and take the turn-off for the rustic **Chiesa di Santa Lucia**, which retains some Romanesque traces and attracts jolly groups of pilgrims on the first days of May. The necropolis, virtually across the road, is made up of around 20 small grottoes carved into the trachyte and dating as far back as 4000 BC. The **Tomba del Capo** contains a series of rooms used as tombs and is by far the most engaging. In the early Christian period three of the main rooms were transformed into a place of worship and partly restored frescoes from the 5th century survive in two of them. Most striking is one of a woman in the room labelled as the *aula*, the 'hall' where the faithful heard Mass.

Getting around this area without your own transport is well-nigh impossible, although a few ARST bus services run from Sassari down to Bonorva (€3.15, 40 to 50 minutes). Two come from Alghero (€4.03, 1½ hours).

PORTO TORRES & THE COAST
Porto Torres
postcode 07046 • pop 21,440

Apart from some Roman remains and the fine Romanesque Basilica di San Gavino, there is little to keep you in this drab port town, busy above all with ferry traffic between it, Corsica and mainland Italy.

History Pliny tells us this ancient maritime centre went by the name of Turris Libisonis. Although the name has led to speculation that Carthiginians (from Libya) may have founded a town here, it was Rome that sent colonists to create a new port town around 46 BC. It remained one of the island's key ports until well into the Middle Ages and was long the capital of the medieval Giudicato di Torres. The twin scourges of pirates and malaria reduced it to a backwater and even today the city is little more than a maritime appendage of Sassari.

Orientation & Information From the main port and Piazza Colombo you enter the heart of town crossing the adjacent square, Piazza XX Settembre, from where the main boulevard, Corso Vittorio Emanuele, pushes south.

The **tourist office** (☎ 079 51 06 59, 079 51 50 00; open 7.30am-1pm & 4pm-8pm daily May-Sept, 9am-1pm & 3.30pm-7.30pm Mon-Sat Oct-Apr) is in an odd little yellow structure in the port area in front of the Capitaneria building – a few hundred metres from where Tirrenia boats arrive. If you want to embark on a tour of Isola Asinara (see later in this chapter) from Porto Torres, you have to purchase tickets here.

The **Banca Nazionale del Lavoro** (Corso Vittorio Emanuele 20) is one of several banks along the main drag with ATMs.

The **post office** *(open 8.15am-1.15pm Mon-Fri, 8.15am-12.15pm Sat)* at Via Ponte Romano is three blocks right off Corso Vittorio Emanuele shortly in from the port.

Torre Aragonese About the only item of vague interest in the centre of town is the yellowish defensive tower erected under Spanish rule. It dominates the port.

Basilica di San Gavino Emperor Diocletian's attempts to stamp out the growing Christian faith in the early 4th century AD were the undoing of the Roman officer Gavino. Converted by Proto and Gianuario to the new faith, Gavino soon found himself under arrest with his new friends and, in 304, all three were beheaded. Evidence for these events is scanty but the legend of the *martiri turritani* (martyrs of Torres) flourished.

The limestone Romanesque Basilica di San Gavino *(open 8.30am-1pm & 3pm-7pm daily)* was started in 1050 on the site of an earlier church in the heart of the old medieval settlement. In Roman times the area was the city's necropolis. The church is the largest of the Pisan-style churches in Sardinia and quite unique. The striped, two-tone colouring typical of most Pisan churches of the time is absent here. More remarkable still, each end of the church is rounded off by an apse – there is no facade. Inside, the presence of 28 marble columns hints at the possibility that a Roman temple may have stood on or near the site. The three saints are commemorated by 17th-century statues in the eastern apse. A series of crypts and remains of the original 7th-century church were at the time of writing closed to visitors. To get here follow the signs down Corso Vittorio Emanuele south from the port for about 1.5km. The basilica is one block to the west of the street.

Parco Archeologico & Antiquarium Most of Turris Libisonis lies beneath the modern port, but some vestiges have been uncovered. Known collectively as the 'archaeological park', it is made up of the remains of public baths, an overgrown Roman bridge and the so-called Palazzo del Re Barbaro. The latter is the centrepiece and actually constitutes the main public bathing complex of the Roman city. Parts of the town's main roads, some *tabernae* (shops)

and some good floor mosaics can also be seen on the site, which is entered via the Antiquarium *(admission €3, Antiquarium only €2; open 9am-8pm Tues-Sat)*. Almost all the items in this museum were found in Roman Turris, and cover a range of ceramics, busts, oil lamps and glassware. Much of the material was found in Roman burial grounds. The site is on the road between the main port and the Grimaldi line's docks, about a five-minute walk.

Places to Stay & Eat Porto Torres is not the kind of place you really want to hang around long, but if you get stuck, there are three hotels.

Hotel Elisa *(☎ 079 51 32 60, fax 079 51 37 68; Via Mare 2; singles/doubles €43.90/67)* is just off Piazza XX Settembre and a spit from the port. Rooms are comfortable and come with TV and phone, and in some cases views across to the port.

Crossing's Cafe *(Corso Vittorio Emanuele 53)* does good *panini* (filled rolls) for €3.

Cristallo *(☎ 079 51 49 09; Piazza XX Settembre 11; meals €35; open Tues-Sun)* is an unassuming-looking place where you can enjoy good seafood and a selection of Sardinian favourites, such as lamb.

Three kilometres out of town on the road to Sassari is **Li Lioni** *(☎ 079 50 22 86; meals €30; open Thur-Tues)*, a sprawling place that presents a solid Sardinian menu. Little in the line of fish here but rather meats and cheeses. Try the *culurgiones* (ravioli-style pasta) filled with ricotta and mint.

Getting There & Away Most buses leave from Piazza Colombo, virtually at the port. Plenty go to Sassari (€1.45, 30 to 40 minutes). Up to six head for Alghero (€2.58, 50 minutes) and another six to Stintino (€2.01, 30 minutes). You can get tickets at **Bar Acciaro** *(Corso Vittorio Emanuele 38)* or at newsstands along the same street.

Nuragica Tour runs three daily buses via Sassari to Olbia airport (€6.77, one hour 50 minutes).

Trains run regularly to Sassari (€1.20, 15 minutes). Direct runs to the capital, Cagliari (€12.95, 4½ hours), run twice a day – otherwise you have to make connections along the way and it can be painfully slow going.

For more information on boats leaving Porto Torres for mainland Italy, Corsica and mainland France, see the Getting There & Away chapter. For information and tickets in Porto Torres, the easiest option is to head for **Agenzia Paglietti** (☎ *079 51 44 77, fax 079 51 40 63; Corso Vittorio Emanuele 19*).

South of Porto Torres

The ancients who built the temple of **Monte d'Accoddi** (☎ *079 201 60 99; admission €2.07, with guide in Italian €3.10; open 9am-6pm daily Apr-June, 9am-8pm daily July-Sept, 8am-5pm daily Oct-Mar*) in the third millennium BC have left us with some intriguing conundrums. Nowhere else in the Mediterranean has such a structure been unearthed. The closest comparable buildings are in fact the fabled ziggurats of the Euphrates and Tigris river valleys in the Middle East, and so this too is often referred to as a ziggurat. Excavations have revealed there was a Neolithic village here as early as 4500 BC. The temple went through several phases and appears to have been finally abandoned around 1800 BC. Soon after, the first nuraghes, perhaps the architectural signature of another race, began to be raised.

Driving from Porto Torres you turn right off the highway after 11km. The ziggurat is a few hundred metres from the road. What you see is a rectangular-based structure, tapering somewhat to a platform and preceded by a long ramp. To either side of the ramp are a menhir and what is believed to be a stone altar for sacrifices from a temple that predates the ziggurat.

East of Porto Torres

Between Porto Torres and Castelsardo, 34km to the east, lies a string of fine but (by Sardinian standards) unexciting beaches. **Platamona**, 7km east of Porto Torres and about 20km north of Sassari, is a cheerful and, on summer weekends, crowded local beach scene for the people of both cities who optimistically like to think of it as the Sassari Riviera. Several seaside restaurants and cafés of indifferent quality operate here and regular buses stream up from Via Eugenio Tavolara in Sassari.

A series of access roads (marked *discesa al mare*) lead through pine stands separating the road from the beach as you head east towards Marina di Sorso. They are all perfectly good and unlikely to be busy midweek. Most boast parking areas and a café or bar. At

Discesa al Mare No 3, for instance, you'll find **Iceberg**, a restaurant and bar (great mozzarella and tomato *panini*) that on some summer weekend evenings hosts dance sessions in the sand.

Three kilometres east of Platamona, **Camping Villagio Golfo dell'Asinara** (☎ *079 31 02 30, fax 079 31 05 89;* W *www.camping asinara.it; per person €10.85; open June-Sept*) is the nicer of the two camping grounds along this stretch of coast.

Shortly after the camping ground the pine stands thin out and the coast becomes rather lacklustre. **Marina di Sorso**, for instance, comprises a restaurant and a building site and has nothing much to recommend it. Beyond the pine stands start up again and last until the Sorso turn-off from the coast road.

From Sassari regular summer buses run up to a point just east of Platamona and then the length of coast as far as Marina di Sorso. Look for the Buddi Buddi bus (line MP) from Via Eugenio Tavolara.

CASTELSARDO
postcode 07031 • pop 5280

Huddled around the high cone of a promontory that juts northward into the Mediterranean, the pastel-coloured houses of Castelsardo constitute an intriguing medieval warren in an exhilarating position high above the sea. Castelsardo is the principal city of the Anglona, a struggling farm district that lies sandwiched between Gallura to the east, Logudoro to the south and the small Romangia district to the west.

Those coming from Gallura will notice the switch from the grey granite that predominates in the island's northeast to the russet tones of trachyte used commonly in building here and further west.

History

Founded in 1102 by the Genoese Doria clan and named Castelgenovese (Genoese Castle), the town was conceived from the beginning as a fortress. The Catalano-Aragonese took over in 1326 and later renamed it Castellaragonese, expelling the Genoese and repopulating the town with Catalans. It became one of Sardinia's seven *città demaniali* (ie, cities directly ruled by the Crown). The Piedmontese changed the town's name to Castelsardo (Sardinian Castle) in 1767. In spite of all the changes of ownership, the town built

The Mysterious Maestro di Castelsardo

Active in the early 16th century, it appears the Maestro di Castelsardo (Master of Castelsardo) studied with the Catalan master Jaume Huguet (1415–92) in Barcelona for a time. Indeed our *maestro* may himself have been Catalan but the fact is we know virtually nothing about him – not even his name. It appears he was also influenced by Il Bermejo (c1440–95), a southern Spanish painter who worked in Barcelona. Experts are confident in attributing to his mysterious hand a variety of works accross the island.

as a fortress has seen precious little military action. The same can be said of the latest 'invasion'. Long neglected by their own people, the houses of the old centre of Castelsardo are slowly being bought up by the renovating Germans, Swiss and other outsiders.

Orientation

Buses pull up in Piazza Pianedda, where the coast road (undergoing several name changes as it passes through town) meets Via Nazionale, the main street that winds up to the top of the old town. You can drive all the way up to the end of this latter road but finding a parking spot is frequently impossible. A more dramatic approach on foot is to follow a path above the sea that cuts around from Via Nazionale beneath the city walls and around to a set of steps leading up to the cathedral.

Information

The **Associazione Turistica Pro Loco** *(Piazzetta del Popolo)* is near the castle in the old town but rarely seems open. Locals say it's best to try in the late afternoon.

Things to See

The best thing about Castelsardo is just wandering the tight web of lanes as you gradually make your way to the top of the town.

The crowning piece is the medieval **Castello** built by the Doria family, or rather what remains of it. The views (as far as Corsica on a clear day) are as good as ever. Inside the castle, the **Museo dell'Intreccio** (closed at the time of writing) provides an instructive lesson on basket-weaving throughout the island.

Just below the castle is the **Chiesa di Santa Maria**, largely a 16th-century makeover whose main interest lies in the 13th-century crucifix, known as the *Critu Nieddu* (Black Christ).

You will no doubt have already noticed the belltower of the **Cattedrale di Sant'Antonio**

Abate, a slender dark finger pointed to the heavens and topped by a brightly tiled cupola. In a setting worthy of northern European fairy tales, the grand church almost appears suspended in mid-air atop the craggy cliffs. A small terrace just nearby and slightly above the church affords views of it and along the northwest coast of the island.

Inside, the main altar is dominated by the *Madonna con gli Angeli*, by the mysterious Maestro di Castelsardo. More of his works can be viewed in the **crypts** *(admission €2; open 10.30am-1pm & 3pm-8pm daily June-Sept)* below the church. A series of small rooms chiselled out of the living rock are what remain of the original Romanesque church that once stood here. You can admire several more works by the Maestro here, the best of them his *San Michele Arcangelo*.

The exit from the crypts takes you past neat lawns that separate you from Spanish-era seaward battlements.

A couple of small **beaches** flank the promontory on either side.

Special Events

On the Monday of Holy Week, the people of Castelsardo celebrate a series of Masses and processions as part of **Lunissanti**, ending with a solemn, evening torchlight parade through the old town that culminates at the Chiesa di Santa Maria.

Places to Stay

It's definitely worth considering staying overnight in Castelsardo.

A few kilometres west of Castelsardo, just outside the average beach resort of Lu Bagnu, is one of the island's three youth hostels. **Ostello Golfo dell'Asinara** (☎ *079 47 40 31, fax 079 58 71 42;* e *ostello.asinara@tisca linet.it; Via Sardegna 1; B&B €10; open Easter & mid-June–mid-Sept)* is set in a leafy location and makes a cheap alternative. You can eat on the big veranda. A bed in a family room costs €13.50 and meals are €8. It also rents out bikes, canoes and the like.

Pensione Pinna *(☎ 079 47 01 68; Lungomare Anglona 7; doubles €48, half board per person €58)* is about the cheapest option in town. Rooms are comfortable enough and they have heating in winter, but there are no frills. You'll have to take half board in summer. Walk a few hundred metres down Via Roma towards the beach and you'll find it on the left.

Hotel Villagio Pedraladda *(☎ 079 47 03 83, fax 079 47 04 99; Via Zirulia 50; singles/ doubles €60/83, half board per person €82.50; open Apr-Oct)* is a more upscale place that draws a mostly Italian crowd. If you are staying for a week or so, you can join its activities club (€16 a week) to use the pool. To find the hotel, take the side street that curves off to the right (east) of Piazza Pianedda.

Places to Eat

La Trattoria *(☎ 079 47 06 61; Via Nazionale 20; meals €20-25)* is a refreshingly modest eating option. Inside try for the one table by the window overlooking the port. The pasta is its strong point; some of the meat dishes are on the dry side.

La Guardiola *(☎ 079 47 07 55; Piazza Bastione 4; meals €35)* does reasonable seafood dishes but its main selling point is the wonderful views from its unbeatable position at the top of the old town.

Su Nuraghe *(☎ 079 47 02 73; Via Sedini; meals €35)*, with even better views *to* Castelsardo from the east, is a more serious culinary experience, leaning towards fish rather than meat. It's about 1km out of town on the road leading east, and signposted up a hill on the right. Reserve a table by the window.

Cormorano *(☎ 079 47 06 28; Via Colombo 5; meals up to €50; closed Tues Oct-May)* is the town's top seafood restaurant. You can try the *linguine con sarde* (a thin pasta with sardines) and all sorts of things from tuna to sea anemones.

Da Ugo *(☎ 079 474124; Corso Italia 7c; meals €40-45; closed Thur Oct-May)*, at the eastern entrance of Lu Bagnu (about 2km from Piazza Pianedda), is the other local star. The main courses are Ugo's strong point, with classics such as *capretto al forno* (oven-baked kid meat) and some fine seafood.

Entertainment

A handful of cafés and bars on and near Piazza Pianedda can get busy of an evening. If you want a dance, head up to **Vogue** *(Via Sedini)*, a disco with a large terrace next door to the Su Nuraghe restaurant.

Shopping

You can't have failed to notice the handicrafts shopping emporia on the way in to Castelsardo. This all started with the basket-weaving for which the town is best known. You can still see the occasional woman settled on her doorstep in the old town, creating baskets and other objects of all shapes and sizes.

Getting There & Away

ARST and other buses stop just off Piazza Pianedda. Up to five make the run each way between Sassari and Santa Teresa di Gallura. The trip to from Sassari (€2.01) takes one hour. To/from Santa Teresa (€4.44) takes 1½ hours. Some buses run to/from Porto Torres too (€2.01, 50 minutes). You can buy tickets for ARST buses from the nameless *edicola* (newsstand) on Piazza Pianedda.

Local orange minibuses run regularly from Piazza Pianedda to Lu Bagnu.

AROUND CASTELSARDO

With your own vehicle you could comfortably take in the following places in a one-day circuit from Castelsardo. If relying on public transport it becomes substantially more difficult.

Tergu

Barely 10km south of Castelsardo lies a fine Romanesque church, the **Nostra Signora di Tergu**. A series of modern statues representing the Stations of the Cross (the episodes of Christ's punishment and death) leads the way into town. The church is set in a pleasant garden, partly made up of the few visible remains of a one-time Benedictine monastery. Built in the 13th century of dark wine-red trachyte and light white limestone, the facade is a particularly pretty arrangement of arches, columns, geometric patterns and a simple rose window.

Nuraghe Su Tesoru & Valledoria

Five kilometres out of Castelsardo heading east you see, on the left of the SS200 road, the Nuraghe Su Tesoru, built towards the end of the era of *nuraghe* construction. There's nowhere really convenient to stop here so blink and you could miss it.

Seven kilometres on brings you to the sprawling settlement of Valledoria, fronted by beaches that stretch more than 10km east to Isola Rossa. West of the settlement shady pine stands provide a thick buffer between the sea and the inland roads. Campers will be happy at **Camping La Foce** (☎ *079 58 21 09, fax 079 58 21 91;* W *www.foce.it; per person* €*13.50, double bungalows* €*100),* which has great facilities (including a pool) and backs onto a lagoon. To get across it to the beach they lay on a free boat.

Park Hotel (☎ *079 58 28 00, fax 079 58 26 00;* W *www.parkhotelweb.it; Corso Europa; doubles* €*77.50, half board per person* €*67)* has pleasant rooms in a quiet location at the western exit of Valledoria. ARST buses running between Santa Teresa di Gallura and Castelsardo stop in the town itself. If you can't convince the bus driver to stop at the hotel or camping ground turn-off, you'll have to hitch or walk.

Perfugas

If touring in this area, you could turn inland from Valledoria and head for Santa Maria Coghinas. Drive straight through and follow the signs for the **Castel Doria**, a lonely tower (now covered in restorers' scaffolding) that sits in a lofty spot above the lake of the same name. The drive down past the lake and its river, the Rio Coghinas, is a pretty one, although the landscape quickly dries out as you approach the sleepy village of Perfugas.

At its centre can be seen what little remains of a nuraghic well temple. At the eastern end of town you can also visit the small **Museo Archeologico** (*admission* €*2.60; open 9.30am-1pm & 4pm-7pm Tues-Sun*) with a modest collection of finds from around the area. Evidence of human settlement around here goes back to Paleolithic times, at least 100,000 years BC.

Two kilometres north of Perfugas (follow the signs from the centre) is a delightful Romanesque church, the **Chiesa di San Giorgio**.

Sedini

With some of its houses built into the living rock, Sedini makes a worthwhile excursion

from Castelsardo, especially for its well looked-after *domus de janas.*

Before you get there, stop at the so-called **Roccia dell'Elefante** (Elephant Rock) a bizarre trachyte rock formation right on the Sedini road at the highway interchange with the SS200 road. Inside are some pre-nuraghic tombs, or *domus de janas.* Across the road a cluster of likely lads hang about trying to sell Sardinian souvenirs – anything from cork-covered bottles to Pattada knives.

Eleven kilometres south you arrive in Sedini, where you will quickly run into the *domus de janas* on the main road (Via Nazionale) through town. By the Middle Ages farmers had made their home in this series of ancient tombs, using the bottom ones as a cellar. The *domus* was then used as a prison until the 19th century, when it was again converted into a house. It now contains a small **display** (*open 9am-8pm daily June-Sept*) of traditional farming and household implements. Otherwise contact the **Cooperative Setin** (☎ *079 58 85 81;* W *web .tiscali.it/sedini*).

Three to six ARST buses run daily from Castelsardo (€1.19, 22 minutes).

San Pietro di Simbranos

The bus from Castelsardo continues as far as Bulzi, from where it's about a 3km hike south to the **Chiesa di San Pietro di Simbranos** (or delle Immagini), a fine example of the Pisan Romanesque style. The striking two-tone banding is well preserved. The church was first built by monks from Montecassino in 1113 and got its Pisan reworking a century later. The crude figures above the main door represent an abbot and two monks. The upper level of the facade is Gothic in style.

Martis & Chiaramonti

The remains of a ruined, mostly Gothic church and a small petrified 'forest' are the minor drawcards at Martis, about 20 winding kilometres south of Sedini.

Just before you enter the village from the northeast a sign directs you left (south) to the **Foresta Pietrificata Carrucana**. 'Forest' is overstating it. At the centre of a modest enclosure some hollow petrified trunks of ancient trees, left over from a Miocene-age forest that was flooded, have been piled up. Curious but not mind-blowing. Also on the edge of town is the ruin of the Gothic **Chiesa di San Pantaleone**, partly shattered and seemingly at peace in its state of abandonment.

Another 6km south brings you to Chiaramonti, a village built onto steep hillsides and capped by the ruins of a 13th-century castle built by Genoa's Doria family. If you think it looks more like the leftovers of a church, you would be right, for in the 16th century the castle was converted into a place of worship.

Only one bus a day makes it down this far from Castelsardo. Up to seven run from Sassari on weekdays.

ALGHERO
postcode 07041 • pop 40,400
Even today, Catalan nationalists in Barcelona, northeastern Spain, think of Alghero (Alguer in Catalan) as 'little Barcelona' (Barceloneta), an integral part of their world. The Catalan tongue may have ceded ground to Italian but the city retains a feel quite distinct from that of other Sardinian cities. Spaniards (Catalan or not) regularly exclaim that they feel as if they had been transported back home.

The city's Catalan identity is still palpable. Many townspeople speak an antiquated form of Catalan. The old Catalan street signs were put up again in the 1970s (next to the Italian ones) and attempts to revive pride in and use of the language have not fallen on completely deaf ears. The occasional magazine in Catalan is available.

In recent years the city seems to have woken up to its own attractiveness and its popularity is such that the population in summer swells to more than 100,000. It is the least Sardinian of the island's cities, open to the sea and outside visitors, and the Algheresi seem to have inherited something of the Catalan business sense, sedulously promoting local tourism and encouraging visitors to come through most of the year (while much of Sardinia seems to snooze outside summer). With its sights, seaside location, restaurants and bars, it is (with Cagliari) the most charismatic of Sardinia's cities.

History
Alghero doesn't appear on history's radar before about the 13th century, by which time it was a small fortress port founded by the Genoese. Theories of an earlier Arab or even Roman settlement abound but enjoy no proof. Little is known of the Genoese settlement except that it was briefly taken by their rivals, the Pisans, in the 1280s.

Alghero remained a focus of resistance to the Catalano-Aragonese invasion of the island in 1323 and was only subdued 30 years later. The local population, part Genoese and part Sardinian, rebelled but in 1354 King Pere the Ceremonious led another force and this time held on to the city. Catalan colonists were encouraged to settle here and after another revolt in 1372 the remaining Sardinians were expelled and relocated inland. From then on Alghero (apparently named after algae that washed up on the coast) became resolutely Catalan and called itself Alguer.

The city remained a principal port of call in Sardinia for its Catalano-Aragonese and subsequently Spanish masters. Raised to the status of city in 1501, Alghero experienced a frisson of excitement when Holy Roman Emperor (and king of Spain) Charles V arrived in 1541 to lead a campaign against North-African corsairs. Unhappily, the discovery of the Americas was bad news for Alghero, whose importance as a trading port quickly ebbed.

In 1720 the town passed to the House of Savoy and lived quietly. The landward city walls were largely torn down in the 19th century, but even in the 1920s the population didn't count much more than 10,000. Bombardment of the historic old centre in 1943 left scars that have never properly healed. Only since WWII has a frenetic process of expansion beyond the old centre taken place.

Orientation
The old town's seaward walls encircle land jutting west into the Mediterranean. On its northern side is the modern port and the new town radiates inland to the north, east and south. Several of the classier hotels and some lively summer bars spread out along the coastal road south, while Alghero's beaches stretch to the north, backed by residential blocks, hotels and a camping ground. The train station is also here but buses terminate just outside the old town on Via Catalogna.

Information
Tourist Office Alghero's **AAST** (☎ *079 97 90 54, fax 079 97 48 81;* W *www.infoalghero .it, Italian only; Piazza Porta Terra 9; open*

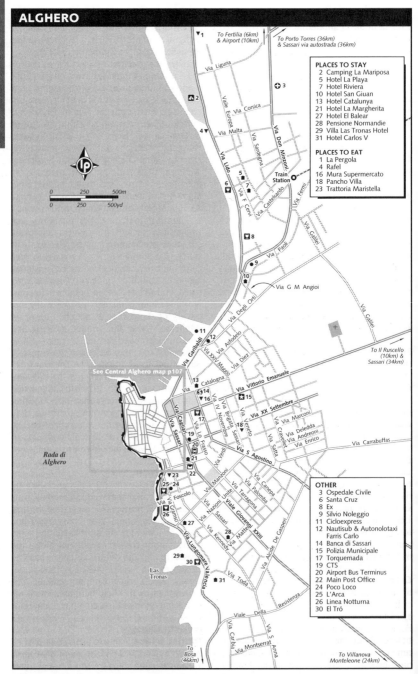

ALGHERO

To Fertilia (6km)
& Airport (10km)

To Porto Torres (36km)
& Sassari via autostrada (36km)

Via Liguria

Via Corsica

Valle Europa

Via Malta

Via Lido

Via Sardegna

Via Don Minzoni

Via Castelsardo

Via Fermi

Via F. Cervi

Train
Station

Via Padri

Via Galilei

Via Degli Orti

Via Garibaldi

Via XXIV Maggio

Via Asfodelo

Via Diez

Via G M Angioi

Via Galilei

To Il Ruscello
(10km) &
Sassari (34km)

See Central Alghero map p107

Via Catalogna

Via Vittorio Emanuele

Via XX Settembre

Via Brigata Sassari

Via IV Novembre

Via Veneto

Via Marconi

Via Craveri

Via Deledda

Via Andreoni

Via Enrico

Via Carrabuffas

Via Lo Frasso

Via Vigoli

Via S Agostino

Via Sassari

Via Cagliari

Via Brigata Sassari

Rada di
Alghero

Via Marconi

Via Foscolo

Via Carena

Via Palomba

Via Tarragona

Viale Giovanni XXIII

Via Nazioni Unite

Via Sassari

Via Kennedy

Via Matteotti

Via Alcide De Gasperi

Via Lungomare Valencia

Via Canoso

Via Resistenza

Las
Tronas

Via Toda

To
Bosa
(46km)

Viale Della

Via Carbia

Via S Anna

Via Montserrat

To Villanova
Monteleone (24km)

PLACES TO STAY
- 2 Camping La Mariposa
- 5 Hotel La Playa
- 7 Hotel Riviera
- 10 Hotel San Giuan
- 13 Hotel Catalunya
- 21 Hotel La Margherita
- 27 Hotel El Balear
- 28 Pensione Normandie
- 29 Villa Las Tronas Hotel
- 31 Hotel Carlos V

PLACES TO EAT
- 1 La Pergola
- 4 Rafel
- 16 Mura Supermercato
- 18 Pancho Villa
- 23 Trattoria Maristella

OTHER
- 3 Ospedale Civile
- 6 Santa Cruz
- 8 Ex
- 9 Silvio Noleggio
- 11 Cicloexpress
- 12 Nautisub & Autonolotaxi
  Farris Carlo
- 14 Banca di Sassari
- 15 Polizia Municipale
- 17 Torquemada
- 19 CTS
- 20 Airport Bus Terminus
- 22 Main Post Office
- 24 Poco Loco
- 25 L'Arca
- 26 Linea Notturna
- 30 El Tró

8am-8pm Mon-Sat, 9am-1pm Sun Apr-Oct, 8am-2pm Mon-Sat Nov-Mar) has to be the best-organised tourist office in Sardinia. If you ask the question, staff almost definitely have the answer.

Money You'll find banks with ATMs and change facilities all over the old town. **Banca Carige** *(Via Sassari 13)* has an ATM. **Banca di Sassari** *(Via La Marmora)* is a Western Union agent.

Post & Communications There's a main post office *(Via Carducci 35; open 8.15am-6.15pm Mon-Fri, 8.15am-1pm Sat)* in town.

Poco Loco *(☎ Via Gramsci 8; open 7.30pm-1am daily)* has three computer terminals where it costs €5 an hour to go online.

Bookshops For a good range of books (mostly in Italian) on all things Sardinian, try **Il Labrinto** *(☎ 079 98 04 96; Via Carlo Alberto 119)*. **Libreria Ex Libris** *(Via Carlo Alberto 2)* has a nice selection of art books. Both stock English novels.

Travel Agencies The national youth travel agent, **CTS** *(☎ 079 98 00 98; c/- Shardana Tours, Via XX Settembre 30)*, has a branch in Alghero.

Medical Services The **Ospedale Civile** *(☎ 079 99 62 00; Via Don Minzoni)* is the town's main hospital. Handy pharmacies include **Farmacia Cabras** *(Piazza Sulis 11)* and **Farmacia Bulla** *(Via Garibaldi 13)*.

Emergencies The **Polizia Municipale** *(Via Vittorio Emanuele 113)* has its headquarters in town.

Old Town (Centro Storico)

The cobbled lanes and honey-coloured walls of this former outpost of the Catalan merchant empire preserve more than a whiff of the centuries of Catalan presence here.

Cattedrale di Santa Maria The bombastic, bright, neoclassical facade of the city's cathedral *(☎ 079 97 92 22; Piazza Duomo; open 7am-noon & 5pm-7.30pm)*, with the fat Doric columns out of all proportion to the square at their feet, is an unfortunate 19th-century addition to what was a bit of a hybrid anyway. Built along Catalan Gothic

lines in the 16th century, the cathedral still preserves some original elements. Inside the style is largely Renaissance, with some late baroque baubles added under the Savoy family in the 18th century.

Of greater interest is the octagonal **Campanile** (belltower) around the back in Via Principe Umberto. This tall pointed reminder of the original Catalan church displays an Isabelline flourish in the gracious lines of its doorway. From June to September guided visits (€1.50) to the tower take place from 7pm to 9.30pm. In August the hours are 6pm to 11pm.

Museo Diocesano In the former Oratorio del Rosario this museum *(☎ 079 973 30 41; Via Maiorca 1; admission €2.50; open 10am-1pm & 7pm-11pm Thur-Tues Aug, 10am-1pm & 5pm-8pm or 7pm-10pm Thur-Tues late Mar–July & Sept-Oct, 10am-1pm & 5pm-8pm Thur-Tues Dec, closed Jan-Mar & Nov)* houses treasures of religious art belonging mostly to the cathedral next door. Pieces include silverware, statuary and a handful of other items. A ghoulish touch is the reliquary of what is claimed to be one of the newly born babies *(innocenti)* slaughtered by Herod in his search for the Christ child. The tiny skull is a chilling affair, but apparently it appealed to the Alghero artist Francesco Pinna, who received it from a Roman cardinal in the 16th century.

The former chapel is itself attractive. The low flat arch above you when you enter is clearly inspired by the Catalan Gothic style.

Piazza Civica Just inside the Port a Mare (Sea Gate) and once the administrative heart of Alghero, this busy, uneven square is still faced by reminders of Alghero's late-medieval splendour. It was from the window of the Gothic mansion, **Palazzo d'Albis**, that Charles V leaned out during his 1541 stay to declare in generous mood: 'You are all knights'.

Chiesa di San Francesco Proceed along Via Carlo Alberto, the Carrer Major (Main Street) of old, now lined with shops and awash with their customers. Along the way you arrive at the restored Chiesa di San Francesco *(Via Carlo Alberto; open 7.30am-noon & 5pm-8.30pm daily)*, a combination of Romanesque and Gothic with an austere stone facade. Inside, most of what you see dates to a late-Renaissance remake of the church, much of which collapsed in 1593. You pass from the church to the tranquil cloister, whose lower level dates to the 13th century. The warm sandstone used in the arcades and columns lends it special warmth and makes it a wonderful setting for summer concerts.

Chiesa di San Michele Further along Via Carlo Alberto you come upon a church (open for Mass only), whose main feature is the brightly coloured majolica dome typical of churches in that other former Catalan territory in coastal Spain, Valencia. The present tiles were laid in the 1960s but this in no way detracts from the visual pleasure.

Just before you reach the church you cross Via Gilbert Ferret. The intersection is known as the *quatre cantonades* (four sides) and for centuries day labourers would gather here in the hope of finding work.

Towers & Walls Much of Alghero's landward defensive perimeter was torn down in the 19th century, in part replaced by the **Giardini Pubblici**, a green space that now effectively separates the old town from the new.

The main land entrance was by the **Torre Porta a Terra** (☎ 079 973 40 45; open 10am-1pm & 6pm-midnight Mon-Sat, 6pm-midnight Sun May-Sept, reduced hrs Oct-Apr). This tower (all that remains of the Porta a Terra, or Land Gate) has been converted into an information office on local entertainment and also has an interesting bookshop.

To the south, another stout tower, **Torre di San Giovanni** (☎ 079 973 16 05; admission €2; open 10am-1pm & 6.30pm-10pm Tues-Sat, 6.30pm-10pm Sun-Mon July-Aug, 10am-1pm & 5pm-8pm Tues-Sun Apr-June) has been turned into a virtual history display on Alghero. A circular panel around the ground floor follows Alghero's history – interactive screens allow you do so in various languages. At the centre of the display is a scale model of the city as it was in 1865. A spiral stairway leads you to the top of the tower, although the views are nothing special.

The **Torre dello Sperone** closes off the defensive line of towers to the south of the old town, while to the north the **Bastione della Maddalena**, with its like-named tower, form

the only extant remnant of the city's former land battlements.

Just west of that bastion is the **Porta a Mare**, by which you can enter Piazza Civica (see earlier). Steps by the gate lead up onto the portside bastions, which stretch around to what remains of the northern **Torre della Polveriera**. The Mediterranean crashes up against the seaward walls of the **Bastioni di San Marco** and **Bastioni di Cristoforo Colombo**, which end at the Torre dello Sperone. Along these seaward bulwarks are some delightful eateries and bars – wonderful for a summer sunset.

Mare Nostrum Aquarium
Sardinia's only aquarium (☎ 079 97 83 33; Via XX Settembre 1; adult/child €5/3; open 10am-1pm & 4pm or 5pm-9pm or 11pm daily June-Oct, 3pm-8pm Sat, Sun & holidays Nov-May) is not a bad diversion and boasts quite a variety of fishy elements, from piranhas to seahorses and leopard sharks to reptiles.

Waterfront
North of Alghero's port, jammed with yachts and other pleasure craft, Via Garibaldi sweeps quickly up to the town's beaches, **Spiaggia di San Giovanni** and the adjacent **Spiaggia di Maria Pia**. Indeed, the line of strands continues pretty much uninterrupted around the coast to Fertilia. The sand is fine and white and the waters a shade of clear turquoise. But they do get awfully crowded in summer and can be inundated with seaweed.

Diving
You can organise dives with a handful of outlets in Alghero. **Nautisub** (☎ 079 95 24 33; Via Garibaldi 45; open year-round) hires out gear for underwater fun.

Organised Tours
In summer, horse-drawn carts trundle around the old town with tourists. The trip takes less than an hour and costs €6/3 per adult/child. The vehicles and their steeds gather on the port side of the Torre della Maddalena.

Otherwise, several agencies scattered about town offer tours of the area around Alghero. Ask at the tourist office for a list.

Special Events
Carnevale and Easter week are both celebrated with reasonable gusto in Alghero,

although in both cases there are more spectacular options around the island.

The **Estate Musicale Internazionale di Alghero** (International Summer of Music) is staged in July and August, featuring classical music concerts in the contemplative setting of the Chiesa di San Francesco cloister.

Places to Stay

A private organisation with B&Bs on its books in and around Alghero is **Margallò** (☎ 079 989 20 19, fax 079 989 20 19; w www .accommodation-alghero-sardinia.co.uk; Via Enrico Costa 26).

Camping La Mariposa (☎ 079 95 03 60; Via Lido 22; per person/tent space €10.50/3, bungalows up to €72; open Apr-Oct), about 2km north of the centre of town, is right on the beach.

Pensione Normandie (☎/fax 079 97 53 02; Via Enrico Mattei 6; singles/doubles €23/ 43.90) is easily the cheapest option. It's a little awkwardly placed and the rooms are basic, although there is heating in winter. There's only one single. Bathrooms are shared.

Hotel San Giuan (☎ 079 95 12 22, fax 079 95 10 73; Via G M Angioi 2; B&B singles/ doubles €41.30/72.30) is a fairly characterless, but perfectly clean and comfortable, spot within stumbling distance of the beach.

Hotel San Francesco (☎/fax 079 98 03 30; Via Ambrogio Machin 2; singles/doubles €44/ 77.40), the only place to stay in the old town, is alone in exuding real charm of another era. Housed in the former convent of the Chiesa di San Francesco, the rooms are simple enough but comfortable – and you cannot get closer to the action.

Hotel La Margherita (☎ 079 97 90 06, fax 079 97 64 17; Via Sassari 70; B&B singles/ doubles €62/99) offers rooms with TV and phone in a big hulk of a building about five minutes' stroll from the old town centre. There is parking too.

Hotel Catalunya (☎ 079 95 31 72, fax 079 95 31 77; Via Catalogna 20; singles/doubles €114/156) boasts the red and yellow of the Catalan flag, colour that has long fluttered over this city. Situated opposite the Giardini Pubblici, the hotel's rooms are comfortable and the top ones benefit from the building's height, with great views. Views are equally enticing from the penthouse restaurant.

A strip of ho-hum hotels in the three- to four-star range fronts Alghero's beaches.

Most close out of season. Some are a little better than others and a couple just back from the waterfront are worth considering.

Hotel La Playa (☎ 079 95 03 69, fax 079 98 57 13; Via Pantelleria 14; B&B singles/ doubles €78/103; open Apr-Oct) is a reasonably quiet spot. Rooms are an average size and en suite, many with balconies. The hotel also has a pool and parking.

Hotel Riviera (☎ 079 95 12 30, fax 079 98 41 19; Via Fratelli Cervi 6; singles/doubles €49/87.80; open Mar-Oct), close by, is if anything a slightly better deal. Rooms come with TV and there is a pool here too.

The southern waterfront, along Lungomare Dante and Lungomare Valencia, is a posher part of town, sprinkled with Art Nouveau villas and the town's star hotels.

Hotel El Balear (☎ 079 97 52 29, fax 079 97 48 47; Lungomare Dante 32; singles/doubles €60/88; open Mar-Oct) is the most modest waterfront option around here, with well-maintained if not luxurious rooms in a good position.

Hotel Carlos V (☎ 079 97 95 01, fax 079 98 02 98; w www.hotelcarlosv.it; Lungomare Valencia 24; singles/doubles €103/134) is a good deal in its range. The hotel is in a fine position, has its own pool and tennis court and the rooms, with all mod cons, are inviting.

Villa Las Tronas Hotel (☎ 079 98 18 18, fax 079 98 10 44; Lungomare Valencia 1; singles/doubles €169.80/234.80, suites up to €427) is a splendid residence that has a whole promontory to itself. Rooms are immaculate and some have stunning coastal views. The hotel has its own pool and gym.

Places to Eat

Seafood clearly dominates the eating here and lobster is the speciality. You'll need to have a special financial disposition to cede to this temptation though!

Centro Storico A good stop for the impecunious but hungry is **Pizzeria Paradiso** (Via Carlo Alberto 8). A big wedge of pizza won't cost more than €4 to take away. **Pata Pizza** (Via Maiorca 89) is in much the same vein.

While on the subject of pizza, **Al Vecchio Mulino** (☎ 079 97 72 54; Via Don Deroma 3; pizzas up to €7, meals €25-30; open Wed-Mon) is worth keeping in mind if you want quality over economy. The pizzas are generous and the vaulted dining areas convivial.

El Pultal (☎ 079 97 47 20; Via Columbano 40; meals €25-30; open Tues-Sun) is locally recommended for pizzas but the seafood dishes are reasonable too.

Osteria Macchiavello (☎ 079 98 06 28; Bastioni Marco Polo 57; meals €30; open Wed-Mon) is a long tunnel of a place stretching to Via Cavour. In summer you will want to dine right up on the fortress walls, watch the sunset and listen to the waves crashing below.

Da Pietro (☎ 079 97 96 45; Via Ambrogio Machin 20; meals €25-30; open Thur-Tues) is a cosy seafood haven. They also have a set menú turistico (set menu) for €20.

Diecimetri (☎ 079 97 90 23; Via Barcelonetta 11; meals €25; open Thur-Tues), around the corner from Da Pietro, is a warm and welcoming spot with paintings of seaside life. The ravioli al sugo di noci (ravioli in a walnut sauce) is great.

Da Ninetto (☎ 079 97 80 62; Via Gioberti 4; meals €25-30; open Wed-Mon) is a bright hole-in-the-wall arrangement and is not a bad spot to indulge in some lobster, which comes in at €9.50 per 100g.

Borgo Antico (☎ 079 98 26 49; Via Zaccaria 12; meals €30-35; open Mon-Sat & lunch Sun) moves a notch up in class, with a more formal air than some of the places above. You can dine in pleasant surrounds inside or opt for the square. The spaghetti all'aragosta (lobster spaghetti) is tempting (€26).

Al Tuguri (☎ 079 97 67 72; Via Maiorca 113; meals €35-40; open Mon-Sat), and its near neighbours, all involve greater fiscal effort but offer exquisite dining experiences. Try the maltagliati con carciofi e fave (a local pasta with artichokes and fava beans).

La Lepanto (☎ 079 97 91 16; Via Carlo Alberto 135; meals €35-40; open Tues-Sun) is mouth-watering at first sight. A grand assortment of fish lies on display and, around the corner, a table swarming with delicious dessert options awaits.

Il Pavone (☎ 079 97 95 84; Piazza Sulis 3/4; meals €40-50; open Mon-Sat) is another classic of the Alghero table although not as grand feeling as La Lepanto. Sit outside and tuck into a good version of culurgiones.

An excellent gelato stop is **Chez Michel** (Piazza Sulis).

Outside the Centro Storico One of the best deals in town is **Trattoria Maristella** (☎ 079 97 81 72; Via Fratelli Kennedy 9; meals €22-25; open Mon-Sat & lunch Sun) if you are looking for moderately priced but reliable grub. The Mediterranean burnt-orange decor is cheerful and in summer you can sit out in the street. Locals pour in so book ahead.

La Pergola (☎ 079 95 05 31; Via I Maggio 3; pizzas up to €9; open Wed-Mon) also does standard meals but is best for its pizzas. As the name suggests, there is a pleasant outdoor dining area. It's a little out of the way if you're on foot.

Rafel (☎ 079 95 03 85; Via Lido 20; meals €25-30; open Fri-Wed), a rough and ready beachside eatery, does better seafood than many of the other options along this beach strip.

Pancho Villa (☎ 079 97 00 49; Via Veneto 47; meals €25; open Tues-Sun) offers a rare alternative to the local fare, a bit of a Tex-Mex trip with tortillas, guacamole and the like. It isn't special but it is different.

Cafés The classiest coffee stop in town is **Caffè Costantino** (Piazza Civica 31) in the basement of the late-Gothic Palazza d'Albis.

Caffè Latino (Bastioni Magellano) is a wonderful spot for a morning cuppa, with tables set out on the fortress-wall walkway above the port.

Self-Catering If you want to put your own meals together you can stock up on fresh produce at the **market** between Via Sassari and Via Cagliari. Anything missing you can pick up at the **Mura Supermercato** (Via La Marmora 28; open 8.30am-10pm Mon-Sat).

Entertainment
Alghero offers a few nocturnal entertainment possibilities and gets pretty busy in summer.

Bars Several bars along or near Spiaggia di San Giovanni can be fun for a drink or two earlier in the evening. Most of these places are open until 2am.

Santa Cruz (Via Lido 2), which also serves up pizza and a few other snacks, is right on the beach and makes a nice spot for drinks earlier in the evening in summer.

There are a few possibilities awaiting in the old town too.

Jamaica Inn *(Via Principe Umberto)* is a cheerful place for a beer and *bruschetta* (a rather un-Sardinian snack of toasted bread that can be covered in all manner of toppings).

The Mill Inn *(Via Maiorca 37; open Thur-Tues)* is one of the busiest and cosiest bars in the old town, with punters crowding in below the stone vaults for a Guinness.

King's Pub *(Via Cavour 123)* has two faces, one the terrace facing the sea out the back on Bastioni di San Marco, the other a pink-lit horseshoe bar approached from Via Cavour.

Buena Vista *(Bastioni di San Marco 47)* is the prime drinking spot for taking in the sunset over an early evening aperitif…or two. If it gets too chilly, retire into the cavernous tavern below decks.

Diva Caffè *(Via Roma 40)* is a more showy affair, where the suntanned take an evening cocktail in the square. It stays open until about 3am on Fridays and Saturdays if the business warrants it.

As the other places fade from about 1am on, the centre of pleasurable gravity shifts across to the chi-chi waterfront area south of the old city. In summer especially, the crowds head here for their drinks until about 4am.

L'Arca *(Lungomare Dante 6)* is a big open bar with masses of seating along the street (closed to traffic). Markets across the road add to the festival atmosphere.

Linea Notturna *(Lungomare Dante 10)*, further down, is a more high-energy spot, with occasional live music and a perpetual dance beat in the air.

CENTRAL ALGHERO

PLACES TO STAY & EAT
5 Caffè Latino
6 Osteria Macchiavello
11 Pizzeria Paradiso
14 Caffè Costantino
19 El Pultal
21 Da Pietro
22 Da Ninetto
23 Diecimetri
24 Hotel San Francesco
28 Al Vecchio Mulino
34 Pata Pizza
36 Borgo Antico
37 Al Tuguri
39 La Lepanto
40 Il Pavone

OTHER
1 Farmacia Bulla
2 Boats to Grotta del Nettuno (Marittima Navisarda)
3 Horse & Cart Tours
4 Bastione della Maddalena
7 Buena Vista
8 Cattedrale di Santa Maria
9 Museo Diocesano
10 Libreria Ex Libris
12 Diva Caffè
13 Palazzo d'Albis
15 ARST & FdS Bus Ticket Office
16 Casa del Caffè
17 Banca Carige
18 AAST Tourist Office
20 Torre Porta Terra
25 Chiesa di San Francesco
26 The Mill Inn
27 Palazzo Machin
29 King's Pub
30 Jamaica Inn
31 Salumeria del Centro
32 Torre di San Giovanni
33 Chiesa di San Michele
35 3° Fuoco
38 Il Labrinto
41 Avis
42 Farmacia Cabras
43 Mare Nostrum Aquarium

El Trò (Lungomare Valencia 3; open Tues-Sun) is the pick of the crop, a kind of beach bar without the beach (but settled right on a rocky outcrop by the sea). People flock here and late at night start to loosen up for a dance – on Fridays and Saturdays they have until 7am the next day.

Clubs & Music Those who have not had enough can make for the summer (June to September) discos outside of town. Entry to these places is generally €10 or so. Drinks can cost €8 and sometimes more.

Il Ruscello (☎ 079 95 31 68) has two dance areas where you will hear mostly mainstream international and local music. It's about 10km out of Alghero on the road to Olmedo.

La Siesta (☎ 079 98 01 37) is another big place, mostly open air, for summertime dancing. Music ranges from Latin to house, but nothing too heavy. Virtually next door, a companion disco, **Il Siestino**, opened in 2002. They are about 10km out of town on the SS292 road to Villanova Monteleone.

In town, **Ex** (Via Lido 17; open Sat & Sun) is the main wintertime music and dance venue.

Shopping

You can barely shoulder past the meandering crowds along Via Carlo Alberto, the Oxford St of Alghero if you will. The street is lined with all sorts of chic shops. Coral is clearly a winner with many.

Salumeria del Centro (☎ 079 97 58 14; Via Simon 2) is a veritable treasure chest of Sardinian goodies, ranging from typical foods

through a selection of wines and handicrafts. They also sell a decent version of the Pattada knives (expect to pay in the region of €60 to €70).

3° Fuoco (☎ 338 964 44 98; Via della Misericordia 20) does a broad range of pottery and ceramics.

Getting There & Away

Air The **airport** (☎ 079 93 50 39) is about 10km north of Alghero. Several car-rental companies have offices here. For more information on flights, see the Getting There & Away chapter.

Bus Intercity buses terminate in and leave from Via Catalogna, by the Giardini Pubblici. You can buy tickets for ARST and FdS buses in a booth in the gardens.

A plethora of buses (ARST and FdS) run to/from Sassari and take 50 minutes to an hour depending on the route (€2.32 to €2.58). ARST runs up to eight buses to Porto Torres (€2.58, 55 minutes).

To Bosa there are four departures, although only two make the quicker, cheaper and more scenic coastal run (€2.85, 55 minutes).

Turmo Travel operates one direct bus to Olbia a day (€7.64, two hours).

Train The train station is situated 1.5km north of the old town on Via Don Minzoni. Up to 11 trains run to/from Sassari (€1.81, 35 minutes).

Car & Motorcycle The quickest route into Alghero from Sassari is via the new

---

Blood Red Gold

Since ancient times the predominantly red coral of the Mediterranean has beguiled and bewitched people. Many believed it to be the petrified blood of the Medusa, attributed to it aphrodisiac and other secret qualities and fashioned amulets out of it.

As early as the 14th century Italian fishermen from Torre del Greco, near Naples, were scouring the Mediterranean for coral to be fashioned into amulets and other objects. The coral was harvested using a sort of boom to simply scrape the seabed (and causing untold destruction in the process), a process which is no longer used; in fact, coral fishing is strictly licensed these days. The Alghero coast was another rich source of this 'red gold', so much so that the Crown of Aragon ordered that all coral boats operating between southern Italy and northern Sardinia must call in at Alghero. A red-coral branch had already been incorporated into the city's coat of arms.

Torre del Greco emerged in the 18th century as a world centre for the working of coral into extraordinary jewellery and sculpture. The raw material, fished around Alghero and elsewhere, mostly wound up in Torre del Greco but nowadays Alghero's own jewellers do a brisk trade themselves.

four-lane highway that connects with the north–south SS131 highway west of the provincial capital. From Porto Torres a similarly new route from the west side of the port town links up with this road. Otherwise you can take the slower but direct SS291.

Getting Around
Your own feet will be enough to get you around the old town and most other places, but you may want to jump on to a bus to get to the beaches.

To/From the Airport Six FdS buses a day run between Piazza della Mercede in Alghero and the airport. They take about 20 minutes and cost €0.57.

A taxi from the airport to central Alghero will cost around €12. If none are around try calling ☎ 079 93 50 35.

Bus Line AO runs from Via Cagliari (by the Giardini Pubblici) to the beaches. Urban buses also operate to Fertilia and several places beyond. You can pick up these buses at stops around the Giardini Pubblici. Tickets (€0.57) are available at Casa del Caffè and most *tabacchi* outlets.

Car & Motorcycle Although summer can get hectic, it is generally possible to find parking not too far from the old centre. Close to the centre (eg, the streets around the Giardini Pubblici) you'll have to pay parking attendants in the order of €0.50 an hour.

Local and international car-rental companies (such as Avis, Hertz and the big Italian company Maggiore) have booths at Fertilia airport. **Avis** *(Piazza Sulis 9)* also has a handy office in town. **Autonolotaxi Farris Carlo** *(☎ 079 95 18 74; Via Garibaldi 45/a)* offers a Fiat Panda for €145 for three days.

You can rent out motorbikes and scooters from several outlets. **Silvio Noleggio** *(☎ 079 98 72 43; Via Garibaldi 113)* has a Honda 600 for €60 a day. Scooters cost from €30 a day. Bicycles cost from €8 a day.

Cicloexpress *(☎ 079 98 69 50; Via Garibaldi)*, on the port side of the road, has bicycles and mountain bikes from €8 to €13 a day and road bikes for up to €75 a day.

Taxi You can find taxis *(☎ 079 97 53 96)* along Via Vittorio Emanuele.

SOUTH & EAST OF ALGHERO
Coast Road to Bosa
One of Sardinia's great scenic drives unfurls itself along the coast south of Alghero to Bosa, 46km away. Since they are both among the most engaging of Sardinia's coastal cities, this road trip (doable by bus) is a must.

The first 8km winds past a series of tiny coves, some blessed with patches of sand, that never attract more than a trickle of bathers. The only serious beach along this road is **Cala Speranza**, a narrow strip of sand below the chapel of the same name. It gets busy in summer, in part because of **Ristorante La Speranza** *(☎ 079 91 70 10; meals €30; open Thur-Tues, daily in summer)*, a popular seafood restaurant and beach bar.

The road twists and turns amid the coastal *macchia* in a desultory fashion for another 7km or 8km, at which point you gain altitude and see before you a magnificent stretch of rocky coastline. From here until the final stretch into Bosa the views are breathtaking, with several spots for photo-stops along the way.

Inland Road to Bosa
An alternative route south out of Alghero (which you could also use to reach Bosa) is the SS292 road via **Villanova Monteleone** (567m). After an initial quick stretch, the road winds up into the hills that lie back from Alghero's southern coast, revealing ever better views across the water to Capo Caccia as you gain height. The road then dips over a ridge into deep woods and takes you out of sight of the coast.

Villanova Monteleone was founded by refugees from Monteleone Rocca Doria when that town, under Genoese control, surrendered to the Crown of Aragon after a three-year siege in 1436. It is a high hill town that you might like to wander around briefly. Up to six FdS buses run here from Alghero (€1.45, 40 minutes).

From Villanova, the road drops into dry plains and skirts the artificial Lago del Temo, named after the river of the same name. Shortly after a turn-off north leads up to **Monteleone Rocca Doria**. This tiny settlement sits atop a sharp rise affording expansive views west over the lake and beyond. For three years, Nicolò Doria resisted a combined force from Alghero, Sassari and Bosa assembled to extirpate this nest of resistance to the Crown of Aragon. His fortress, the Rocca Doria, was dismantled and is now little more than a small fenced off patch of rubble. The few people living here (most scarpered to Villanova) have struggled ever since. So much so that in the 1950s they tried, unsuccessfully, to sell the whole village.

You then meander southeast. The first towns you encounter, such as Padria and Pozzomaggiore, are not enormously engaging, although the former does have a small archaeological museum. From here you could make east for Bonorva or northeast for Torralba (see Logudoro & Meilogu earlier in this chapter). One ARST bus (departure 2.05pm) runs as far as Pozzomaggiore from Alghero (€3.72, 1½ hours).

Otherwise, follow the SS292 south from Padria as it swings southwest towards Bosa (via Suni).

NORTH OF ALGHERO

The northwestern corner of the island, of which Alghero is the main city, is historically known as the Nurra. The area takes in Porto Torres and extends up to the Stintino peninsula.

Nuraghe di Palmavera & Necropoli di Anghelu Ruiu

The main excursion into this corner of Sardinia's ancient past is a two-stage operation.

Most interesting is the Nuraghe di Palmavera *(admission €2.10, with Necropoli di Anghelu Ruiu €3.60; open 9am-7pm daily Apr-Oct, 9.30am-4pm Nov-Mar)*, about 10km northwest of Alghero on the road to Porto Conte.

At the heart of this 3500-year-old nuraghic village stands a limestone tower and an elliptical building with a secondary sandstone tower that was added later. To access them enter a small courtyard from the east. The ruins of smaller towers and bastion walls surround the central edifice and beyond the walls are the packed remnants of circular dwellings, of which there may have been about 50 originally. From the air it looks like some divinity has lost his rag and scattered a bunch of stone curtain rings about the place.

The circular **Capanna delle Riunioni** (Meeting Hut) is the subject of considerable speculation. Its foundation wall is lined by a low stone bench, perhaps for a council of elders, and encloses, in the middle, a pedestal

topped by a model *nuraghe*. One theory suggests there was actually a cult to the nuraghes themselves.

Take the AF bus (€0.57, 15 to 20 minutes) from central Alghero (ask for one heading to Porto Conte, and get the driver to drop you off as near as possible to the site).

About 7km north of Alghero, just to the left (west) of the road to Porto Torres, lie scattered the ancient burial chambers of the Necropoli di Anghelu Ruiu *(admission €2.10, with Nuraghe di Palmavera €3.60; open 9am-7pm daily Apr-Oct, 9.30am-4pm Nov-Mar)*. You need your own vehicle to get here.

The tombs, 38 in all, of the necropolis date to between 2700 BC and 3300 BC. They are divided into two types, the more ancient ones with *a pozzetto* (well-shaped) entrances and an irregular disposition of individual chambers around it, and the later 'open passage' type. These feature a straight ramp leading down to the entrance, beyond which lies a series of chambers. A torch might be handy for peering into these nooks and crannies. In some of the chambers in these tombs, difficult to make out, are lightly sculpted bull's horns, perhaps the symbol of a funeral deity. Although curious enough, to those of us without a specific passion for ancient archaeology the site is only of passing interest. A half hour of scrabbling about and staring into the uninformative penumbra was enough for us.

Several other minor archaeological sites are scattered about the area north and northwest of Alghero. The tourist office can provide details.

Tenute Sella & Mosca

The name of the Anghelu Ruiu necropolis is sported by a fine dessert wine produced just 2km up the road by Sella & Mosca. This prestige wine producer is the best known on the island. You can pop into the immaculately maintained property to visit the **wine cellars** *(☎ 079 99 77 00; admission free; tour 5.30pm Mon-Sat mid-June–Sept)*. Around the low buildings and exquisite gardens spread 600ha of vineyards – which have been going since 1899. The cellar tour gives you some insight into old and modern production methods. You can always visit the **wineries** *(open 8.30am-8pm daily)* or *enoteca* to admire and perhaps purchase some wine.

Fertilia

This odd Fascist creation is an almost disturbingly quiet enclave. The rather bare, rationalist architecture of the 1930s lends it an unreal atmosphere, as do the references (such as street names) to Italy's northeast. The town, originally populated by farmers from around Ferrara, was designed to be the focal point of a land-reclamation programme throughout the Nurra. After the war, refugees arrived from Friuli-Venezia Giulia and adjacent territories lost to Tito's Yugoslavia, bringing with them the lion of St Mark, symbol of Venice. An appropriate statue now dominates the waterfront.

Fertilia evinces little more than fleeting curiosity in its visitors. The grand memorial to the noble farmer that graces the seaside end of Via Pola is a reminder of the town's founding raison d'etre.

A few kilometres west of Fertilia is the charming **Spiaggia delle Bombarde**. When coming from Alghero take the turn-off left (south) for Hotel dei Pini (before reaching the Nuraghe Palmavera). It is a favourite with locals, set amid lots of green, with a play area for kids back from the beach and views across to Alghero. If it's too crowded you could try the next one along, **Spiagga del Lazzaretto**. You'll find parking and bar-cafés at both.

Places to Stay & Eat Halfway between Fertilia and Alghero, **Camping Calik** (☎ 079 93 01 11, fax 079 93 05 95; per person €11.88; open June-Sept) backs on to the Stagno Calich lagoon. To reach a modest beach all you have to do is cross the road.

Camping Nurral (☎ 079 93 04 85, fax 079 93 06 46; per person €10.50; open year-round) is just on the north side of the crossroads as you head out of Fertilia on the road to Santa Maria La Palma. The main disadvantage of staying here is the camping ground's disco.

Hostal de l'Alguer (☎/fax 079 93 20 39; e hostalalguer@tiscalinet.it; Via Parenzo; B&B €13), one of the island's three youth hostels, is set at the western end of town (about a 500m walk from where the Alghero–Fertilia bus stops in Piazza Venezia Giulia), with rooms spread over a series of modern houses set in a dusty compound.

Hotel Bellavista (☎ 079 93 01 24, fax 079 93 01 90; Lungomare Rovigno 13; singles/doubles €51/93) is an ugly building on the seafront but rooms are reasonable and most have balconies looking out to sea.

Hotel Fertilia (☎ 079 93 00 89, fax 079 93 05 22; singles/doubles €62/75) is a couple of kilometres north of Fertilia on the road to Santa Maria la Palma. Rooms are generous and it's a leafy location.

Da Bruno (☎ 079 93 00 98; road to Santa Maria la Palma; meals €40; open Thur-Tues), located in the same spot as Hotel Fertilia, does some great seafood. Try the gnocchetti alla Bruno.

Acquario (☎ 079 93 02 39; Via Pola 34; meals €35; open Tues-Sun) is a popular seafood eatery right in Fertilia. It is just off the waterfront road about 50m east of Hotel Bellavista.

For heartier traditional Sardinian fare, seek out some of the agriturismi inland from Fertilia.

Barbagia (☎ 079 93 51 41; Regione Fighera, Podere 26; meals around €40) offers wonderful Sardinian cooking. From Fertilia, head north towards Santa Maria la Palma and take the second right after the intersection with the Alghero–Porto Conte road. It's about halfway along on the left (north) side of the road.

Sa Mandra (☎ 079 99 91 50; Regione Sa Segada, Podere 21; meals €30-35), about 2km north of Fertilia airport on the airport road, is another fine choice for meaty Sardinian cooking.

Getting There & Away The local AF bus from Alghero (€0.57, 15 minutes) runs every 40 minutes from 7.50am to 9.50pm. Up to 10 of these go on to Porto Conte and stop at the turn-off for Spiagge delle Bombarde.

Porto Conte

The signs to Porto Conte lead you along the southern flank of this broad bay past bobbing yachts, spruce gardens, discreet but costly residences and a trio of posh hotels. The road ends at a Catalano-Aragonese tower and lighthouse. The road to Capo Caccia actually leads you west around the expanse of the bay, along which there are several **beaches**, among them the one at the plush but clumsy-looking Hotel Baia di Conte.

Inland around Monte Timidone (561m) is the **Foresta Demaniale Porto Conte** (open 8am-4pm Mon-Sat, 9am-5pm Sun & holidays), also known as the Arca di Noé (Noah's

Ark) because of the variety of animals introduced here since the 1970s. They include deer, unique white donkeys from the Isola Asinara, little horses from the Giara region and wild boar. They get about in an area of 1200ha, made up largely of *macchia*, oaks and conifers. Griffon vultures and falcons fly its skies.

You can drive into the park area from the main road just south of the Hotel Baia di Conte and follow a restricted route. Walkers and cyclists have greater liberty.

The AF bus runs from Alghero to Porto Conte up to 10 times a day (€0.88, 30 minutes).

Capo Caccia & Grotta di Nettuno

The road down the east flank of the park skirts the waters of Porto Conte on its way to this impressive headland. Stop at the marked lookout point, from where you have a dramatic view to the sheer cliff walls of Capo Caccia and the wave-buffeted offshore island of Isola Foradada.

The end of the road is marked by the entrance to the Grotta di Nettuno (☎ 079 94 65 40; adult/child €8/4; open 9am-7pm Apr-Sept, 10am-5pm Oct, 9am-2pm Jan-Mar & Nov-Dec). You can't proceed to the lighthouse as it is on military land.

The grotto is an underground fairyland of stalactites and stalagmites. You are guided along 200m of path and stairs around the grotto. It has taken several million years for the stalactites and stalagmites to develop into all sorts of curious shapes, such as the organ, church dome (or warrior's head) and so on. Another longer path, closed to tourists, leads to seven little fresh-water lakes deep inside the cave system.

One FdS bus from Via Catalogna in Alghero (€3.25 return, 50 minutes) leaves daily at 9.15am (returning at midday) and a couple of extra services are put on from June to September. Once at the terminus, you have a walk down the several hundred steps, known as the **Escala del Cabirol** (Roe Deer's Stairway in Catalan), that hug the cliff walls down to the entrance of the grotto.

Traghetti Navisarda (☎ 079 95 06 03) runs several boats a day from April to October (on condition they have at least 20 passengers) and allow you a fish-eye view of the coast from Alghero to Capo Caccia before depositing you at the grotto. The

return-trip costs €10 (not including entry to the grotto) and takes about 2½ hours.

Warning In the case of bad weather, the grotto is closed. Ask at Alghero's tourist office if you are uncertain.

Torre del Porticciolo & Around

The road north of Porto Conte leads to a couple of lovely getaways. The first turn-off takes you to the coast at Torre del Porticciolo. A tower stands atop the northern promontory that protects this tiny natural harbour, backed by a small arc of a beach. High *macchia*-stained cliffs mount guard on the south side, and you can explore adjacent coves along narrow walking trails.

Shady **Campeggio Torre del Porticciolo** (☎ 079 91 90 07, fax 079 91 92 12; per person/car/tent space €12/5/3.50, 2-person bungalows from €78) is just a few steps from the beach and offers a restaurant, pool and shop. About 1km back towards the main road, you could also stay at **Agriturismo Porticciolo** (☎ 079 91 80 00; w www.agriturismoporticciolo.it, Italian only). In low season a little apartment can cost €30 a day but in summer (June to September) they are frequently rented out on a weekly basis for €627. You should at least try to eat in the grand dining area, made welcoming with its heavy timber ceiling and huge fireplace. The food is excellent – you can opt for a set of *antipasti*, followed by a Sardinian pasta (such as *ravioli di ricotta*) and meat favourites like *porceddu* or *agnello* (lamb). Book ahead.

Six kilometres north of Torre del Porticciolo is one of the island's longest stretches of wild sandy beach, **Porto Ferro**. Waves often crash in from the west, attracting the occasional surfer. In summer a snack bar sets up just back from the beach. To get there, take the Porto Ferro turn-off and, before reaching the end of the road (which is where the bus from Alghero stops), take a right (follow the 'Bar Porto Ferro' signs). The summer bus from Alghero (€1.45, 35 to 65 minutes depending on route and traffic) runs three times a day.

Da Gino (☎ 079 99 91 38; meals €30), 2km west of Santa Maria la Palma on the SS291 to Sassari, is a fine *agriturismo* where you can eat good local food. Call ahead.

From Porto Ferro a series of back roads lead about 6km around to **Lago Baratz**, the island's only natural lake. You can walk down to the marshy edge of the lake from the road that sidles up against its southwestern flank. Surrounded by low hills, the lake attracts some birdlife, although the winged fellows tend to hang about the less-accessible north side. A 3km dirt track connects the lake with the northern tip of Porto Ferro beach.

A few kilometres farther east tipplers might visit the **Cantina Sociale di Santa Maria la Palma** (☎ 079 99 90 44; open 8am-1pm & 3.30pm-8pm daily June-Sept, 7.30am-1pm & 2.30pm-5.30pm Mon-Fri Oct-May) in the eponymous village. It is the Nurra's second winery after the grand Sella & Mosca spread. You can mosey around the *enoteca* (winestore) and may be taken on a tour of the winery.

Argentiera

Huddled up back from a pebble beach stand the crumbling, haunting ruins of this one-time silver-mining town. The Romans first started extraction here and the Sardinians finally abandoned the activity in the 1960s. Since then the area has been left to sink into decay. Almost. In more recent years people from Sassari and around have started to restore houses and a handful reside here year-round. In summer the settlement is served by a small general store, bar and restaurant.

Directly in front of the mining ruins is the aforementioned beach, and there's another broader strand a few metres farther around to the north.

From Lago Baratz it's 13km to **Palmadula**. From there the road unfurls 5.5km to the west, amid spectacular coastline. The sunsets here can be wonderful. Shortly before reaching the town you pass a caravan park and another fine beach. The occasional bus runs here from Sassari.

STINTINO & ISOLA ASINARA

The northwestern tip of Sardinia, once the preserve of a small coterie of fishing families, has become a minor beach resort. Frequently whipped by the *maestrale*, the prevailing wind from the northwest, the undulating countryside has an empty, even desolate feel. Little farming is done, although throughout the northern Nurra you will see cattle grazing.

Once at the top of the narrow peninsula, the main attractions are Spiaggia della Pelosa's limpid waters and the wild clifftops of Capo Falcone. Over the strait, the Isola Asinara, long a penitentiary, is slowly being developed as a protected park. A couple of small beaches and the unique white donkeys from which it takes its name tempt people across.

Stintino

postcode 07040 • pop 1230

Gathered around two inlets that make natural harbours, a tight community of about 1000 lives in Stintino. Many are descended from the 45 families forcibly removed from Isola Asinara in 1882, when the state decided to turn the island into a prison and quarantine station. Stintino developed a reputation for its tuna hunt, a bloody annual event known as the *mattanza* (slaughter).

Although the Sassaresi had discovered the beauties of Stintino's beaches as early as the 1930s, tourism in the modern sense only began to make inroads in the 1960s.

Arriving from the south, you pass **Spiaggia Le Saline** and, inland, the **Stagno Casaraccio**, a big lagoon where you might just see flamingos at rest.

The pleasant enough town of Stintino is wedged between its two harbours, the main Porto Mannu and the smaller Porto Minori on the south side of the promontory. Up the middle between them runs Via Sassari.

The **tourist office** (☎ 079 52 37 88; Via Sassari 77; open 9.30am-1pm & 5pm-8pm Mon-Sun June-Sept, 9.30am-1pm Mon-Sat Oct-May) has information on accommodation and boat excursions. Stintino is the place to get onto tours to Isola Asinara (see later).

Museo della Tonnara Just south of Stintino, the town's fishermen long made their living by the annual *mattanza*, the trapping and killing of vast quantities of tuna that from April to June would course down the Golfo di Asinara during the mating season.

The bloody scenes of their capture and slaughter are captured on film in this museum (adult/child €2/1; open 10am-1pm & 6pm-9pm Mon-Sun June-Sept) on Porto Mannu. The six rooms are ordered as the six chambers of the *tonnara* (the net in which the fish are caught) and in documents, seafaring memorabilia, photos and film recall this centuries-old trade. The *tonnara* here was shut down in 1974, although locals attempted to revive them briefly in the late 1990s for scientific purposes. It still takes place in Carloforte and Portoscuso, in the south, as well as a couple of spots in Sicily. For more on the *mattanza*, see the Southwest Sardinia chapter.

Just on the south side of Porto Mannu is a tiny beach, and that about wraps it up for Stintino.

Spiaggia della Pelosa & Capo del Falcone Continuing up the coast, the hotels, holiday residences and restaurants fill in the gaps between the town of Stintino and the northern tip of the peninsula. People stream up for Spiaggia della Pelosa, a beautiful strip of fine white sand and shallow turquoise waters facing a Catalano-Aragonese watch tower placed on a lonely offshore islet. Unfortunately, the beach is not quite what it used to be as storms in 2002 carried off a good wodge of sand. But the water remains amazing.

In front of you lie the bare Isola Piana and, behind it, the expanse of Isola Asinara (see later). A moderately fit swimmer can easily reach Isola Piana.

An hourly summer bus service runs from Spiaggia Le Saline via Stintino to Spiaggia della Pelosa and Capo del Falcone. If driving you must pay an attendant (up to €4.50 for half a day) to park around Spiaggia della Pelosa.

Some lucky chaps have built their holiday residences on the craggy reaches of Capo Falcone, at the northern tip of the peninsula. You can walk around to the cliffs and the sunset can be awesome.

Places to Stay & Eat There are three hotels in Stintino town and another dozen, mostly medium to upper range, dotted along the coast.

Albergo Lina (☎ 079 52 30 71, fax 079 52 31 92; Via Lepanto 38; doubles €72; open year-round), just in front of Porto Minori, has simple rooms with their own bathroom.

Albergo Geranio Rosso (☎ 079 52 32 92, fax 079 52 32 93; Via XXI Aprile 4; singles/doubles €70/105, half board per person €80) is an immaculately kept place two streets back from Porto Minori. Rooms are comfortable and have air-con.

Albergo Silvestrino (☎ 079 52 30 07, fax 079 52 34 73; Via Sassari 14; singles/doubles

€64.50/111, half board per person €95) is another perfectly decent choice on the main street. Rooms are a good size, light and decorated with intriguing paintings.

All three hotels have their own restaurants. The one at Albergo Silvestrino is quite good.

Le Delizie della Nonna (Via Sassari 67) does great *panini* and other takeaway gourmet snacks.

Ristorante Da Antonio (☎ 079 53 70 77; Via Marco Polo 16; meals €30-35; open daily) is a bright family-run place just off Porto Minori. The strong points are fish and local vegetables.

Ristorante L'Ancora (☎ 079 527 90 09; meals €35; open daily June-Sept) has a charming veranda with magnificent sea views where you can indulge in good seafood. It's not obvious from the main road – turn right into the Ancora residential complex and follow the signs.

Ristorante Valentina (☎ 079 52 00 80; meals €30-35; open daily June-Sept) is a similar deal a little farther south from L'Ancora. With the views it offers good meat dishes, even a Chateaubriand (€18).

Getting There & Away Up to eight buses run from Sassari to Stintino and Spiaggia della Pelosa in summer (€3.15, one hour 10 minutes). As many as six run from Porto Torres (€2.01, 30 minutes).

Isola Piana

There is nothing much to this flat and featureless island. However, if you are around at the right time you may catch the traditional migration of cows in early winter and late spring to/from the island Piana. The cows, tied one after the other, swim across from north of Spiaggia della Pelosa.

Isola Asinara

Known to the ancients as the Isle of Hercules, this rather bare island's modern name comes from the unique white donkeys *(asini)* that stroll about it. Now a national park, the island was from the end of the 19th century until the mid-1990s a maximum-security prison and quarantine station.

The island has been the object of some controversy. The Justice Ministry has still not ceded all its land to the regional government and competing private interests want to build villas and even tourist complexes in spite of its national park status. Much remains to be done to get the park properly up and running.

A couple of beaches are off limits, including **Cala Sant'Andrea**, which is a breeding ground for turtles.

You can book the return trip for an excursion around the island from either Porto Torres (€21.56) or Stintino (€14.20). There are two departures a day from Stintino (9am and 3pm) and one from Porto Torres (9am). Add other standard charges of €7.45 per head. The return trip departs at 7.30pm.

Once debarked at the southern end of the island at Porticciolo Fornelli you will take a bus (€6.60) along the island to **Cala d'Oliva** beach in the northeast. From there you can hire bicycles (€5.80) or join a 4WD tour (€27).

If you opt for the afternoon trip from Stintino, you will be taken on a guided hike about one quarter of the way up the island via a ruined castle (the Castellaccio) and back.

Bring your own lunch as there is nowhere on the island to buy anything. Tickets are available at **Agenzia La Nassa** (☎ 079 52 00 60; Via Sassari 6) in Stintino and the tourist office in Porto Torres, or you can book by calling a toll-free phone number (☎ 800 56 11 66) or online at W www.parcoasinara.it.

Boat cruises around the island generally include lunch on board and swimming at a beach. **Stintours** (☎ 079 52 31 60; W www .stintours.com, Italian only; Via C Colombo, Stintino), for instance, has old-fashioned boats hoisting the traditional *vela latina* (triangular sail). It costs €55 a head (minimum of six).

BOSA
postcode 08013 • pop 7856
Bosa lies within the fat finger of Nuoro province that slips its way to the west coast between Sassari and Oristano provinces. The only important Sardinian town on a river, Bosa is a pretty stop that combines the curiosity of the medieval town and its monuments with the broad sandy beach nearby. Watching over it all are the ruins of the medieval Castello Malaspina.

History
There may have been a settlement near modern Bosa as early as the 11th century BC and certainly a Roman town thrived on the banks of the Temo river. By the early 12th century the Malaspina family (a branch of the Tuscan clan of the same name) had moved in and built their castle, below which the townspeople huddled in feudal vassalage. The town prospered on the back of fishing, farming and trade. For a while Bosa was used by the Giudicato d'Arborea as a base against the Catalano-Aragonese, under whom it later declined despite its status as city under direct rule of the Crown. Things looked up under the House of Savoy as coral fishing, tanning, lacework and the production of gold and silver jewellery all took off. Modernity put an end to the lucky streak: cut off from the island's main transport links, Bosa sunk into gloomy depression by the end of the 19th century and today sets much store by tourism.

Orientation & Information
Bosa is about 3km inland on the north bank of the Temo. To the east the castle walls dominate the town. Sa Costa, the old town, is like a tight plaster web stretched around the west face of the hill. Below it, Corso Vittorio Emanuele, the main boulevard, runs east to west, taking in the Cattedrale and Piazza Costituzione before running into the straggly grid of the modern town.

From the Cattedrale, the charming Ponte Vecchio spans the river, on whose southern bank are lined up the former tanneries. Via Nazionale runs west 3km to Bosa Marina, the town's seaside satellite.

Tourist Offices The **Pro Loco** (☎ 0785 37 61 07; cnr Via Alberto Azuni & Via F Romagna; open 9.30am-1pm & 6pm-8.30pm daily May-Sept), the main tourist office, is seconded by another **tourist office** (☎ 0785 37 71 08; W www.infobosa.it, Italian only; open 10am-1pm & 7pm-10pm daily June-Sept) in Bosa Marina train station.

Money You can change money and extract cash from the ATM at the **Banco di Sardegna** (Piazza IV Novembre).

Post & Communications There's a **post office** (Via G A Pischedda; open 8.15am-1.15pm Mon-Sat) located in town.

Web Copy (☎ 0785 37 20 49, fax 0785 37 21 91; Via Gioberti 12; open 9am-1pm &

SASSARI & THE NORTHWEST

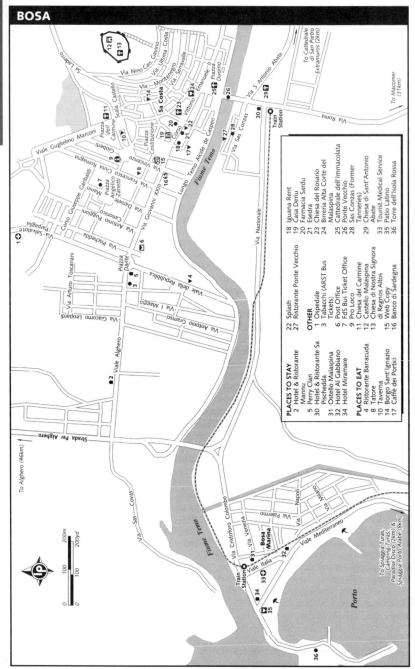

BOSA

PLACES TO STAY
2   Hotel & Ristorante Mannu
5   Perry Clan
30 Hotel & Ristorante Sa Pischedda
31 Ostello Malaspina
32 Hotel Al Gabbiano
34 Hotel Miramare

PLACES TO EAT
4   Ristorante Barracuda
8   Tatore
10 Taverna
14 Borgo Sant'Ignazio
17 Caffè dei Portici
22 Splash
27 Ristorante Ponte Vecchio

OTHER
1   Ospedale
3   Tabacchi (ARST Bus Tickets)
6   Post Office
7   FdS Bus Ticket Office
9   Pro Loco
11 Chiesa del Carmine
12 Castello Malaspina
13 Chiesa di Nostra Signora di Regnos Altos
15 Web Copy
16 Banco di Sardegna
18 Iguana Rent
19 Casa Deriu
20 Farmacia Sardu
21 Esedra
23 Chiesa del Rosario
24 Birreria Alta Corte del Malaspina
25 Cattedrale dell'Immacolata
26 Ponte Vecchio
28 Sas Conzas (Former Tanneries)
29 Chiesa di Sant'Antonio Abate
33 Tourist Medical Service
35 Patio Latino
36 Torre dell'Isola Rossa

6pm-10pm Mon-Sat) has six fast computers you can surf for €6 an hour.

Medical Services The unwell can try the local **Ospedale** *(☎ 0785 37 31 07; Via Salvatore Parpaglia)* or a **tourist medical service** *(☎ 0785 37 46 15; Viale Italia)* just off the beach at Bosa Marina. **Farmacia Sardu** *(Corso Vittorio Emanuele 51)* is a handy pharmacy for medication.

Things to See & Do

The walls and towers of the **Castello Malaspina** *(closed at the time of writing)*, also known as the Castello di Serravalle, still dominate the town despite having seen much better days. Inside is the humble-looking castle chapel, the **Chiesa di Nostra Signora di Regnos Altos**, which houses an extraordinary and anonymous 14th-century fresco cycle, a veritable who's who of famous saints ranging from a giant St Christopher through a party of Franciscans to St Lawrence in the middle of his martyrdom on the grill.

You can get here by virtually any route climbing up through the maze of lanes in **Sa Costa** (the old core of town). Most of the houses are a mongrel mix and in sorry condition after long years of neglect. They share as a common feature an opening onto two streets, one much steeper than the other.

At the bottom of the hill, the **Cattedrale del'Immacolata** *(Piazza del Duomo)* is a rare if not overly riveting example of rococo (officially called Piedmontese baroque), the result of a late-18th-century makeover of the original 16th-century church. From it the main boulevard, Corso Vittorio Emanuele, leads west past elegant 17th-century houses lent a certain Aragonese *je ne sais quoi* by their airy wrought-iron balconies.

On the same street, the **Chiesa del Rosario** is known above all for the unsightly clock that juts out into the street from its whitewashed facade.

Casa Deriu *(Corso Vittorio Emanuele 59; open 10am-1pm & 7pm-11pm Tues-Sun)* is a grand mansion that today doubles as a museum with a mixed vocation. The main (2nd) floor is a charming remake of a 19th-century interior. On the 1st floor you can see a display on the old tanning business that took place across the river, as well as

typical products from the surrounding region. The top floor is dedicated to Melkiorre Melis (1889–1982), an important exponent of the applied arts in Italy.

At the northern end of the old town, the **Chiesa del Carmine**, located on the square of the same name, is from the same period as the cathedral.

Fishing boats still tie up on the palm-lined Temo river in the shadow of the **Ponte Vecchio**. Across it line up the former 18th-century tanneries known as **Sas Conzas**, which were still in business shortly after WWII and are now a heritage site. One or two restaurants operate in them in summer.

To the left of the Ponte Vecchio is the little **Chiesa di Sant'Antonio Abate**, focus of a town festival dedicated to the saint on 16–17 January and again at Carnevale time.

Two kilometres upstream is the isolated former **Cattedrale di San Pietro Extramuros** *(open 10am-7pm daily)*, with its Gothic facade (look at the detail above the central doorway) and largely Romanesque interior.

After all the exploration you will find it hard to resist the fine golden sand of Bosa Marina's broad beach. It can get pretty full in summer. Wind-surfers like this spot and it is possible to hire gear on the beach. A couple of diving outfits operate here too.

The squat Catalano-Aragonese **Torre dell'-Isola Rossa** (watch tower) stands watch over the mouth of the Temo and beach. Occasionally temporary exhibitions are held here.

Those interested in making excursions or doing some trekking in the area around Bosa could approach **Esedra** *(☎ 0785 37 42 56; Corso Vittorio Emanuele 64)*. They also sell Isola handicrafts.

Special Events

Bosa's **Carnevale** kicks off with a burning pyre outside the Chiesa di Sant'Antonio Abate and follows with all sorts of parades in the succeeding days. The last day, *martedì grasso*, is the most intriguing. The morning funereal lament for the end of the Carnevale is followed in the evening by the search for the *giolzi*, symbol of carnival and sex, by groups of boisterous locals dressed in white. It's not clear what happens if they find it, nor indeed just what it is!

For four days around the first Sunday of August Bosa celebrates the **Festa di Santa**

Maria del Mare. Fishermen form a colourful procession of boats to accompany a figure of the Virgin Mary along the river from Bosa Marina to the Cattedrale.

In the second week of September folk celebrate the **Festa di Nostra Signora di Regnos Altos**. The old-town streets are bedecked with huge palm fronds, flowers and *altarittos* (votive altars).

Places to Stay

A handful of hotels in Bosa are complemented by another half dozen down the track at Bosa Marina. They are open year-round.

Camping Turas (☎ *0785 35 92 70, fax 0785 37 35 44; per person €8.80, bungalows €50-73)* is the nearest camping option, about 1.5km south of Bosa Marina and just back from the beach in Località Turas. It's shady if fairly basic.

Ostello Malaspina (☎/fax *0785 37 50 09; Via Sardegna 1; B&B per person €11.05)* is a pleasant option on a quiet shady street in Bosa Marina, a quick walk from the beach. Meals cost €8.

Perry Clan (☎ *0785 37 30 65, fax 0785 37 70 54; Viale Alghero, cnr Piazza Dante; singles/ doubles €25.80/41.30)*, set on the road into central Bosa, is a no-nonsense stop. Rooms come with own bath, TV and phone and it's cheap.

Hotel Mannu (☎ *0785 37 53 06, fax 0785 37 53 08; Viale Alghero; singles/doubles €42/ 62)* is not substantially different, although rooms do have air-con and are a little classier.

Hotel Sa Pischedda (☎ *0785 37 30 65, fax 0785 37 70 54; Via Roma 2; singles/doubles €47/52)* is easily the most attractive choice in town. The wine-red facade of this restored house greets you just on the south side of the Ponte Vecchio. The rooms are a little spare but some have arched balconies out the back. It is the only place in Bosa that can be said to have character.

Hotel Miramare (☎/fax *0785 37 34 00; Via Colombo; singles/doubles €42/52)* is virtually on the beach. Rooms are clean and simple, with TV and own bathroom.

Hotel Al Gabbiano (☎ *0785 37 41 23, fax 0785 37 41 09; Viale Mediterraneo; singles/ doubles €54/72, half board per person €77)* looks bland enough from the outside but the rooms, most with balconies looking out to sea, are kept spick and span.

Places to Eat

Caffè del Portici (*Piazza Costituzione 4)* is a great spot for breakfast – sit down with a paper at one of the tables in this grand square.

Taverna (*Piazza del Carmine)* invites you to stop for a *panino* in the shade.

Tatore (☎ *0785 37 31 04; Via Giuseppe Mannu 13; meals €25-30)* dishes up whatever its owners find in the fish markets that day. Hardly surprisingly the seafood pasta is good, as is the *zuppa di pesce* (fish soup).

Borgo Sant'Ignazio (☎ *0785 37 46 62; Via Sant'Ignazio 33; meals €24; open Tues-Sun)* hides amid the web of lanes in the heart of the old town. The tastefully decorated dining area provides an enticing setting for typical Sardinian dishes.

Ristorante Sa Pischedda (☎ *0785 37 30 65; Via Roma 2; pizzas up to €8, meals €25)*, out the back of the hotel on Via Nazionale, has pleasant indoor dining area and a pergola for summer. Its strong point is pizza.

Ristorante Ponte Vecchio (☎ *0785 37 52 18; Lungo Temo Emilio Scherer; meals €30-35; open daily June-Sept)* has a delightful seating arrangement right on the river with views across to the north side of Bosa and the Ponte Vecchio. The pasta is good, as are some of the fresh fish options. Other seafood mains are not so great.

Ristorante Barracuda (☎ *0785 37 45 10; Viale della Repubblica; meals €25-30)* seems like a suburban house and is indeed a family operation. The emphasis is on seafood.

Ristorante Mannu (☎ *0785 37 53 06; Viale Alghero; meals €30-35)* has a reputation as one of Bosa's best. The location ain't nothing wonderful but the range of traditional Sardinian and standard Italian dishes is good.

Splash (*Corso Vittorio Emanuele 62)* invites you to slurp on a gelato for a *passeggiata* after you've finished your meal.

Down in Porto Alabe, look out for **Ristorante Lizu'e Rena** (☎ *0785 35 93 24; meals €25-30; open Mon-Sat)* on the beach. The menu offers a reasonable spread of seafood and meat dishes and the quality is high.

Entertainment

In Bosa itself, you could start the evening with a few quiet ones at **Birreria Alla Corte del Malaspina** (*Corso Vittorio Emanuele 39)*, one of a couple of café-bars with tables out in street. The cafés on Piazza Costituzione are also pleasant for an evening tipple. While in Bosa try the Malvasia, a heavy, sticky dessert wine.

The summer nocturnal action takes place on the beaches at Bosa Marina and beyond. Several beach bars operate along Bosa Marina's strand. For dancing you will most likely wind up at the **Patio Latino** at the northern end. It pumps out Latin rhythms until the wee hours. Seaside club music is also on hand at **Paradise**, about 2km down the coast road in Località Turas. Most elect to dance outside, but on chillier evenings there's an internal dance floor too.

Getting There & Away

Bus All buses terminate at Piazza Zanetti. Most services are run by FdS, which has a ticket office on the square. Up to four buses run to/from Alghero. The quicker ones take the scenic coastal route (€2.89, 55 minutes). As many as nine run to/from Macomer (€2.01, 50 minutes). Sassari is a long haul (€5.84, 2¼ hours), with several intermediate stops. Some ARST buses also run to/from Bosa, with services to Oristano for example.

Train In July and August a *trenino verde* service connects Bosa Marina with Macomer on Saturdays. The train leaves Macomer at 9.30am but the return trip is by bus at 2.05pm (€8.50 one way, 1¾ hours). Macomer is in turn connected by a year-round train service to Nuoro.

Car & Motorcycle Parking on the beach front can cost €0.50 an hour or €3 a day, although you can probably find space in side streets. In central Bosa parking is a little way out of the old town.

You can rent mountain bikes (€7 for 24 hours) and 50cc scooters (€25 for 24 hours) at **Iguana Rent** (☎ 339 833 94 10; Piazza Costituzione 2).

Getting Around

Up to 21 daily FdS buses run from central Bosa (Piazza Zanetti) to Bosa Marina (€0.62, 10 minutes).

AROUND BOSA
The Coast

The only problem with Bosa Marina's beach is that it gets crowded in summer. If you want fewer people and, in exchange, accept less sand, there are options. Stretching south are **Spiaggia Turas**, **Spiaggia Porto Alabe** and **Cala Torre Columbargia**. The first two are respectively a 1.5km and 8km drive from Bosa Marina and can get busy in high season too. The last of them is reached from Tresnuraghes and involves some dusty trail driving. It's about 18km from Bosa Marina.

Macomer
postcode 08015 • pop 11,110

A quick drive through mostly flat country brings you 31km west to Macomer. Scene of the last stand by the Sardinians against the Catalano-Aragonese in 1478 and once a Roman military base, the modern agricultural town of Macomer offers little to the modern transient but a modest **Museo Etnografico** (☎ 0785 7 04 75; Corso Umberto 225), where you can see typical furnishings and utensils from the farming and small-town world set in a mid-19th century house. If you are dependent on public transport, you could easily end up here, as Macomer is a rail and bus junction.

Near the town, *nuraghe*-buffs have a couple of options. **Nuraghe di Santa Barbara**, an impressive 15m-high structure with several towers and defensive walls, stands just north of the SS131 about 2km north of Macomer. Not far off and on the other side of the highway is the more ruinous **Nuraghe Ruiu**. Finally the **Nuraghe di Santa Sabina** is south of Silanus and 15km east of Macomer. It has a cute neighbour in the form of a Byzantine chapel.

Three fairly ordinary hotels make it possible to sleep over if you get caught between connections.

Hotel Su Talleri (☎/fax 0785 7 14 91; Via Cavour; singles/doubles €26/42) is probably the best and is marginally the cheapest. Rooms with own bathroom, TV and air-con are reached by an odd external spiral staircase. It is just off Corso Umberto and a stone's throw from the museum.

Ristorante Su Talleri (☎ 0785 7 16 99; Corso Umberto I 228; meals €30; open Mon-Sat) does a great version of *ravioli di ricotta* (ravioli filled with ricotta cheese) and some fine grilled meats. It has the feel of an anonymous roadside diner but you'll have no argument with the grub.

Macomer is a junction town situated on the SS131 highway. Up to 12 Trenitalia trains travel to Macomer from Oristano; six of them originate from Cagliari (1¾ to 2½ hours depending on the train). Five leave from Sassari (1½ to 1¾ hours). A handful of FdS trains and up to four buses make the journey between Macomer and Nuoro (1¼ hours).

The Trenitalia and FdS train stations, along with the *autostazione* are handily located together around the appropriately named Piazza Due Stazioni at the western edge of town along Corso Umberto.

Olbia & the Gallura

They say the chichi Costa Smeralda, the granite Gallura coast, the magical Arcipelago di La Maddalena and a handful of ancient monuments attract up to 80% of all Sardinia's tourism to this northeastern corner of the island. It sure seems so when you drive around here in summer!

The hilly green Gallura region is bordered off to the west by the Coghinas River and to the south roughly by the Monte Limbara and a line of hills stretching east to Olbia. Along with the undeniably beautiful beaches and coves of the Costa Smeralda, some of the wilder northern beaches are also a big draw (this is good windsurfing territory). The rolling countryside, dotted in parts by *stazzi* (farmsteads) and hiding a series of curious ancient reminders of Sardinia's nuraghic past, is among the prettiest on the island. The Arcipelago di La Maddalena should not be missed and while around here you could even hop across to Corsica.

Gallurese cooking has its quirks, including *suppa quata* (or *cuata*). This is a casserole made of layers of thick bread, cheese and a mixed meat ragout all drenched in broth and baked to obtain a crispy crust. Look out for some fine Vermentino white wines too.

For many the Costa Smeralda and surrounding area *is* Sardinia. The beauty and interest of the Gallura are undeniable but it would be a shame to devote all your time to this, the most touristed part of the island. Plenty of great beaches, countryside, ancient sites and engaging cities lie beyond.

OLBIA
postcode 07026 • pop 43,820

Take a miserable malaria-riddled town huddled back from the sea amid mosquito-infested swamps; drain said swamps, add tourism, port and airport and voilà: you have Olbia. Now a sprawling city characterised by that dusty, half-finished feel that so often accompanies fast-buck tourist development in the Mediterranean, Olbia offers little but a convenient way in and out of Sardinia.

To be fair, it does have some points in its favour: a couple of minor monuments and above all the sensation that you are in a 'real' working town. Hotels and restaurants open year-round. With planes, trains, buses and

Highlights

- Join an island-hopping excursion around the Maddalena Archipelago
- Clamber all over the granite seascapes of Capo Testa
- Take a boat to the dramatic Isola Tavolara
- Search out the fine coves of the Costa Smeralda
- Discover the little-visited ancient sites, like the Coddu Ecchju *tomba dei giganti*, inland from Arzachena
- Head up cool Monte Limbara for the views

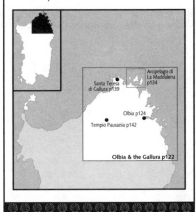

boats all converging on it, you may well find Olbia makes a convenient overnight stop. Much more would be overdoing it.

History

Little light has been shed on Olbia's past but it was almost certainly founded by the Carthaginians. A natural port set back inside the deep Golfo di Olbia, the town was an important port of call in Roman times – a dozen or so relics of Roman vessels were unearthed near the port in the 1990s. Known as Terranova, the town seems to have muddled along in the Middle Ages but declined under Catalano-Aragonese and later Spanish rule. Not until the arrival of the highways and railway in the 19th century did the town show signs of life again. The surrounding area was slowly drained and turned over to agriculture and even some light industry. The port cranked back to life. Since the 1960s Olbia has boomed. The major bridgehead for the mainland, Olbia has continued to expand rapidly and with little regard for good taste.

With a major airport, port facilities and a big chunk of the island's tourist industry a mere jaunt up the coast on the Costa Smeralda, Olbia is pushing to have a new province created around it. Most (if not all) of the territory would be carved away from Sassari, the largest province in Italy, and many feel it is only a matter of time.

Orientation

The waters of the Golfo di Olbia carve a deep wound into the northeastern Sardinian coast,

creating an ideal situation for a port. The heart of the town stretches west from that port. Boats dock at the Stazione Marittima, at the end of a narrow lick of land jutting 2km into the gulf.

The town's main drag, Corso Umberto I, runs from the waterfront inland about 1km to the train and bus stations. On its way it passes the central interlocking squares of Piazza della Regina Margherita and Piazza Matteotti. The town fathers have seen fit to pipe pop music through loudspeakers up and down the street and in the squares all day long. One wonders if this is supposed to put locals and visitors into a summer holiday mood, although the inescapable dulcet tones of Laura Pausini and Eros Ramazzotti might have the opposite effect on some.

The web of narrow streets to either side of Corso Umberto I constitute what might be called the 'old town' although nothing much dates to more than a century ago. The bulk of the hotels, restaurants and bars are crowded into this small area.

Information
Tourist Office The **AAST tourist office** (☎ 0789 2 14 53, fax 0789 2 22 21; Via Catello Piro 1; open 8am-1pm & 3.30pm-7pm Mon-Sat, 8.30am-12.30pm & 5pm-7pm Sun June-Sept, 8am-1pm Mon-Sat Oct-May) is located just off the port end of Corso Umberto I.

Money You can change money at the **Banca di Sassari** (Corso Umberto I 3) and **Banco di Sardegna** (Corso Umberto I 142). The former represents Western Union.

Post & Communications The nearest **post office** (Viale Aldo Moro; open 8am-1pm Mon-Fri, 8am-12.30pm Sat) to central Olbia is on the corner of Via Amedeo, north of the hospital.

Medical Services There is a **hospital** (☎ 0789 55 22 00; Viale Aldo Moro) in town. In an emergency you can call ☎ 0789 55 22 01 or ☎ 0789 55 24 41 for a night doctor.

Things to See & Do
A stroll along the Corso and side streets, culminating in a drink at either Caffè Mary or Caffè Cosimino on Piazza della Regina Margherita, is an agreeable way to kill an hour or two. You'll notice the occasional vaguely Liberty (Art Nouveau) style building from the early 20th century but that's about it.

Just off Corso Umberto I is the **Chiesa di San Paolo**, a curious granite church with a pretty Valencian-style tiled dome (added after WWII) raised in 1747. It appears a Punic and then Roman temple stood on the same site.

To leap centuries back into the city's history, head past the train station and track down the **Chiesa di San Simplicio** (Via San Simplicio; open 9am-1pm & 4pm-7pm), a Romanesque jewel set aside from the town hubbub. Built entirely of granite, it is a curious mix of Tuscan and Lombard styles.

Places to Stay
With more than a dozen hotels, Olbia could well be a haven if you have nothing booked in the surrounding area.

Hotel Minerva (☎/fax 0789 2 11 90; Via Mazzini 7; singles/doubles €33.50/51.60) is the cheapest deal in town, right in the midst of the narrow lanes of 'old' Olbia. Rooms are basic and on weekends the streets can be rowdy.

Hotel Terranova (☎ 0789 2 23 95, fax 0789 2 72 55; Via Garibaldi 6; singles/doubles €67/98) is nearby. Rooms come with aircon, phone and TV and most have balconies over the narrow cobbled lane below. You're just a spit from your morning coffee on Piazza della Regina Margherita.

Hotel Gallura (☎ 0789 2 46 48, fax 0789 2 46 29; Corso Umberto I 145; B&B singles/doubles €56.80/82.60) is Olbia's touch of faded elegance. Rooms are a little fusty but nicely decorated in an antique sort of way.

Hotel Cavour (☎ 0789 20 40 33, fax 0789 20 10 96; Ⓦ www.cavourhotel.it; Via Cavour 22; B&B singles/doubles €62/87.50) has nicely appointed rooms behind double-glazed windows (handy in this part of town) in a stylishly renovated building. It has parking too.

Hotel President (☎ 0789 2 75 01, fax 0789 2 15 51; Via Principe Umberto 9; B&B singles/doubles €60.90/104), something of a minor colossus, is Olbia's grand old dame. She's faded around the edges but some of the rooms look out over the ferry landing (at least they would if the entire area were not in a state of chaos due to unending roadworks!).

Hotel Martini (☎ 0789 2 60 66, fax 0789 2 64 18; Ⓔ hmartini@tin.it; Via Gabriele D'Annunzio 2; B&B singles/doubles €87/137) is the town's top establishment, housed in a hulk of a building overlooking the rather grand-sounding Porto Romano, in fact a small fishing harbour.

B&B Lu Aldareddu (☎ 0789 6 85 79; Ⓦ http://web.tiscali.it/lualdareddu; Località Monte Plebi; doubles €90) is a classy and relaxing alternative about 10km north of the town centre on a low olive-tree covered hill. The 18th-century house has been nicely restored and the proprietors put on courses of anything from cooking through photography to pottery. From here you are within reasonable cycling distance of the Costa Smeralda's finest beaches.

Places to Eat
The best spot for breakfast is Piazza della Regina Margherita, where two historic cafés

offer spacious surroundings and ample shady terraces. **Caffè May** and **Caffè Cosimino** are next door to one another and either is just the ticket for a cappuccino, pastry and a read of the paper.

Olbia is blessed with any number of eateries and not all of them cater slavishly to floods of tourists. Most close on Sunday.

Ristorante Gallura (☎ 0789 2 46 48; Corso Umberto I 145; meals €30-35), in the hotel of the same name, has a reputation for fine seafood and homemade pasta. Booking ahead is essential and neat casual dress advised, as this restaurant has quite a name. It is also a rather romantic outing.

Zhanto (☎ 0789 2 26 45; Via delle Terme 1b; meals €25-30) is like a welcoming family home. The garden is a bonus and the food

is good. Try the *ravioli di mazzancolle* (ravioli stuffed with king prawns).

Ristorante da Paolo (☎ 0789 2 16 75; Via Cavour 22; meals €25-30; closed lunch Sun) offers several variations on that favourite Sardinian theme, horsemeat. Gobble it up in the cosy atmosphere created by the exposed stone walls and timber ceilings.

Hostaria Sa Fenisi (☎ 0789 2 78 25; Piazza Matteotti; meals €25), with its timber beams and long brick arches (and summer dining on the square too), is a welcoming spot for a mix of seafood and meat dishes.

Barbagia (☎ 0789 5 1 64 02; Via Galvani; meals €30), out of the centre, is one of the best spots in Olbia to get a taste of the traditional Sardinian cuisine of the interior. All sorts of odd names in Sardinian, which no

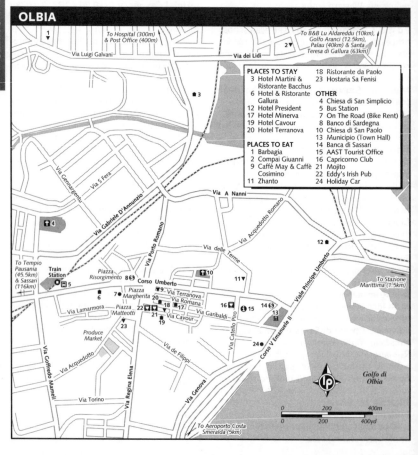

OLBIA

PLACES TO STAY	18 Ristorante da Paolo
3 Hotel Martini & Ristorante Bacchus	23 Hostaria Sa Fenisi
6 Hotel & Ristorante Gallura	**OTHER**
12 Hotel President	4 Chiesa di San Simplicio
17 Hotel Minerva	5 Bus Station
19 Hotel Cavour	7 On The Road (Bike Rent)
20 Hotel Terranova	8 Banco di Sardegna
	10 Chiesa di San Paolo
PLACES TO EAT	13 Municipio (Town Hall)
1 Barbagia	14 Banca di Sassari
2 Compai Giuanni	15 AAST Tourist Office
9 Caffè May & Caffè Cosimino	16 Capricorno Club
	21 Mojito
11 Zhanto	22 Eddy's Irish Pub
	24 Holiday Car

amount of Italian will help you recognise, pop out of the menu at you.

Compai Giuanni (*☎ 0789 5 85 84; Via dei Lidi 15; meals €25*) is also a hike from the centre and an unlikely looking spot. If you want to try splendid fish and seafood soups or the Gallurese speciality, *suppa quata*, this is your place.

Ristorante Bacchus (*☎ 0789 2 16 12; Centro Martini, Via Gabriele D'Annunzio 2; meals €35*) is Olbia's senior restaurant. Try for a seat overlooking Porto Romano. It does a mix of local and standard Italian fare and desserts to die for.

Entertainment

Not too many people hang about in Olbia for fun, especially not in summer, when anyone who is anyone heads directly up the coast to the Costa Smeralda and most of the rest of us to points beyond.

Still, Corso Umberto I, cut off to traffic from 7pm, becomes an ebullient scene for the *passeggiata*, with pizzerie, gelaterie and bars all setting up tables outside and punters packing in for food and drink. At the lower port end of the boulevard, marketers add a little more colour with their stands of knick-knacks.

If you are in town of an evening, especially out of season, amble along to **Eddy's Irish Pub** (*Via Cavour 3*) for the rather extraordinary combination of the Black Stuff and Mexican food. Across the nameless lane at **Mojito** (*Piazza della Regina Margherita*) you can try hard to pretend you're in Latin America.

For a little local dance fun, toddle along to **Capricorno Club** (*☎ 0789 2 31 09; Via Catello Piro 4*), the local disco that opens from October to May.

Getting There & Away

Air Olbia's **Aeroporto di Costa Smeralda** (*☎ 0789 6 90 00*) is about 5km southeast of the centre. For information on flights and air fares, see the Air section in the Getting There & Away chapter.

Bus The intercity *autostazione* (bus station) is on Corso Umberto I. For tickets head to the ticket window at the train station next door.

ARST has buses to destinations all over the island, including: Arzachena (€1.76, up

to 11 a day); Golfo Aranci (€1.19, eight a day, summer only) and Porto Cervo (€2.58, up to five a day). Further afield you can get to Dorgali (€6.30, three a day), Nuoro (€6.30; up to seven a day), Santa Teresa di Gallura (€3.72, up to six a day) and Sassari (€5.84, two a day Monday to Saturday) via Tempio Pausania (€2.89).

Turmo Travel (*☎ 0789 2 14 87*) has a daily bus (except Sunday) from Cagliari. It arrives in Piazza Crispi. Another daily bus operates to/from Alghero (€7.64, two hours) – it arrives in Corso Umberto I in front of the Municipio building. **FdS** has a morning bus from Sassari to the port (Monday to Saturday). **Sunlines** (*☎ 348 260 98 81*) has several daily runs between Porto Torres and Olbia (including port and airport). Similarly, it runs buses from Palau and down the Costa Smeralda to Olbia.

Train The Trenitalia station lies parallel to Via Gabriele D'Annunzio – walk through the bus station.

One direct train a day runs to Cagliari (€12.95, four hours). Otherwise you have to change at Chilivani (and sometimes Macomer as well!) and wait for a connection. Up to three trains run to Sassari (€5.60, one hour 50 minutes) and up to seven to Golfo Aranci (€1.75, 25 minutes).

Car & Motorcycle All the big international rental outfits are represented at the airport. Some local ones are also dotted about town. **Holiday Car** (*☎ 0789 2 84 96; Via Genova 71*) will rent you a Fiat Panda from €35 a day in high season, or a Fiat Punto for €40. This includes 150km and insurance. If you rent for more than three days the price comes down (€31 a day for three to six days) and you get unlimited kilometres.

To rent scooters up to 150cc or mountain bikes, try **On The Road** (*☎ 0789 20 60 42; Via Sassari 8*).

Boat Regular ferries arrive in Olbia from Civitavecchia and Livorno. For more details see the Getting There & Away chapter.

Getting Around

You are unlikely to need local buses, except for getting to the airport and the Stazione Marittima. Buy tickets at tobacconists and some bars.

OLBIA & THE GALLURA

To/From the Airport Bus No 2 (€0.55) runs every half hour from 7.30am to 8pm from the airport to the town centre (Corso Umberto I). A **taxi** (☎ 0789 6 91 50) will cost about €12.

Several buses for destinations around the island leave direct from the airport. Among them is a service for Nuoro run by **Deplano** (☎ 0784 29 50 30), which operates five times a day from June to September.

Bus A handful of bus routes operate around Olbia but the only ones of interest to visitors are those running to/from the airport (see earlier) and the port. The latter, No 3 (€0.55), can be picked up in Via Genova and Via Principe Umberto for the short trip to the Stazione Marittima.

Car & Motorcycle Entering the heart of town (Corso Umberto I and around) is forbidden from 7pm to 2am. To park in the centre in the blue parking spaces you must purchase a one-hour parking ticket (€0.62) from certain bars (listed under the P signs around town). Scratch in the appropriate day and arrival time and leave on the dash.

Taxi You can sometimes find taxis (☎ 0789 2 27 18) at the rank on Corso Umberto I near Piazza della Regina Margherita.

SOUTH COAST
The coast south of Olbia is a busy stretch with a handful of beaches that attract locals and a sprinkling of Italian holiday-makers. The settlements, until you reach San Teodoro about 25km south, are largely uninspiring but some of the coast is well worth exploring. Looming offshore is Isola Tavolara, which can be reached by boat excursion from several locations, most conveniently from Porto San Paolo.

The first beach of any note is **Lido del Sole**, busy with locals (catch bus No 5). Just beyond the last promontory of this part of Sassari province, **Capo Ceraso** juts out. The views north across the Golfo di Olbia from the cape are great but you'll have do a little yomping to enjoy them as cars can't make it too far in.

Porto San Paolo & Isola Tavolara
Another winding 6km brings you to the tidy holiday residence of Porto San Paolo. Turn east off the main road to enter the settlement proper, a quiet cluster of modest bougainvillea-embraced holiday houses.

The main reason for stopping in is to join an excursion to Isola Tavolara. Several boats ferry people out at least hourly from 9.30am (€10, 25 minutes) from the little port at Porto San Paolo. You cannot fail to be impressed by the rock walls at either end of this island. Facing Porto San Paolo they rise 565m. Once you arrive, seek out one of the beaches. The best is **Spiaggia Spalmatore**, which is where most boats land. Aside from snacking at a couple of beachside eateries, there is nothing much to do but splash about in the translucent water, admire the incredible view of Tavolara's heights (and across to Sardinia) or, alternatively, your navel. Several return services start around midday.

You could also opt for a tour that would take you around the island, the neighbouring island of **Molara** and possibly also **Capo Coda di Cavallo** (Cape Horsetail), a promontory on the mainland south of Molara. Expect to pay up to €30 – you should get some swimming time on either Tavolara or Molara.

Back in Porto San Paolo, you probably won't have any desire to stay (and could do so only in a rather pricey hotel). You might still want to hang about for a nice seaside meal at **Il Portolano** (☎ 0789 4 06 70; Via Molara 11; meals €35), a charming spot for seafood (few meat dishes make it onto the menu). Bare stone walls and soft music complete the pretty picture.

San Teodoro
postcode 08020 • pop 3500
A sprint down the SS125 brings you to what has become a summer hot spot in recent years. Young Italians have taken San Teodoro (in Nuoro province) by storm. It's a pleasant town with no real sights but some good beaches and an accessible feel. Add a small sprinkling of bars and clubs and you have a winning combination.

On your way down, you pass the aforementioned **Capo Coda di Cavallo**, a low promontory from whose tip you have great views up the coast and to the Tavolara and Molara Islands.

Past the beaches of **Porto Brandichini** you arrive in San Teodoro following the banks of a major lagoon, the **Stagno di San**

Teodoro. It is home to a lot of birdlife and if your luck's in you may see pink flamingos wading about.

On the seaward side stretches an uncommonly long and broad strand, **Spiaggia della Cinta**. It finishes where the village begins. San Teodoro has its own little beach too, **Cala d'Ambra**, about half a kilometre downhill from the centre.

Places to Stay & Eat Of the three camping grounds in and around town, the more attractive choice is **Camping Cala d'Ambra** (☎ 0784 86 56 50; per person/tent space €11/6.20; open June-Sept), 300m back from the seaside.

Hotel L'Esagono (☎ 0784 86 57 83, fax 0784 86 60 40; Via Cala d'Ambra; doubles up to €77, half board per person €93; open Apr-Oct) is also down by the sea in the same spot. A series of single-storey buildings, it makes a nice place to sleep, although the nearby disco can make shuteye problematic on some summer nights. It also has a restaurant.

Other hotels are scattered back inland, but most close out of season. **Le Mimose** (☎ 0784 86 51 39, fax 0784 86 57 97; Via Nazionale; singles/doubles €75/103) is one of the few exceptions. The rooms are comfortable enough if unexceptional and the hotel has its own pool and tennis court.

Apart from lying about on the beaches, the main activity is nocturnal. On and around the main street, Largo E Lussu, you will find a series of noisy pizzerias that double as music bars (the live efforts can be strained), as well as some quieter restaurants.

Gallo Blu (☎ 0784 86 60 41; Via degli Afodeli; meals €25-30) tends to concentrate more on seafood, with reasonable results.

At Puntaldìa, a tiny spot on the Punta Sabbatino promontory just north of the Stagno di San Teodoro (and about 8km from San Teodoro itself), **Il Covo** (☎ 0784 86 30 43; meals €35-40; open Apr-Sept) is a fine feeding choice for fresh seafood. Try the *insalata di aragoste* (lobster salad).

Entertainment Once loaded up with food, people promenade and the more excitable ones step out. Along Largo E Lussu are several bars with terraces, including **Birreria In Bocca al Luppolo**. These start closing around 2am, at which point a couple of clubs kick in. Local opinion suggests that **L'Ambra Night**,

virtually in front of Hotel L'Esagono, is the best, but a couple of others also operate in summer (sometimes August only). **Ripping** is a popular summer dance spot at the southern exit from town.

Getting There & Away As many as seven ARST buses stop en route between Olbia (€2.58, 40 minutes) and Nuoro (€6.30, one hour).

South of San Teodoro

Heading farther south, the coast remains flat and comparatively dull, although beaches are not in short supply. Perhaps the nicest is the shallow **Cala di Budoni**, a spacious strip near the sprawling holiday centre of the same name. Beyond, the SS125 heads towards Posada and the spectacular Golfo di Orosei (see the Nuoro & the East chapter).

GOLFO ARANCI TO COSTA SMERALDA

North of Olbia lies another port town, Golfo Aranci, quieter than its busier cousin. The next promontory up marks the beginning of a remarkable slice of the island, the Costa Smeralda (Emerald Coast). Playground of the rich and famous (less-prominent persons manage to filter in, wallets permitting), it features a handful of fine beaches, twee but on the whole not entirely tasteless resort development, expensive yachts and one or two options for staying without going bankrupt. It's definitely worth a look around although you may not be inclined to stay long.

Golfo Aranci

postcode 07020 • pop 1950

The busy coast road streaming northeast out of Olbia takes you past several popular beaches, such as **Pittulongu** and the more pleasant **Sos Aranzos**, which lies about 7km short of Golf Aranci. It is signposted to the right (east), but you must take the first left as soon as you leave the main road or you'll miss your mark. It is a quiet strip with good views across to Golfo Aranci and Isola Tavolara.

Golfo Aranci, a one time fishing village that since the 1880s has also served as a port connecting with the mainland, is an odd place. Via della Libertà, the main drag, winds and curls its way endlessly past houses, shops and the occasional restaurant and hotel to end up finally in the 'centre', that is the final few hundred metres of town and the port. Behind the port rise the craggy heights of **Capo Figari** (340m), converted into a minor nature reserve. The cape stands in counterpoint to the sheer cliffs of Isola Tavolara, eminently visible across the gulf to the south. Coquettishly placed just off the coast is the Isola di Figarolo islet.

There's little incentive to search out Golfo Aranci but it could be your first port of call if you arrive in Sardinia from Civitavecchia, Fiumicino or Livorno. If that is the case, the town has several acceptable beaches should you not feel sufficiently energetic to move straight on.

Places to Stay & Eat
Hotel La Lampara *(☎/fax 0789 61 51 40; Via Magellano; doubles up to €98)*, just off Via della Libertà, is about the handiest and one of the more economical of the town's half dozen hotels. Rooms are simple but will do the trick.

A string of restaurants on or near Via della Libertà keep hunger at bay. Those closer to the port have a grittier look but can be quite good for seafood. Try **Ristorante Miramare** *(☎ 0789 4 60 85; Piazzetta del Porto 2; meals €25)*.

Getting There & Away
Regular buses (€1.19, 30 minutes; up to eight a day in summer) and trains (€1.75, 25 minutes, seven daily) link Golfo Aranci with Olbia. For information on boats between Golfo Aranci and mainland Italy, see the Getting There & Away chapter.

Porto Rotondo
Porto Rotondo is just that, a round port. To anyone coming from Sydney or San Francisco it might look like a miniature version of a posh harbourside suburb. Light pastel shaded villas fill up the land rising back from the port, in which are ranged boats of varying dimensions, all bobbing up and down in moneyed contentment.

Around the central Piazzetta San Marco are scattered priceless boutiques, the occasional gelateria and bar. All perfectly pleasant if somewhat akin to a leafy mall. Apart from a quick wander around, there's not much reason for nonresidents to pop in. There certainly isn't any room at the inn for people without strong dollar reserves. Prime

Minister and media magnate Silvio Berlusconi has a huge villa set in ample grounds, La Certosa, around here.

Bright young things crowd into **Mantra** *(Piazzetta Rudargia; open Tues-Sat)* on summer nights. Dance floor fun (mostly house) can be mixed with sushi or pasta and entry costs a mere €40.

As if in defiance of all the displays of wealth here and on the Costa Smeralda, a highly strategic camping ground has been placed. **Villaggio Camping La Cugnana** *(☎ 0789 3 31 84, fax 0789 3 33 98; w www.campingcugnana.it; Località Cugnana; 2 people & car €33.60, 2-person bungalows per week €511.30; open May-Sept)* is on the road running along the southern side of Golfo di Cugnana, between Porto Rotondo and the north–south road leading to Porto Cervo. It has a supermarket, backs onto the sea and, perhaps best of all, puts on a free shuttle bus to some of the better Costa Smeralda beaches, including Capriccioli, Liscia Ruia and Spiaggia del Principe (see later). Book ahead for bungalows. Prices come down by half in May, June and September.

Cala di Volpe & Around
The Costa Smeralda really begins on the Golfo di Cugnana at Cala di Petra Ruja and takes in the Capo Ferro headland to the north before swinging around to Liscia di Vacca – in all 55km of coast and about 8000ha.

From Villaggio Camping Cugnana continue 1.5km west and then turn north (right) at the junction. This coast road north takes you towards the heart of the Costa Smeralda. Beach bums will be chuffed around here. Keep your eyes peeled for a turn-off to **Spiaggia Liscia Ruia**, shortly before reaching the grand Moorish fantasy that is the Hotel Cala di Volpe, with its private beach, marina and endless luxury. Past the hotel, you will see signs for **Capriccioli**, another splendid choice of beach with crystalline water and a pleasant setting.

A further sign leads you to Romazzino. One of the best beaches around here is **Spiagga del Principe** (aka Portu Li Coggi). To find it, turn right at Via degli Asfodeli before reaching Hotel Romazzino. You'll soon have to follow the example of others and park your vehicle (unless you've come with the shuttle bus from the Cugnana camping ground) before the barrier. From there it's about a

10-minute walk to a beach with limpid water and little development to spoil the backdrop. **Spiaggia Romazzino**, easier to find, is also fine.

There's nowhere much for anyone (except for the rich and famous) to stay or eat around here, so bring a sandwich.

Porto Cervo

Some of the villas facing onto the hushed but wealthy port seem based on sets for Star Wars desert town scenes. The oddly rounded, pseudo-Moroccan fantasy feel they exude clearly owes more to imagination than reality!

Still, with the kind of money floating around here, why not? In early July 2002 the New York Yacht Club's commodore, Charles Dana III, came to town to sign a joint training deal with the Aga Khan's Costa Smeralda Yacht Club. They have even touted possible team efforts for future America's Cup challenges.

When you look past the yachts, fancy villas, impossibly expensive hotels, swimming pools, tennis courts and carefully studied if unconvincing architecture, what you have is a shopping mall and stage for the international jet set.

The heart of 'town' is the Piazzetta, graced by a couple of restaurants and surrounded by a warren of discreet shopping alleys. Stairs lead down to the Sottoportico della Piazzetta, where the theme continues. During the day the place is dead as a doornail. From about 8pm the playboys and playgirls of the Western world come out to cavort in the bars and eateries, do a little shopping, see and be seen. And that is basically it.

The beautiful people hang around in several bars. The portside **Lord Nelson Pub** attracts a yachty brigade for cocktails. After 11pm they crank up the music a little. **La Regata**, also by the marina, keeps the drinks coming until about 2am.

The real action happens a few kilometres south of Porto Cervo in a grouping of the Costa Smeralda's most exclusive clubs. **Sopravento** (☎ 0789 9 47 17; Località Abbiadori) and, across the road, **Sottovento** (☎ 0789 9 24 43; Località Abbiadori) are strictly for the money or, at least, the look. The not always so charming door people will decide whether you have what it takes.

Just before this pair and on the same road, the macro disco **Billionaire** (☎ 0789 9 41 92; Località Alto Pevero) joined the scene in 1999. Anybody who's anybody, and then

---

The Aga Khan's Dreamworld

Karim Aga Khan IV (born 1937) is the Imam of the Ismaili Muslims, a community spread across 25 countries. He's not short of a quid either and when he landed up along the northeastern coast of Sardinia in his early 20s he decided to buy some of it. And so in 1961 he and some moneyed chums signed the founding act of the Consorzio (Consortium) della Costa Smeralda (the name was cooked up at the same time) after acquiring the land from struggling farmers. The plan was to build an exclusive luxury resort and within three years the first hotels were operating. Thus tourism was kicked off in Sardinia at the top end of the market.

Strict rules governed taste and contributed to the artificial yet not displeasing jet-set resort: the introduction of non-native plants was prohibited, all electricity cables and water conduits had to be laid underground, no street advertising was allowed and buildings had to be in keeping with the surroundings. The whole was conceived as a kind of ideal Mediterranean village cocktail.

In 1963 the Aga Khan also founded Alisarda, the first airline to connect Sardinia with the mainland. In 1964 it transported 186 passengers. Four years later more than 20,000 climbed aboard and in 1991 the airline, by now an important European player, changed its name to Meridiana.

Although now surrounded by tourist resorts catering to all classes, the Costa Smeralda remains strictly for the well-to-do and retains a distinctive aura. Each summer Italian celebs are joined by an international brigade of beautiful people. Mere mortals make day trips to the beaches and wander into Porto Cervo to marvel at the luxury yachts and the cost of a coke (€5 in case you were wondering).

The Aga Khan still comes each year, although he no longer runs the place. The present owners, Starwood Hotels, planned to sell the lot for €350 million to a Sardinian-Venetian consortium in December 2002, which plans to sink in €1 billion in new hotels and services over the following 15 years.

some, can crowd into this place – thousands do. Let's hope you haven't lost too much on the stock market, as entry is a mere €50.

Getting There & Away Twice a day (except Sunday) the **Deluca bus company** (☎ 0789 5 00 87) has two daily buses to Porto Cervo from Olbia. They leave Piazza Crispi in Olbia at 9am and 1pm and take half an hour. The service runs from mid-June to mid-September. Otherwise, **ARST** has up to five connections, which make more stops and take anything from one to 1½ hours (€2.58).

Baia Sardinia

From Porto Cervo the coast road swings north then west 4.5km to Baia Sardinia, whose attraction is its main beach, **Cala Battistoni**. The shades of blue are remarkable and its popularity wholly understandable but it is jammed solid in mid-summer. The resort is heavy handed, with plenty of holiday complexes overlooking the bay, clearly not in the same spirit as the Costa Smeralda.

L'Approdo (☎ 0789 9 90 60; meals €25-30) is a cheery, glassed-in eatery on the beach. Offerings range from pizza to seafood. A few kilometres south of Baia Sardinia on the road to Cannigione you'll see the **Ristorante Grazia Deledda** (☎ 0789 9 89 90; meals €30-35). This once-proud holder of a Michelin star may have come down a little over the years but you can still eat decent Sardinian fare here.

The bright young things start strutting their evening stuff at **News Café** in the town's little square. Another popular drinks hang-out facing the beach is **Barracuda**. Once suitably revved up it's time for the club, of which they have several choices. **Ritual** (☎ 0789 99 90 32) is just out of town on the way to Porto Cervo. **Mokambo** (☎ 0789 99 86 17), in the nearby Località Tilzitta, is another big dance spot with a garden. You may be treated to a little fashion show or art expo too.

From Olbia, the Deluca bus service to Porto Cervo continues 15 minutes to Baia Sardinia.

Cannigione

Anyone from the New World will think they have turned up in the 'burbs. Cannigione has decent but unexciting beaches and is a rather dull place. Unobtrusive villas, little shops

and the occasional café make up the sum total of the business.

One of the more popular nocturnal hangouts for Costa Smeralda VIPs is **Reggae Bar** (☎ 0789 8 63 86), a few kilometres north up the road opposite the Villaggio Isuledda holiday village. From there a narrow coast road winds north to Palau (see later).

ARZACHENA & AROUND
Arzachena
postcode 07021 • pop 10,150

Arzachena sits well behind the front lines of coastal tourism and serves as a springboard to some inland treasures: a series of mysterious nuraghic ruins and two *tomba de gigantic* (giants' tombs) – the most impressive of such sites in Sardinia.

The **AAST** (☎ 0789 8 26 24; Viale Paolo Dettori 43; open 8am-2pm & 2.30pm-6.30pm Mon-Fri, 8am-2pm Sat), on the road leading south out of town, can help with accommodation lists but otherwise is a little ropey.

The town is devoid of interest save for the bizarre **Mont'Incappiddatu**, a mushroom-shaped granite rock at the end of Via Limbara, a quick stroll from the central Piazza del Risorgimento. Archaeologists believe the over-arching rock may have found use as a shelter for Neolithic tribes people as long ago as 3500 BC. You can almost see them huddling here with their spears and pots on a miserable rainy day. 'If you think I'm going out hunting in this bloody weather...'

Places to Stay & Eat The tourist office has a long list of apartments available for short-term lets and *affittacamere* (private houses that rent out rooms) in and around Arzachena. It also has accommodation lists for the coast.

In Arzachena itself there are four hotels. Probably the best bet if you don't have unlimited euros at your disposal is **Casa Mia** (☎ 0789 8 27 90, fax 0789 8 32 91; Viale Costa Smeralda; singles/doubles €67/115; half board per person €83), which has perfectly good rooms with TV, phone and aircon. It also has a reasonable restaurant, of which there are not too many in town.

Getting There & Away ARST runs regular buses to Porto Cervo via Baia Sardinia and intermediate stops. More than 10 buses arrive from Olbia and several north from

Santa Teresa di Gallura and Palau. Occasional services run to/from Castelsardo, Sassari and Nuoro.

In summer the *trenino verde* between Palau and Tempio Pausania passes through here. See Palau later.

Arzachena's Ancient Sites

What really makes Arzachena interesting lies in the countryside around it. Nuraghes and *tomba dei giganti* litter the countryside. Five sites in particular monopolise the interest of visitors, lay people and experts alike.

You can actually walk to some of them from central Arzachena, although to reach all of them would become quite an undertaking. You really need wheels to see them all comfortably in a long morning's gadding about.

Since 2000 the town authorities have attempted to inject a little order into things and you now pay to visit the sites, run by a group called **Lithos** (☎ 0789 8 15 37). Each site costs €2, or you can enter two/three/four/all five of the sites for €3.50/5/7/8.50. It is possible to join guided tours, sometimes with English and French-speaking guides. The sites open from 9am to 8pm daily June to September. There is also talk of opening some of them in the off season. Tickets for one or more are available at all sights, and you can purchase literature on them at information centres at the **Malchittu** and **Coddu Ecchju** (also known as Coddu Vecchiu) sites.

Nuraghe di Albucciu & Malchittu Just 3km east of Arzachena and just off the road to Olbia the Nuraghe di Albucciu is curious for several reasons. It is built partly into the natural granite on the site and has a vaguely rectangular form. To the right of the entrance is an elliptical chamber covered not with the 'tholos' style roof more readily associated with nuraghic towers but more simply a flat slab of granite. Beyond, a tunnel seems to have served as an emergency escape route. Opposite is another chamber in the shape of a brief corridor while yet another corridor leads right (south) to the biggest room, where several people could have slept. Half way along the corridor stairs lead up to the terrace on the next level.

Some 2km farther on by a walking track, past the information office, is the temple of Malchittu. Shaped like an elongated zero, the temple dating to 1500 BC is made up of a principal chamber, accessed by an atrium. It is one of only a few temples of its kind in Sardinia but the experts can only guess at its true uses. It appears it had a timber roof and was closed with a wooden door, as was Nuraghe di Albucciu. From this relatively high point fellows who gathered to do whatever it was they did had extensive views over the surrounding territory.

Coddu Ecchju The *tomba dei giganti* of Coddu Ecchju is one of the most important of its kind. The most visible part of it is the two-part, oval-shaped central stele. Both slabs of granite, one balanced on top of the other, show an engraved frame that apparently symbolises a false door, passageway to the hereafter impenetrable to the living. At the base is a small entrance to the long-covered tomb behind. You'll be aching to peer through and see what's on the other side. The answer is not much. On either side of the stele stand further slabs of granite, forming a kind of guard of honour, arranged in vaguely semicircular form, in front of the tomb itself. The site is one of the most important of its kind in Sardinia.

If you don't want to pay to get in, you can see the set-up, albeit not close up, from the roadside. If you follow the road south for a little less than a kilometre and turn left down a dirt track, you'll see on your right the **Nuraghe di Capichera**, closed for restoration and partly covered by vegetation.

To get to this site take the Arzachena–Luogosanto road south out of Arzachena and follow the signs.

Li Muri & Li Lolghi From Coddu Ecchju return to the Arzachena–Luogosanto road and turn left (west) for Luogosanto. After about 3km you take a right (signposted) for Li Muri and Li Lolghi. After 2km (partly of dirt trail) you reach a junction.

The left fork leads uphill along another dirt track 2km to the necropolis of Li Muri. This curious site is made up of four interlocking megalithic circular burial grounds, possibly dating to 3500 BC. Archaeologists believe that VIPs were buried in the rectangular tombs, made simply of stone slabs and a stone cover. At the rim of each circle was a menhir or betyl, an erect stone upon which a divinity may have been represented. The rings of stone may have been designed to keep in hills of earth that may have covered the tombs. Interesting parallels have been drawn between this site and others in Corsica and elsewhere in the Mediterranean.

Back down at the junction, the right fork (asphalt) takes you about 1km to the entrance to Li Lolghi, another *tomba dei giganti*, similar to that of Coddu Eccju. The central east-facing stele, part of which was snapped off and later restored, dominates the surrounding countryside from its hilltop location.

From there you can continue 2km north to reach a road that will take you east back to Arzachena.

Palau
postcode 07020 • pop 3400

Palau is a strange animal, living from a mix of tourism (ie, people passing to and from Isola della Maddalena) and the NATO presence in the islands of the Arcipelago di La Maddalena. While not wholly objectionable, the town itself has little to offer.

If you need information on the town or the surrounding area, including the Arcipelago di La Maddalena , try the **tourist office** (☎ 0789 70 95 70; Via Nazionale 96; open 8am-1pm & 4pm-8pm Mon-Sat, 8.30am-1.30pm & 5pm-8pm Sun). These hours are reduced October to May. Go online at **Web Time** (Via Fonte Vecchia 52; open 9am-9pm daily June-Sept), above Il Grillo bar near the little pleasure boat port, for around €5 an hour.

About 3km west on the road to the resort of Porto Rafael stands the late-19th-century **Fortezza di Monte Altura** (☎ 329 224 43 78; admission €2.50; open 9am-noon & 5pm-8pm June-Aug, 9am-noon & 3pm-6pm Apr-May, 9am-noon & 3pm-5pm Sept-Oct). Join a guided visit (40 minutes) in Italian to tour this position, built to help defend the north coast and Arcipelago di La Maddalena from invasion, something it was not ever called on to do.

The **Roccia dell'Orso** is a strange weather-beaten sculpture cut into the granite on a high point 6km east of Palau. Known to ancient navigators and mentioned by Ptolemy, Bear Rock looks a little less bear-like up close but you can see how the name came about. The views from here are fabulous. The occasional local bus trundles out this way from Palau.

A fleet of tour operators offers boat excursions to various of the Maddalena islands.

Trips, usually taking in several stops with time to swim on well-known beaches, cost in the region of €30 a person. Ask at the tourist office.

Places to Stay & Eat If you get stuck for a place to stay, you could try here, as the town has quite a few hotels and a couple of camping options.

Camping Acapulco (☎ 0789 70 94 03; per person €14.50; open Apr-Sept), about 500m west of the centre of Palau on the coast near Punta Palau, is in an attractive spot not far from a decent beach just the other side of the trickle that is the Rio Surrau.

Albergo Serra (☎ 0789 70 97 13, fax 0789 70 97 13; Via Nazionale 17; singles/doubles €31/44) is a basic affair on the main drag just up from the port. Rooms come with own bath and TV and it's the cheapest deal in town.

Hotel La Roccia (☎ 0789 70 95 28, fax 0789 70 71 55; Via dei Mille 15; singles/doubles €70/105) has a dominating position high up in the town, and the views from some of the balconies are not bad at all. The rooms are decent, with bath, telephone, TV and air-con.

Ristorante Da Franco (☎ 0789 70 95 58; Via Capo d'Orso 1; meals €25-30) is a warm, inviting spot with brick walls and timber ceiling.

Ristorante Da Robertino (☎ 0789 70 96 10; Via Nazionale 18; meals €30) makes a big deal of its lobster, which you can see served up with great ceremony. If you opt for the deep boiled sea critter, expect a fatter bill.

La Taverna (☎ 0789 70 92 89; Via Rossini 6; meals €25) is a cosy side-street dining option. Pop in for some *risotto marinaro* (seafood risotto) at €10.

Several interesting options line the SS133 west of town. At the **Agriturismo Lu Palazzeddu** (☎ 0789 70 40 28; Ponte Liscia; set meals €23.25), about 6km out of Palau, you can sit down to a reasonable set meal in a rustic roadside situation.

There is no shortage of little bars to indulge in a post-dinner drink. Many are overrun by US servicemen and their families, which lends the town a surreal air.

Getting There & Away Boat, trains and buses get you in and out of Palau.

Bus There are **ARST** buses connecting Palau with destinations around the north and east coast, including Olbia, the Costa Smeralda, Santa Teresa di Gallura and Castelsardo.

Caramelli buses run frequently to nearby destinations like Isola dei Gabbiani and Capo d'Orso. All buses leave from the port.

Train The **Trenino Verde** (☎ 079 24 57 40; w www.treninoverde.com) is an olde worlde train (sometimes of the steam variety) that runs from Palau twice daily to Tempio Pausania (€13 return, 1¾ hours) from mid-June to mid-September. It is a slow ride along a narrow-gauge line through some great countryside – bring some snacks because there is no onboard service. Trains leave from a station in the port.

Boat Several companies have regular car ferries to Isola della Maddalena. **Tris** (Traghetti Isole Sarde; ☎ 199 76 76 76, 0789 70 84 84) has runs from 7.10am to 10.20pm. The 20-minute crossing costs €2. A small car costs €5.50. **Saremar** (☎ 199 12 31 99, 0789 70 92 70) and **Tremar** (☎ 0789 73 00 32) also operate regular services. The latter has an hourly service late at night until dawn. Ticket prices are similar on all vessels.

Tris has occasional vessels running between Genoa, Savona and La Spezia on the northern Italian mainland and Porto Vecchio (in Corsica) via Palau. It also runs fast boats between Palau, Genoa and Porto Vecchio. There is also a service to Naples. See the Getting There & Away chapter for more details.

Porto Pollo & Isola dei Gabbiani

Seven kilometres west of Palau, windsurfers converge on Porto Pollo (also known as Portu Puddu) for what are considered some of the best conditions for this sport on the island.

You can hire gear and get lessons at several places. **Paolo Silvestri**, right on the Isola dei Gabbiani headland that separates Porto Pollo from the next bay, Porto Liscia, rents out full kit for €16. A one-hour lesson costs €35. If sailing is more your thing, **Sporting Club Sardinia** (☎ 0789 70 40 01) offers courses at various levels. Five 80-minute lessons for beginners cost €170.50.

The narrow isthmus separating Porto Pollo from Porto Liscia ends in a rounded promontory called Isola dei Gabbiani. It is largely occupied by **Camping Isola dei**

Gabbiani (☎ 0789 70 40 19, fax 0789 70 40 77; w www.isoladeigabbiani.it; per person €15.50), which also offers caravan and bungalow accommodation. A bungalow for two in high season costs €76 a day. But you are obliged to book it for two weeks!

Buses on the Palau–Santa Teresa di Gallura route can stop off at the road junction, from where you have to walk about 2km.

ARCIPELAGO DI LA MADDALENA

The seven main islands and more than 40 islets that constitute this archipelago form the Parco Nazionale dell'Arcipelago di La Maddalena (declared in 1996 and including several small islands to the south). The islands are in fact the high points of a valley that once joined Sardinia and Corsica in one landmass. When the two split, waters filled the strait now called the Bocche di Bonifacio. The *maestrale* (northwest) winds that prevail here have over centuries helped mould the granite into the bizarre natural sculptures that festoon the archipelago. There are plans to merge the park with islands belonging to Corsica to create the Parco Marino Internazionale delle Bocche di Bonifacio.

Known to the Romans as the Cuniculariae (Rabbit Island), they were later settled by Benedictine monks in the 10th century. Until the 18th century, however, they remained barely inhabited.

The bulk of the population lives in the town of La Maddalena, on the island of the same name, a couple of nautical miles north of Palau. A handful of people also live on Isola Caprera, linked to La Maddalena by a causeway, and on Santo Stefano, which houses a US Navy base for atomic submarines. To the west of La Maddalena lies Isola Spargi, while further to the north are grouped the three lovely islands of Santa Maria, Budelli and Razzoli. All put together, the islands and islets cover just 49.3 sq km.

Isola della Maddalena
postcode 07024 • pop 11,105
After a 20-minute crossing from Palau you land at La Maddalena, the only significant settlement on the islands. It is a pleasant, cheerful port town and makes for a nice stroll between the odd gelato or glass of wine at any of the numerous bars dotted along and just back from the waterfront.

OLBIA & THE GALLURA

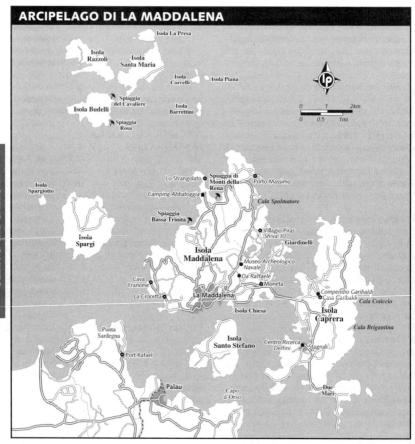

ARCIPELAGO DI LA MADDALENA

Until the end of the 17th century the island's meagre population lived mainly in the interior, but were attracted to the growing village by the presence of the new Sardinian Navy (ie, of the Savoy Kingdom of Piedmont and Sardinia), founded by one Baron Des Geneys and given a base here. It later became an important Italian military base and remained so until the end of WWII. Nowadays the tradition continues with a navy school and the presence of US Navy personnel serving on the US submarine base on Isola Santo Stefano.

The island boasts some lovely coastal stretches but in parts is also rather drab. Strewn with granite, the soil is poor for farming and in places the scrub gives the island a rather unkempt feel.

Information The **tourist office** (☎ 0789 73 63 21; Cala Gavetta; open 8.30am-1pm & 4.30pm-7.30pm daily June-Sept, reduced hrs Oct-May) has information on the entire archipelago. The Banco di Sardegna on Via Amendola has an ATM.

Things to See & Do The only sight as such in town is the **Museo Diocesano** (☎ 0789 73 74 00; Via Baron Manno; admission free; open 10.30am-12.30pm, also 6.30pm-8.30pm May-Sept), at the back of the modern Chiesa di Santa Maria Maddalena on the square of the same name. The present church was built in 1814. The museum contains a modest collection of religious objects, including some statues, paintings and other bits and bobs. The best thing to do is stroll around the port and call in at the many cafés, bars and restaurants.

A vaguely circular road system leads around the island, allowing easy access to several beaches. Island buses stop at some useful points along the way. Heading anti-clockwise around the island, you could make first down a dirt track north of Moneta for the **Giardinelli** headland – a couple of pretty shallow beaches await.

Popular in the north is **Cala Spalmatore**, a small sandy strand at the end of a protected inlet. As the road curves around to the west it passes the wilder beaches of **Monti della Rena**. Buses stop at both of these. Another good one (follow the signs for the Camping Abbatoggia) is **Lo Strangolato**, for which you'll need wheels or to walk about 15 minutes from where the bus leaves you.

Another decent strand, with clear blue waters, is the **Spiaggia Bassa Trinità**, on an asphalted spur road in the island's north-west.

While touring around you could stop in at the **Museo Archeologico Navale** (admission €2.50; open 9.30am-1.30pm & 4.30pm-7.30pm Tues-Sun), a little over 1km out of La Maddalena on the road to Cala Spalmatore. The museum contains finds from ancient shipwrecks in its two modest rooms, presided over by an impressive remake cross section of a Roman vessel containing more than 200 amphorae.

Places to Stay & Eat The best of the island's handful of camping grounds is **Camping Abbatoggia** (☎ 0789 73 91 73; per person €10.50; open June-Sept), in the north. It has access to a couple of good beaches, including Lo Strangolato.

Da Raffaele (☎ 0789 73 87 59; La Ricciolina; doubles €41.50, half board per person €44; open May-Sept) is about as cheap and basic as hotel accommodation gets around here. To find this rambling place head out of town and follow the signs right off the main road just after the Museo Archeologico Navale.

Hotel Il Gabbiano (☎ 0789 72 25 07; Via Giulio Cesare 20; singles/doubles €62/83) is a nice option just outside the western end of town. Rooms are comfortable and some have good sea views.

Da Roby's (☎ 0789 73 77 27; Via Amendola 2) does great *foccacine* filled with

mozzarella, tomato and ham for €5. You can eat in or take away. The US Navy boys like this place too.

Osteria Enoteca da Liò (☎ 0789 73 75 07; Corso Vittorio Emanuele 2-6; meals €25-30) is a quiet eatery just off Piazza Santa Maria Maddalena, where you can indulge in Liò's culinary whims, which might run from *carpaccio di salmone* to various fish options in white wine sauce.

Ristorante Il Galleone (☎ 0789 73 51 52; Via Zonza 7; meals €25-30) has signs pointing its way from all over town. It needs them, as you'd be unlikely to stumble on it otherwise. What you find is an earthy backstreet diner where you can eat good seafood.

Ristorante al Faone (☎ 0789 73 87 63; Via Ilvia 10; meals €25) is not quite as hidden and is an old stalwart. Try the *gnocchetti sardi alla campidanese* (little gnocchi in a sausage and tomato sauce) followed by a meat or seafood main.

Entertainment It's hard to resist a tipple at any one of a series of relaxing waterfront bars. Further bars and snack spots line the lively Via Garibaldi. Or you could try **The Penny Drops** (Piazza Santa Maria Maddalena 7), an Irish establishment. To dance head out of town to **Shiva 30** (☎ 349 469 02 95), in Villaggio Piras, less than 1km short of Cala Spalmatore.

Getting There & Away See the Palau section for information on ferries to La Maddalena from the mainland. They arrive (and leave) at separate points along the La Maddalena waterfront.

Getting Around Two local buses run from Via Amendola on the waterfront. One goes to the Compendio Garibaldi complex on Isola di Capra (see later) and the other heads around the island, passing the Museo Archeologico Navale and several beaches, including Cala Spalmatore and Spiagga Bassa Trinità. Tickets cost €0.65.

You can rent mountain bikes (€10 a day) and scooters (around €30 a day) from **Noleggio Vacanze** (☎ 0789 73 52 00; Via Mazzini 1), just off the waterfront.

Isola Caprera

The road out of La Maddalena town towards the east takes you through desolate urban relics towards the narrow causeway (first built towards the end of the 19th century) that spans the Passo della Moneta stretch of water between Isola della Maddalena and Isola Caprera. Once on the island, a turn left is signposted to the **Compendio Garibaldi** *(admission €2; open 9am-1.30pm & 4pm-7pm Tues-Sun June-Sept, 9am-1.30pm Tues-Sun Oct-May)*, an object of pilgrimage for many Italians. Entry is by guided visits (in Italian).

Giuseppe Garibaldi, professional revolutionary and apotheosised in the folklore of Italian unification, bought half the island in 1855 (he got the rest 10 years later). He made it his home and refuge, the place he would return to after yet another daring campaign in the pursuit of liberty and Italian unification.

This dry and now uncultivated island was as tough then as now to work. Garibaldi used about 60ha as farmland, watered by a series of wells he dug himself. He soon had a flourishing garden of fruit and vegetables, made his own wine and raised cows, sheep and pigs – all now long gone.

The red-shirted revolutionary first lived in a hut that still stands in the courtyard while

building his main residence, the Casa Bianca. Off the courtyard you are first taken into a long outhouse full of farming utensils and Garibaldi's bathtub. You enter the house proper by an atrium adorned with his portrait, a flag from the days of Peru's war of independence and a reclining wheelchair donated to him by the city of Milan when he became infirm a couple of years before dying. You then proceed through a series of bedrooms where he and family members slept. The kitchen had its own freshwater pump, a feat of high technology in such a place in the 1870s. In what was the main dining room are now displayed all sorts of odds and ends from binoculars to the general's own red shirt. The last room contains his deathbed, facing the window and the sea, across which he would look longingly, dreaming until the end that he might return to his native Nice.

Outside in the gardens are his rough hewn granite tomb and those of several family members (he had seven children by his three wives and one by a governess).

About 1km south of Garibaldi's place is the **Centro Ricerca Delfini** in the one time

Garibaldi's Travels

Born into a fishing family in Nice, the young sea captain Giuseppe Garibaldi (1807–82) began his quixotic revolutionary career early on by joining a botched republican mutiny in the Sardinian Navy in 1834. Condemned to death by a Genoese court, Garibaldi fled to France and then in 1836 on to South America, where he spent 12 years battling in independence wars in Brazil and Uruguay and in between doing odd jobs. He and his Italian legion of Red Shirts won quite a name for themselves as tenacious guerrillas. During the Brazilian campaigns he also met his first wife Anita, who was to fight by his side until her death in 1849.

Garibaldi was a firm believer in the cause of Italian unification and independence. In 1848, the year of uprisings across Europe, he and some of his legionnaires were in Milan fighting its Austrian masters. Hounded across into Switzerland, he was soon back to lead the short-lived Roman Republic's defence after the city had chased away the Pope. When the French intervened on behalf of the Pope, Garibaldi resisted siege through the month of July 1849. His futile but heroic stand captured the imagination of Italians but Garibaldi soon found himself in exile again, in the USA and Peru. Allowed back to Italy in 1854, he was made a major general in the Piedmontese Army in 1858 and undertook several campaigns against the Austrians. In the meantime, he had discovered Isola Caprera.

Garibaldi was by now a symbol of Italian patriotism and in 1860 embarked on his most daring venture, invading Sicily with 1000 Red Shirts. To the astonishment of all he had conquered the island and southern Italy in five months, and handed the lot to King Vittorio Emanuele of Piedmont. The king welcomed the successes, which led to the declaration of a unified Italy the following year. The king and his wily Prime Minister Count Cavour considered Garibaldi a loose cannon and shunted him aside but beyond Italy he had become a legend. Abraham Lincoln is even said to have offered him a command in the American Civil War. He conducted several more battles in the cause of Italian unity (completed in 1870) and even fought with the French against Prussia in 1870–71. He lived out his remaining days in his Caprera home, increasingly crippled by rheumatism.

hamlet of Stagnali. You won't see any dolphins here but rather encounter an education centre with short films and other didactic material. Given it's all in Italian it is probably of limited interest.

Otherwise, the island is dotted by several tempting beaches. Many people head south for the two strands that make up the **Due Mari** beaches on a narrow isthmus. You could, however, head north of the Compendio Garibaldi for about 1½km and look for the walking trail that drops down to the steep and secluded **Cala Coticcio** beach. Marginally easier is **Cala Brigantina** (signposted), southeast of the Garibaldi complex.

Other Islands
The five remaining main islands can only be reached by boat. Numerous excursions leave from Isola della Maddalena, Palau (see earlier) and Santa Teresa di Gallura (see later) and approach the islands in various combinations. Or you can hire motorised dinghies and do it yourself.

Isola Santo Stefano is partly occupied by the military and so mostly inaccessible. **Isola Spargi**, west of Isola della Maddalena, is surrounded by little beaches and inlets. One of the better-known ones is **Cala Corsara**. To the north lies a trio of islands, **Isola Budelli**, **Isola Razzoli** and **Isola di Santa Maria**. With your boat and time to paddle about you could explore all sorts of little coves and beaches. On tours you are likely to be taken to see **Cala Rosa** (Pink Cove, so-called because of the sand's unique crimson tinge) on Isola Budelli (since 1999 swimming at the environmentally threatened Cala Rosa has been banned), **Cala Lunga** on Isola Razzoli and the oft crowded **Cala Santa Maria** on the island of the same name. The beautiful stretch of water between the three islets is known as the **Porto della Madonna** and is on most waterborne itineraries through the archipelago.

SANTA TERESA DI GALLURA
postcode 07028 • pop 4060
Although the area was inhabited in Roman and medieval times, the present town was established by the island's House of Savoy rulers in 1808 to help combat smugglers. The neat grid streets in the centre were designed by an army officer but most of the town today is the result of the tourism boom since

the early 1960s. The red-tiled roofs could almost be a picture of Australian or American suburbia and fill with as many as 50,000 people at the height of summer. At other times of the year a strange quiet descends on the place, with most of the houses, flats and even hotels empty.

Santa Teresa's history is as much caught up with Corsica as Sardinia. The local dialect is similar to that of southern Corsica and down through the centuries numerous Corsicans have settled in the area.

Orientation & Information
Santa Teresa is a straightforward grid-plan town, its centre resting on a rise. To the north roads drop down to the Rena Bianca beach, while to the south they decline slowly towards the town exits.

The **AAST** (☎ 0789 75 41 27, fax 0789 75 41 85; Piazza Vittorio Emanuele I 24) has information on the town and surrounding area.

You can change money at the **Banca di Sassari** (Piazza Vittorio Emanuele I) and the **Banco di Sardegna** (Via Nazionale).

There's also a **post office** (Via Eleonora d'Arborea; open 8am-1pm Mon-Fri, 8am-12.30pm Sat) handy. You can go online at **InfoCell Computers** (☎ 0789 75 54 48; Via Nazionale; open 9am-1pm & 4.30pm-8.30pm Mon-Sat) for €5 an hour.

Libreria Roggero (☎ 0789 75 50 83; Piazza Vittorio Emanuele I 30) is a handy place full of all sorts of tomes, guides and maps on Sardinia (mostly in Italian).

Things to See & Do
Apart from wandering about the tidily arranged streets, there is not an awful lot to do in Santa Teresa. The **Torre di Longonsardo** (admission €1.50; open 10am-12.30pm & 4pm-7pm daily June-Sept) was probably built under Spanish rule in the 16th century as a watchtower. It is in a magnificent position, overlooking the natural deep port to one side and the entrance to Spiaggia Rena Bianca on the other. With the binoculars set up atop the tower (€0.50) you can observe the goings on in Bonifacio, nine nautical miles across the strait.

For those wishing to expend minimum effort to arrive at a beach, the town's crowded **Spiaggia Rena Bianca** is the shot. Umbrellas and sun lounges are available for €5 apiece.

Boat Excursions Various boat excursions set out from Santa Teresa di Gallura to the Arcipelago di La Maddalena Islands (see later) to the east.

The **Consorzio delle Bocche** (☎ *0789 75 51 12*) offers two full-day trips. The first (€34 per person) takes in the western islands of the archipelago and La Maddalena itself with bathing stops on Isola Santa Maria and Isola di Spargi. The other trip (€38.50) carries on down the Costa Smeralda with brief swimming stops and time in Porto Cervo. Lunch is served on board.

Diving The diving off Santa Teresa and around the islands in the Bocche di Bonifacio is good and several outfits operate in and around Santa Teresa. **Centro Sun Marina di Longone** (☎ *0789 74 10 59; Via Tibula 11*), on the way to Capo Testa (see later), organises dive trips and PADI courses.

Places to Stay

Many places open only in summer and most charge *mezza pensione* (half board). Still, there's plenty to choose from.

The nearest camping ground is **Camping Gallura Village** (☎/fax *0789 75 55 80; Località Li Luccianeddi; per person €12*), a few kilometres out of town on the road to Castelsardo. It's a big ground and gets crowded. Nicer is **Camping La Liccia** (☎/fax *0789 75 51 90; per person/car €11/2.60*), 4km farther west. Both sites have bungalows.

Pensione Scano (☎/fax *0789 75 44 47; Via Lazio 4; half board €59; open year-round*) is about the cheapest all-round deal in Santa Teresa. Rooms are perfectly fine and, on price, the extra you pay for a full meal is less than you'd pay to eat out.

Hotel L'Ancora (☎ *0789 75 45 64, fax 0789 75 46 52; Via Calabria; B&B singles/ doubles €60/103*) is a perfectly comfortable back-street option. Rooms are spacious and come with TV, phone and heating in winter.

Hotel Bellavista (☎/fax *0789 75 41 62; Via Sonnino 8; singles/doubles €33.50/56.80, half board €59; open May-Oct*) is a surprise deal given its location looking down to the sea. You will have to take half board in high season.

Hotel Moresco (☎ *0789 75 41 88, fax 0789 75 50 85; Via Imbriani 16; doubles up to €114, half board per person up to €115; open mid-Apr–Oct*) is a rambling place with

lovely tiled floors throughout and a splendid position overlooking the sea. Rooms with arched balconies have decent views and the hotel reserves a strip of the beach for its guests. The restaurant is good.

Hotel Marinaro (☎ *0789 75 41 12, fax 0789 75 51 87; Via Angioi 48; singles/doubles €77.50/87.80*) is an elegant choice in a leafy street just downhill from the centre. Tastefully decorated rooms are kept in top order.

Places to Eat

Most places shut from about December to March. On the other hand most open seven days a week from May to September.

Ristorante Papé Satan (☎ *0789 75 50 48; Via Lamarmora 20; pizzas up to €8*), with its wood-fired oven, is one of the best pizza options in town. The place has a nice internal courtyard and the service is prompt and friendly.

Azzurra (☎ *0789 75 47 89; Via del Porto 19; meals €30*) is a popular place with a long list of pasta dishes and a reasonable selection of fish and seafood. Try the *fritto misto* (mixed fry up) of calamari, shrimps and fish.

Ristorante Canne al Vento (☎ *0789 75 42 19; Via Nazionale 23; meals €30-35*), in the hotel of the same name, is a classier affair. Try the *zuppa di pesce* (fish soup) or one of the handful of Sardinian options.

Ristorante Moresco (☎ *0789 75 41 88; Via Imbriani 16; meals €35*), in the hotel of the same name, proposes a Sardinian meal for €18, which at least gives you a taste of some classic local dishes and sweets like the omnipresent *seadas* (light pastry filled with cheese and covered in honey).

Ristorante La Torre (☎ *0789 75 46 00; Via del Mare 36; meals €30*) is at its best with risotto and seafood. Locals recommend it.

Ristorante La Medusa (☎ *0789 75 41 60; Piazza della Libertà 2; meals €25-35*) offers various options, including a *cena sarda*, or Sardinian dinner set menu at €20.70. This gives you the chance to taste a reasonable (if not first class) version of local dishes.

Entertainment

Hanging around any of the three café-bars on Piazza Vittorio Emanuele I is a pleasant option. At **Bar Central 80** there are often musicians playing outside on the square. **Groove Cafe** is a more laid back spot to sit down for a soothing beer, while **Bar Conti** is more introverted, with people sipping mixed drinks inside.

Caffè Mediterraneo (☎ 0789 75 90 14; Via Amsicora 7; open 7.30am-3.30am daily), just off the square, is one of the hippest spots. A cavernous locale loaded with beautiful people drinking cocktails and listening to the music.

Primabase (Via Carlo Alberto 31) is another decent little bar, with seating outside on the street to watch the passing late-night shoppers at the market stands.

For something more lively you need to head 3km south of town. Follow the signs for Palau and Olbia and soon you meet a turn-off to the right for Buoncammino. A quick jaunt down this road brings you to Santa Teresa's late-nightlife hub. **Free Jazz Café** (☎ 0789 75 58 11) is a late-night bar that happens to serve pizza. Right next door is the area's only club, the noisy outdoors **Estasi's** (☎ 339 763 09 67), which opens Friday and Saturday night in the summer season.

Shopping

Coral, some of it fished locally, is the big item here, and you'll find no shortage of boutiques and jewellery shops selling mostly silver jewellery encrusted with mainly crimson and azure coral. The pedestrianised Via Umberto and Via Carlo Alberto, leading south of Piazza Vittorio Emanuele I, together host a nightly (June to September) market where you can find cheapish jewellery, strange lampshades and other items.

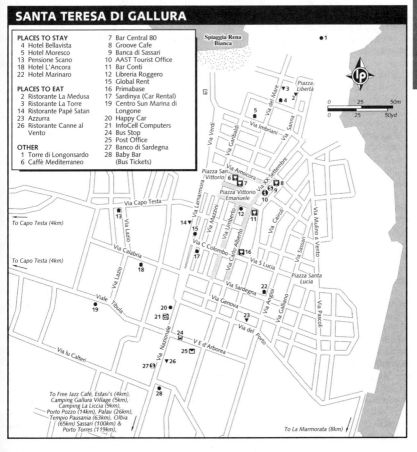

SANTA TERESA DI GALLURA

PLACES TO STAY
4 Hotel Bellavista
5 Hotel Moresco
13 Pensione Scano
18 Hotel L'Ancora
22 Hotel Marinaro

PLACES TO EAT
2 Ristorante La Medusa
3 Ristorante La Torre
14 Ristorante Papé Satan
23 Azzurra
26 Ristorante Canne al Vento

OTHER
1 Torre di Longonsardo
6 Caffè Mediterraneo
7 Bar Central 80
8 Groove Cafe
9 Banca di Sassari
10 AAST Tourist Office
11 Bar Conti
12 Libreria Roggero
15 Global Rent
16 Primabase
17 Sardinya (Car Rental)
19 Centro Sun Marina di Longone
20 Happy Car
21 InfoCell Computers
24 Bus Stop
25 Post Office
27 Banco di Sardegna
28 Baby Bar (Bus Tickets)

Getting There & Away
Bus Most of the buses terminate at Via Eleonora d'Arborea, near the post office. **ARST** buses operate up to seven times a day between Olbia and Santa Teresa (€3.72, one hour 50 minutes). The same company has up to five daily connections from Sassari (€5.85, 2½ hours). These buses stop at numerous places (like Castelsardo) en route. Get tickets from the nearby Baby Bar.

Autobus Turmotravel (☎ 0789 2 14 87) has a daily run from Cagliari (€17.30, six hours) at 5.30am (!), returning at 2.30pm. The same company runs a summer service (June to September) between Olbia airport and Santa Teresa (1½ hours) via Arzachena and Palau six times a day.

Sardabus has two runs to Tempio Pausania (one hour), but none on Sunday or holidays.

From June to September Sardabus runs five circle line buses connecting Baia Santa Reparata, Capo Testa, Santa Teresa and La Marmorata. The run takes a half hour.

Car & Motorcycle You can rent a Fiat Panda for €57 a day or a Fiat Puntos for €65 from **Global Rent** (☎ 0789 75 50 80; Via Maria Teresa 40). Various sizes of scooter and motorbike cost €26 to €40 a day.

Sardinya (☎ 0789 75 90 90; Via Maria Teresa 29) offers a Ford Fiesta for €57, while **New Happy Cars** (☎ 0789 75 47 41; Via Nazionale 6) is one of the cheaper deals, with a Panda for €50 and the Punto for €55.

Taxi If you're in a tearing hurry to get to Olbia airport you can get a special **airport taxi** (☎ 0789 74 10 35) for just €65.

Boat Santa Teresa is the main regular jumping off point for Corsica. Two companies run car ferries on this 50-minute crossing.

Saremar (☎ 0789 75 41 56) has from four to eight departures each way depending on the season. Adult one-way fares range up to €8.52. A small car costs up to €27.89. Those landing in Bonifacio pay a €3.10 port tax per person and €1.29 per vehicle.

Mobyline (☎ 0789 75 14 49) has 10 daily crossings in July and August and four during the rest of the year. Prices are virtually the same.

Rental You don't need a licence to rent the smaller rubber speed boats. At **Capo Testa**

Yachting (☎ 0789 74 10 60), down in the town port, you can get a four-seater for €130 per day in high season.

AROUND SANTA TERESA
For more serious beach action than the perfectly serviceable Rena Bianca beach in Santa Teresa, you need to head a few kilometres out of town, east or west. Buses will get you to some of the following spots but life is a lot easier with your own transport.

East Coast
Back roads lead about 4km east of Santa Teresa, past a growing array of villas set in among the *macchia*-covered rises back from the coast, to what is no doubt a good beach, **La Marmorata**. You can also take a longer cut by following the SS133b highway out of Santa Teresa towards Olbia.

This long, deep strand of fine sand is protected to the west by **Punta Falcone**, mainland Sardinia's northernmost point, and is a calm, enticing spot. Or it would be. There is something off-putting about arriving (having parked your car at €1 an hour) to hear the sounds of Abba pouring from the sandwich stand as a group of package tourists provide an unstable display of morning calisthenics beside the serried ranks of beach umbrellas and sun lounges. Behind them, like some science-fiction vision of troglodyte living, curve the hundreds of terraced rooms of an enormous holiday complex.

A better bet lies another 4km farther east down the SS133b road towards Olbia. Turn left (north) for **La Licciola**. About 3km on you reach a small holiday settlement. Head right up through it and half a kilometre on you drop down to a good beach, relatively wild and utterly free of beachside build-up. Virtually next door is the Valle dell'Erica resort, which you can safely skip.

Another 4km down the road lies **Porto Pozzo**, an unexciting fishing hamlet on a long inlet. There is little to hold you up here, except for some cheapish lodgings. **Camping Arcobaleno** (☎ 0789 75 20 40; per person €8.80) is a pleasant enough shady ground in the town itself.

Locanda Porto Pozzo (☎ 0789 75 21 24; Via Aldo Moro; singles/doubles €26/41) has neat, simple rooms (that can suffer from traffic noise) and is surely one of the cheapest hotels in the entire northeast!

The place livens up a bit for the Festa di San Tommaso at the end of the first week of July, with markets, music and religious processions. Boat trips to the Arcipelago di La Maddalena leave from here.

Another 5km down the SS133b takes you to the junction with the SS133, which leads east to Palau and southwest to Tempio Pausania.

Capo Testa

Four kilometres away from central Santa Teresa, this extraordinary granite headland seems more like a divine sculpture garden. Nature has contrived to make this pocket of rock a unique scene – the undulating, curvaceous forms look as though they were squeezed and moulded by a master dessert maker. The Romans quarried granite here, as did the Pisans centuries later.

The place also has a couple of beaches. **Rena di Levante** and **Rena di Ponente** lie either side of the narrow isthmus that leads out to the headland itself. From the smaller north-facing Rena di Levante you can see the coast of Corsica, while from the longer Rena di Ponente, with its impossibly turquoise water, the view stretches southwest along the Sardinian coast.

Right on Rena di Ponente you can rent windsurfing gear at **Nautica Rena di Ponente** (☎ 348 033 31 66). Full kit costs €15.

Progressing along to the headland you pass a couple of minor beaches, hotels and restaurants before reaching the end of the road, marked in summer by a snack stand. Follow the trails out amid the weird rock formations.

Just where the road ends you can gingerly climb down to a tiny pocket of sand at **Cala Spinosa**, one of a couple of such 'beachettes'. If you clamber about to the southwestern extremity of the headland you'll find the ironically named **Cala Grande**, actually rather small too!

West Coast

Just before you reach Capo Testa, a turn-off to the left takes you to the low-key **Baia Santa Reparata** tourist complex, fronted by several decent beaches, although they can get choppy when the wind is up.

To head further southwest down the coast, you need to take the SS90 road for Castelsardo from Santa Teresa. There is any number of beaches along this run. The first one

of any size, and consequently never too crowded, is **Rena Maiore**, signposted off the road about 10km out of Santa Teresa. Here, as with many of the other beaches, you can take a vehicle part of the way along a dirt track and then walk down to the beach. Rena Maiore is long and backed by dunes. A coastal walking track heads as far west as Vignola. ARST buses between Santa Teresa and Castelsardo stop at the turn-off.

Five kilometres on is **Spiaggia Montirussu**. Curving round from the headland of the same name, it is also known as **Spiaggia Piana**. To its west, past another rocky stretch, lie several more fine beaches, including **Spiaggia Lu Littaroni** and **Spiaggia Naracu Nieddu**, rarely crowded even in high summer. A trail off the SS90 road to the first of these is signposted 3km on from the Spiaggia Montirussu trail. About 3km farther on again you come to **Vignola Mare**, whose good beach is dominated at one end by a Spanish-era watchtower. It's 25 minutes by ARST bus from Santa Teresa.

Fourteen kilometres farther down the SS90 is the turn-off for a rather bizarre location, the **Costa del Paradiso** (45 minutes by bus from Santa Teresa), a private resort set amid striking granite formations, thick greenery and a rugged coastline. The low slung, mostly uniform houses of this select holiday villa complex lend it a vaguely surreal air. Still, at least it has been done with some minimum of taste. You can drive into the complex and down to the coast. If you get that far, it is possible to clamber about 2km west along the shore to the little-visited beach of **Cala Tinnari**, in the shadow of the 216m hill of the same name.

Another 10km from the Costa Paradiso turn-off brings you to the one for **Isola Rossa**, a small promontory (with the predictable Spanish era watchtower) off which lies the red islet that gives the place its name. The beaches are nice and not too crowded even in summer. It also has a couple of modestly priced hotels. **Hotel Vitty** (☎/fax 079 69 40 05; Via Lungomare 11; doubles €57.80, half board €70) has reasonable rooms with TV and phone. Some have balconies out the back from which you can glimpse the tiny port. It also has a restaurant.

Several more average beaches line the coast west towards Castelsardo (see the Sassari & the Northwest chapter).

Tempio Pausania

postcode 07029 • pop 13,950 • elev 566m
An appealing town surrounded by cork oak woods deep in the heart of Gallura, Tempio Pausania has been a key town since Roman times, when it was known as Gemellae. To the south looms the mountain range of Monte Limbara, whose ascent (by car or on foot) makes a fine excursion.

The old town's buildings, almost all built from the local grey granite, don't date beyond the 18th century and many are more recent but the place has the appeal of being a real (albeit small) city, something you may have come to miss amid the tourist settlements along the coast.

No matter from which direction you come you will find yourself amid thick woods of cork oak, long a pillar of the economy in this part of the island. The minor road leading south from the coast via Aglientu is one of the prettiest.

Information The **Pro Loco** (☎ 079 67 99 99; *Piazza Gallura; open 10am-7pm Mon-Sat, 10am-1pm Sun mid-June–mid-Sept, 10am-1pm & 4pm-7pm Mon-Fri, 10am-1pm Sat rest of the year*) has loads of information.

Several banks with ATMs are scattered about. **Banco di Napoli** (*Piazza Gallura 2*) is handy.

There's a **post office** (*Largo A de Gasperi; open 8.15am-1.15pm Mon-Sat*) in town.

In a medical crisis you could pop into the emergency rooms of the **Ospedale Civile** (☎ 079 67 10 81; *Via Grazia Deledda 19*).

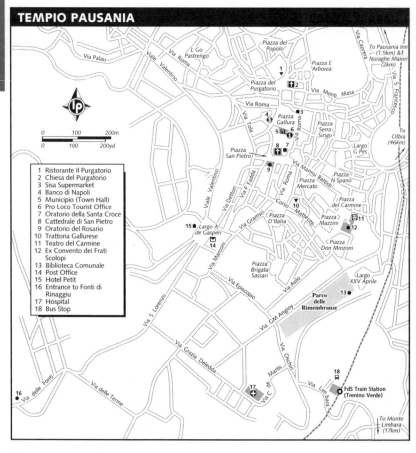

TEMPIO PAUSANIA

1 Ristorante Il Purgatorio
2 Chiesa del Purgatorio
3 Sisa Supermarket
4 Banco di Napoli
5 Municipio (Town Hall)
6 Pro Loco Tourist Office
7 Oratorio della Santa Croce
8 Cattedrale di San Pietro
9 Oratorio del Rosario
10 Trattoria Gallurese
11 Teatro del Carmine
12 Ex Convento dei Frati Scolopi
13 Biblioteca Comunale
14 Post Office
15 Hotel Petit
16 Entrance to Fonti di Rinaggiu
17 Hospital
18 Bus Stop

Things to See & Do The centrepiece of the town is the imposing **Cattedrale di San Pietro**. Unfortunately, all that remains of the 15th-century original are the belltower and main entrance. Across the square, the **Oratorio del Rosario** dates to the time of the Spanish domination of the island.

Behind the cathedral, the town's main square, Piazza Gallura, is fronted by the suitably grave **Municipio** (town hall). A couple of cafés here make good spots for people watching. The nearby Piazza del Purgatorio is presided over by a modest **church** of the same name. The story goes that a member of the noble Misorro family was found guilty of carrying out a massacre on this very spot. To expiate his sins, the Pope ordered the man to fund the building of this church, where to this day it is the custom of townspeople to come and pray after a funeral.

Tempio is littered with churches and an indication of the town's former importance lies in the presence of the former 17th-century **Convento degli Scolopi** (*Piazza Mazzini*). It is now a college but you can peer through the gates to the leafy cloister from Piazza del Carmine.

If you want to see a couple of rusty old steam locomotives, head down to the train station.

Since Roman days Tempio has been known for its springs, the **Fonti di Rinaggiu**, a pleasant 1km walk southwest from the centre (take the shady Via San Lorenzo and follow the 'Alle Terme' signs).

Two kilometres north of town on the SS133 road to Palau is the **Nuraghe Maiori**, signposted off to the right and immersed in thick cork oak woods. As the name ('major') suggests, it is a good deal bigger than many of the simple ruined single towers you will repeatedly spot around the countryside here. Off the entrance corridor is a chamber on each side, and a ramp leads you to a third, open room at the back. Stairs to the left allow you to walk to the top.

Special Events Members of *confraternita* (religious brotherhoods) dress up in sinister looking robes and hoods for the **Via Crucis** night procession on Good Friday, a clear echo of the days of Spanish rule.

Places to Stay & Eat The only central hotel is the drab and overpriced **Petit Hotel**

(☎ *079 63 11 34, fax 079 63 17 60; Largo A de Gasperi 9/11; singles/doubles €93/114).*

Pausania Inn (☎ *079 63 40 37, fax 079 63 40 72;* w *www.hotelpausaniainn.com; Località Battino; singles/doubles €57/83, half board per person €54.23)* is a better deal, about 1km north of the town on the road to Palau (and the Nuraghe Maiori). The place is new and extensive, with comfortable rooms, own restaurant and pool.

Trattoria Gallurese (☎ *079 67 10 48; Via Novara 2; meals €20-25; open Sat-Thur & lunch Fri)* welcomes you upstairs to a simple homespun dining area for local food. It has a good value set menu for €12. If you want something like *porceddu* (suckling pig) or *capretto* (kid meat), order a day in advance.

Ristorante Il Purgatorio (☎ *079 63 43 94; Piazza del Purgatorio; meals €30-35; open Wed-Mon)* is one of the town's classiest restaurants. Soft lighting off the bare stone walls creates an intimate setting in which to try a variety of local and national dishes.

To make your own meals, try the **Sisa supermarket** (*Piazza Gallura*).

Entertainment A couple of cafés on Piazza Gallura are good for an evening drink and people watching. At the **Teatro del Carmine** (☎ *079 67 15 80; Piazza del Carmine)* a variety of performances, from operetta to classical concerts, can be enjoyed, especially in the summer Festival d'Estate, which runs from July to mid-August.

Getting There & Away ARST buses from Olbia, Palau and Sassari, among others,

---

The Voice of Tempio

In 1902, at the age of 21, Bernardo de Muro took a chance and left his malaria-struck home town of Tempio for Rome where he hoped to get a break as a singer. One year later he was admitted to the Conservatorio Musicale di Santa Cecilia, from where he was launched on the path to international success on the opera stage. In a long career he performed in classics ranging from *Carmen* to *Il Trovatore*, finally leaving this mortal world in Rome in 1955. He is buried in Tempio and a tiny museum in his memory operates in the Biblioteca Comunale (municipal library) downstairs from the Parco delle Rimembranze.

arrive in the square in front of the train station. The station itself comes to life for the summertime *trenino verde* service to/from Arzachena and Palau.

Around Tempio Pausania

Aggius Eight kilometres northwest of Tempio, Aggius is a quiet village set dramatically amid granite walls and cork woods. Not much goes on here, although the cafés along the main road get lively with chattering folk in the late afternoon. The town is known for carpet weaving – back in the first half of the 19th century some 4000 looms were said to have been busy in the area. By the early 1900s local demand had declined and this cottage industry was on the brink of disappearing until it was revived with a view to selling pieces as exotica to markets beyond Sardinia. Some 80% of production nowadays is aimed at tourists. The carpets and rugs typically are fairly conservative with simple designs, and you can see a good display at the **Pro Loco** (☎ 079 62 02 06; *Largo Andrea Vasa; usually open 10am-noon & 5pm-8pm daily*) from mid-July to mid-September.

The **Valle della Luna**, a strange boulder-strewn landscape, stretches northwest a few kilometres from Aggius.

FdS buses run to Aggius from Tempio Pausania.

Calangianus & Luras As a major centre of cork production, you can expect to find plenty of the stuff on sale in all imaginable forms in Calangianus, about 10km east of Tempio. If you get talking to some of the artisans, you may find them showing you how corks are made for your bottle of Vermentino. Three kilometres north at Luras, the main attraction is the **Dolmen de Ladas**. To find it follow the road to Luogosanto north out of town for 1km. The dolmen, a collection of funerary stones dating back as far as the third millennium BC, is signposted off to the right. To be honest, you really have to like these items to warrant the effort.

Monte Limbara The most interesting excursion from the town is to make for the summit of Monte Limbara (1359m), about 17km south. The most convenient way to do so is with your own vehicle, winding slowly along the ribbon of road that snakes up to the summit. From Tempio, drive south out

of town past the train station and follow the SS392 road for Oschiri. After 8km you will hit the left turn-off for the mountain.

The initial stretch takes you through thick pine woods. As you emerge above the tree line, a couple of *punto panoramico* (viewing spots) are indicated from where you have terrific views across all of northern Sardinia. One is marked by a statue of the Virgin Mary and child, near the simple little **Chiesa di Santa Maria della Neve** church.

The road then flattens out to reach **Punta Balistreri** (1359m), where the RAI national TV has stacked relay and communication towers. The air is cool and refreshing even on a midsummer's day, and the views west towards Sassari and beyond and north to Corsica are breathtaking.

Lago di Coghinas, Berchidda & Oschiri

Those with wheels could make another excursion south of Monte Limbara. Once down from the mountain, turn left on the SS392 and head for Oschiri. This road skirts around the west side of the Limbara massif, at first amid thick green woods of cork oak and pine, tops the Passo della Limbara (646m) and then begins its descent. After about 12km, the green gives way to scorched straw-coloured fields dotted by the occasional cork tree, the temperature rises and the blue mirror of the artificial Lago di Coghinas comes into view.

Just before the bridge over the lake, a narrow asphalted road breaks off east towards Berchidda around the northern flank of Monte Acuto (493m). Berchidda is a fairly nondescript farming town with a wine tradition. This is Vermentino territory and you can find out about local wine-making traditions and taste some of the area's drops at the **Museo del Vino** (☎ 079 70 45 87; *admission €2; open 9am-1pm & 4pm-10pm June-Sept, 9am-1pm & 3pm-7pm Oct-May*).

From Berchidda you can walk to the top of Monte Acuto and inspect what little remains of the **Castello di Monte Acuto**, one-time stronghold of Ubaldo Visconti and later of the Doria and Malaspina families. A road leads 4km west from Berchidda to a dirt trail, from where it's another couple of kilometres, the first part possible in 4WD.

Should you need to stay in Berchidda there are a couple of modest hotels with their own restaurants. **Sos Chelvos** (☎ 079 70 49 35, *fax 079 70 49 21; Via Umberto I 52; singles/ doubles €23.30/41.30)* is a functional and friendly place.

Three or four buses a day pass through from Olbia and Ozieri. Berchidda is also on the Olbia–Chilivani train line but the station is 2km out of town.

The bridge across Lago di Coghinas leads 5km south to Oschiri. There's not an awful lot to this town, apart from the tiny Romanesque **Chiesa di San Demetrio**. Oschiri is however, the home of *panadas*, a kind of pie that can contain anything from meat to eel fished out of Lago di Coghinas.

Nuoro & the East

If Sardinia is a world apart from the Italian mainland, Nuoro is an island within the island. Much of Sardinia's most rugged mountain territory is concentrated in this defiant and inward-looking province. The uncompromising territory provides the island's most exhilarating walking and climbing (and even a smidgin of modest skiing!), but since few trails are adequately marked you should always consider using guides; excessively independent-minded hikers go missing every year. Several fine nuraghic sites await discovery and the province boasts some of Sardinia's most breathtaking coastline, particularly the Golfo di Orosei.

Other Sardinians will warn you to be circumspect with the village folk of Nuoro. While they can seem taciturn and guarded at first, on the whole they are a hospitable breed – you just have to crack the ice and not go charging in like a bull in a china shop.

Nuoro is to Sardinia what Calabria is to mainland Italy. To outsiders the locals appear brooding and introverted, yet with a rough-diamond beauty. Both have a history of banditry, and kidnappings were as popular in Nuoro in the 1980s and early 1990s as in Calabria. For centuries a tough peasant population has learned to expect only oppression and taxes from governments and the upper classes. Hardened by their unforgiving environment as much as by their circumstances, a small fraction of men have chosen violence as the only way to break a vicious cycle. The Nuoresi are aware of their province's reputation and understandably can be defensive about it. Not a few blame the media for beating the story up.

Rome continues to consider Nuoro a difficult province in a thorny region. The area has more than its share of police and *carabinieri* but their frequent patrols and roadblocks seem to accomplish little. Accounts between families and rivals are still occasionally settled with the shotgun, but locals rarely say anything to the authorities, in whose protection they have little confidence.

None of this is likely to touch the outsider, and the unruliness of the place is part of its charm, albeit sometimes in a perverse manner. The dark majesty of the Supramonte and Gennargentu mountains and the inland

Highlights

- Hire a speedboat to explore the stunning beauty of the Golfo di Orosei's beaches and coves
- Allow yourself to be dazzled by the traditional island costumes on parade for Nuoro's August Festa del Redentore
- Trek along the deep Gola Su Gorroppu gorge
- Seek out the Fonte Sacra Su Tempiesu, a remarkable ancient sacred site
- Stare up at Europe's tallest stalagmite in the Grotta di Ispinigoli
- Tuck into some fine *culurgiones*, a much-favoured pasta dish
- Join in the pagan January fun of the *mamuthones* in Mamoiada
- Explore the Santuario Santa Vittoria, the most extensive nuraghic settlement on the island

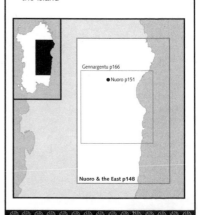

Gennargentu p166

● Nuoro p151

Nuoro & the East p148

Barbagia region (also known as Le Barbagie, a plural collective noun indicating the several distinct areas that make up the region) is matched by the oppressive breezeblock wildness of most of the province's towns and villages. The Nuoresi are the uncontested kings of the half-finished house and some of their towns would not look out of place in a battle scene. Often downright ugly, they frequently stand in stunning positions arranged like mountainside balconies, so steeply terraced that you wonder how they have any purchase on the soil they occupy.

Fine country restaurants of all classes purvey heaped dishes of solid comfort food and you will want to wash it down with a robust Cannonau red, produced here and appreciated as far away as North America.

NUORO

postcode 08100 • pop 37,615 • elev 554m

A handful of museums and churches and the town's pleasant hilly position in the shadow of Monte Ortobene make the provincial capital well worth a stopover – you could easily make a relaxing day of it in the birthplace of Sardinia's most celebrated writer, Grazia Deledda.

History

A handful of archaeological remains indicate the site of Nuoro was settled as early as the 5th century AD, while circumstantial evidence suggests there could have been a village here in Roman times. Little is known about the town prior to the 14th century, although it appears to have passed from the control of the Giudicato di Torres to that of Arborea. Subsequently Nuoro (Nugoro in the local dialect) passed from one feudal family to another, under the overall control of the Crown of Aragon (and later Spain), in the course of the 15th and 16th centuries.

By the end of the 18th century the town boasted a population of not more than 3000 souls, mostly farmers and shepherds, and had clearly become the 'urban' centre of this part of the island. If reports by the island's rulers of the time are to be believed, Nuoro was also a violent nest of bandits and outlaws. Many Nuoresi were no doubt pushed to lawlessness by the precariousness of peasant life and the centuries of oppression to which the whole area had been subject.

In 1820 a law to privatise common land (effectively handing it to rich landowners) sparked a series of peasant revolts. Backed into an impossible corner, the desperate rebels even burned down Nuoro's town hall. In 1859 Nuoro was demoted as its province was brought under the administration of Sassari, a situation not reversed until 1927. The decision was possibly influenced by the new Italian state's view of the whole Nuoro district

as a 'crime zone', an attitude reflected in its treatment of the area, which only served to further alienate the Nuoresi and cement their mistrust of authority.

After 1927 Nuoro quickly grew into a bustling administrative centre, attracting internal migrants from all over the province to its haphazardly expanding suburbs. Although the problem of banditry has subsided and the town presents a cheerful enough visage, Nuoro remains troubled. Its population is falling as high unemployment drives people away.

Orientation

The old centre of the town is bunched together in the northeastern corner of the city on a high spur of land that swings slowly eastward to become Monte Ortobene. Viale Francesco Ciusa and the Colle Sant'Onofrio afford pleasant views east across the valley.

The heart of the town is contained in the warren of tidy streets and lanes around Piazza San Giovanni and Corso Garibaldi, the main street. Several restaurants, but little in the way of hotels, dot the area. Apart from a couple of options near the centre and on Monte Ortobene, most of Nuoro's few hotels are oddly placed west of the centre near the hospital.

The train and main bus stations are also west of the city centre.

Information

Pro Loco (☎ 0784 3 00 83; Piazza Italia 19; open 9am-1pm & 4pm-7pm Mon-Sat) tourist office is in the same building as the provincial EPT tourist administration office.

Punto Informa (☎ 0784 3 87 77; W www .viazzos.it, Italian only; Corso Garibaldi 155; open 9am-1pm & 3.30pm-7pm Mon-Sat) is a private initiative run by FdS (Ferrovie della Sardegna, bus and train services) Miffed by a lack of cooperation from the public sector for a service they provide free (in addition to normal FdS business), they sometimes threaten to close the information service. Let's hope they do not.

The **main post office** (Piazza Francesco Crispi; open 8.15am-6.40pm Mon-Fri, 8.15am-1pm Sat) is in the heart of town.

You can change money at the **Banco di Sardegna** (Corso Garibaldi 69) or the **Banco Nazionale del Lavoro** (Via Alessandro Manzoni 26).

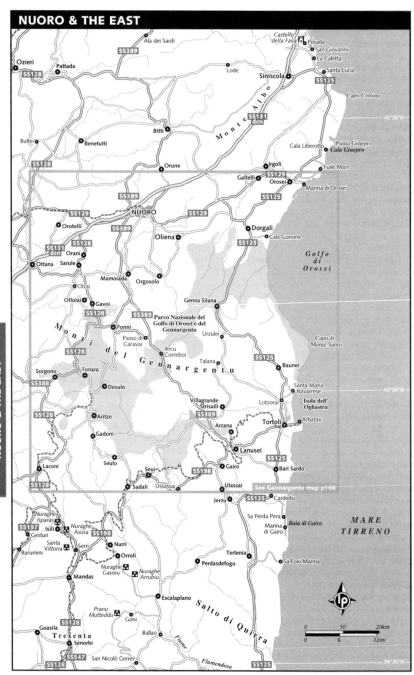

NUORO & THE EAST

The national youth travel agent, **CTS** (☎ 0784 25 40 18; Via Deffenu 41-43), has a branch in town.

Libreria Mondadori (☎ 0784 3 41 61; Corso Garibaldi 147) is a handy bookshop although there's little in English.

The city's main hospital is the **Ospedale Civile San Francesco** (☎ 0784 24 02 37; Via Mannironi), west of the centre. The central **police station** (☎ 0784 3 21 00; Viale Europa) is just north of the action.

Things to See & Do

The compact centre with its leafy squares and narrow lanes is a pleasure to wander around.

Museo Archeologico Nazionale The museum (Via Mannu 1; admission free; open 9am-1.30pm & 3pm-6pm Wed & Fri, 9am-1.30pm Tues, Thur & Sat), housed in the neoclassical Palazzo Asproni, opened its doors in 2002. For the moment, only one of the three available floors has been restored and converted into museum space but the other floors will follow. The collection of artefacts, ranging from ancient ceramics and fine bronzetti (bronze figurines) to a drilled skull from 1600 BC and Roman and early medieval finds, concentrates on objects dug up at sites in the province of Nuoro.

Duomo The orange-rose neoclassical facade of this 19th-century cathedral (Piazza Santa Maria Della Neve) stands imperiously above a tree-lined square on the edge of the old town. The church, completed in 1853 and dedicated to Santa Maria della Neve, is not overly exciting in artistic terms, although it contains a couple of interesting works inside, including Disputa de Gesù Fra i Dottori (Jesus Arguing with the Doctors), a canvas attributed to the school of Luca Giordano and located between the first and second chapels on the right as you enter. Half the panels of the Via Crucis are by Giovanni Ciusa-Romagna.

Piazza Sebastiano Satta The square was completely remade in 1967 to celebrate the centenary of the birth of Nuoro's second literary claim to fame, the poet Sebastiano Satta. Rough-hewn granite blocks reminiscent of ancient menhirs rise up out of the square, each with a niche containing a little bronze (a clear wink at nuraghic bronzetti) representing the poet in various poses. They are the inimitable work of Costantino Nivola. The house where Satta lived (now a closed, run-down building) stands where Via Sebastiano Satta enters the square.

Museo d'Arte (MAN) The MAN (☎ 0784 25 21 10; Via Sebastiano Satta 15; adult/child €2.58/1.55; open 10am-1pm & 4.30pm-8.30pm Tues-Sat, 10am-1pm Sun) offers a look at modern and contemporary art in Sardinia. Among the more important names are Antonio Ballero, Giovanni Ciusa-Romagna, Mario Delitalia and the sculptor Francesco Ciusa.

The permanent exhibition is frequently accompanied by temporary showings, on the ground floor, of work by painters and sculptors from elsewhere in Italy and beyond.

Casa di Grazia Deledda Also known as the Museo Deleddiano (☎ 0784 25 80 88; Via Grazia Deledda 53; adult/child €2.58/0.52; open 9am-8pm Tues-Sat, 9am-1pm Sun mid-June–Sept, 9am-1pm & 3pm-7pm Oct–mid-June), the birthplace of Sardinia's most celebrated writer has been converted into a museum. All sorts of memorabilia relating to the writer and her works are spread over the building's three floors.

Chiesa di San Carlo This early-17th-century church, on the square of the same name, is itself of little interest, but the Sardinian sculptor Francesco Ciusa is honoured with a memorial, as well as a bronze copy of his Madre dell'Ucciso, which won a prize at the Venice Biennale in 1907.

Nearby Piazza San Giovanni contains a curio. Mussolini remains immortalised in faded Fascist-era propaganda written large in party graffiti on a building wall: 'Fascism believes now and forever in sanctity and heroism – Mussolini'. Can't argue with that now, can we?

Museo della Vita e delle Tradizioni Sarde This extensive, rambling museum (☎ 0784 25 70 35; Via Antonio Mereu 56; adult/child €2.58/0.52; open 9am-8pm Tues-Sat, 9am-1pm Sun mid-June–Sept, 9am-1pm & 3pm-7pm Oct–mid-June) is the most interesting in town. It is basically an ethnographic collection but, unlike many of its country-town confreres, represents a broad and engaging entry into many aspects of traditional Sardinian life.

Highlights include the generous display of traditional costumes from around the island, some still in use in more remote villages. In addition come the many pieces of jewellery and decorative items in gold and silver used to adorn the more boisterous of the costumes. Traditional Sardinian woollen carpets and rugs, tapestries, arms, musical instruments and household items make up the rest of the display.

Parco Colle Sant'Onofrio A short wander up from the museum is this quiet hilly park. From the highest point you can see across to Monte Ortobene and, further south, to Oliena and Orgosolo. There are swings for kids and benches for the pooped. You can also head to Il Fortino for a drink or meal (see Entertainment later).

Chiesa della Solitudine Sitting in leafy isolation at the beginning of the road that leads up to Nuoro's sacred mount, Monte Ortobene, this lacklustre 1950s granite church *(Viale della Solitudine)* is important for what it contains rather than what it is. Here lie, to the right of the altar in an undemonstrative sarcophagus, the remains of writer Grazia Deledda. On the eve of 28 August, the religious high point of Nuoro's Festa del Redentore, a solemn torchlight parade starts here at 9pm and winds up at the Duomo.

Monte Ortobene The road continues about 6.5km up to what is for the Nuoresi a place of veneration and escape. Monte Ortobene (955m) is a favourite picnic and lunch spot for locals but never more so than during the Festa del Redentore in August. On the 29th (starting bright and early at 6am) the faithful make a pilgrimage from the Duomo to the statue of the Redentore (Christ the Redeemer) that looks out in windswept pose across the valleys below. Afterwards Mass is celebrated in the nearby Chiesa di Nostra Signora del Monte, followed by another late-morning Mass at the feet of the statue.

After taking care of the spirit, the thoughts of Nuoresi turn to more terrestrial needs. Many fan out in the woods (full of ilex, pine, fir trees and poplars) and open picnic hampers, while others crowd into a couple of bars or grab a restaurant table.

The statue itself was raised in 1901 in response to a call by Pope Leo XIII to raise 19 (representing the 19 centuries of Christianity) statues of Christ around the country. Grazia Deledda was in part behind the push by Nuoro to be one of the selected few. Since then, the statue, which represents Christ victoriously trampling the devil underfoot, has been the object of pilgrims who attribute to him all manner of cures and interventions.

The views across the valley to Oliena and Monte Corrasi are at their most breathtaking from the road to the left shortly before you reach the top of the mountain.

The No 8 local bus runs up to the mountain seven times a day from Piazza Vittorio Emanuele. The last one back down leaves at 8.20pm.

Centro Sportivo Farcana About 4km up Monte Ortobene from Nuoro, this sports centre (☎ 0784 3 23 57) is signposted off to the left. It's main attraction is the outdoor Olympic pool, a treat in summer if you haven't the energy to go to the seaside.

Special Events
The **Festa del Redentore** (Feast of Christ the Redeemer) in the last week of August is the main event in Nuoro and since its inception in 1901 has become one of the most exuberant folkloric festivals on the island's calendar. For more information on this festival, see the special section 'Viva la Festa!'.

Places to Stay
There are five hotels in town but most are well out of the centre. Also ask at the tourist offices about a handful of B&B options.

Casa Solotti (☎ 0784 3 39 54; w www .casasolotti.it; B&B per person €25) makes it worth the hassle of getting up to Monte Ortobene. It's a charming house set in a grand garden and exposed to wonderful views down into the valleys below.

Of the mainstream hotels, **Hotel Grillo** (☎ 0784 3 86 78, fax 0784 3 20 05; Via Monsignor Melas 14; singles/doubles €50/66) is the most central. A biggish place with comfortable, spacious rooms (the colour green predominates), it is the best first port of call.

Hotel Sandalia (☎/fax 0784 3 83 53; Via Einaudi 12/14; singles/doubles €50.50/71)

NUORO

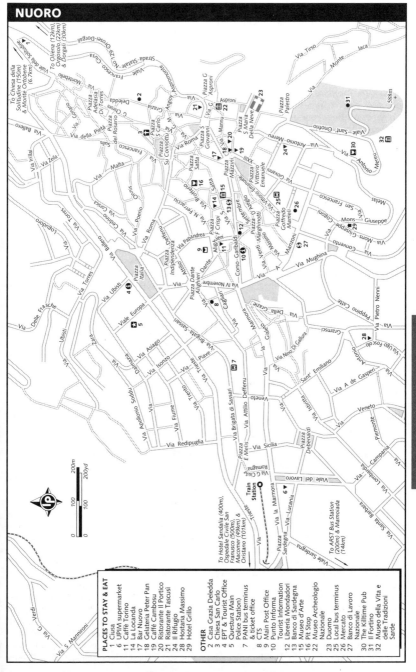

To Chiesa della
Solitudine (150m)
& Monte Ortobene
(6.7km)

To Ollena (12km),
Orgosolo (22km)
& Dorgali (30km)

Strada Statale
No 129 Orosei-Dorgali

Via Tirso

Monte
Jaca

Piazza G
Asproni

Piazza
Adelasia
Di Torres

Piazza G
Asproni

Piazza
Palestro

588m

Montebello

Piazza
del Rosario

Piazza
S Carlo

Piazza
S
Giovanni

Piazza S
Maria
Della Neve

Viale Sant'Onofrio

Via della Pietà

Piazza
Satta

Piazza
Satta

Via Antonio Mereu

Via
Malta

Via Zola

Via Irifilai

Via
Torres

Via Trieste

Via della
Pietà

Viale Europa

Piazza
Italia

Via Ubisti

Via Torres

Via Brigata Sassari

Via Asiago

Via Isonzo

Via Piave

Via Tireno

Via Fiume

Via Redipuglia

Piazza
Dante
Alighieri

Corso Garibaldi

Via IV Novembre

Via Della Grazie

Via Brigata di Sassari

Via Attilio Deffenu

Veneto

Piazza
E Melis

Via C Ciuc
Romana

Train
Station

Via la Marmora

Piazza
Sardegna

Via Sicilia

Piazza
Debenardi

Via Ugo Foscolo

Via Peppino Catte

Via Pietro Nenni

Via Gramsci

Sant' Emiliano

Via A de Gasperi

Veneto

Piemonte

Via Lombardia

Via Campania

Via Santa Barbara

Viale Sardegna

To Hotel Sandalia (400m),
Ospedale Civile San
Franusco (500m),
Macomer (49km) &
Oristano (101km)

To ARST Bus Station
(200m) & Marmoiada
(14km)

NUORO & THE EAST

PLACES TO STAY & EAT
1 Ciusa
6 UPIM supermarket
11 Caffè Torino
14 La Locanda
17 Bar Nuovo
18 Gelateria Peter Pan
19 Caffè Cambosu
20 Ristorante Il Portico
21 Ristorante Tascusi
24 Il Rifugio
28 Hostaria Massimo
29 Hotel Grillo

OTHER
2 Casa Grazia Deledda
3 Chiesa San Carlo
4 EPT & Tourist Office
5 Questura Main
  Police Station)
7 PANI bus terminus
  & ticket office
8 CTS
9 Main Post Office
10 Punto Informa
  Tourist Information
12 Libreria Mondadori
13 Banco di Sardegna
15 Museo d'Arte
22 Museo Archeologio
  Nazionale
23 Duomo
25 Local bus terminus
26 Mercato
27 Banco di Lavoro
  Nazionale
30 The Killtime Pub
31 Il Fortino
32 Museo della Vita e
  delle Tradizioni
  Sarde

has plenty of comfortable rooms with parquet floors, TV and en-suite bathroom. They also have a couple of spacious suites.

Places to Eat
Restaurants Possibly the cheapest full meal in Sardinia can be enjoyed at **La Locanda** *(Via Brofferio 31; set meals €8.50; open Mon-Sat)*. It is not haute cuisine but you get two filling courses and some wine. Locals pile in for lunch.

Hostaria Massimo *(☎ 0784 3 38 60; Via Ugo Foscolo 3; pizzas up to €7, meals €25; open daily)* attracts packs of punters into its bustling terrace, especially in summer. The pizzas (about 30 options) are good but you can dine well on other dishes too.

Il Rifugio *(☎ 0784 23 23 55; Via Antonio Mereu 28-36; set lunch €16, meals €25-30; open Thur-Tues)* is an age-old trattoria in a brand-new locale. The restaurant has been serving up delicious *malloreddus* (sea shell–shaped pasta) in a tomato and basil sauce, and many other fine dishes, since the late 1980s. In 2002 they moved to their present address. Simple elegant dinner tables and chairs, along with old photos of Nuoro on the wall, lend the place a welcome warmth.

Ciusa *(☎ 0784 25 70 52; Viale Francesco Ciusa 53; meals €30; open Wed-Mon)* turns out a decent pizza and some tempting pasta dishes. Among the latter are *maccarones de busa al ragù d'anatra* (a chunky pasta in duck sauce).

Il Portico *(☎ 0784 25 50 62; Via Monsignor Bua 13; meals €30-35; open Mon-Sat)*, with its lemon-coloured walls and rose-painted arches, is a pleasing little enclave for a range of local and seafood dishes.

Ristorante Tascusi *(☎ 0784 3 72 87; Via Aspromonte 11; meals €25-30; open Mon-Sat)*, in the heart of the old town, offers a limited but reliable range of pastas and mains.

Su Redentore *(☎ 0784 3 15 38; meals €25-30; open Tues-Sun)*, at the top of Monte Ortobene, is a cheerful and popular eatery with a varied menu of seafood and more traditional local dishes, which are the better option.

Gelateria Peter Pan *(Piazza Mazzini)* is a good spot to pick up an after-dinner gelato and start an evening promenade.

If you want to stock up and make your own meals, pick up fresh produce at the *mercato* on Piazza Goffredo Mameli and

other stuff at the **UPIM** *(Viale del Lavoro)* supermarket near the train station.

Cafés Corso Garibaldi is lined with several cafés that are good for taking a load off.

Caffè Torino *(Piazza Crispi 2)*, opposite the main post office, is a busy place from breakfast to the early evening tipple time.

Bar Nuovo *(Piazza Mazzini)*, strategically placed between two converging streets, makes optimum use of the position with a good people-watching terrace outside. It's as good for the morning paper as for an evening's beer.

Caffè Cambosu *(Via Monsignor Bua 4)* runs close competition to Bar Nuovo. You can sit outside or in one of several charming rooms inside with little marble-topped tables on which to rest your wine glass.

Entertainment
Pit Stop *(☎ 0784 25 70 30; Via Brofferio 19)* is a lively bar that opens out onto Piazza Satta as well as Via Brofferio. You can eat here but the main diversion is a drink or two in the square until around midnight.

The Killtime Pub *(Via Antonio Mereu 45)* draws in night owls in search of a libation from all over town. The pub atmosphere is more in the name than in the reality but the pints will keep you happy until about 2am.

Il Fortino, in the Parco Colle Sant'-Onofrio, is another good option. They do grills and drinks, and a few cocktails late into the night here away from the city bustle seem to taste all the better.

Getting There & Away
Bus PANI buses run to/from Cagliari (€11.31, 3½ hours) four times a day via Oristano (€5.84, two hours) and to/from Sassari (€6.77, 2½ hours) up to six times a day. Three continue on to Porto Torres (€7.64, three hours). You can get tickets at the **office** *(Via Brigata di Sassari 19)*, where the buses terminate.

ARST buses run from a station on Viale Sardegna all over the province and beyond. Runs to the coast are frequent, with up to seven daily runs to places like Orosei (€2.32), Cala Liberotto (€2.89, one hour 10 minutes), La Caletta (€3.72, one hour), Posada (€4.91, one hour 20 minutes) and San Teodoro (€6.30, one hour 50 minutes). The south coast is less well served, with only two or three daily runs to places such as Baunei (€4.91, two hours), Santa Maria Navarrese (€5.37, two hours 25 minutes) and Tortolì (€5.84, two hours 40 minutes).

Deplano runs up to five daily buses to Olbia's airport (1¼ hours) from the Viale Sardegna bus station in Nuoro via Budoni and San Teodoro. A couple of daily buses also run to Alghero and Fertilia airport (2½ hours).

To get into town from the bus station catch the No 8 bus from Viale Sardegna to Piazza Vittorio Emanuele.

Train The train station is west of the town centre on the corner of Via La Marmora and Via Ciusa Romagna. FdS trains run from Nuoro to the interchange station of Macomer, where mainline Trenitalia trains make it possible to link up with other destinations in the island. From Cagliari the run costs €10.80 and can take 3½ hours or more.

Car & Motorcycle The SS131 DCN cross-country, dual-carriage highway between Olbia and Abbasanta (where it runs into the north–south SS131 Carlo Felice highway) skirts Nuoro to the north. Otherwise, the SS129 is the quickest road east to Orosei and Dorgali. Several roads head south for Oliena, Orgosolo and Mamoiada.

Getting Around
Local buses can be useful for the train station (Nos 2, 3 and 4), the ARST bus station (No 8) and heading up to Monte Ortobene (also No 8).

You can call for a taxi on ☎ 0784 3 14 11 or try to grab one along Via La Marmora.

AROUND NUORO
Fonte Sacra Su Tempiesu
Much ignored by visitors, owing to the lack of publicity and transport, the well temple of Fonte Sacra Su Tempiesu (☎ 0784 27 67 16; adult/child €2/1; open 9am-6pm daily), named after the farmer who came across it in 1953 (he was from Tempio), is unique among the nuraghic temples in Sardinia. Set in dramatic hill country looking east to Monte Albo and, on a clear day, to the sea, the temple was built over a spring and dedicated to the cult of water.

The temple displays the standard characteristics such as a keyhole-shape arrangement

with stairs leading down to the well bottom. It is oriented towards the rising sun in such a fashion that on the day of the summer solstice sunlight penetrates directly into the well. Water brims to the top of the stairs and trickles down a runnel to another small well, part of the original, more primitive temple built around 1600 BC. The newer temple, dating back to about 1000 BC, is a (partially restored) masterpiece. Above the well and stairs rises an A-shaped structure of carefully carved, interlocking stones of basalt and trachyte (sealed watertight with lead). The stone was transported from at least as far away as Dorgali! Stretch the imagination and this place has the shape of a mountain chalet, with a steep, pointed roof to allow rainwater to run off. No other such structure has been found in Sardinia and this one, excavated from 1981, was for centuries hidden by a landslide that had buried it back in the Iron Age.

Getting here is a problem without your own transport. Head for **Orune**, 18km northeast of Nuoro (turn off the SS131 DCN highway at the Ponte Marreri exit for the 11km climb to the town). From Orune it is a 7km drive southeast down a narrow country route (signposted). Buses run only as far as Orune. From the ticket office you walk 800m downhill to the temple. You may be accompanied by a guide (in Italian).

SUPRAMONTE
The bare walls of the Supramonte dominate the interior of eastern Nuoro province and attract hikers from all over Europe.

Oliena
From Nuoro you can see the fetching little town of Oliena across a deep valley to the south, especially when lit up like a Christmas tree at night. Behind it rises the magnificent spectacle of Monte Corrasi.

Follow the road up past the petrol station to Piazza Santa Maria, where buses stop and the town's 13th-century church of the same name is located. On the square you will find **Servizi Turistici Corrasi** (☎ 0784 28 71 44; Piazza Santa Maria 30), which has information on the town and mountains. It organises treks to Tiscali, the Gola Su Gorroppu and elsewhere. Another source of information is **Tourpass** (☎ 0784 28 60 78; Corso Deledda 32; open 9am-1pm & 4pm-7pm daily).

Hotel Cikappa (☎/fax 0784 28 87 33; Corso Martin Luther King; singles/doubles €36/49), towards the southwest end of the town, is a cheerful hikers' hotel. Rooms are surprisingly comfortable and the hotel also hosts a hearty restaurant.

Ristorante Masiloghi (☎ 0784 28 56 96; Via Galiani 68; meals €30; open daily) is a good little spot at the eastern exit of town with tables out on the veranda. It specialises in lamb and young wild boar. You could also try the special gourmet set menu (€38).

Hotel Monte Maccione (☎ 0784 28 83 63, fax 0784 28 84 73; singles/doubles €32.50/53), run by the Cooperativa Eris, is buried deep in the woods of Monte Maccione (700m), 4km south of Oliena and a good way uphill (the narrow road up is like so many hairpins placed one above the other). The restaurant, where you can eat well for €25 to €30, is a favourite getaway with locals. Oliena is a centre of good Cannonau reds, so always ask for local drops.

Hotel Su Gologone (☎ 0784 28 75 12, fax 0784 28 76 68; singles/doubles €119/176, half board per person €119; open Mar-Sept & mid-Dec–mid-Jan), 7km east of Oliena, is one of the best hotel/restaurant complexes on the island. A discreet series of ivy-covered buildings contains the comfortable and charmingly decorated rooms. The restaurant, which concentrates on fine reinventions of local cuisine, is rated as one of Sardinia's best and is likely to relieve you of €50 including wine.

Orgosolo
postcode 08027 • pop 4900 • elev 620m
A dusty, grey rural town in the typical half-finished style of so many Nuoro towns, and backed by the dramatic grey wall of the Supramonte, Orgosolo means sheep-rustlers and bandits to most people. Feuds and murder marked much of the town's 20th-century history. The legends surrounding Orgosolo's wild past inevitably attract curious visitors, who are greeted by more than a hundred *murales* (murals) rather than gunfire. For years locals have been adding a splash of colour to the mostly drab housing with imaginative wall paintings, many taking up social and political causes both local and international.

Make for the Chiesa di San Salvatore in the centre and begin exploration of the colourful streets and lanes around here. The town otherwise looks a little like a war zone

---

Shoot 'Em Up

The people of Nuoro province will often be the first to tell you they know exactly what kind of a reputation their province has elsewhere. Reports may be exaggerated but a Wild-West whisper runs through the place. Where else in Italy can you wander into a tough town like Orgosolo and see the locals whooping it up with horse races down the main street on a Saturday afternoon? And perhaps most worrying for the newcomer is a tangible sign that gun laws are not so strictly enforced in these parts. As you drive around the province you will find it hard to come by street signs that have not been well peppered with rifle shots. 'Drunken youths', people will explain. So long as it's just the signs being shot to pieces, that's probably OK!

---

and playing softball at the local pitch next to an open garbage dump can hardly be attractive. Still, the place has atmosphere. Where else (even in deepest central Sardinia) can you turn up on a Saturday evening and find the locals lining the main road for some impromptu horse racing?

Five kilometres south of town, the SP48 local road heads up to the **Montes** heights. Another 13km south is the **Funtana Bona**, the spring at the source of the Cedrino river. On the way you pass through the tall oaks of the **Foresta de Montes**.

The townspeople and folk from all around the province's Barbagia area converge on Orgosolo (on the northern fringes of Le Barbagie) on 15 August for the **Festa dell'Assunta**, with colourful if solemn parades to mark the Feast of the Assumption.

Should you want/need to stay the night, you have two options. **Petit Hotel** (☎/fax 0784 40 20 09; Via Mannu; singles/doubles €28.50/38.80) is a basic place in the centre of the sprawling town. Don't expect much else but the bed and loo. If you prefer to save a few euros, you can take a room without a private bath.

Slightly better, but awkwardly located in a dead-end (and one might also be tempted to say deadbeat) lane at the western end of town, is the **Hotel Sa 'e Jana** (☎/fax 0784 40 24 37; Via E Lussu; singles/doubles €37/47). It is a slightly more comfortable choice than

Petit Hotel but still rather basic. You can also eat here.

Regular buses make the 30-minute run to/from Nuoro (€1.45).

NORTH NUORO COAST

The northern coast of Nuoro province actually starts with Capo Coda Cavallo and, a little further south, the happening little beach town of San Teodoro (see the Olbia & the Gallura chapter). From here to Orosei, 58km south, a succession of good, clean beaches with generally crystal clear water unfolds before you. They are not always exciting in terms of scenery and you may want to hurry on to see the marvels of the Golfo di Orosei, but they are generally peaceful, even around the minor resorts like La Caletta, Santa Lucia and Cala Liberotto (the most attractive of the lot).

Budoni to Cala Liberotto

Approaching from San Teodoro, a series of low-level tourist settlements dot the coast on the way south to Orosei and the gulf of the same name.

About 10km south of San Teodoro you wind up in the minor beach resort of Budoni. It's nothing special but around here, especially at **Agrustos** just to the north, you'll find a string of hotels and camping grounds should you need to call a halt.

Posada lies another 12km south of Budoni and makes a more interesting stop. Climb the **Castello della Fava** (admission €2.10; open 9am-8pm daily June-Sept, 9am-6pm Oct-May), where only the monolithic central tower remains, for sweeping views to the coast and inland. The 'bean castle' is so-named after a myth in which an invading Arab force abandoned a one-year siege of Posada in the wake of a clever stratagem by the besieged. They caught a pigeon, stuffed it with fava beans and damaged its wings so that they could be sure it would fall in the Arabs' camp. Sure enough it did and when the Arabs discovered the half-digested beans in the bird's stomach as they prepared to cook it, they concluded they could not starve Posada out. In fact, the besieged were down to their last beans! A few paces downhill from the castle, the modest **Chiesa di Sant'Antonio** was the scene of peace talks between the Eleonora d'Arborea and the Catalans in 1388.

Medieval Posada, its gaily painted houses hugging the hillside, is quite an attractive spot and could make a decent base for a couple of days. You could stay at **Hotel Sa Rocca** (☎ 0784 85 41 39, fax 0784 85 41 66; Via Eleonora d'Arborea; singles/doubles €30/ 50, half board in summer €50) in the old town below the castle. The place has its own restaurant and the views from some rooms and dining tables across to the coast are an attraction in themselves. Rooms come with TV and phone.

A couple of kilometres south of the town, on the road to La Caletta, another nice choice, set back from the SS125 road amid plenty of greenery, is **Hotel Corallo** (☎ 0784 81 03 04, fax 0784 81 21 84; singles/doubles €31/51.65). Rooms are simple and some without own bath cost a little less.

A couple of decent beaches line Posada's coast, but for the best, **Spiaggia Su Tiriarzu**, head out of town towards La Caletta. Turn left (east) at the sign for the beach settlement of San Giovanni. North along a bridge that crosses the lagoon you arrive at this pristine beach.

About 4km south of Posada is the low-key resort of **La Caletta**, where six budget to mid-range hotels and several restaurants await. It is not an overly prepossessing place, but a handy stop. The beach starts south of town and continues down to quieter **Santa Lucia**, 5km further on, where you'll find a couple of camping grounds.

The wild and woolly **Capo Comino** is Sardinia's easternmost point. To its north, the long beach of the same name doesn't get too crowded but is often full of seaweed.

South of the cape, a more pleasing series of beaches unwinds before you. Follow the SS125 south for a few kilometres to the turn-off for **Spiaggia Berchidda**. The whole stretch of strands around here is fine but the best is **Spiaggia Bidderossa**, a couple of kilometres walk to the south. In summer you are supposed to get a ticket (numbers limited) for this beach from the Pro Loco in Orosei (mornings only and clearly a pain if you are approaching from the north!), as it is part of a protected area.

Moving closer to Orosei, **Cala Liberotto** is yet another resort, this time made up of a series of pretty little beaches broken up by rocky intrusions. In the background the discreet holiday villas are partly obscured by

NUORO & THE EAST

the thick pine woods. The biggest and north-ernmost of the beaches is **Spiaggia Mat-tanosa**. Some 3km north of the resort centre, around a small promontory, is another good beach, **Cala Ginepro**.

Several camping grounds and hotels are spread out about the area. The best of the four is **Camping Cala Ginepro** (☎ 0784 9 10 17, fax 0784 9 13 62; per person/tent space €11.40/15.50, 4-person bungalows up to €134; open May-Oct). Just behind it you can pick up a meal at **Pizzeria Mariposa**. **Hotel Quasar** (☎/fax 0784 9 12 59; doubles €82) is about the cheapest option and a short walk from the central beaches of Cala Liberotto.

ARST buses running between Olbia and Orosei stop on the SS125 highway at Posada and Cala Liberotto. Other local buses run up to seven times a day from Camping Cala Ginepro and Cala Liberotto to/from Orosei. The trip takes about 25 minutes to/from the camping ground.

GOLFO DI OROSEI

Sardinia's most memorable stretch of coast-line has its northern beginning at Marina di Orosei, the coastal extension of Orosei. The gulf attracts many tourists in summer but even if you arrive in August you will not re-gret having made the effort to see its cliffs, coves and stunning water.

Orosei

postcode 08028 • pop 5265

Follow the 'centro' signs to wind up in **Pi-azza del Popolo**, its centre a pretty green, tree-lined garden and its edges guarded by churches.

The **Cattedrale di San Giacomo**, up a flight of steps, presents an unusual picture. Its blank, white neoclassical facade flanked by a set of tiled domes is strangely reminis-cent of churches in the coastal Mediter-ranean region of Valencia in Spain.

Across the square is the more modest 17th-century **Chiesa del Rosario**, with a baroque facade. The lane leading up from its left side takes you to Piazza Sas Animas and the **church** of the same name, a pleasant stone building with a vaguely Iberian feel about it. Opposite rises the empty hulk of the **Prigione Vecchia**, also known as the Castello, a tower left over from a medieval castle.

Another lane leading from the right side of the Chiesa del Rosario passes out of the old town and down into Piazza Sant'Antonio, a shady square off which lies the equally shaded and modest **Chiesa di Sant'Antonio**, dating largely from the 15th century. The broad uneven courtyard surrounding the church is lined with squat *cumbessias*, or pil-grims' dwellings, and a solitary Pisan watch-tower.

Hotel options are not abundant. Just off the road that runs around the centre, **Hotel S'Ortale** (☎ 0784 9 98 05, fax 0784 9 98 06; Via S'Ortale; singles/doubles €43.90/69.70) is a perfectly good choice. Rooms are of a decent size, with own bathroom and TV and the hotel has a restaurant.

Otherwise, for food you might head for **La Taverna** (☎ 0784 99 83 30; Piazza G Marconi 6; meals €25) with tables spilling out on to the pleasant leafy square (just off Piazza Sas Animas). Try its *gnocchetti sardi al ragù d'asino* (small gnocchi in donkey-meat sauce). It also sometimes have a few rooms to rent – it's a pleasant central location and worth a try.

Several daily buses run to Orosei from Nuoro (€2.32, about one hour) and Dorgali (€1.19, 25 minutes).

Around Orosei

Once a relatively poor area, frequently flooded by the Rio Cedrino, the area around Orosei now bursts with wellbeing. Tourism has contributed a great deal but the damming of the Rio Cedrino (creating the Lago Cedrino upstream) in 1983 went a great way to turning things around. Instead of being victims of the water, the area's farmers now have controlled access to water for irrigation.

Marina di Orosei This beach marks the northern end of the gulf, which from here you can see arched in all its magnificence to the south. A broad sandy strip, the strand runs 5km south and undergoes several name changes along the way: **Spiaggia Su Barone**, **Spiaggia Isporoddai** and **Spiaggia Osalla**. All are equally tempting and mostly backed by pine stands, giving you the option of re-treating to the shade for a picnic or even a BBQ (facilities are scattered about the pines). Even in August you can find plenty of space to stretch out – most of the punters tend not to wander too far from where they park their cars. The water is a cool, clear emerald green

Narrow roads run from Orosei and Marina di Orosei along the coast here, giving you several access points along the way. The Marina di Orosei beach is closed off to the north by the Rio Cedrino and behind the beaches stretch the **Stagni di Cedrino** lagoons.

Past a big breakwater you can wander from Spiaggia Osalla around to **Caletta di Osalla** (the second stretch of sand after the main beach). It is cute, with the Rio di Osalla, a small river, running into the beach down the valley behind it. A couple of bars and an *agriturismo* (farm stay) cater for the lunch and snack needs of punters, who can be numerous in August.

Galtellí If you take the inland SS129 route from Orosei to Nuoro (which you might wish to do in order to visit the nuraghic sites of Serra Orrios and S'Ena 'e Thomes on the way to Dorgali – see later in this chapter), you will pass through this unremarkable farming town. A short way into the town, a road left leads to the cemetery and what little remains of the Romanesque **Chiesa di San Pietro**, cited in Grazia Deledda's *Canne al Vento*. The house of the Nieddu sisters, characters in the same book, is signposted 20m off as the **Casa delle Dame Pintor**. It is occasionally open for a modest photo exhibit dedicated to Deledda.

Occasional buses run between Galtellí, Orosei and Cala Liberotto.

Grotta di Ispinigoli Mexico is home to the world's tallest stalagmite (40m) but you shouldn't worry about settling for second best here – the natural spectacle of its slightly shorter counterpart is every bit as awe-inspiring. The Grotta di Ispinigoli *(adult/ child €7/4.50; open 9am-7pm daily Aug, reduced hrs Apr-Jul & Sept-Nov, closed Dec-Feb)*, 4km north of Dorgali, is extraordinary for several reasons.

Unlike most caves of this type, which you enter from the side, here you descend 60m inside a giant 'well', at whose centre stands the magnificent 38m-high stalagmite that has made the cave a must on many tourists' sight list in Sardinia. Water has long ceased to filter in to this cave, which means what you see will be unlikely to change in coming centuries.

Exploration of the caves began in earnest in the 1960s. In all, a deep network of 15km

of caves with eight subterranean rivers has been found. Cavers can book speleological tours of up to 8km through one of the various tour organisers in Dorgali and Cala Gonone. People have been poking around here since ancient times. Nuraghic artefacts were discovered on the floor of the main well, and Phoenician jewellery on the floor of the second main 'well', another 40m below. On the standard tour you can just peer into the hole that leads into this second cavity, known also as the **Abbisso delle Vergini** (Abyss of the Virgins). The ancient jewellery found has led some to believe that the Phoenicians launched young girls into the pit in rites of human sacrifice. The theory that the Phoenicians indulged in such blood-curdling activities has, however, been poo-pooed by some historians. The artefacts found are now on display in three window cases at Dorgali's archaeological museum.

Hotel Ispinigoli *(☎ 0784 9 52 68; singles/ doubles €72/98, half board per person €67)* is a good hotel located just below the entrance to the cave, and also happens to be home to a well-known restaurant. Rooms are spacious and nicely decorated and some have fine countryside views. You can eat à la carte or choose one of a series of set menus. The mostly meat *menú barbaricino* (€23) is a good taste of local cuisine, while the *menú marinaro* (€28) is a seafood option. The wine list is endless.

Dorgali
postcode 08022 • pop 8200 • elev 387m
Although of no real intrinsic interest, Dorgali is a handy base at the crossroads for traffic south to Arbatax and beyond, north to Orosei and the coast road to Olbia, east 10km to Cala Gonone and west towards Oliena and Nuoro.

The **Pro Loco** *(☎ 0784 9 62 43; Via La Marmora 108b)* can book rooms in hotels and B&Bs in Dorgali and Cala Gonone – a handy service when things fill up in summer. You can change money (and have Western Union wire you some) at the **Banca di Sassari** *(Corso Umberto 48)*. The **Cartolibreria La Scolastica** *(Via Lamarmora 75)* sometimes has IGM hiking maps.

The **Museo Archeologico** *(Via Vittorio Emanuele; adult/child €2.50/1.50; open 9am-1pm & 4pm-7pm Tues-Sun)* holds a modest collection of local archaeological finds, including those dug up in the nearby Grotta di Ispinigoli.

Several groups can get you onto 4WD excursions, hikes and caving expeditions. **Gennargentu Escursioni** *(☎ 0784 9 43 85; Via La Marmora 197)* organises one-day trips into the Gola Su Gorroppu (€25) and into the Supramonte (€41) for instance – another is **Escursioni Ghivine** *(☎ 349 442 55 52, fax 0784 9 67 21,* W *www.ghivine.com; Via La Marmora 69E)*.

The town has some B&Bs and two reasonable hotels should you have no luck (or inclination) on the coast at Cala Gonone.

Hotel Il Querceto *(☎ 0784 9 65 09, fax 0784 9 52 54; Via La Marmora; singles/doubles €50/75)* is a comfortable if charmless option about half a kilometre outside the southwestern town exit. **Hotel S'Adde** *(☎ 0784 9 44 12, fax 0784 9 41 35; Via Concordia; singles/doubles €46/76)* is a more attractive option at the high northeastern end of town and next to a small park with kids' rides. Rooms are comfortable, with TV and air-con, and the hotel restaurant opens out onto a 1st-floor terrace.

Ristorante Colibrì *(☎ 0784 9 60 54; Via Gramsci 14; meals €27-30; open Mon-Sat)* is tucked away off the main drag (follow the signs) and is a slightly overlit haven for carnivores. Mains range from *porcetto* (suckling pig) through to lamb and goat (done in thyme). The pasta is excellent – try the *culurgiones,* a kind of ravioli.

ARST buses run up to nine times a day from Nuoro (€2.01, 45 minutes) and twice from Olbia (€6.30, one to 1½ hours). Up to 10 shuttle back and forth between Dorgali and Cala Gonone (20 minutes). You can pick up buses at several stops along Via La Marmora. Buy tickets at the bar on the junction of Via La Marmora and Corso Umberto.

Serra Orrios & Thomes

The nuraghic village of Serra Orrios *(adult/child €5/2; open for hourly visits 9am-1pm & 4pm-6pm daily)*, while not as remarkable as the site at Santa Vittoria (see later this chapter), is worth a stop. The remnants of more than 70 huts are clustered around what is left of two temples. The site lies 11km northwest of Dorgali (3km north off the Dorgali–Oliena road).

From there you could continue north to see a fine example of a *tomba di giganti.*

Continue 3km north of the crossroads with the Nuoro–Orosei route and the **Tomba dei Giganti S'Ena 'e Thomes** *(open dawn-dusk)* is signposted to the right. Just open the gate and walk on about 200m. The stone monument is dominated by a central, oval-shaped stone stele that closed off an ancient burial chamber.

Cala Gonone

Back in the 1930s Italian aristocrats and well-placed Fascists rather liked Cala Gonone and used it as a privileged summer meeting place. A tiny fishing port in those days, and lying just outside the northern end of the Parco Nazionale del Golfo di Orosei e del Gennargentu, it only began to see the first postwar tourists trickle through in the mid-1950s. Things have developed and Cala Gonone is now a summer favourite with masses of Italian and foreign visitors. Surrounded by imposing grey peaks, like **Monte Tului** (917m) to the southwest, **Monte Bardia** (882m) to the west and **Monte Irveri** (616m) to the north, it is an impressive setting and some fine beaches are within easy reach. The settlement, with its string of hotels and restaurants, is in itself nothing remarkable but pleasant enough. Most importantly, Cala Gonone's pleasure-craft port is a starting point for boat excursions to the magical coves and cliffs to the south.

Information The **Pro Loco** *(☎ 0784 9 36 96; Viale Bue Marino 1a; open Apr-Oct)* has hours that change according to the month – up to 9am to 11pm in July and August. Staff are enthusiastic and have plenty of info on the area.

Things to See & Do Just south of the port is a modest arc of beach, the **Spiaggia Centrale**, in front of an ugly cement wall. If you want to have some idea of how the Germans in Normandy felt on D-Day, come down here in the late afternoon and watch wave after wave of high-speed dinghies land and disgorge battalions of tourists returning from a day at the beaches to the south!

South along the waterfront, **Spiaggia Palmasera** is a sequence of extremely narrow patches of sand interrupted by rocky stretches. For something better, walk 1km south to **Spiaggia Sos Dorroles**, backed by a striking yellow-orange rock wall. Spiaggia Centrale was a smaller version of the same thing until the town council decided to cement it over to avert the threat of a land-slide (which, according to some geologists, is unlikely to happen for a few thousand years yet!).

The last easily accessible beach south of Cala Gonone is the smaller, rockier **Cala Fuili**, a couple of kilometres south at the end of the road (follow Via Bue Marino out of Cala Gonone). It is backed by a deep green valley and is a taste of what lies further south. From here it is possible to take a walking trail inland and up into the cliff tops to reach Cala Luna (see later in this chapter), about two hours' hike to the south.

A worthwhile excursion takes you north of Cala Gonone to the beautiful and wild-feeling beach of **Cala Cartoe**. In August it's predictably busy, but come out of season and it will probably be all yours. You need a vehicle to get there. Take Via Marco Polo from behind the port and follow to a T-junction; the cala is signposted to the right (north). Follow this narrow road, in itself worth the effort as it ascends rapidly, affording breath-taking views across the Golfo di Orosei. Over the pass you descend for a short while to another T-junction where you turn right. One kilometre on brings you to the turn-off (right) for Cala Cartoe, 4km on. A kiosk sells drinks, ice cream and snacks in summer. The beach, fine white sand leading you into crys-talline emerald water, is backed by a small stream and an amphitheatre of dense wood-land. No wonder it was chosen as a set for the saccharine film, *Swept Away*, starring Madonna and released in 2002.

Back up on the main road, you could turn right and head on another kilometre to the turn off for **Caletta di Osalla**, 5km away (see Around Orosei earlier in this chapter). The main road then arches back inland to the Grotta di Ispinigoli (see earlier in this chapter).

A couple of kilometres short of Cala Gonone on the road from Dorgali a track leads south to the **Nuraghe Mannu** *(adult/child €4/2; open 9am-7pm daily June-Sept, 9am-5pm Mar-May)*, a modest nuraghic village that might be worth the effort if you don't get to see more important nu-raghic sites elsewhere. The narrow road continues southward and offers some wide views of the gulf before petering out into a dirt track. Along the way you will espy a

few conical-shaped huts, or *cuiles* once used by local shepherds.

You can get onto all sorts of boat excur-sions or hire your own to explore the extra-ordinary coast south of Cala Gonone (see later this chapter). Diving is another option. Several operators offer diving courses and trips in the Golfo di Orosei, one is **Dimen-sione Mare** *(☎/fax 0784 9 67 66; Viale Col-ombo)*. Several excursion and hiking outfits will put you onto the trail (on foot or in 4WD) for the Supramonte, including de-scents of the Gola Su Gorroppu gorge and visits to the Tiscali nuraghic village: try **Dol-men** *(☎ 0784 9 32 60;* **w** *www.sardegnadas coprire.it, Italian only; Via Vasco da Gama 18)*.

Places to Stay & Eat A little way back from the waterfront along the main road from Dorgali is **Camping Cala Gonone** *(☎ 0784 9 31 65, fax 0784 9 32 55; per per-son €15, bungalows up to €130; open Apr-Oct)*. It gets crowded in August but is shady.

Piccolo Hotel *(☎ 0784 9 32 32; Viale Col-ombo; B&B singles/doubles €41/51)* is the cheapest place in town and a cheerful enough option with simple but acceptable rooms a short stroll back from the port.

La Favorita *(☎/fax 0784 9 31 96; Viale Palmasera; B&B singles/doubles €47/57)* is, if anything, more basic still but, at just a stumble from the town beach, is perfectly all right. You may be obliged to take half board in high season.

Pensione L'Oasi *(☎ 0784 9 31 11, fax 0784 9 34 44; Via G Lorca; singles/doubles €88/111)* is tucked away high up over the port on the road to Cala Cartoe, about 1km from the centre. Rooms are big and fresh, most with balconies opening to privileged views of the gulf below.

Hotel Miramare *(☎ 0784 9 31 40, fax 0784 9 34 69; Piazza Giardini; singles/doubles €56.80/100.70)* was the first hotel to go up here in 1955 and it remains a good upper-range option. Rooms are arranged with style and have satellite TV, phone/fax and minibar. The garden restaurant is a shady retreat where good Sardinian dishes are served.

There are plenty of other hotels on or near the waterfront but you will definitely need to book ahead in July and August. Most close in winter.

Pizzeria 2P *(☎ 0784 9 31 45; Via Vasco da Gama 7; pizzas from €4.50)* is a good spot

NUORO & THE EAST

for a pizza in a shady terrace just back from the more expensive (and frequently inferior) eateries on the waterfront. Pizzas are thin, crispy and delicious.

Ristorante Acquarius *(☎ 0784 9 34 28; Lungomare Palmasera 34; meals €35)*, on the waterfront, is one of the best dining options in Cala Gonone, but portions are a trifle stingy for the prices asked. You can sit in a pleasant garden and choose from a mix of Sardinian and standard Italian dishes. Try the *anzelottos* (ricotta-filled ravioli) followed by the *cozze alla marinara* (mussels).

Entertainment A couple of waterfront bars are good for whistle-wetting from about midnight. **Pub Road House Blues** *(Viale Palmasera)* and **Birreria Il Gufo**, next door, both have tables overlooking the beach and get fairly busy.

A lot of dance punters head for the disco tents set up at the southern end of Spiaggia Palmasera – you can hear them all over Cala Gonone!

Lo Skrittiore *(☎ 339 330 37 08)* is a big summer disco that rocks the Centro Sportivo, a couple of kilometres uphill off the Dorgali road and given over to more serious sporting activities for most of the year. Musical tastes range from Latin American to house hits.

Getting There & Away As many as 10 ARST buses run from Dorgali (€0.67, 20 minutes), 10km away, and pull up at Via Marco Polo near the port in summer. Seven of these come in from Nuoro.

Cala Luna to Cala Goloritzè

If you do nothing else in Sardinia, you should try to make an excursion along the 20km southern stretch of the Golfo di Orosei by boat. Intimidating limestone, *macchia*-topped cliffs plunge headlong into the sea, interrupted periodically by pretty beaches, coves and grottos. The English language, for all its richness, cannot provide the words to describe the shades and nuances of blue, green and turquoise that characterise the water. With an ever-changing base of sand, rocks, pebbles, seashells and crystal-clear water, the unfathomable forces of nature have conspired to create sublime tastes of paradise. The colours are at their best until about 3pm, when the sun starts to

drop behind some of the higher cliffs. You can only reach most of the coves and beaches by sea, although keen hikers can plan walks to some of them from inside the Parco Nazionale del Golfo di Orosei e del Gennargentu.

Clearly this is big business for the locals, and August is especially busy – don't expect splendid isolation. This coast is paradise, but in high summer you'll have to share. The local town councils find themselves sharing too – every year images of this coast wind up in holiday publicity for places as far off as Calabria and even Spain! The councils fluster and rage, threatening to sue whomever they can but generally end up having to live with it.

From the port of Cala Gonone you head south and pass that town's beaches. You will have already noticed the deep royal to midnight blue of the 'high seas' off the coast.

The first stop after Cala Fuili (see earlier) is the **Grotta del Bue Marino**, touted as the last island refuge of the monk seal, although none have been seen around for a long time. The watery gallery is certainly impressive, with shimmering light playing on the strange shapes within the cave. Guided visits take place up to seven times a day. In peak season you may need to book this in advance in Calagonone or Santa Maria.

The first beach after the cave is **Cala Luna**, a crescent shaped strand closed off by high cliffs to the south and a series of limestone caves to the north. Thick vegetation covers the mountains that stretch back from the beach. The strand (part sand, part pebble) is lapped by rich turquoise and deep emerald-green waters close in, changing to a deep dark blue further out. Some enterprising individuals run a little restaurant amid the greenery behind the beach.

A long stretch of cliffs follows, peppered with several grottos and lovely stopping-off points for those in their own boats.

Cala Sisine is the next beach of any size, also a mix of sand and pebbles and equally backed by a deep verdant valley. The site is a little less dramatic than that of Cala Luna. **Cala Biriola** quickly follows, and then several enchanting spots where you can bob below the soaring cliffs – look out for the patches of celestial blue and poke about.

Cala Mariolu is arguably one of the most sublime spots on the coast. Split in two by

Orgosolo, Le Barbagie

Farmlands around Oristano

Cala Mariolu, Golfo di Orosei

Balconies, Oristano

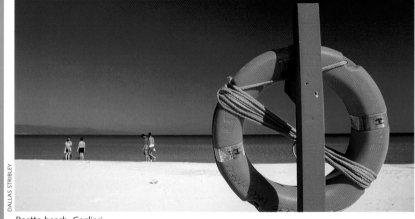

Poetto beach, Cagliari

Chiesa, Cagliari

Ruins of Nuraghe Su Nuraxi, La Marmilla

a cluster of bright limestone rocks, there is virtually no sand here. Don't let the smooth white pebbles put you off. The water that laps these beaches ranges from a kind of transparent white at water's edge through every shade of light and sky blue and on to a deep purplish hue. Several little grottos close off the north side. Words cannot convey what it is to swim about here.

Two somewhat less-exciting beaches, **Cala delle Sorgenti** and **Cala dei Gabbiani**, follow, but hey, it's all relative. The last beachette of the gulf, **Cala di Goloritzè**, rivals with the best. Again, the water's hues beggar description. At the south end bizarre granite figures soar away from the cliff side. Among them is **Monte Caroddi**, a 100m-high pinnacle loved by climbers.

Beyond the beach you can proceed in the shadow of the coast's stone walls towards **Capo di Monte Santo**, the cape that marks the end of the gulf. The cliffs lose altitude as you approach the cape and some have been 'rusted' by iron in the stone. Shortly before reaching the cape an inlet invites exploration.

From here the implacable cliffs continue south to **Santa Maria Navarrese**, another fine choice of base from where you can also undertake excursions of the coast just described.

There are several ways to approach these wonders from Cala Gonone. A fleet of boats, from large high-speed dinghies to small cruise boats and graceful sailing vessels are on hand, with a broad range of excursions on offer. The most basic option would see you joining a band of punters to be transported to one of the beaches along the coast.

The basic cost of such trips starts at €8.50 for the returning trip only from Cala Luna (for those who elect to walk there). The return trip to Cala Luna or Grotta del Bue Marino is €14.50. The two together cost €23.50. The return trip to Cala Mariolu costs €22. Prices drop in the slower months.

Full-day cruises, with visits to (but usually not all) the various beaches and other beauty spots can cost from €21.50 for a mini-cruise. Much nicer is the day-long trip on a sailing boat, costing €67 a head. If you want lunch on board (instead of taking your own), add €18. Contact **Cala Gonone Charter** (☎ 0784 9 37 37; Via S'Abba Irde 3).

The final option is the most tempting and the most expensive. If you have saved about €60 to €80 a head, think about hiring a *gommone* (a big motorized dinghy). They start at €120 for a smaller one with a two-stroke engine for two people, or €150 for two people in a slightly bigger craft with a four-stroke engine; calculate €10 to €15 extra in petrol. Nothing quite beats the freedom this offers, and if you are a beginner, don't worry, so was the author! Nothing compares with the freedom to tool about the coves, call in at beaches or simply anchor in a pretty inlet and swim in the impossibly coloured waters. The only minus is you can't get into the Grotta del Bue Marino this way.

Boats operate from March until about November – dates depend a lot on demand. Prices vary according to season, of which there are four. 'Very high season' is around 11 to 25 August. You can get information at agencies around town or at a series of booths direct at the port.

OGLIASTRA

The southeastern sector of Nuoro province is known as the Ogliastra. From Dorgali the SS125 (Orientale Sarda) highway winds south through the high-mountain terrain of the eastern end of the Parco Nazionale del Golfo di Orosei e del Gennargentu. The 18km stretch south to the **Genna 'e Silana** pass (1017m) is the most breathtaking. To the west your eyes sweep across a broad valley to a high chain of mountains, including **Monte Oddeu** (1063m) and, behind it, the impressive Supramonte. Various hiking maps of the area exist although the best are the IGM's 1:25,000 sheets. Unfortunately these are not easy to come by but you could try in Dorgali (see earlier in this chapter). A useful local website for this area is Welcome in Ogliastra (W www.turinforma.it).

Tiscali

A first detour, if you're in the mood for ancient sites, comes a few kilometres south of Dorgali with a road dropping off to the southwest past Monte Sant'Elena towards the nuraghic village of Tiscali *(admission €5; open 9am-7pm daily May-Sept, 9am-5pm Oct-Apr)*. The village is thought to date only to the 3rd or 4th century BC, and was built in the white limestone *dolina* (sinkhole) inside the modest Monte Tiscali (515m) at an altitude of 360m.

From Dorgali, you drive about 14km to a bridge where a walking trail (1½km) to the

NUORO & THE EAST

site is signposted. Another approach for walkers is from the north down the Valle di Lanaitto. If on a tour, you will be taken by 4WD down this valley and to within about an hour's walk of the site.

Gola Su Gorroppu

When you reach the Genna 'e Silana pass (hard to miss as a hotel and restaurant mark the spot on the east side of the road at km183), you could stop for a morning's hike to the Gola Su Gorroppu. The trail is signposted to the right (east) side of the road and is easy to follow. You reach the gorge with its claustrophobically tight high walls after two hours' hiking. There's nothing to stop you wandering a little either way along the Rio Fluminedda river bed, but don't be tempted to go too far without being properly equipped and preferably with a guide. This magnificent gorge offers myriad possibilities and in autumn, when the river is fuller, becomes a serious challenge.

Although some people go it on their own, you will be safer going on longer walks with a guide. You could do worse than approach the **Cooperativa Gorropu** (☎ 0782 64 92 82; Via Sa Preda Lada 2, Urzulei), whom

you will find also in the Sa Domu 'e S'Orcu building at km177.6 on the SS125 just north of the Urzulei turn-off. These guides organise treks of varying duration in and to the gorge, as well as all over the inland territory of the Golfo di Orosei and the Supramonte. They also organise meals with shepherds in the countryside and might be able to swing rooms in private houses for you.

For more tips on hiking in this area see also Lonely Planet's *Walking in Italy* guide.

Urzulei to Baunei

A side road drops off the SS125 west to Urzulei, another of those Nuoro towns that looks only half built. There is nothing of real interest here and no accommodation. Still, if you feel like a drive through some back country take the lonely road to **Talana**, 16km south. Much more forlorn it is hard to get to but if you happen to be around in August you might encounter a local oddity – ostrich races!! From here you can follow inland roads out of the mountains and down to the coast at Lotzorai (see later), 20km away.

If instead of turning off for Urzulei you keep moving south along the SS125, you will reach Baunei, 20km on. Again, there is little

Deadly Serious Jocu de Sa Murra

The scene is tense. Two pairs of men lean in towards one another in deadly earnest competition. Tempers can be short as they each launch hands at one another and scream out numbers in Sardinian in what appears for all the world like an excitable version of the rock, paper, scissors game.

The rules of the 'Game of the Murra', a pastime with centuries of colourful history in central Sardinia and especially the Barbagia region of Nuoro, are not that complicated. Two or four men can participate – in the latter case it works a little like a tag team match. One on each side stretches out a hand and shows some of his fingers. They both scream out numbers in an attempt to guess the total of fingers shown by both players. The operation is repeated in rapid fire manner until one side guesses correctly and so wins a point. At each successful guess (in the case where four are playing) the winner of the round then continues with the loser's partner. The side to reach 16 points (sometimes 21) first with a two-point advantage wins. Where both teams run neck and neck at 16 (or 21), they pass to a sudden death round – the first to five points wins.

The game is played with extraordinary passion and speed, and at the increasingly popular organised competitions the passions grow as wine bottles are emptied. The numbers are cried out amid oaths and taunts. Men with heart conditions are advised not to participate.

Traditionally the game was an impromptu affair played on street corners or wherever idle men came together. The problem is no one liked to lose and accusations of cheating often flew. Frequently the game ended with knives drawn and used, so much so that for long periods the *murra* was banned. Since the late 1990s championships have been organised, especially at Urzulei and Gavoi, but also on the Montiferru outside Seneghe in Oristano province. The competition takes place in the morning, followed by a long and boozy lunch and then impromptu bouts in the afternoon. To the outsider these post-prandial bouts can seem more inflamed than the official morning sessions!

about the town to keep you long but you could sit at the **Cafe Belvedere**, halfway along the main road, for a drink and soak in the mountain valley views to the west.

What is seriously worth your while in Baunei is a 10km detour up onto the mountain plateau known as the **Altopiano del Golgo**, signposted from the middle of town. A steep 2km (10° incline) set of switchbacks gets you up to the plateau and sailing north through heavily wooded terrain. After 8km you see a sign to your right to Su Sterru (also known as Il Golgo). Follow the sign (less than one km), leave your vehicle and head for this remarkable feat of nature – a 270m abyss just 40m wide at its base. Its funnel-like opening is now fenced off but, knowing the size of the drop, just peering into the dark and damp opening of this eroded karst phenomenon is enough to bring on a case of vertigo. Cavers who like abseiling just love it.

At the end of the dirt trail is the **Locanda Il Rifugio** (☎ 0782 61 05 99, mobile 337 81 18 28), which the Cooperativa Goloritzè has carved out of a one-time shepherd's farmstead. Rooms with up to four beds can cost €37 a double, or you can opt for full board and take your meals in the excellent restaurant, where they prepare such specialities as *capretto* (kid meat) and *porcetto*. All the meat is raised by the shepherds' cooperative – the place is surrounded by cattle, pigs and donkeys. The cooperative organises horse riding, excursions in 4WD and hiking. The 4WD trails from the plateau lead to within 20 minutes' hiking distance of the marvellous Cala Goloritzè and Cala Sisine beaches (see earlier in this chapter). The place opens roughly for spring and summer. Staff can arrange to pick you up in Baunei if you don't have your own transport.

Just beyond their stables is the late-16th century **Chiesa di San Pietro**, a humble affair flanked to one side by even humbler *cumbessias*, rough, largely open stone affairs – not at all comfortable for passing pilgrims.

Santa Maria Navarrese

Located at the southern end of the Golfo di Orosei, this delightful spot is a tempting alternative to its busier northern counterpart, Cala Gonone. Shipwrecked Basque sailors built a small church here in 1052, dedicated to Santa Maria di Navarra on the orders of the princess of Navarra who happened to be one of the survivors. The church was built in the shade of a grand olive tree that still thrives today – some say it is nearly 2000 years old.

The pleasant pine-backed beach (with more beaches stretching away further to the south) is lapped by transparent water and the setting is a gem. Offshore are several islets, including the **Isola dell'Ogliastra**, and the leafy northern end of the beach is topped by a watchtower built to look out for raiding Saracens.

About 500m further north is the small pleasure port, where **Nautica Centro Sub** (☎ 0782 61 55 22) organises dives and rents out the same kind of high-speed *gommoni* (dinghies) that you find in Cala Gonone. They start at €100 a day for two people and allow to you inspect the same wonderful spots described previously, but in reverse order. Similar excursions to those from Cala Gonone to some or all of these beauty spots also depart from here. Inquire at the kiosks in the port or at the **Tourpass office** (☎ 0782 61 53 30; Piazza Principessa di Navarra; open 8.30am-1pm & 5pm-8pm daily, also 9pm-11.30pm in summer) in the centre of town.

Three hotels lie within 200m of one another. **Hotel Plammas** (☎ 0782 61 51 30; Viale Plammas 59; singles/doubles €31/62) is the cheapest deal and is a perfectly pleasant spot about 200m up the hill from the central square. The rooms are straightforward and a little sparsely furnished but fine. The restaurant has a name, especially for its pasta (try the fish-based *culurgiones*) and seafood mains. If money is tight, go for the €13 set menu.

For more comfort, head 50m down the road to **Hotel Santa Maria** (☎ 0782 61 53 15, fax 0782 61 53 96; Viale Plammas; singles/doubles €68/124). It's a charming place set amid florid gardens, and has its own restaurant too.

You'll find several other little eateries and a handful of bars dotted about within quick strolling distance of the centre. **Bar L'Olivastro** has tables and chairs set up on shady terraces below the weird and wonderful branches of a huge olive tree at the northern end of the beach.

In the last week of August the *sagra della carne di capra* is held, a goat roast and eating frenzy for all those who happen to be present at the right time (the meat is usually cooked by about 9pm).

NUORO & THE EAST

Some of the ARST buses on the route between Tortolì and Dorgali call in here.

Lotzorai

A few kilometres further south, Lotzorai is not of enormous interest in itself, but sits behind more glorious pine-backed beaches, such as **Spiaggia delle Rose**. To find it follow the signs to the three camping grounds that are clustered close to one another just behind the beach.

If passing through here you are struck by hunger pangs and have some cash to lose, make for **L'Isolotto** (*☎ 0782 6 69 43; Via Ariosto 4; meals €40-45; open Tues-Sun*), off Via Dante and not far from the centre (signposted). The place looks unprepossessing enough but the homemade pasta and seafood mains make the money spent a good investment.

Tortolì

postcode 08048 • pop 9673 (including Arbatax)

Five kilometres further south, this cumbersome provincial centre has little appeal. You won't need to grace it with your presence unless of course you arrive in Sardinia at the nearby airport or by boat at Arbatax. Should you find yourself in need of a room, Tortolì offers four choices. The best value is **Hotel Splendor** (*☎/fax 0782 62 30 37; Viale Arbatax; singles/doubles €45/55*), but the pale green building is awkwardly placed on the north side of the railway tracks just out of town on the way to Arbatax.

Da Lenin (*☎ 0782 62 44 22; Via San Gemiliano 19; meals €30; open Mon-Sat*) is signposted to the south of the main road connecting Tortolì with Arbatax (a little closer to the former) and worth seeking out for the homemade pasta and good seafood. In summer their terrace fills quickly.

Local bus No 2 connects central Tortolì with both Arbatax and its nearest popular beach at Porto Frailis. ARST and FdS buses connect the two towns with destinations along the coast and deeper into Nuoro province

Arbatax

postcode 08041

Just 4km east of Tortolì is the almost equally uninspiring Arbatax, a minor industrial outgrowth of Tortolì and its port. Still,

this may be your point of arrival if coming by ferry. You should make an attempt to proceed elsewhere rather than hang about

Just by the port is the terminus for the FdS *trenino verde* summer tourist train to Mandas. In the train station is also housed the **Pro Loco**, whose opening hours vary maddeningly with ferry arrival times.

Across the road behind the petrol station is Arbatax's main attraction, the *rocce rosse* or 'red rocks'. These bizarre, weather-beaten rock formations dropping into the sea are well worth a closer look. In the distance your gaze is attracted by the imperious cliffs of the southern Ogliastra and Golfo di Orosei.

About 100m farther along the waterfront road, Via Lungomare, you'll see the Tirrenia boat ticket office a block away on Via Venezia 10. Local buses Nos 1 and 2 stop on this street on the way to Tortolì and, in the case of the latter service, the beach and hotels at nearby **Porto Frailis**. If you need to stay overnight around here, about the only cheapish option is the **Hotel Il Gabbiano** (*☎ 0782 62 35 12; singles/doubles €46.20/51.65*) in Porto Frailis, which has basic rooms, some without own bathroom. Otherwise you should consider heading for Tortolì or heading farther afield. If you can make bus connections, the camping grounds at Lotzorai or, better still, the hotels at Santa Maria Navarrese should be your nearest objective.

The tiny Arbatax-Tortolì **airstrip** (*☎ 0782 62 49 00*) is about 1½ km south of Tortolì. No scheduled buses or taxis run here but most people arriving by air are coming on some sort of package with transport arranged.

The *trenino verde* runs along a slow scenic route towards Mandas to the west (4¾ hours, two trains daily). Stops include Lanusei, Arzana, Ussassai and Seui.

For more information on the ferries arriving in Arbatax, see the Getting There & Away chapter.

South of Arbatax & Tortolì

Although the beaches immediately south of Arbatax, starting with Porto Frailis, are OK, much better ones lurk about 4km to the south. You'll need a vehicle to reach them.

To get to **Spiaggia Orrì**, take the SS125 out of Tortolì and then the left fork (signposted) for the beach shortly after. It is a long and broad sandy beach with beautiful clear water and fascinating, smooth granite-rock outcrops at various points along the strand. The next beach down, **Spiaggia Musculedda** has finer sand still, while the selling point of **Spiaggia Is Scogliu Arrubius**, about 4km south of Orrì, is the view to the strangely red rocky outcrops offshore.

The SS125 proceeds south to Cardedu. Beach fanatics can take a side road from here to the coast. Follow the coast road down past the little resort village of **Sa Perda Pera** (which itself has a charming beach) to the Marina di Gairo area. The object is **Spiaggia Cala Francese**, better known by the name of a long-disused beach hotel, Su Sirboni. You need to park your car and walk for about 500m along the rocky shoreline to reach this near pristine beach.

Another 17km south takes you through Tertenia (following the Rio Quirra), from which a minor road branches east to the beaches around **Sa Foxi Manna**, a nice arc of white sand closed off by a hilly promontory to the north. The highway continues 15km south across the provincial border to Cagliari and into the Cagliari & the Southeast chapter.

Arzana & Around
A big town, **Lanusei** is the kind of place to pass through.

Arzana is one of those brooding mountain towns that impresses mostly for its precarious position. A main road winds round the hillside and to either side houses sprawl up and down the slopes. On a clear day you can see the sea – a world away.

If wandering this part of the island, you could do worse than stop here. **Da Danilo** (☎ 0782 3 73 93; Via Eleonora d'Arborea 33; singles/doubles €18/31, half board €35) has comfortable if unspectacular rooms, and the home-cooked meals are abundant – in fact, you'll feel like you have become part of a big chaotic household. The hotel owners can put you in touch with local guides to go hiking in the Parco Nazionale del Golfo di Orosei e del Gennargentu. To find the hotel, head for the main church and then follow the signs. When you reach a building with the sign 'Ristorante', you're home.

Another reason for coming here is the food at **La Pineta** (☎ 0782 3 74 35; meals €25-30; open Mon-Sat), on a side street off a back road leading out of the town to the north – follow the signs. The place, backed by pines,

seems ordinary enough but serves some of the best meat dishes in central Sardinia.

Three daily buses connect Nuoro with Arzana (€4.44 or €4.91 depending on the route, one hour 10 minutes). FdS buses run west towards Seui and Seulo.

You could head southwest towards **Gairo** and turn south for **Ulassai** to visit the nearby **La Grotta di Su Marmuri** (open Apr-Oct). The caves, full of stalactites and stalagmites are open for guided visits (about an hour) which take place three to five times a day, depending on the month, and cost €6.50 per person. You can call ahead on ☎ 0782 7 98 59.

The drive further south along this route is a breathtaking windy meander on the east side of a deep valley, eventually dropping down into the plains en route to Tertenia.

Back at Gairo, the road proceeds west towards Seulo (see Aritzo to Lanusei later in this chapter), a pretty route, although the towns warrant little more than quick pit stops.

North of Arzana, you could head for the **Lago Alto della Flumendosa** and follow the route suggested in reverse. Before doing so, a quick diversion suggests itself. **Villagrande Strisaili** is another high mountain village with little to it but its impressive altitude (700m). Make the detour for the food at **Il Bosco** (☎ 0782 3 25 05; Località Santa Barbara; meals €25; open Tues-Sun), just outside the village. Culurgiones, wild boar dishes and decent pizza all figure on the menu.

LE BARBAGIE
The tough, uncompromising territory of Le Barbagie, spread out north and south of the Monti del Gennargentu, is at the geographical heart of Sardinia. This is perhaps fitting, since many would argue it is the most truly Sardinian part of the island. Dialects of the Sardinian tongue are widely spoken in its villages and people still cling to many local traditions, from Sardinian wrestling and ancient Carnevale rites to traditional costumes. It is still possible to see older women getting about in the curious vestments of another era.

At its heart are the bald, windswept heights of the Gennargentu massif, the highest points on the island.

Mamoiada
postcode 08024 • pop 2605 • elev 644m
Just 14km south of Nuoro, this undistinguished town is the scene of a remarkable

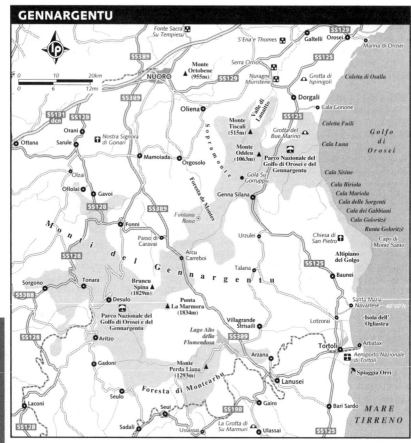

winter celebration for the **Festa di Sant'Antonio** on 17 January that dates to pagan times. For more information on the *mamuthones* (people wearing animal-like masks), see the special section 'Viva la Festa!'.

If you can't be here for Carnevale, you can get an idea of what it's all about at the **Museo delle Maschere** (☎ *0784 56 90 18;* Ⓦ *www.museodellemaschere.it; Piazza Europa 15; adult/child €4/2.60; open 9am-1pm & 3pm-7pm Tues-Sun).* After a 12-minute multimedia presentation of the tradition you head into a small room with mannequins dressed up as *mamuthones, issohadores* and other like figures from Sardinia and elsewhere in mainland Italy and Europe.

An enthusiastic cooperative of locals runs the museum and also provides exhaustive explanations (usually delivered in Italian). Some 200 of Mamoiada's men are involved each year in all the festival fun, and they all take it in turns to join in and dress up for the occasion.

For a bite to eat, try **La Campagnola** *(Corso Vittorio Emanuele 59; meals €20; open Tues-Sun).* They do pizzas and a limited range of pasta and main courses.

The wooden masks worn by the *mamuthones* have become fairly uniform over the years as only a few artisans make them and demand is great. A couple of shops around the village sell them – don't expect to pay less than €100 for a good one.

Regular buses travel to Mamoiada from Nuoro (€1.19, 20 minutes) and Fonni (€2.01, 55 minutes).

Fonni

postcode 08023 • pop 4501 • elev 1000m

Fonni is a sizeable rural town and the island's highest. In winter it becomes a minor ski base – Sardinia's only one – for those enjoying the couple of runs south at Bruncu Spina (see later).

The imposing **Basilica della Madonna dei Martiri**, built in 1610 and remodelled around 1700, lies off Piazza Europa at the highest point in town. You enter through an archway and the light-rose facade of one of the most important baroque buildings in Sardinia stands to the right. Around it line up *cumbessias*. A couple of trees have been curiously transformed by sculptors into religious scenes, notably one showing Christ and the two thieves crucified. Inside the church (on the right), a shrine contains a revered image of the Madonna that is paraded about by townsfolk in traditional costume on the occasion of Fonni's two main feast days, the **Festa della Madonna dei Martiri** on the Monday after the first Sunday in June and the **Festa di San Giovanni** on 24 June.

Of the town's two hotels, **Hotel Cualbu** (☎ 0784 5 70 54, fax 0784 5 84 03; Viale del Lavoro; singles/doubles €56.90/79.70) is the handiest. Rooms are modern, comfortable and a little gaudily coloured. The hotel also has a restaurant, pool, sauna and small gym. Given the prices, it's a pretty good deal.

Up to seven ARST buses serve Fonni from Nuoro (€2.01 to €3.15, 40 minutes to one hour depending on the route). The faster and cheaper ones go via Mamoiada.

Gavoi

postcode 08020 • pop 2979 • elev 777m

A not unpleasing stop above the broad **Lago di Gusana**, Gavoi boasts the late-Gothic **Chiesa di San Gavino**, with a red trachyte facade and fine rose window. Inside, note the richly decorated wooden pulpit half way down the left side of the nave. Just inside the main entrance to the right is another timber masterpiece, the 1706 baptismal font.

Hotel Taloro (☎ 0784 5 30 33, fax 0784 5 35 90; [w] www.hoteltaloro.it; singles/doubles €39/67, half board per person €47), on Lago di Gusana on the way to Fonni, is a new brand of hotel for Sardinia. You don't just come for a nice room but to improve your physical and mental state with a little thalassotherapy (therapy using sea water and

marine products), a mud bath or two and a few stints in the solarium.

In Gavoi itself, when hunger strikes head for **Ristorante Sante Rughe** (☎ 0784 5 37 74; Via Carlo Felice 2; meals €25-30; open Mon-Sat), a charming place with bare stone walls and a host of good local fare close to the San Gavino church.

Up to seven ARST buses trundle through here daily from Nuoro (€2.58, 55 minutes).

Orani & Ottana

Some 14km north of Gavoi, Orani is a surprisingly big place blessed with an inordinate number of churches.

The main attraction is, however, the **Museo Nivola** (☎ 0784 73 00 63; Via Gonare 2; adult/child €1.55/0.77; open 9am-1pm & 4pm-9pm June-Sept, until 8pm Oct-May), just inside the southern entrance into town up a hilly side street. The museum is a representative collection of Costantino Nivola's works (see also Arts in the Facts about Sardinia chapter), housed in the town's former public washhouse. The works, mostly carried out in his adopted home of the USA, are sculpted in marble, travertine and bronze. Some of the bronzes bear an uncanny resemblance to the *bronzetti* of Nivola's ancient nuraghic ancestors. Others, representing male and female figures, are a wink at Sardinia's menhirs.

Five kilometres south of Orani, the town of Sarule doesn't warrant a stop but a narrow side road east leads to the **Santuario di Nostra Signora di Gonare**, a grey buttressed church and sanctuary atop a lone conical hill (1093m). The church dates mostly to the 17th century, but the site has been occupied by a religious sanctuary that has attracted pilgrims from all over the island since at least the early 14th century.

The road west of Sarule leads to lacklustre Ottana, said to be the dead centre of Sardinia. The place comes to life in February for the parades of its traditional Carnival characters, the *boes* and *merdules*.

Tonara & Sorgono

Tonara is known for its *torrone*, wonderful nougat available all over the province and to a lesser extent throughout the island. The town's interest ends there.

Sorgono, 10.5km west of Tonara, is notable mainly for being the last stop on the FdS

Biting the Dust

For thousands of years Sardinian men have clashed in unarmed trials of strength known as *S'Istrumpa*, but by the 20th century this home-grown version of wrestling was still practised only in the somewhat ornery Barbagia district. Men would embrace for a tussle at festivals, marriages, harvest festivities and even when the army came to town looking for recruits. On occasion they might lock horns on a wholly impromptu basis!

Traditionally there were few rules – whoever bit the dust two out of three (or three out of five) times lost. A key feature is that the only real contact between the two wrestlers is the grip used (taking the opponent's wrists, hands and/or waist) in the attempt to force one another on to the ground. No blows are exchanged.

Fearing that this age-old tradition might die out, enthusiasts in Ollolai organised the first ever official *S'Istrumpa* tournament in 1985 and four years later held the island's first championships. These are still held in Ollolai every summer, governed nowadays by more rules than was traditionally the case (including time limits on rounds). Enthusiasm for the sport has spread around the island, although its heartland remains Nuoro province.

In 1994 the Federazione S'Istrumpa was founded and a year later it joined the FILC (International Federation of Celtic Wrestling). The *istrumpadores* (Sardinian wrestlers, also known as *gherradores*) have found that their techniques are similar to those used since ancient times by wrestlers as far away as Scotland!

Uncharitable observers say of the wrestlers that *prima bevono, poi stringono* ('first they drink, then they grapple'), which on less-organised occasions may well have once been the case – a few rounds of wrestling could easily ensue after a friendly handshake – clearly a sign of real manhood. At any rate, a good *istrumpador* these days takes his sport too seriously to be mixing it with pre-match tippling.

trenino verde line. Unless on that train, there is precious little point in turning up here.

Desulo
postcode 08032 • pop 2954
Along with Fonni (see earlier in this chapter), this long string of a town (it was in fact three villages that have with time become one) sticking determinedly to the hillside is another popular spot with locals. There's access to the limited skiing on Bruncu Spina in winter and hiking at other times of the year.

The town can be lively enough in August too with local holiday-makers but there is little of intrinsic interest to the place.

Albergo La Nuova (☎/fax 0784 61 92 51; *Via Lamarmora; singles/doubles €18/31)*, with only a handful of simple rooms (shared bathroom in the corridor) and about two-thirds of the way along the main road through town from the southwest, is the cheapest sleeping option here.

Hotel Lamarmora (☎ 0784 61 94 11, fax 0784 61 91 26; *Via Lamarmora)*, at the northern end of town by the hairpin bend that leads to Fonni, has spacious if chaotic rooms (some with good views over the town and valley).

Both places have restaurants but at Hotel Lamarmora the kitchen closes early. You'll have more joy at La Nuova (walk upstairs from the street-level bar), where a straightforward meal of pasta and meat main will cost about €20 with wine, water and coffee.

Just two ARST buses run here (€3.72, one hour 20 minutes) from Nuoro via Fonni.

Bruncu Spina & Punta La Marmora
Given the challenges involved in trekking in many parts of the Parco Nazionale del Golfo di Orosei e del Gennargentu, reaching the island's two highest peaks is surprisingly easy.

Head first for Bruncu Spina (1829m) by car. The approach road to this, the second-highest summit in Sardinia and the island's only downhill ski centre (one lift!), leads east off the Desulo–Fonni road, 5km short of Fonni. The 10km road winds through mostly treeless territory up to the base of the ski lift, where you will also find a snack bar. To reach the summit, however, you take a steep dirt trail that branches to the right off the mountain road 1km short of the snack bar. This road leads three long kilometres up to the top, easily identifiable by the communications antennae. From here you have broad sweeping views across the island in all directions. Some claim you can even glimpse Corsica on a crisp clear day! For a view from 5m higher, you need to march about 1½ hours south to Punta La Marmora (1834m). Although it looks easy enough from Bruncu Spina, you need a good walking map or a guide not to get into difficulty.

Belvì
postcode 08030 • pop 788 • elev 660m
Southwest of Desulo on the road to Aritzo, there is little reason to stop at this cherry-producing town unless you want to take a peek at the **Museo delle Scienze Naturali** (*Via San Sebastiano; admission by optional donation; open 8am-noon & 2pm-7pm June-Sept, 9am-noon & 3pm-5pm Oct-May*), a modest collection of minerals, stuffed animals and fossils put together by local enthusiasts just off Via Roma at the Aritzo end of town.

Aritzo
postcode 08031 • pop 1522 • elev 796m
Caressed by a breath of cool mountain air even at the height of August, Aritzo is a comparatively lively spot.

Entering from the north, you see signs to the **Museo Etnografico** (*admission €1.55; open 10.30am-1pm & 4.30pm-7pm Tues-Sun*), down a side street to the right just after the IP petrol station and housed in a school building. The collection ranges from farm implements and household objects to old black-and-white photos of Aritzo and the surrounding area.

The same ticket gets you into **Sa Bovida Prigione Spagnola**, the 16th-century Spanish-era prison just off the main drag on the narrow Via Scale Carceri.

A few metres south and across the road, the originally Gothic (few traces remain) **Chiesa di San Michele Arcangelo** contains an 18th-century *Pietà* and a 17th-century portrait of *San Cristoforo*, in the second and last chapels respectively on the right hand side. Across the road from the church is a viewpoint across to the odd, box-shaped **Monte Texile**.

On the last Sunday of October the town fills up with people in search of chestnuts at the **Sagra delle Castagne**. Great piles of chestnuts are roasted up in the streets and given away.

The town's hotels are clustered towards the southern exit from town. **Hotel Castello** (*☎ 0784 62 92 66; Corso Umberto; singles/doubles €26/41.50*), right at a bend in the road, is the cheapest place to stay. A rather tall edifice, the hotel's rooms are functional and many have decent views.

Hotel La Capannina (*☎/fax 0784 62 91 21; Via A Maxia; singles/doubles €46.50/56.80*) is a nicer option. The hotel is fronted by gardens and some of its comfortable rooms enjoy good views out the back. All the hotels have their own restaurants.

A smattering of buses link towns around here, and ARST has up to two daily connections with Nuoro (€4.44, two hours).

Aritzo to Lanusei
From Aritzo the main road carves its way through the hills to the south via Gadoni before swinging southwest to towns like Seulo and Seui, a route plied by the occasional FdS bus.

It is the location more than anything that makes **Seulo** a pretty stopover. If you need a place to stay or eat, try the **Agriturismo S'Armidda** (*☎ 0782 5 83 08; località Bau' Asei*) 4km on a side road leading above the town. They say that on a good night you can see the lights of Cagliari from here.

The road from Seulo winds pleasantly along to **Seui**, which conserves a few traditional houses in local stone and timber, with wrought-iron balconies. Proceed another 9km towards Ussassai before taking a nice detour north. If you don't have the time for trekking around this side of the Gennargentu massif, this drive at least takes you nicely off the beaten track for a bit.

Nine kilometres north of the turn-off you see **Nuraghe Ardasai** on your left. Built on a rocky outcrop dominating the deep Rio Flumendosa valley to the north, it is worth a stop for the views, although the *nuraghe* itself has seen better days. Six kilometres farther on is a turn-off for the dense **Foresta Montearbu**, towered over by the mount of the same name (1304m). A few kilometres farther on is a turn-off that leads you to the more impressive **Monte Perda Liana** (1293m), which in the distance looks rather like an erect nipple. You are in deeply wooded country here, full of pines and firs. As you head for the mountain lake of **Lago Alto della Flumendosa**, a turn-off to the west leads to a dirt road that peters out in the heart of the southern Gennargentu massif.

The main road follows the lake's south bank eastward for about 10km before crossing over the scenic *trenino verde* train line a couple of times and reaching the main Nuoro–Lanusei road.

SARCIDANO

This southwestern corner is more arid and flatter than much of the rest of the province but boasts four objectives that repay the effort of exploring here – the delightful town of Laconi (a rare bird in central Sardinia), the important Nuraghe Arrubiu, the menhirs of Pranu Muttedu and, above all, the fascinating nuraghic settlement of Santa Vittoria.

Laconi

postcode 08034 • pop 2359 • elev 550m

When you see grand banners reciting '*Sant'-Ignazio, prega per noi*' (St Ignatius, pray for us), you know you're in Laconi, an airy mountain village blessed with a fine archaeological museum and a refreshing, wooded park.

Down behind the neoclassical Municipio (town hall) on Corso Garibaldi (the main drag) is the inventive **Museo delle Statue Menhir** (☎ 0782 86 62 16; Via Amsicora; adult/child €3.50/2; open 9.30am-1pm & 4pm-7.30pm daily Apr-Sept, 9am-1pm & 4pm-6pm Oct-Mar, closed 1st Mon of each month). The Sarcidano area, as well as neighbouring La Marmilla (see the Southwest Sardinia chapter) and the area south of the Sarcidano is where the bulk of the island's menhirs have been found. Some of these ancient anthropomorphic statues have been put on display here, while others remain *in situ*, such as at Pranu Mutteddu (see later in this chapter). The museum display spreads over seven rooms, with detailed and well-presented explanations (in Italian) and some multimedia on computers by the entrance.

From the Municipio, cross the road and head down Via St Ignazio to the **Casa Natale di Sant'Ignazio** (admission free), a simple two-roomed house where the town's St Ignatius is said to have been born (he died in 1781). Out the back in the second room is a shrine to the saint and a few seats that the faithful use.

Once in Via Sant'Ignazio again continue past the saint's house and take the first left.

This brings you to the **Parco Laconi**, a rare retreat full of dense woods, exotic trees (such as an impressive Cedar of Lebanon), springs, lakes, grottos and the remains of the **Castello Aymerich**. Originally built in 1051, its most interesting elements are the Moorish-seeming windows in the now roofless upstairs hall. From here you have wonderful views across the park and the greenery surrounding Laconi.

One or two buses connect Laconi with Isili, Aritzo, Barumini and other surrounding towns. The FdS *trenino verde* calls in here on its way north from Mandas. The station is about 1km west of the town centre.

Isili

You will pass through here on your way from Laconi to get to the Santuario Santa Vittoria. Just to the north of this unexciting town is the **Nuraghe Isparas** (admission free; open 9am-1pm & 2pm-5pm daily). It is a strange light grey colour and its interior *tholos* is the highest in Sardinia.

What the town lacks in interest it makes up for in hotels. Three of the four establishments are on Via Vittorio Emanuele, the main street, and none charge more than €42 for a double.

ARST buses and the *trenino verde* pass through here.

Santuario Santa Vittoria

By far the most intriguing and important nuraghic settlement in Sardinia if you except the grand *nuraghes* themselves, the Santuario Santa Vittoria (adult/child €4/2; open 9am-7pm daily) warrants some effort if you are at all interested in the island's ancient origins.

Archaeologists first got to work on the site in 1907 and restoration work was carried out in the 1960s. Still, only four of about 22 hectares have been fully uncovered. The site is seen as a central point of worship in all Sardinia.

What you see today is divided roughly into three zones. The central area, the *recinto delle riunioni* (meeting area) is a unique enclave thought to have been the seat of civil power. A grand, oval-shaped space is ringed by a wall within which are towers and various rooms.

Beyond it is the religious area, with a *tempietto a pozzo* (well temple), a second temple,

Much Musing on the Meaning of Menhirs

Much has been made of the meaning of menhirs, found on Stone Age sites across Europe and in varying shapes and forms. Among the best known are those of Stonehenge and Avebury in England and Carnac in France. These megalithic monuments were erected singly or in groups and served a religious purpose, sometimes adorning burial grounds (as in the case of Pranu Mutteddu). Although many have been found in Sardinia, neighbouring Corsica is better known for them.

The simplest, with virtually no sculptural relief, have been dubbed 'protoanthropomorphic', meaning that they appear to represent (often life size) human figures, but with no hint as to whether male or female. Of the more sophisticated menhirs, the male ones found in Sardinia outnumber female ones about ten to one.

The males nearly all display similar features, some more developed than others. The top carving, like a distorted McDonalds arch, presents eyebrows and nose. The main trident figure below has also been interpreted as a figurative image of a man upside down on his way into the afterlife – the middle 'prong' of the trident being a phallic symbol, as is the image of the dagger, sometimes with a blade on either end, below the trident.

Female figures are less clearly portrayed, with sometimes barely protruding points for the breasts and on occasion what looks like a doorway around the position of the womb. This has been variously interpreted as a celebration of the woman's capacity to give life or as a symbol of the Gate of Life. On some female menhirs a groove around the 'head' is seen as representing women's head gear or hair dressing.

a structure thought to have been the *capanna del sacerdote* (priest's hut), defensive trenches and a much later addition, the Chiesa di Santa Vittoria, a little country church after which the whole site is now named. Separated from both areas is the *Casa del Capo* (Chief's House), so-called perhaps because it is the most intact habitation, with walls still up to 3m high. Finally, a separate area, made up of several circular dwellings, is thought to have been the main residential quarter.

The only way to get here is with your own wheels. From Isili, drop 8km south to Serri and follow the signs 6km to the west.

Nuraghe Arrubiu & Beyond

Rising out of the Sarcidano plain, 5km south of Orroli, the Nuraghe Arrubiu *(adult/child €4/2, night guided visits €6; open 9.30am-1pm & 3pm-8.30pm daily Mar-Oct, 9.30am-5pm Nov-Mar)* takes its Sardinian name (meaning 'red') from the curious colour lent it by the trachyte stone from which it is built. It is an impressive structure. The central

tower, about 16m high, is thought to have reached 30m. It is surrounded by the five-tower defensive perimeter and, beyond, the remains of an outer wall and nearby settlement. The artefacts found on the site indicate the Romans made good use of it.

Pranu Mutteddu

Fans of all things ancient will be hard pressed to resist pursuing the road south from Nuraghe Arrubiu to reach this menhir-studded necropolis. Follow the road south 11.5km to **Escalaplano** and from there 8km towards **Ballao**. Take the first turn west to **Goni** (you are now just inside Cagliari province), which you hit after 9km. A few kilometres further on and you reach the site, just north of the road.

The site is dominated by a series of *domus de janas* tombs and some 50 menhirs, 20 of them lined up east to west, presumably in symbolic reflection of the sun's trajectory. The scene is reminiscent of similar ones in Corsica and is quite unique in Sardinia.

Oristano & the West

Carved out of bits of surrounding Cagliari, Nuoro and Sassari in 1974, Oristano is the most overlooked of the island's provinces. With the exception of the classical site of Tharros and a couple of nearby beaches on the Sinis peninsula, it attracts little attention from foreigners. A typical declaration from one heard in Tharros was: 'Next stop Cagliari'. It's a shame because the area deserves more attention.

The sleepy capital, Oristano, is not without its charm and the hinterland hides several interesting points, including the extraordinary well temple of Santa Cristina, the nearby Nuraghe Losa, the Roman baths of Fordongianus and the olive country of the Montiferru. This is also good territory for flamingo-spotting, and some of the local festivals, especially Oristano's Sa Sartiglia (February) and the equestrian folly of Sedilo's Ardia (July), are unforgettable.

If you are looking to stay in a private house rather than a hotel check out **Sardinian Way** (☎ *0783 7 51 72, fax 0783 77 77 50;* [w] *www .sardinianway.it; Via Carmine 14)* in Oristano. Another possibility is **La Mia Casa** *(☎/fax 0783 41 16 60;* [w] *www.lamiacasa.sardegna .it; Posidonia Tourist Services, Via Umberto I 64, 09070 Riola Sardo)*, with more than 20 B&Bs in seven villages in the province.

Oristano looks more to the sea than is generally the case in Sardinia. Mullet *(muggine)*, fished from the Stagno di Cabras lagoon and Golfo di Oristano, is so common that it is also known as *pesce di Oristano* ('Oristano fish'). A local speciality is *mrecca*, mullet that is boiled, wrapped in pond grass and then dried and salted. Grilled eel is popular, as are *patelle*, a limpet like dark clams.

ORISTANO
postcode 09170 ● pop 32,890

A rather provincial place, Oristano is nevertheless worth a visit. A handful of churches, the archaeological museum and a few remnants of the old city will keep you occupied for a half day or so. Oristano can make a handy base for the surrounding area too.

History

Oristano emerged as the main settlement of this western chunk of Sardinia in the early

Highlights

- Inspect the ruins of Tharros, an ancient Phoenician and Roman seaside settlement

- Gather in Oristano for the masked elegance of the Sa Sartiglia equestrian tournament at carnival time

- Relax in the cool tranquillity of San Leonardo de Siete Fuentes

- Visit the incredible nuraghic temple of Santa Cristina and the nearby Nuraghe Losa

- Behold the thundering madness of Sedilo's chaotic Ardia horse race

- Head for the long Is Arenas beach for a relaxing day by the seaside

Oristano p176

Oristano & the West p174

Middle Ages as people abandoned ancient Tharros which, since the arrival of the Phoenicians in the 8th century BC, had been *the* urban and trading centre.

Little is known of the city's origins, although medieval sources suggest that by the 11th century the city had become the capital of the Giudicato d'Arborea (which reflects the area of the modern province), one of four such entities into which Sardinia was divided in the Middle Ages prior to its takeover by the Crown of Aragon. Eleonora di Arborea (c1340–1404) became head of the Giudicato in 1383 and has gone down in history for her wise administration and resistance to the

Catalano-Aragonese. Her death in 1404 led to final capitulation but her Carta de Logu, an extraordinary law code, outlived her. The invaders saw its value and applied the code to all of Sardinia. It remained in force until the early 19th century.

Oristano, meanwhile, slid into misery. Under the Catalano-Aragonese and then the Spaniards, trade collapsed and the city was subject to appalling administration, plague and famine. The arrival of the Piedmontese in 1720 did little to alter matters and the 18th century was marked by repeated riots and rebellions.

Creation of the Carlo Felice highway in the 1820s and, a century later, Mussolini's programmes to drain swamps to the city's south, gave Oristano a much-needed boost, but it retains the feel of provincial torpor even today.

Information

Tourist Offices Oristano is well endowed with tourist offices. The most helpful is the **EPT** (☎ 0783 3 68 31; |e| enturismo.oristano@ tiscali.it; Piazza Eleonora 19; open 8am-2pm & 4pm-7pm Mon-Fri, hrs vary Sat). Nearby, you can get city information at the **Pro Loco** (☎ 0783 7 06 21; Via Vittorio Emanuele 8; open 9am-noon & 5pm-8pm Mon-Fri, 9am-noon Sat May-Sept, 9am-noon & 4.30pm-7.30pm Mon-Fri, 9am-noon Sat Oct-Apr). There is also a **booth** (Piazza Roma; open 9am-1pm & 4pm-9pm, til 10pm Sun & public holidays July–mid-Sept) in town during summer.

Caviar of the Mediterranean

Many a potential mullet never makes it to adult fishhood, as mullet roe, bottarga in Italian, is a popular delicacy in Oristano. The roe is salted, pressed between planks of wood and then sun dried before consumption. Known as the 'caviar of the Mediterranean', it is used for hors d'oeuvres or on pasta (usually spaghetti). In the latter case it is either grated over the pasta or heated up with olive oil and mixed in. Oristano's fishermen have been making bottarga for centuries, but local output is falling. Water pollution and the declining mullet population are obliging producers of bottarga to increasingly import the raw material from as far off as Africa and Mexico.

Money Several banks, among them the **Banca Nazionale del Lavoro** (Piazza Roma), congregate in central Oristano.

Post & Communications The main **post office** (Via Mariano IV; open 8.15am-6.15pm Mon-Fri, 8.15am-noon Sat) in town is centrally located.

You can get email at **Internet Haus** (Via Brancaleone Doria 28; open 9.30am-1pm & 5.30pm-9.30pm Mon-Fri, mornings Sat) for €4 an hour.

Bookshops An excellent range of books on all aspects of Sardinia is available at **La Pergomena** (☎/fax 0783 7 50 58; Via Vittorio Emanuele II 24), although they are mostly in Italian. You can also pick up a handful of novels in English, French and German.

Travel Agencies The national youth travel agent **CTS** (☎ 0783 77 20 33; Via Grazia Deledda 9) has a branch in Oristano.

Medical Services You can get help at the **Guardia Medica** (☎ 0783 7 43 33; Via Carducci). The main **hospital** (Viale Fondazione Rockefeller) is away from the centre. There's also a handy **pharmacy** (Corso Umberto 51) in town.

Duomo

The city's cathedral (Via Duomo; open 7am-noon & 4pm-7pm Mon-Sat, 8am-1pm Sun) is unmistakable with its onion-domed bell tower dominating the central Oristano skyline.

Most of what you see today is a baroque makeover, although some elements, including the apses and a chapel, survive from its Gothic predecessor. The 14th-century wooden sculpture of the Annunziata or Madonna del Rimedio, in the first chapel on the right as you enter, is believed to be the work of Nino Pisano, a Tuscan sculptor whose late-Gothic works stand on the cusp of the Renaissance. Among the other riches held by the church, but no longer on view, are two marble panels that once fronted the statue. They bear 11th- to 12th-century biblical scenes following Byzantine lines on one side and depictions of prophets, saints, apostles, the Annunciation and Christ in judgement. All these were carved by an unknown Catalan artist. It is hoped they will

ORISTANO & THE WEST

one day go on display as part of a church museum.

Chiesa di San Francesco

The broad dome and neo-classical facade of this 19th-century church *(Via San Antonio; open 8am-noon & 5pm-7pm Mon-Sat; 8am-noon Sun)* are barely of passing interest, as is the rather bland interior. However, inside, on the left as you enter, is a fine wooden sculpture, the so-called *Crocifisso di Nicodemo*. This 14th-century masterpiece by a Catalan artist conveys all the pain of a skin-and-bones Christ on the cross.

Antiquarium Arborense

This archaeological museum *(☎ 0783 79 12 62; Piazzetta Corrias; adult/child €3/1; open 9am-1.30pm & 3pm-8pm daily)* holds one of the most important collections on the island.

The ground floor is generally given over to temporary exhibitions and the permanent collections are on the 1st floor.

The centrepiece is a model of the classical city of Tharros as it might have appeared around the 4th century AD. Explanatory texts are in Italian only.

Over the rest of the floor and in glass cases along a raised gallery is a broad collection of artefacts found at Tharros and on the Sinis peninsula. The items stretch from pre-nuraghic and nuraghic (mostly fragments of ceramics, along with axeheads and spearheads and other tools) through to Phoenician, Carthaginian, Roman and even early medieval finds. Ceramics predominate, but

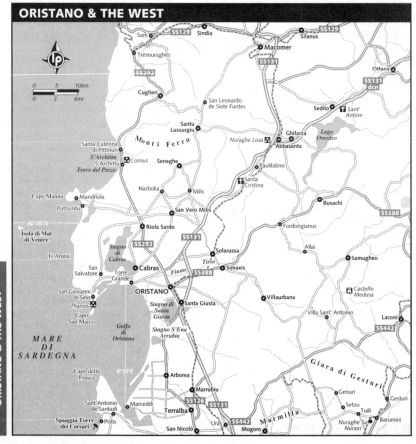

ORISTANO & THE WEST

there are also Carthaginian figurines and some splendid Roman glassware. Amphorae, the trading containers of ancient times, abound, along with a range of pots, plates, cups and oil lamps.

Next door to the main room is the museum's **pinacoteca**, which hosts a small collection of *retabli* (painted altar pieces). One series of panels, *Retablo del Santo Cristo*, done by the workshop of Cagliari's Pietro Cavaro in 1533, depicts a series of Franciscan saints. Take a closer look at them because this group of apparently beatific fellows are depicted with their instruments of martyrdom. They each have swords, daggers or saws slicing through their heads, necks or hearts and yet quiver not one jot!

Piazza Eleonora & Around
Piazza Eleonora became the city's central square through 19th-century urban reforms. Today it is presided over by a proud **statue** of the grand old lady herself and the neoclassical facade of the **Municipio** (town hall). She holds scrolls of the Carta de Logu, her famed law code, and panels below extol her famous victories.

Pedestrianised Corso Umberto runs north off the square to Piazza Roma. It is a charming promenade, flanked by the restored pastel facades of Aragonese houses and an array of boutiques. Piazza Roma itself is wholly dominated by the thickset presence of the **Torre di Mariano II**, one of the only vestiges of the medieval walls that once protected the city. It can only be visited on rare occasions.

About the only other reminder of the city's medieval past is the squat round tower located just off Via Mazzini to the east, the so-called **Portixedda** (admission free; open 10am-12.30pm & 4pm-6.30pm Tues-Sun) or 'little gate'. It contains a small exhibition on the city's one-time defences, pulled down in the late-19th century.

Eleonora, said to be buried in the city's **Chiesa di Santa Chiara**, is also remembered by a crumbling 16th-century house in Via Parpaglia. Dubbed **Casa di Eleonora** by locals, it was in fact built long after the heroine's death.

Special Events
Some say the citizens of Oristano have gathered to watch the annual masked horse race, **Sa Sartiglia** (held in February), since

the days of the Giudicato. Whatever the truth of this, it is the highpoint of the city's Carnevale celebrations. For more information on this festival, see the special section 'Viva la Festa!'.

Places to Stay
You're not likely to want to hang about in Oristano long, but it can make a handy base for excursions, especially if you are relying on buses. The city's hotels (five open at the time of writing) are bland affairs.

Hotel Piccolo (☎ 0783 7 15 00; Via Martignano 19; singles/doubles €31/51.65) is aptly named since most of the rooms are rather pokey. It's relatively cheap and central but that's all that can be said for it.

Hotel Mistral (☎ 0783 21 25 05, fax 0783 21 00 58; Via Martiri di Belfiore; singles/doubles €43/68) is probably the ugliest option, at least on the outside. Rooms are stock standard, with bathroom, TV, phone and air-con.

Hotel Mistral 2 (☎ 0783 21 03 89, fax 0783 21 10 00; Via XX Settembre; singles/doubles €56/84) is a bigger and slightly more cheerful version of the former, with functional rooms over several storeys and a leafy terrace above street level.

Villa delle Rose (☎ 0783 31 01 01, fax 0783 36 01 01; Piazza Italia 5; singles/doubles €44/80) is discreetly tucked away on this nondescript square. Singles may not be easy to come by but the doubles are comfortable and well maintained.

Hotel ISA (☎/fax 0783 36 01 01; Piazza Mariano 50; singles/doubles €50/83) is the most appealing of the hotels, even if it's getting a little crumbly around the edges. The better rooms have little semicircular balconies overlooking the square.

Places to Eat
La Torre (☎ 0783 30 14 94; Piazza Roma 52; pizzas up to €6; open Tues-Sun) is a perfectly acceptable spot for a cheap and cheerful pizza.

Bonsai (☎ 0783 7 35 46; Via San Martino 15; meals €20-25; open Wed-Mon) is a rough-and-ready local place where you can get a square meal of pasta and meat or fish main course.

Da Gino (☎ 0783 7 14 28; Via Tirso 13; meals €25-30; open Mon-Sat) has been around in one form or another since the 1930s. Seafood dishes, using freshly caught

ORISTANO & THE WEST

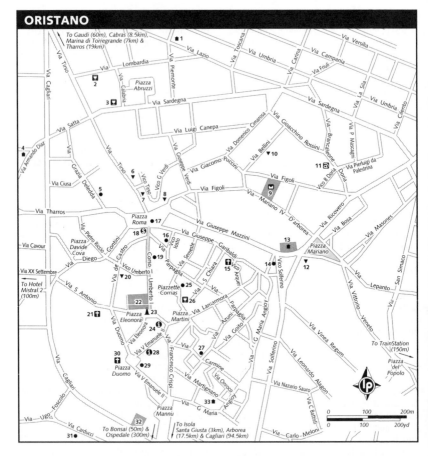

ORISTANO

beasties from the nearby lagoons and coast, stand out. *Aragosta* (lobster) is one of the house specialities. It also has an enticing *antipasti* trolley and does great risottos prepared in various ways.

Ristorante Craf (☎ 0783 37 06 89; Via De Castro 34; meals €30; open Mon-Sat) is another quality option. You enter a cosy vaulted cavern and sit down to carefully prepared dishes, including some good soups and, if you're game, donkey meat.

Faro (☎ 0783 7 00 02; Via Bellini 25; meals €30-35; open Mon-Sat) specialises in mostly Sardinian dishes. The place is overly bright but the food, especially the pasta, is good.

Cocco Desì (☎ 0783 30 07 35; Via Tirso 31; meals €40-45) has been in business since the early 20th century. In its present gourmet incarnation you are offered a pleasing variety of local and Italian cooking. Try the *sa cassola* (fish soup).

Pinna (☎ 0783 7 00 32; Piazza Mariano 38; open Mon-Sat) is a great *gelateria*. Alongside all your favourite flavours are some lesser-known concoctions. Wine gelato is becoming a hit in Italy and here you can try the Passito di Sardegna Duchessa ice cream: an intoxicating cone.

Entertainment

Oristano's young and restless gather at the local bar **Lola Mundo** (Piazzetta Corrias 14). It sets up a few tables outside for those warm summer evenings. A grungier spot to drop in

ORISTANO

PLACES TO STAY		OTHER		21	Chiesa di San Francesco
1	Villa delle Rose	2	Blu Bar (PANI Buses)	22	Municipio (Town Hall)
4	Mistral Hotel	3	Pub Tira Tardi	23	Statue of Eleonora
13	Hotel ISA	5	CTS	24	EPT Tourist Office
33	Hotel Piccolo	9	Post Office	25	Antiquarium
		11	Internet Haus		Arborense
PLACES TO EAT		14	Portixedda	26	Lola Mundo
6	Cocco Dessi	15	Chiesa di Santa Chiara	27	Sardinian Way
7	Da Gino	16	Casa di Eleonora	28	Pro Loco Tourist Office
8	La Torre	17	Torre di Mariano II	29	Libreria Pergomena
10	Faro	18	Banca Nazionale	30	Duomo
12	Gelateria Pinna		di Lavoro	31	Guardia Medica
20	Ristorante Craf	19	Pharmacy	32	Autostazione

for a quick beer is **Pub Tira Tardi** (*Via Sardegna 17a; open Wed-Mon*).

For anything busier you need to head down to Marina di Torregrande or fan out across the province's coast for summertime discos (some are listed in the course of this chapter). In winter you can do a little dancing at **Gaudí** (*Via Tirso 171*) on the way north out of town towards Cabras.

Shopping
Isola (*Via Cagliari*) has a showroom for Sardinian crafts on the road leading to Santa Giusta.

Getting There & Away
Bus The main intercity *autostazione* (bus station) is on Via Cagliari. ARST buses leave for destinations all over the province as well as longer distance objectives like Sassari (four a day) and Cagliari (three a day).

PANI buses also serve Cagliari (€5.84, 1¼ hours) four times a day and Sassari (€7.18, 2½ hours) three times a day. Several head east to Nuoro (€5.84, two hours). These buses arrive and leave from Via Lombardia, north of the city centre. Buy tickets at **Bar Blu** (*Via Lombardia 30; open 6am-10pm Mon-Sat*) or on the bus on Sundays.

Train The main Trenitalia train station is in Piazza Ungheria west of the town centre. Six or seven trains run between Oristano and Abbasanta and Paulilatino.

As many as 20 trains, sometimes involving a change en route, run between Cagliari and Oristano (€4.55) and can take from one hour to almost two hours, depending on stops made. As few as four make the run from Sassari to Oristano (€7.75) and take around 2½ hours. For Olbia there are only two through trains (three hours), otherwise you have to change at Chilivani.

Car & Motorcycle Oristano is on the SS-131 highway between Cagliari, Sassari and Porto Torres. Branch highways head off to the northeast for Nuoro and Olbia.

Getting Around
Bus The town centre is easily done on foot, although you will probably want to use buses to get in from the train station. The *rossa* (red) and *verde* (green) lines stop at the station and terminate in Piazza Mariano.

Car & Motorcycle Parking is fairly easy if you leave your car a little out of the centre (such as in the streets south of Via Cagliari). To park in the blue spaces in the centre you pay €0.52 for the first hour, €0.78 for the second and €1.03 for each hour thereafter (8.30am to 1pm and 4pm to 7.30pm Monday to Saturday).

Taxi You'll find that taxis tend to congregate at the train station and around Piazza Roma. You can also call a taxi on ☎ 0783 7 02 80 or ☎ 0783 7 43 28.

AROUND ORISTANO
Santa Giusta
postcode 09096 • pop 4416
Dominating a high point in the centre of Santa Giusta, virtually a satellite of Oristano just 3km south on the Stagno di Santa Giusta lagoon, is the proud basilica of the same name. The town grew on the site of ancient Othoca, a Punic foundation later expanded by the Romans.

The Romanesque **Basilica di Santa Giusta**, built in 1135-45, was one of the earliest in a string of Tuscan-style churches to go up on the island. It makes a striking sight today above an unusually green public park. Typical of the Tuscan style are the two columns resting on lion's backs at the main entrance.

Inside, the central nave and lateral aisles are separated by a series of columns, some looted from Tharros. They come in all shapes and sizes and with varying capitals. You can wander down below the altar into the low crypt, whose ceiling is held up by further recycled and truncated columns.

The church is the centre of four days of celebrations around May 14, the **feast day of Santa Giusta** (for more information on this festival, see the special section 'Viva La Festa!').

Buses from Oristano's main bus station leave once every half hour or so for the 10- to 15-minute trip (depending on traffic).

Marina di Torregrande

Oristano's main beach lies 7km west – a long sandy strand stretching east to west along the northern end of the Golfo di Oristano. Behind the sand is an esplanade with cheerful restaurants and chirpy bars to keep people animated. It's a very Italian scene, with suntanned locals promenading, kids running about and some awful but jaunty local pop tunes emanating from the terrace bars. In winter it's a ghost town. Aside from a quick inspection of standard Catalano-Aragonese defensive round tower, there is nothing to do but swim, eat and drink.

Camping Torregrande (☎/fax 0783 2 22 28; per person/tent space €5.20/7.80, bungalows €65.50; open May-Sept) is a few hundred metres short of the waterfront as you come in from Oristano.

Giovanni (☎ 0783 2 20 51; Via Colombo 8; meals €35; open Tues-Sun) is the pick of the culinary crop. Don't be fooled by its unprepossessing location a few hundred metres back from the sea on the road to Cabras. The pasta using local seafood are the strong suit.

The beach strip is lined with summertime drinkeries. A local favourite is **Coco Loco Café**. A few kilometres inland on the road to Cabras is **Banana Disco**, which does everything from eurotrance to mainstream Italian and international disco pop.

Oristano city buses on the *azzurra* (blue) line run from Via Cagliari to Marina di Torregrande.

Mucking About in Fassois

Among the 4th-century black-ink drawings found in the subterranean chamber at San Salvatore (see later in this chapter) is an image of *fassoi*, little boats made of rushes fastened together. With a raised prow and stubby rear end, these little fishermen's vessels (rarely more than 4m long and 1m wide) have remained unchanged to the present day. Designed for a lone occupant, the *fassoi* was all most lagoon fishermen could afford in their daily search for mullet. You are unlikely to see many out on the lagoons nowadays, but on the first Sunday of August the town of Santa Giusta organises a *fassoi* race on the Stagno di Santa Giusta lagoon.

Cabras
postcode 09072 • pop 8940

Drive around the confusing labyrinth of ill-lit, abandoned-looking streets of Cabras on a balmy summer evening and you could be forgiven for asking yourself if someone has started a war and not bothered to inform you.

Things to See The area around Cabras has been settled for thousands of years. In the course of the 1990s important finds were made on the site of **Cuccuru is Arrius**, 3km to the southwest, dating back as far as the fourth millennium BC. Some of these have been housed in the imaginative building that is the **Museo Civico** (☎ 783 29 06 36; Via Tharros 121; admission including site of Tharros €4; open 9am-1pm & 4pm-8pm Tues-Sun June-Sept, 9am-1pm & 3pm-7pm Tues-Sun Oct-May) at the southern end of town. The collection is divided into two parts. The first is dedicated to the prehistoric artefacts dug up at Cuccuru is Arrius. The second, more interesting for archaeological neophytes, consists of material from Tharros (see Sinis Peninsula later). Items range from Carthaginian milestones to fragments of Roman sculpture.

Special Events On the first Sunday of September, the Festa di San Salvatore, several hundred young fellows clothed in white mantles set off on the **Corsa degli Scalzi** (Barefoot Race) – an 8km dash to the sanctuary of San Salvatore (see later). They bear with them an effigy of the Saviour to commemorate an episode in 1506, when townspeople raced to San Salvatore to collect the effigy and save it from Moorish sea raiders. They race back to Oristano in similar fashion the following day.

Places to Eat From Cabras' lagoon and the nearby Mediterranean coast comes the raw eating material for a surprisingly fine phalanx of restaurants.

Sa Funtã (☎ 0783 29 06 85; Via Garibaldi 25; meals €30; open Mon-Sat) is a curious centuries-old house with its own stone well (you are invited to take a look) in central Cabras. The menu is recited and service can be pushy, but the food in this rustic establishment is good. Try the bavette alle patelle and finish with the house dessert, mustazzolus, and a glass of Vernaccia.

Il Caminetto (☎ 0783 39 11 39; Via Cesare Battisti 8; meals €30-35; open Tues-Sun), barely 100m away, is a bigger place with a classier feel. It's generally packed and again fishy delights are the main melody.

L'Oliveto (☎ 0783 39 26 16; Via Tirso 23; meals €30-35; open Wed-Mon) is hard to find (make for the northern end of town and ask) but worth the effort. Set in gardens (you can eat inside on cooler evenings), it is another centre of seafood excellence. Sit back over coffee to the wafting sounds of Bob Marley as you finish up.

Getting There & Away ARST buses run every 20 minutes or so from Oristano (€0.88, 15 minutes).

SINIS PENINSULA

Most people visit this part of Sardinia for the Sinis peninsula, home to one of the island's most important ancient classical sites and some fine beaches.

Tharros

The ancient city of Tharros (☎ 0783 37 00 19; admission including Museo Civico in Cabras €4; open 9am-sunset daily), set impeccably by the sea, reached the height of its importance under the Carthaginians. What is visible today, however, largely dates to the Roman era. It is interesting enough but don't expect grand temples and amphitheatres – an effort of imagination is required to picture what Tharros might really have been like.

The original Phoenician trading town was raised on the site of a nuraghic settlement and subsequently absorbed by Carthage. Until the end of the First Punic War, in which Rome defeated Carthage, Tharros flourished as a trading port and naval base. After the war in 238 BC, Carthage ceded control of Sardinia to Rome.

Tharros remained a key naval town but lost its pre-eminent role when Rome constructed its main inland road from modern-day Cagliari to Porto Torres. Nevertheless, the city got a thorough overhaul under the Empire, particularly in the 2nd and 3rd centuries AD. The city's basalt streets were laid, and baths, the aqueduct and other major monuments built. From the 4th century Tharros had to deal with increasingly frequent enemy raids from North Africa, starting with the Vandals and culminating with the Arab Muslims in the early Middle Ages. The by-then Christian rulers of the Giudicato d'Arborea finally decided in the 11th century that enough was enough and quit the shimmering waters of Tharros in favour of the relative inland safety of Oristano. Much of the ancient city was subsequently stripped – it was easier to cart ready-cut stone to Oristano to expand the new capital than start from scratch.

From the entrance you follow a brief stretch of the cardo (typically the main street in Roman settlements) and reach, on the left, the castellum aquae (the city's water reserve). Two lines of pillars can be made out within the square structure. Turn left towards the sea and you pass remains of a **Punic temple** before arriving at the seaside. Here was one set of **thermal baths**, and a little to the north the remains of a **paleochristian baptistery**. At the southernmost point of the settlement along the coast is another set of baths, dating to the 3rd century AD. On the bare rise north of the ticket office was the nuraghic village and, later, the Phoenician and Punic tophet (for more on this see the Facts about Sardinia chapter).

You may visit the nearby late-16th century **Torre di San Giovanni** (admission €2; open 9am-sunset) watchtower, which is occasionally used for photo and art exhibitions and commands magnificent views north along the coast and south to Capo San Marco. There is nothing to stop you wandering down the dirt tracks to Capo San Marco and the lighthouse.

ORISTANO & THE WEST

A series of pizzerias and bars lines the parking area as you approach Tharros. Parking is free around the church of San Giovanni di Sinis (see next), but you pay as you get closer to Tharros – up to €1 an hour.

On summer weekend evenings, music and theatre bring the ruins of Tharros to new life. Tickets cost around €15 (available at the site's ticket office) and shows begin at 10pm.

Four ARST buses per day travel here from Oristano in summer (€1.45, 20 to 30 minutes).

San Giovanni di Sinis

About 1km north of the ancient site is one of Sardinia's oldest Christian churches, the sandstone **Chiesa di San Giovanni di Sinis**. You probably saw it as you passed by in the direction of Tharros. The church dates to about the 11th century, but includes its domed, square-based predecessor from the 6th century. The church was abandoned in the 18th century and by the early 1800s was being used as a shepherds' refuge. It was partly restored in 1838 and again in the 1960s and 1990s. In summer you will almost certainly find the church open. It was long-surrounded by a makeshift fishermen's village, most of whose thatched *domus de cruccuri* have long been demolished. A couple, used by holidaymakers, remain on the east side of the peninsula.

San Salvatore

Welcome to the Wild West, folks. All that's missing in the broad, empty square of this pilgrim town, 8km from Cabras, is the tumbleweed. Back in the 1960s several spaghetti westerns were shot here, and the little, tiled *cumbessias* (pilgrims' houses) piled up next to each other play the part of dusty Mexican village rather well.

The place has a much longer and less frivolous history. The unobtrusive 16th-century **Chiesa di San Salvatore** is a *chiesa novenara*, open for nine days only to celebrate the feast of the saint after which it is named. Pilgrims flock from all around for this expression of faith in late August and early September, taking up temporary lodgings in the *cumbessias*.

The church was built atop a site of ancient pagan worship. If you get lucky and find it open, you will be able to head downstairs to the 4th-century rendition of the site, with faded frescoes and intriguing black-ink drawings and graffiti.

The September **Corsa degli Scalzi** (Barefoot Race) that starts in Cabras ends here, before turning around to return to Cabras (see earlier for more details) the next day.

Beaches

One of the most attractive beaches of the Sinis coast is the **Spiaggia di San Giovanni di Sinis**, the golden strand nearest Tharros. It has the advantage over most of the more northern beaches of being relatively free of rocks and algae. On the other hand, it gets busy.

Of the many beaches further north, one of the more interesting is **Is Arutas**. Mingled in with the minute pebbles and sand is a good quantity of quartz – walking along the beach is like getting a foot massage, but making a souvenir of the quartz is illegal. The beach is signposted 5km west off the main road leading north from San Salvatore. Unfavourable winds sometimes leave great rollers of rotting algae on the beach – not such a great olfactory experience.

Putzu Idu is a long and sandy, if untidy, strand backed by a motley set of holiday homes and beach bars. Two kilometres south along a minor trail is the smaller and more captivating **Spiaggia S'Arena Scoadda**. From Putzu Idu and Mandriola, immediately next door, you can take boat excursions to the nearby **Capo Mannu** (€6 per person) or the colourfully named **Isola di Mal di Ventre** (Stomach Ache Island), 10km off the coast to the southwest. It takes about 15 minutes to get there and depending on the tour you'll get to circumnavigate the uninhabited isle before being dropped off on one of the little beaches. One such tour is run on the **Motonave Azzurra** (☎ 329 324 90 03) from Mandriola.

The lagoon inland from Putzu Idu often hosts some of Sardinia's flamingo population. The road north splutters to an end at Su Pallosu, from where you can see the vast strip of the **Is Arenas** beach to the northeast (see North of Oristano later).

A trio of hotels (one each in Putzu Idu, Mandriola and Su Pallosu) offers the option of staying here and a handful of restaurant-pizzerias keep hunger at bay. In Putzu Idu the **Le Saline** disco, a hit in the mid-1990s, reopened for business in 2002.

MONTI FERRU

The thickly wooded highland of Monti Ferru (Iron Mountain), culminating in the 1050m peak of Monte Urtigu, closes off the province of Oristano to the north and forms a natural protective line for the medieval Giudicato d'Arborea.

The area is largely unknown to foreign travellers. The mountains are thick with a wealth of Mediterranean flora, including plenty of cork oak, and it is possible to see deer and mouflon on walks here.

To the west the slopes quickly drop to the coast and some fine beaches, while from the eastern heights of Monti Ferru you can gaze across the hot dry plains of the Campidano. The towns that huddle below the hills to the south produce some of the island's best olive oil.

Milis & Around

Surrounded by the citrus gardens that enchanted the French poet Paul Valéry and made it a more prosperous village than most of its neighbours, Milis seems to all intents and purposes a quiet and happy place. People from surrounding villages like Seneghe will tell you the people of Milis (all 1666 of them) are a little smug too. Centuries-old rivalries have not abated, and while only a few kilometres separate Milis from other towns, a gulf divides them. Even now, they say, Milis lads wouldn't dare go looking for girls in neighbouring towns, nor vice versa!

The **Chiesa di San Paolo**, a Romanesque church at the entrance to town, is Tuscan in style and contains several interesting paintings executed by Catalan masters in the 16th century. Closer to the centre is the 14th-century **Chiesa di San Sebastiano** with its basalt bell tower and, opposite, the crimson-coloured **Villa Boyle**, an 18th-century residence now used as a cultural centre.

Five kilometres north lies **Seneghe**, a quiet village on the lower slopes of Monti Ferru. Typical of this olive oil–producing area, Seneghe's narrow streets are lined by dark stone houses. The oil is among the best in Italy and a brand to look for is Cosseddu. From Seneghe an 8km road winds up northwest into the heart of the mountains. Towards the end of the trail you'll find a picnic area and bar, open on summer weekends.

A useful point of reference for hikers wanting to get to know Monti Ferru and the surrounding area is the Seneghe-based **Benthos** (☎/fax 0783 5 45 62; W www.bentho sardegna.com, Italian only) agency run by Raimondo Cossa, who knows this part of the island like the back of his hand.

Another good reason for stopping by is to call in at **Il Bue Rosso** (☎ 0783 54384; Piazzale Montiferru 3/4; meals around €25; open daily). The speciality is local beef but you have a choice of plenty of traditional dishes, including fish on Fridays and pizza on the weekends. The organically produced house wine is good and you are welcome to just sit back and enjoy the views of the surrounding hills. Housed in a 1920s dairy, you'll find it near the town's Narbolia exit.

From Milis or Seneghe you can make for the village of **Bonarcado** (no great friends of the Milesi either!) at whose northern exit stands the modest Romanesque **Chiesa di Santa Maria** (once part of a medieval monastery) and, a short walk away, the curious **Santuario della Madonna di Bonacattu**, a rudimentary chapel built on a Greek cross plan and topped by a simple dome. Although expanded in the 13th century, the original structure dates to about the 7th century.

Santu Lussurgiu

postcode 09075 • pop 2676 • elev 503m

Eight kilometres north of Bonarcado, Santu Lussurgiu lies inside an ancient volcanic crater on the eastern edge of Monti Ferru and is worth a visit just to view the original location. Whichever way you approach it you will end up on the main road that follows the crater's rim with panoramic views of the town. Some nice 18th-century houses huddle together with a trio of churches in the old heart of the town, long known for its crafts (less so nowadays). Santu Lussurgiu was a centre of carpet weaving and woodwork, and had something of a name for its knives too.

La Bocca del Vulcano (☎ 0783 55 09 74; Via Alagon 27; meals €40-45) located high up in this crater town is an unassuming looking house where you can eat such house specialities as cinghiale alla Montiferru (wild boar). From Bar-Pizzeria La Cascata on the main road, follow the signs up to the restaurant (a long walk!).

San Leonardo de Siete Fuentes

The Santu Lussurgiu–Cuglieri road is a refreshing mountain route that leads north and then west towards the coast. Just 4km out of Santu Lussurgiu, a branch road runs north for Macomer but you only need to follow it 2km, admiring the sweeping panorama across the eastern plains, to arrive in this watery oasis.

To those accustomed to the dry Sardinian landscape, this cool, lush retreat comes as a shock. Wander up through the shady park, full of oaks and elms, to the seven taps (the name of the place suggests there are seven springs) from which pours abundant fresh water. Even in the heat of midsummer you can almost feel chilly here. Water, water everywhere and all of it to drink!

The charming 12th-century **Chiesa di San Leonardo**, now a mix of Romanesque and Gothic styles, became the property of the Knights of St John of Jerusalem. In 1295, Guelfo, son of Ugolino della Gherardesca, died in the hospital that once flanked the church.

Hotel Malica *(☎/fax 0783 55 07 56; Via Macomer 5; singles/doubles €21/35)* is an uncomplicated place to sleep, surrounded by greenery and the first place you pass (on your left) as you enter the hamlet.

Pizzeria da Franceso *(open year-round)* on the corner of the main road and the pretty cobbled lane behind the church is a handy spot to eat.

Cuglieri
postcode 09073 • pop 3099 • elev 483m
Instead of proceeding north to Macomer, turn back south and head west for Cuglieri. The road passes through the northern hill country of Monti Ferru and slowly snakes down through dense forest towards Cuglieri. Long before you reach the town, you'll see the silvery dome of the **Basilica di Santa Maria della Neve**.

Up close the 17th-century church is not so inspiring, but the square before it makes a great platform from which to watch the sun set over the coast far below. The steep, narrow lanes of the old centre invite a little aimless wandering.

Albergo Desogos *(☎/fax 0785 3 96 60; Via Cugia 6; singles/doubles €18/36)* is the only hotel in town, tucked away in a leafy lane in the middle of the old town. The handful of rooms are basic but quite OK and the restaurant is known all over the Monti Ferru area.

Santa Caterina di Pittinuri & Around
A low-key resort with two hotels and an untidy smattering of holiday homes, Santa Caterina offers a reasonable beach, closed off at the southern end by dramatic cliffs.

A few kilometres south are the remains of the ancient town of **Cornus** and an adjacent early Christian site. The latter is the more interesting part but it may no longer be possible to wander in as the area was closed off by the police in mid-2002 to protect it from vandals.

For those who wish to try their luck, a yellow sign to Cornus 1km south of Santa Caterina points to several kilometres of dirt road leading to the site.

What you first see is the early Christian site of Columbaris, raised in the 4th to 7th centuries AD. It appears the area developed as a major cemetery next door to Cornus and then grew in religious significance with the construction of three churches in among the tombs.

As you enter the site, to your right is the outline of one church and further down to the left are two basilicas built side by side with apses pointing in opposite directions. In the middle of the smallest one is a well-preserved circular baptismal font.

A few hundred metres further on are the limited remains of Cornus, probably founded by the Carthaginians and taken over by the Romans. The whole area was abandoned for Cuglieri in the face of repeated raids by Muslim Arabs in the early Middle Ages.

The cliffs of the headland at the southern end of Santa Caterina di Pittinuri separate it from the next bay, **S'Archittu**. There's not an awful lot of sand but the water is a deep emerald green and enticing. Around the next bend, **Torre del Pozzo** (also known as Torre Su Putzu) has a small sheltered beach.

From here the SS292 road curves gently away from the coast, but if you're looking for a long, broad stretch of sand don't travel too far. About 3km south of Torre del Pozzo you'll see signs for the first of three **camping grounds**, the Europa. A couple of hundred metres on are the other two – turn off here (if you have a car) to access the northern end of the long **Is Arenas** strand. Apart from the occasional influx of algae, the water is clear and even in mid-August it is pretty easy to find a fair patch of space to yourself.

Places to Stay & Eat Right on the waterfront of Santa Caterina, **La Scogliera** (*☎/fax 0785 3 82 31; Corso Alagon; singles/doubles €26/47; half board per person €47*) has seven modest rooms and a wonderful restaurant with some tables right over the crashing waves and views to the cliffs. The many different pizzas (up to €5) are recommended.

Otherwise, a couple of more expensive hotels (one in Santa Caterina and the other in Torre del Pozzo), along with one or two B&Bs, make up the accommodation possibilities in this trio of holiday villages.

Alternatively, campers can make for one of the three camping grounds that back onto the Is Arenas beach. **Camping Europa** (*☎/fax 0785 3 80 58; per person/tent space €10.33/12.91*) has bungalows too. **Camping Nurapolis** (*☎ 0785 5 22 83, fax 0785 5 22 55; per person/tent space €8.30/13*) has the advantage of being open year-round.

La Capanna is a classic summer club in Torre del Pozzo. It has been going since the early 1980s and still attracts clubbers from all over the province on Friday and Saturday nights. As you enter Santa Caterina from the south you'll notice another choice, **Menhir**. On the main dance floor everything from eurotrance to Latin dance rules, while on the terrace you can relax to chill-out tunes.

Buses between Oristano and Bosa stop at Santa Caterina, S'Archittu (from Oristano 1/2 hour, €1.76) and Cuglieri (one hour, €3.58). They will stop on request at the camping grounds.

LAGO OMEDEO CIRCUIT

Although it is possible to reach some of these places by public transport, it is frequently difficult and time consuming. Your own vehicle is infinitely preferable, especially for the nuraghic sites of Santa Cristina and Nuraghe Losa.

Santa Cristina

For thousands of years men and women have practised their faith here. Nuraghic people gathered around the extraordinary well temple in the remote past and Christian pilgrims still visit the Chiesa di Santa Cristina today. If you visit no other ancient temple sites in Sardinia you should see this one.

The site (*admission including Paulilatino archaeological museum €3.10; open 8.30am-11pm daily May-Sept, 8.30am-9pm Oct-Apr*)

is just east off the SS131, a few kilometres south of Paulilatino. The centrepiece is the extraordinary nuraghic well temple, which dates perhaps to the late-Bronze Age (11th to 9th century BC), but around it spread the remains of an ancient settlement.

Buy tickets in the bar and wander out through the garden to the cheerful Chiesa di Santa Cristina (built around 1200) and its surrounding *muristenes* (pilgrims huts originally for Camaldolesi monks). The church and huts open for nine days to celebrate the feast days of Santa Cristina (around the second Sunday in May) and San Raffaele Arcangelo (4th Sunday of October).

Beyond lies the nuraghic village (1500–1200 BC) set in a woods. Of special note are the modest *nuraghe* and several long stone huts. The site was inhabited not only by ancient Sardinians but even up to the early Middle Ages.

About 150m east of the church is the incredible well temple, which looks like it was built to a Stanley Kubrik design although it was only excavated in the 1960s. The temple was built around 1000 BC of perfectly cut and fitted blocks and follows some standard norms. The bottom, triangular half of the keyhole-shaped temple has stairs leading down to the well (the inclusion of stairs meant that one could reach the water no matter what its level). The well itself is topped by a tholos up to ground level. If you look down through the tiny aperture at ground level you will see your face reflected in a perfect circular frame in the water below. The temple is oriented northwest to southeast in such a way that at the equinox in March and September the sun completely lights the stairway.

Paulilatino
postcode 09070 • pop 2531

Finds from the Santa Cristina site have been put on display in the small **Museo Archeologico-Etnografico** (*admission including Santa Cristina nuraghic site €3.10; open 9am-1pm & 4.30pm-7.30pm Tues-Sun May-Sept, 9am-1pm & 3.30pm-5.30pm Tues-Sun Oct-Apr*), set in a proud village mansion in Paulilatino. The museum also contains a few items typical of ethnographical museums, including farm and domestic implements from tougher rural days. The Santa Cristina ticket allows you to visit the museum on a separate day.

Nuraghe Losa

A few kilometres north of Paulilatino and barely a few hundred metres west off the SS131 highway stands one of the more impressive of Sardinia's nuraghes (☎ 0785 5 48 23; admission €3.50; open 9am-1pm & 3pm-7pm daily).

The grand basalt *nuraghe* is a three-cornered structure dominated by an unusually smooth conical tower, dated to the Middle Bronze Age (1500 BC). To get inside the complex, whose use remains the subject of speculation, you first pass a 'tower hut' just in front of the entrance. Once inside a narrow corridor leads directly into the main tower. The keystones at the top of the conical structure could be moved to let in more light. Off each side of the central corridor, passages lead left and right to two lateral towers, one fully enclosed, the other open. Stairs lead from the left passage to the next level but you cannot follow them beyond to get on to the terrace. A tiny entrance on the north corner of the triangle leads into the small north tower.

In the ticket office you can admire three small glass cases of bits and bobs unearthed on the site.

Ghilarza

postcode 09074 • pop 4664

Unless you are a fan of one of the key figures of Italian 20th-century Socialism, you could with few qualms skip this nondescript town. Antonio Gramsci (1891–1937), born in Ales more than 30km south as the crow flies, for a time lived in a modest house on the main street of Ghilarza, about 80m from the ugly parish church on Piazza Parocchia. Gramsci, a fervent opponent of Mussolini's Fascists, campaigned for workers' rights, suggested an alliance of north Italian industrial workers with impoverished southern peasants and founded what would become the country's Communist daily, *L'Unità*. Arrested in 1926 by the Fascists, he died in Rome after a long illness.

You can visit the **Casa di Antonio Gramsci** (☎ 0785 5 41 64; Corso Umberto 57; admission free; open 10am-1pm & 4.30pm-7.30pm Wed-Mon) to view a small collection of memorabilia related to the man and his beliefs.

Lago Omedeo & Sedilo

The SS131 DCN motorway leads east from Ghilarza towards Nuoro along the northern flank of Lago Omodeo, the island's largest artificial lake. In the summer of 2002 it was almost dry – a keen indicator of the extent of Sardinia's water problems.

The unremarkable rural town of Sedilo lies just north off the highway and may at first draw your attention because virtually all the street and highway signs have been so thoroughly peppered with gunshot. Sedilo is, however, known first and foremost for the **Ardia**, a thoroughly exciting display of equestrian bravado held to honour a saint who wasn't – the Roman Emperor Constantine (San Costantino, but also rendered Santu Antine in these parts). The **sanctuary** and **victory arch** dedicated to Constantine lie about 1.5km outside the town centre, south along a narrow road that passes over the main highway. From here you have views across to Lago Omodeo (or what's left of it). See also the special section 'Viva La Festa!'.

If you need a bite to eat you'll find a couple of pizzerias in the village.

Fordongianus

postcode 09083 • pop 1072 • elev 35m

The Romans had an infallible nose for healthy hot springs. When they found those at Fordongianus, already recorded by Ptolemy, they renamed the place Forum Traiani (of which the present name is a deformation) and expanded the earlier settlement on what was in any case a strategic position along the Tirso river.

The **Terme Romane** (☎ 0783 6 01 57; admission including Casa Aragonese €3; open 9.30am-1pm & 3pm-7.30pm daily, til 5.30pm Oct-Mar) are just outside the town centre on the river bank. The core of the baths, built in the 1st century AD, is a rectangular pool that was once surrounded by a portico (of which only one side now stands). Around it were other pools and service rooms.

You can actually see the complex pretty much in its entirety from outside the perimeter. Also outside the perimeter are two 'baths' into which steaming hot water pours. In one locals are allowed to wash clothes as they have done for centuries and in the other they may clean containers of milk and other non-toxic materials. In winter the steam floating off the Tirso river as the thermal water gushes in is an eerie sight.

In town itself, don't be tempted to drink from the many water fountains scattered about the place – the water is 48°C and far from drinkable! It *is* good for taking home to hand wash clothes. The red trachyte stone of which everything is built lends the village a strange air. As red as the rest is the lovely late-16th century **Casa Aragonese** *(admission including Terme Romane €3; open 9.30am-1pm & 3pm-7.30pm Tues-Sun, til 5.30pm Oct-Mar)*. Although there isn't a great deal to see inside, it is worth a quick look just to see how a local, noble Catalan family lived. The strange statues outside, also in the ubiquitous trachyte, are the result of an annual sculpture competition held here. Fordongianus is about 40 minutes (€1.76) from Oristano by bus.

Samugheo & Castello di Medusa
postcode 09086 • pop 3556 • elev 370m
The route south out of Fordongianus turns towards Allai and then gains altitude on its way to the textile centre of Samugheo, an unlovely place that becomes almost interesting for its August textiles fair – a good time for buying rugs.

Otherwise you pass through here mainly for the drive. Much the same can be said for the trip in search of the Castello di Medusa, a defensive fortress built in the days of the Giudicato d'Arborea. Four kilometres south of Samugheo, take the turn left (east) down a narrow country road that has you passing into high mountain country on an exhilarating serpentine route. After 5km, you hit 700m of steep, downhill, dirt hairpin bends to wind up at the scant remains of this lonely castle.

If you get stuck here you can stay at **Hotel Bittu** *(☎ 0783 6 41 90; Via Vittorio Emanuele 37; singles/doubles €16/32)*, a straightforward hotel with clean, comfortable and unexciting rooms.

SOUTH OF ORISTANO
The fertile plains south of Santa Giusta were once carpeted by thick cork oak woods, completely cut down over the centuries in a process that left behind a series of malaria-infested, uninhabitable bogs. The farmland is now criss-crossed by a grid pattern of roads, some leading to beaches along this quiet coast.

In 1919, a programme of drainage and reclamation was set in motion and then accelerated under Mussolini. A system of irrigation canals replaced the bogs and the

coastal strip was reforested. At the heart of it all a new town, Mussolinia, was established. Most of the colonists encouraged to come here were from the north Italian Romagna and Veneto regions. After the war Mussolinia was rebaptised Arborea and the land gradually distributed to independent farmers, again mostly northern Italians.

Among the fruits of all this effort are the light Terralba red wines and occasional rosé.

Stagno S'Ena Arrubia
Six kilometres south of Santa Giusta, this lagoon is one of several in the province to host flamingos. There is a good chance you will see some even in summer, although you'll need binoculars to get a decent look.

If you are taken with the place, you can stay in the quiet and basic **Camping S'Ena Arrubia** *(☎/fax 0783 80 20 11; per person/tent space €6.50/7; open July-Aug)*. It's on the southwest side of the lagoon (follow the signs from the main Santa Giusta–Arborea road).

Arborea
postcode 09092 • pop 3928
At the very heart of Mussolini's grand land-reclamation scheme lies the extremely odd town that at first took his name, Mussolinia. A small, quiet place, its focus is the immaculate Piazza Maria Ausiliatrice, a patiently tended and flourishing garden. On all sides it is flanked by architectural whimsy of the 1920s and '30s: such neo-Gothic efforts as the **Chiesa del Cristo Redentore**, delightfully decorated inside, vie for attention with Art Nouveau buildings like the **Municipio** (town hall).

Inside the latter, on the 1st floor, six glass cases contain a collection *(admission free; open 10am-1pm & 3.30pm-5.30pm Mon & Tues, 10am-1pm Wed-Fri, 9am-10.30am Sat)* of ceramics and other artefacts dug up in the area. Most of the material is from the Imperial Roman period and, while a curiosity, is not to cry over if missed.

Hotel Gallo Blanco *(☎/fax 0783 80 02 41; Piazza Maria Ausiliatrice 10; singles/doubles €22/39)* has nine pleasant rooms, some overlooking the square. You can also get a square meal in its restaurant.

Marina di Arborea
The turn-off for this pleasant and much-ignored beach, fronted by a couple of houses,

a seaside hotel and pine stands further back, is 2km north of Arborea.

Il Canneto *(☎ 0783 80 05 61; singles/ doubles €40/80)* offers, apart from simple rooms in what is more like a sprawling family house, its own modest restaurant and the possibility of horse riding.

Marceddi

This dusty fishing settlement couldn't be much further off a tourist trail. Fisherfolk paddle about in the shallows and a cheerful little congregation of passers-by stop to lunch on what they have caught at **Da Lucio** *(☎ 0783 86 71 30; Via Lungomare 40; meals €25-30; open lunch Fri-Wed Sept-June, lunch & dinner daily July-Aug).*

Across the Stagno di Marceddi rise the hills of the Costa Verde in the Cagliari province. If you have your own vehicle it will be hard to resist the temptation to cross the narrow causeway and start exploring one of the wildest and most beautiful stretches of Sardinian coast. For more information on Costa Verde, see the South-west Sardinia chapter.

Southwest Sardinia

From the magnificent and little-visited beaches of the Costa Verde to the abandoned zinc mines of the Iglesiente, the southwest of the island presents some stunning contrasts. The Iglesiente is a hilly and, in places, mountainous zone that fills in the southwestern corner of the island between Capo della Frasca in the northwest and Sarroch in the southeast. Since ancient times the northern half of this sector has been known for its mines. Lead and silver were of prime importance to the Romans and their predecessors, while zinc dominated the renewed extraction activities from the mid-19th century until the 1970s. Iglesias remains a surprisingly attractive city for a (former) mining capital, and the crumbling installations of the mines and their villages scattered round about are fascinating.

Offshore, the islands of San Pietro and Sant'Antioco seem to lead an almost autonomous existence. The latter is especially curious for its ancient sites, catacombs and good beaches.

These islands and the south coast are historically known as the Sulcis. The Phoenicians, Carthaginians and later the Romans all favoured this southern coast facing Sicily. Of their settlements (if you exclude Cagliari), the most intact today is seaside Nora, with its ruined theatre, temples, public baths and mosaics.

Inland stretch the hot plains of the Campidano and the adjacent Marmilla, a strange territory of conical hillocks. In among the latter are some of Sardinia's most important ancient sites, including the important Su Nuraxi *nuraghe* of Barumini, and the high plateau of the Giara di Gesturi, last haven to the Sardinian *cavallino*, a kind of wild pony.

Finding accommodation is not always easy in these parts. Aside from the hotel and camping ground suggestions that follow, a handful of *agriturismi* (farm stays) operate in the countryside, as well as a few B&Bs and other rooms for rent. For B&Bs, a useful centralised point of contact is **Domus Amigas** (☎ *0781 3 63 19;* W *www .domusamigas.it)*. They have houses on the books in various locations across the southwest, with per person costs ranging up to about €25.

Highlights

- Revel in the crystal waters of some of the island's best and least-developed beaches on the Costa Verde
- Feel the spooky echoes of hard times gone by in the abandoned mines of the Iglesiente
- Soak up the Spanish-style atmosphere of Iglesias
- Cast your mind back to Roman times amid the ruins of the ancient port town Nora
- Behold the Nuraghe Su Nuraxi, one of the most important on the island
- Search for the wild 'mini-horses' of the high plateau of La Giara di Gesturi

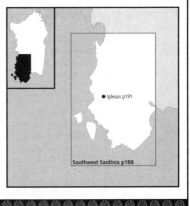

Iglesias p191

Southwest Sardinia p188

IGLESIAS
postcode 09016 • pop 29,700

As mining towns go, Iglesias is a surprisingly charming spot little visited by outsiders. The Spaniards are long gone but the place retains an Iberian feel, with chatter in the air, deep summer heat, Aragonese-style wrought-iron balconies and that touch of decay you find in many a Spanish town.

History
The Romans called it Metalla, for around here they mined precious metals, especially lead and silver. It was not a fun activity and the mines were largely worked by slaves

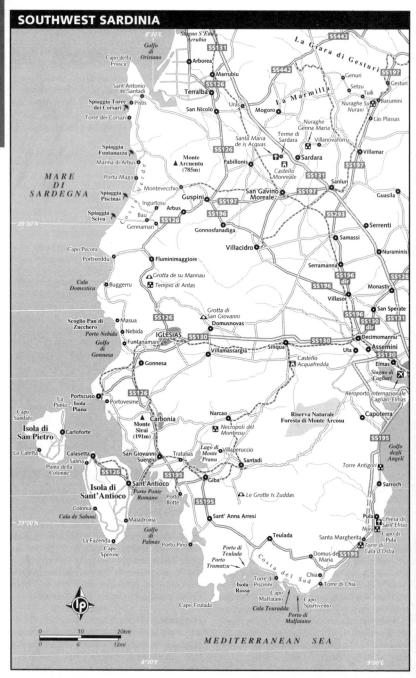

condemned *ad metalla* (to the metal mines). The Romans were not the first to work mines around here. At the San Giorgio mines just outside Iglesias, mining equipment dating to the Carthaginian era was discovered when the mines were reopened in the 19th century.

The collapse of the Roman Empire brought mining to a halt and it was not until the Middle Ages that it was resumed. The town, meanwhile, had come to be known as Villa di Chiesa, owing to the dense concentration of churches belonging to various groups of immigrants in the area.

Onto this stage stepped the colourful character of Ugolino della Gherardesca, head of a powerful Pisan family who took control of the town and surrounding area after Pisa had assumed control of what had been the Giudicato di Cagliari 1258. Ugolino soon had the mines working at full speed, developed local agriculture and trade, and turned the rapidly growing city into a Tuscan-style *commune* (self-governing town or city) with its own laws and currency. In short, Ugolino catapulted the city into its golden age.

Ugolino subsequently left Villa di Chiesa to his eldest son, Guelfo, and returned to the messy political battlefield of Pisa. Guelfo and his brother Lotto realised the game was up when their father was arrested in 1288 (see boxed text 'The Ugly Fate of Ugolino') and abandoned Villa di Chiesa, which from then on was administered directly from Pisa. They made several attempts to regain control of the town in the ensuing years but finally ran out of friends and resources. After the last of these efforts, Guelfo died in San Leonardo de Siete Fuentes in 1295.

In 1323 Catalano-Aragonese troops landed at what is now Portovesme and soon laid siege to the town that, after it fell the following year, they renamed Iglesias (Spanish for 'churches'). Under Iberian rule the mining activity was gradually wound down, more through lethargy than anything else, and it was not until the mid-19th century that interest in the mines was rekindled by the nascent heavy industry of a resurgent and soon-to-be-united Italy. Iglesias again became the nerve-centre of the island's mining operations, which started to decline after WWII and finally shut down for good in the 1970s.

Orientation

The old town is bunched together in the northwestern corner of the city, bounded by Via Roma, Via Gramsci, the leafy, broad and busy Piazza Sella, Via Eleonora d'Arborea and Via Campidano, the latter still lined by remains of the medieval walls that are now only a memory on the other streets.

Main street in the old town is Via Matteotti, scene of the nightly *passeggiata* (the

The Ugly Fate of Ugolino

Ugolino della Gherardesca, master of Villa di Chiesa and power broker in Pisa, headed one of the Tuscan city state's key clans. But Ugolino was going to make an error in judgement that would plunge the entire family into misery.

Having spent 10 years in Sardinia's Villa di Chiesa personally directing affairs, he returned to Pisa. Originally a Ghibelline, in 1275 he switched sides and plotted a Guelph takeover of Pisa. (In the impenetrable bog of medieval Italian politics, there was a ferocious divide between the Guelphs, supporters of the Pope, and Ghibellines, who backed the Holy Roman Empire in its interminable squabbles with Rome.)

The plot was discovered and Ugolino banished, but he soon returned and, after Pisa's crushing defeat by Genoa in the sea battle of Meloria in 1284, became *podestà* (ruler) of Pisa.

Four years later the Ghibellines rebelled and Ugolino was thrown into a tower with two of his sons and two grandsons. They were left to starve to death and a particularly ghoulish story has Ugolino eating his offspring to stave off the inevitable. Ghibelline Dante thought Ugolino's betrayal to the Guelphs so reprehensible that he shoved him into the very depths of hell in his *Inferno* (Canto 33, verses 1–78), where the tale of cannibalism is strongly hinted at. Mind you, the vicious Archbishop Ruggieri, who not only betrayed Ugolino but gave the order to throw him and his children into the tower, ended up in the same spot. Dante has the two of them in the icy depths of hell, condemned to an eternal cannibalistic frenzy, each munching away on the other.

traditional evening stroll). It leads to a series of squares, Piazza La Marmora, Piazza Collegio, Piazza Piscini and Piazza del Municipio. Scattered about are some of the many churches from which the town takes its name.

In medieval times the city was divided into quarters, but you'll only realise this during festivities, when the standards of each quarter flutter from the crowded balconies of the old town.

The real fulcrum of the city hubbub in the evening is Piazza Sella, just beyond the old town at the southern end of Via Matteotti.

Information

Tourist Information The **Pro Loco** (☎ 0781 4 17 95; Via Gramsci 11-13; open 9.30am-1pm & 4pm-7pm Mon-Fri, 9.30am-12.30pm Sat) has information on the town and the rest of the Iglesiente.

Money You can change money at the **Credito Italiano** (cnr Via Matteotti & Piazza Sella) and **Banco Nazionale del Lavoro** (Via Roma 29). Both have ATMs.

Post & Communications The main **post office** (Via Montevecchio; open 8.15am-6.15pm Mon-Fri, 8.15am-1pm Sat) is centrally located.

Things to See & Do

In Iglesias, as elsewhere in Italy, the twilight decades of the 19th century brought a burst of optimism and activity. Mining had again been cranked up into a key motor for local development, and as if to herald in the new age, the bulk of the medieval walls were demolished and the grand spacious Piazza Sella laid out in what had been a field just outside the walls. From that time on it became the townsfolk's central meeting place and still today the young and old gambol about in the shadow of the 1885 statue of Quintino Sella, Sardinian statesman and vigorous promoter of the reborn mining industry.

Just off the square amid pleasant hillside sculpted gardens stand the remains, mainly a stout square tower, of **Castello Salvaterra**, a Pisan fortress finished under Catalano-Aragonese rule. It's an almost bucolic little stroll and from up here you can appreciate fine views of the old town.

To get an idea of what the city looked like before the walls came down, proceed to Via Campidano, where a stretch of the 14th-century northwestern perimeter built by the Catalano-Aragonese, complete with towers, remains defiantly in place.

Back in Piazza Sella, head into the old city along its main boulevard, the shop-lined Via Matteotti, which on a summer day seems like central Manhattan at rush hour as evening descends and the locals come out, all fresh and dressed to the nines, for the *passeggiata*.

You will soon notice that the compact space of old Iglesias lives up to its name. The **Duomo** (cathedral) dominates the eastern flank of Piazza del Municipio. Built under Count Ugolino della Gherardesca, it retains its Pisan-flavoured Romanesque-Gothic facade, as does the belltower with its chequer-board variety of stone. At the time of writing the cathedral was closed, making it impossible to view the internal makeover Catalan architects gave it in the 16th century. Directly across the square is the bishop's residence, while the grand neoclassical **Municipio** on the west side houses the town's politicians.

A short walk off the square brings you to the dainty rose-red trachyte **Chiesa di San Francesco** (Piazza San Francesco). Although possibly older than the cathedral in origin, it now only sports its Catalan Gothic wardrobe, some of it dating to the 15th century. Inside, the single nave is flanked by chapels inserted between the buttressing.

Up Via Pullo and then Via della Zecca you reach the **Chiesa di Santa Maria delle Grazie** (Via Manzoni), which is closed. From its 13th-century origins it preserves only the lower half of the facade. The rest dates to the 17th and 18th centuries, a thorough plastic-surgery job demonstrating questionable judgement.

While on the theme of churches, two are worth seeking out a short distance from the centre. The **Chiesa di Nostra Signora del Valverde** is about a 15-minute walk southeast from Piazza Sella near the cemetery. Its facade recalls that of the cathedral and repeats its two series of blind arches in the Pisan style. Adjacent are some remains of the convent that once stood here.

You reach the **Chiesa di Nostra Signora del Buon Cammino** by following a steep incline north of Via Campidano. It takes about 10 to 15 minutes and the views on arrival are the main attraction.

When you have had your fill of the Lord's many houses, try something a little earthier. The **Museo dell'Arte Mineraria** (☎ 333 447 99 80; W www.museoartemineraria .it; Via Roma 17; admission free; open 7pm-10.30pm Wed-Sun June-Aug, 6pm-8.30pm Sat & Sun Sept-May) is indeed a curio. The building was raised in 1911 as a mining school and many of the materials and displays downstairs that recreate the reality of the mines were used by the school to train senior mine workers. The tunnels downstairs were in fact dug by mining students and during WWII found an unexpected use as air-raid shelters.

Upstairs is a collection of specimens of rock and minerals dug up here and around the world.

Special Events

If you are in Iglesias for **Settimana Santa** (Easter) you will think you have been transported to central Spain. From Holy Tuesday to Good Friday, the town is transformed into a stage for nightly processions. Hooded and white-robed members of religious brotherhoods, bearing candles and crucifixes and accompanied by a slow deathly beating of deep drums, carry around effigies of the Virgin Mary and Christ dead in *sa lettera* (his bed). All slightly sinister but fascinating.

Much cheerier is Iglesias' **Estate Medioevale Iglesiente** (Iglesias' Medieval Summer).

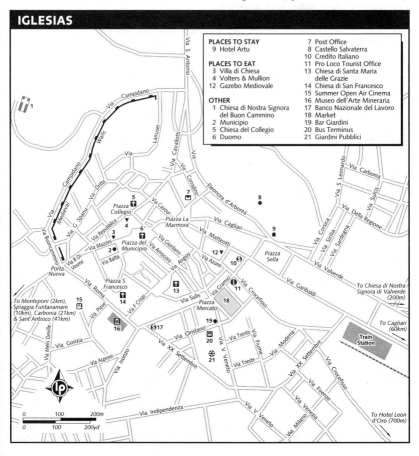

IGLESIAS

PLACES TO STAY	7 Post Office
9 Hotel Artu	8 Castello Salvaterra
	10 Credito Italiano
PLACES TO EAT	11 Pro Loco Tourist Office
3 Villa di Chiesa	13 Chiesa di Santa Maria
4 Volters & Mullion	delle Grazie
12 Gazebo Mediovale	14 Chiesa di San Francesco
	15 Summer Open Air Cinema
OTHER	16 Museo dell'Arte Mineraria
1 Chiesa di Nostra Signora	17 Banco Nazionale del Lavoro
del Buon Cammino	18 Market
2 Municipio	19 Bar Giardini
5 Chiesa del Collegio	20 Bus Terminus
6 Duomo	21 Giardini Pubblici

Since the mid-1990s the town has dressed up for medieval processions and other antique antics, including markets, costume events and feasting.

Places to Stay & Eat

Iglesias is short on lodgings and not much longer on eateries.

Hotel Artu (☎ *0781 2 24 92; fax 0781 3 24 49;* **w** *www.hotelartuiglesias.it, Italian only; Piazza Sella 15; singles/doubles €54/82.40)* is the only central option. An ugly building, its rooms are fine and of a reasonable size, some looking out onto the busy square.

Hotel Leon d'Oro (☎ *0781 3 35 55, fax 0781 3 35 30; Corso Colombo 72; singles/ doubles €60/90)* is well south of the centre. A functional place where you might expect to bump into lonely commercial travellers, it has comfortable rooms and even a swimming pool.

Volters & Mullion (☎ *0781 3 37 88; Piazza Collegio 1; meals €25; open daily)* is a cheerful eatery tucked into a corner of Piazza del Collegio. It has a nice range of pasta and main courses. It's not fine cuisine but perfectly reasonable. The place is one of the best for a couple of summer evening tipples too.

Gazebo Medioevale (☎ *0781 3 08 71; Via Musio 21; meals €25-30; open Mon-Sat)* is a good winter alternative. Take a table beneath the long stone-and-brick arches and settle in for a mostly seafood menu. Staff prepare some fish dishes with couscous.

Villa di Chiesa (☎ *0781 2 31 24; Piazza del Municipio 8; meals €25)* is busy. You can eat inside or on the square and it does a reasonable pizza.

Entertainment

The cafés around Piazza Sella, Piazza La Marmora, along with the Volters & Mullion restaurant, are about the sum of the average evening's options.

Ask at the tourist office about the summer **open-air cinema** programme.

Getting There & Away

Bus All intercity buses arrive at and leave from the Via Oristano side of the Giardini Pubblici. You can get timetable information and tickets from **Bar Giardini** (open 5.30am-2.30pm & 3.30pm-9pm Mon-Sat) across the road. As many as 10 FMS buses run from Cagliari to Iglesias (€2.89, one to 1½ hours).

To Carbonia there are as many as eight runs (€1.45, 45 minutes).

Train As many as 16 trains run between Iglesias and Cagliari (€2.56, 50 minutes to one hour).

Car & Motorcycle With the exception of the fast dual carriageway SS130 from Cagliari (less than an hour), approaches by road to Iglesias are slow. From the south, the coast road from Cagliari joins the road from Sant'Antioco to pass via Carbonia to Iglesias. The most direct road from the north is the SS126, which drops south from Oristano province (see the Oristano & the West chapter) to Guspini and then heads through the mountains via Arbus and Fluminimaggiore.

AROUND IGLESIAS
Monteponi Mines

Just outside Iglesias to the southwest, the hillside is still occupied by the eerie buildings of the now-silent Monteponi mines, still partly lit up at night. It is possible to join a tour of the **Galleria Villamamna** (☎ *348 540 42 30)*, one of the tunnels in the mining complex, but only by arrangement (usually for groups only).

You can get a local Linea B FMS bus from Via Oristano eight times a day (€0.57, 20 minutes).

Grotta di Santa Barbara

A few kilometres further along the Carbonia road, you come across the abandoned San Giovanni mines. Back in the 1950s the Grotta di Santa Barbara (☎ *348 526 24 72; adult/child €12/6; visits 9.30am, 11.30am, 3.30pm & 6.30pm July-Aug)* was discovered on the mine site. The cave consists of one enormous chamber, its walls covered in crystals of various types.

You can turn up for a visit in summer but it could be hit and miss. Otherwise you can only visit by prior arrangement.

East of Iglesias

Grotta di San Giovanni About 10km east of Iglesias on the SS130 road to Cagliari lies the unremarkable town of **Domusnovas** (regular FMS buses from Iglesias). Four kilometres to the north, however, lies the altogether

[Continued on page 200]

Viva la Festa!

Mamuthone masks, Mamoiada

Festa del Redentore, Nuoro

Mural of the Ardia horse race, Sedilo

Ardia horse race at San Constantino Church, Sedilo

ince time immemorial Sardinians have marked the coming and going of the seasons with traditional festivals. The most important predate Christianity and are linked to the farming calendar. As elsewhere in the Christian world, these feast days were often 'Christianised' and so appropriated by the Church simply by attaching the celebration of one saint or another to the original pagan ritual. In other words, 'if you can't beat 'em, join 'em'. With time, more saints' days were added to the calendar and in any case the common people soon forgot that their now Christian holidays in fact had predated the arrival of their faith. Well, perhaps not entirely forgotten. The Church was able to commandeer the feast days and institute moments of Christian solemnity, but could hardly deter people from doing what they most liked about their festivals – indulging in the liberating, hedonistic opportunity to eat, drink and be merry.

In the wake of WWII and the economic boom years of the 1960s, many of these traditions began to die off. Old beliefs and superstitions weakened as agriculture lost its pre-eminent place for the populace and education was made accessible to all. Many minor traditions have no doubt disappeared for good, but Sardinians have remained doggedly faithful to some of their most important dates and since the 1980s have resurrected others.

Sardinia's festivities are not completely unique. Some of the big dates are common across the Christian Mediterranean from mainland Italy to Spain. Indeed, the long Spanish occupation of the island inevitably left an indelible mark and numerous Sardinian celebrations have a distinctly Iberian flavour.

There isn't a village that doesn't make some effort at least once a year to celebrate a saint's day or some other occasion, but clearly some festivals are of greater interest than others. More popular saints' days are marked in towns and villages up and down the island, while more obscure ones might only rate a muted *festa* once a year in an out-of-way hamlet. A selection of the most important festivals follows.

January

Festa di Sant'Antonio Abate
16 January • All over Sardinia

With the winter solstice passed, people of many towns and villages across Sardinia, especially in Nuoro province, seem intent on giving the chill weather a push towards spring with great bonfires in central squares on this evening. According to the myth, Sant'Antonio stole fire from hell to give to man. After the blessing of the fire and perhaps a procession, townsfolk turn to the serious business of drinking. Among the places where you can be sure of seeing a good bonfire are Orosei, Orgosolo, Sedilo and Paulilatino.

Mamuthones
16–17 January & Carnevale • Mamoiada

Warranting special mention are the celebrations that take place in the otherwise nondescript town of Mamoiada, south of Nuoro. Traditional costumes are used in processions here to represent the *mamuthones*,

Title page:
Crowds at the Ardia festival, Sedilo
(Photograph by Stefano Cavedoni)

where a dozen townspeople don heavy hairy costumes and masks with a half-human, half-animal allure. Weighed down by up to 30kg of *campanacci* (massive cowbells), these beasts make quite a racket. Ritually chasing them are eight *issohadores*, in the guise of outmoded gendarmes. The two figures can be interpreted as representing good and evil or the cycles of life. Their importance down through the centuries was capital to the superstitious, who hoped by this ritual to appease nature and hurry along the advent of spring for the coming year. The din of the cowbells was designed to ward off evil spirits. Although adopted by the Christian Church, this noisy parade was essentially a pagan affair. They generally come out to play again in Carnevale (see later).

Festa di San Sebastiano
19 January • All over Sardinia
A cluster of towns that don't celebrate Sant'Antonio set up their winter bonfires three days later for San Sebastiano. The idea is virtually the same and some towns (like Dorgali, Paulilatino, Seui, Seulo and Torralba, among others) indulge in double dipping, celebrating both occasions with equal fire.

February
Carnevale
All over Sardinia
During the period running up to Ash Wednesday, many towns stage carnivals and enjoy their last opportunity to indulge before the 40 days of Lent. Traditionally processions and parties take place from Thursday to *martedí grasso* (fat Tuesday, the last chance to eat and drink whatever you want before Ash Wednesday). In most towns nowadays, activities start on the weekend and for many Lent is no longer a period of abstinence, so Tuesdays are not as 'fat' as they once were. Carnevale is celebrated with more vim and vigour in some places than others. In Alghero the effigy of a French soldier is tried and condemned to burn at the stake on *martedí grasso*. Similar 'executions' take place at other towns, including Cagliari. Bosa celebrates Carnevale in lively fashion, as do the following places listed separately for the uniqueness of their particular festivities.

Mamuthones & More
The *mamuthones* of Mamoiada (see earlier) usually get a second outing at Carnevale. At the same time similar figures appear in two other towns in the province of Nuoro: the *thurpos* in Orotelli and the *boes* and *merdules* in Ottana.

Sa Sartiglia
Sunday & Tuesday before Lent • Oristano
This is the highlight of Carnevale celebrations at Oristano. It involves a medieval tournament of horsemen in masquerade, armed with lance or sword, who charge at high speed towards a ring suspended high up on a rope. Processions of locals in traditional costume precede the knightly challenge. Horse races of a less disciplined and fancy nature

take place at Santu Lussurgiu (the *sa carrera 'e 'nanti* race), Scano Montiferro and Sedilo (in both cases the race is known as the *corsa a sa pudda*), all in Oristano province.

March/April

Pasqua (Easter)
All over Sardinia

Holy Week, which can take place any time from 22 March to 25 April depending on the lunar calendar, is marked by solemn processions and Passion plays all over the island. Some are more striking than others. The Spanish-influenced Good Friday Via Crucis procession in Tempio Pausania, for instance, is an almost sinister affair featuring the hooded members of religious societies known as *confraternite*. The people of Iglesias celebrate Easter with equally Iberian vigour. The most engaging Easter procession is probably Castelsardo's Lunissanti (Monday of Holy Week), an evocative torchlit parade through the old town. Other places well worth visiting for Easter celebrations are Cagliari and Alghero (where Passion plays are done in the Catalan language).

Festa di Sant'Antioco
Second Sunday after Easter • All over Sardinia

Celebrated in various points across the island, St Antioch's feast is rightly greeted with most enthusiasm in the town named after him, Sant'Antioco (on the island of the same name in Sardinia's southwest).

May

Festa di Sant'Efisio
1–4 May • Cagliari

One of the island's most colourful festivals takes place to honour the memory of Sardinia's patron saint. On 1 May the saint's effigy is paraded around the city on a baroque, bullock-drawn carriage amid a colourful costume procession. Back in AD 303 the Roman commander

Right: Traditional *mamuthone* model at Ruggero Mameli's workshop, Mamoiada

DALLAS STRIBLEY

Ephisius, who had converted to Christianity, was beheaded on Diocletian's orders on the beach at Nora. Since then the crypt in Stampace where he was said to have been imprisoned became a site of pilgrimage. In 1652 Cagliari suffered the plague for two years with no sign of it abating; the people turned to Sant'Efisio for help and lo!, the plague ended. Thus was born the festival that has continued every year to this day. After the day's parades, the effigy is accompanied on a procession to Nora, from where it returns on 4 May, arriving in the capital at nightfall to be greeted by still more street celebrations.

Festa di Santa Giusta
14 May • Santa Giusta
Held in the town of the same name just south of Oristano, the festival involves parades and music over four days.

Cavalcata Sarda (Sardinian Parade)
Second-last Sunday in May • Sassari
Hundreds of Sardinians wearing colourful traditional costume gather at Sassari to mark a victory over the Saracens in AD 1000. They are followed up by horsemen who make a spirited charge through the streets at the end of the parade.

June
Festa della Madonna dei Martiri
Monday after the first Sunday of June • Fonni
The people of Fonni dress in traditional costume and stage a procession with a revered image of the Virgin Mary, starting at the grand basilica of the same name.

Festa di San Giovanni Battista
24 June • All over Sardinia
Although handed a saint's name, the traditional feast of 24 June marks the passing of the summer solstice. It is not as big in Sardinia as in other parts of the Mediterranean (like Catalunya and the Balearic Islands in Spain) but a few towns, including Olbia and Portoscuso, celebrate with traditional flaming bonfires the night before. Fonni, for the second time in the same month, puts on a colourful procession in traditional costume to mark this feast day.

July
Ardia
6–7 July • Sedilo
More dangerous than Siena's famed Il Palio horse race, this impressive and chaotic equestrian event celebrates the victory of the Roman emperor, Constantine, over Maxentius in AD 312 (the battle took place at the Ponte Milvio in Rome). An unruly pack of skilled horsemen (frequently the jockeys who ride at Il Palio are Sardinians) race around a dusty track by the chapel erected in Constantine's name (aka Santu Antine) and, the most dangerous moment, rumble under the arch just

outside the town. It was at the foot of this arch than one veteran of the races was killed when he fell from his mount on the first day of racing in 2002. The following day, muted but defiant, his chums again sat in the saddle for the second day's competition – their companion would have wanted it that way. Copious draughts of wine and gunfire accompany the general cacophony. Don't underestimate these horsemen, who are considered among Italy's best and frequently provide the jockeys for the much better known Il Palio races in Siena, Tuscany.

Festa della Madonna del Naufrago
Second Sunday of July ● Villasimius
This striking seaborne procession takes place off the coast of Villasimius where a statue of the Virgin Mary lies on the seabed in honour of shipwrecked sailors.

August

Estate Musicale Internazionale di Alghero (International Summer of Music)
July & August ● Alghero
This festival features, in particular, classical music concerts.

Festa di Santa Maria del Mare
First Sunday of August ● Bosa
Bosa's fishermen celebrate their devotion to the Virgin Mary with a river parade of boats bearing her image. Town celebrations continue for four days.

Is Fassois
First Sunday of August ● Stagno di Santa Giusta
A race of these tiny, traditional rush fishing boats is held to the south of Oristano.

Matrimonio Maureddino
First Sunday of August ● Santadi
The Matrimonia Maureddino, or Moorish Wedding (so named because of the centuries of contact this and other southern towns had with the Moors of North Africa in the Middle Ages), wedding festival is held in the southwest. In this colourful ceremony a local couple is married in the main square in full traditional rural costume. The whole town turns out to see the couple, driven to the square in *is traccas*, a cart drawn by the island's red bulls. After the couple and their immediate guests return home for the wedding banquet, the rest of the town lets loose with folk dancing, eating and drinking in the square well into the night.

I Candelieri (The Candlesticks)
14 August ● Sassari
Sassari's big traditional feast is I Candelieri held on 14 August. In the 16th century the city's trade guilds (*gremi*) organised a thanksgiving parade to the Virgin Mary for ending one of the city's many bouts of plague. Giant timber 'candles' were created. Nine guilds are represented. In the

weeks preceding the big day, guild members who have been elected to bear the candles can be seen practising. On the big day the traditional highpoint is the Faradda, when the nine guilds parade their candles, accompanied by drummers and pipers, from Piazza Castello to the Chiesa di Santa Maria di Betlem.

One member of each guild is named standard bearer, an honour and a burden, for he must collect money to organise a grand banquet. You don't have to practise the trade of the ancient guilds (which range from tailors to stonecutters, shoemakers to farmers) but it is generally an honour passed down from father to son.

The celebrations are held to honour a vow made in 1652 for deliverance from a plague but are also connected with the Feast of the Assumption (15 August). Another important location for similar festivities in honour of the Virgin Mary on 14 August is Nulvi.

Festa dell'Assunta
15 August • Orgosolo
Held in this rough and ready town, this is one of the most important festivals in the Barbargia area of central Sardinia. The event is marked by processions of religious fraternities and the colourful local costumes worn by the women.

Estate Medioevale Iglesiente
mid-August • Iglesias
Since the mid-1990s, Iglesias has hosted an increasingly popular 'Medieval summer', whose highpoint is the Corteo Storico Medioevale (Historic Medieval Parade), a grand costumed affair.

Festa del Redentore
Second-last or last Sunday of August • Nuoro
Possibly the grandest procession of traditional Sardinian costume dominates this festival in Nuoro in the last week of the month. Groups from towns and villages all over the island, but especially Nuoro province, proudly parade their widely varying festive dress. Among them parade strapping horsemen and dance groups. At night spectators are treated to folk dancing displays. The religious side of the festivities has its roots in the placement of a statue of Christ at the top of Monte Ortobene at the turn of the 20th century. A torchlit procession winds through the city on the evening of 28 August and an early morning pilgrimage to Monte Ortobene takes place the following day.

September
Festa di San Salvatore
First Sunday of September • San Salvatore
Several hundred young fellows clothed in white set off on the Corsa degli Scalzi (Barefoot Race), an 8km run to the hamlet and sanctuary of San Salvatore, from Cabras. They bear with them an effigy of the Saviour and the whole event commemorates an episode in 1506, when townspeople raced to the San Salvatore sanctuary to collect the effigy and save it from Moorish sea raiders.

Festa di Nostra Signora di Regnos Altos
Mid-September • Bosa

The people of the old town of Bosa decorate their streets with huge palm fronds, flowers and *altarittos* (votive altars) in honour of the Virgin Mary.

October

Sagra delle Castagne
Last Sunday of October • Aritzo

This Nuoro province town livens up for its Chestnut Festival. The streets fill with the smoky perfume of roasting chestnuts, which thousands of people from all around come along to munch on.

December

Natale (Christmas)
25 December • All over Sardinia

During the weeks preceding Christmas there are numerous processions and religious events. Many churches set up elaborate cribs or nativity scenes known as *presepi*. The day itself is a quiet family affair.

[Continued from page 192]

remarkable Grotta di San Giovanni. It is a giant cave that, until 2000, you could drive your car through. Since the local council decided it would be better for the cave to drive around it and built a road to this effect, access has been left to pedestrians alone.

The SS130 speeds east on to Cagliari, with few recommendable stops along the way. One is the Castello di Acquafredda (see later in this chapter).

North of Iglesias

A pretty but nauseatingly windy 26km stretch of road meanders north out of Iglesias to **Fluminimaggiore**, a sleepy place with an ethnographical museum and a couple of bars and eateries. The town holds little interest but along the way are two notable stops. Up to eight FMS buses link Iglesias with Fluminimaggiore (€1.76, 45 minutes), and you can get off along the way to visit these sights.

Tempio di Antas Even before reaching the right-hand turn-off about 15km north of Iglesias, you can spot this sand-coloured Roman temple *(☎ 347 817 49 89; adult/child €2.60/1.30; open 9am-1pm & 3pm-8pm daily May-Sept; 9am-1pm & 3pm-6pm Sat, Sun & holidays Oct-Apr)* on the high ground across the valley.

Before you get too excited about the marvels of Roman engineering, let's clear one thing up straight away – the eight columns you see standing were re-erected during excavation and restoration between 1967 and 1976. The temple in its present form dates to the era of Emperor Caracalla and was dedicated to Sardus Pater, an obscure nuraghic deity and, according to one myth, founder of Sardinia. At the foot of the resurrected columns at the front of the temple are the fenced-off remains of its Carthaginian predecessor (dedicated to the Punic god Sid Babi), which the Romans cannibalised to erect their version.

Between the ticket office and the temple, a narrow trail marked as *sentiero romano*, or Roman way, leads (after about five minutes) to what little remains of a nuraghic settlement, the existence of which seems to confirm speculation that the Carthaginian temple was preceded by an earlier place of worship. Following the trail for 1½ hours

would theoretically take you to the Grotta de Su Mannau, but we haven't tried it out.

Another 20-minute walk (signposted) from the temple takes you to the quarries the Romans used to provide extra building material for the temple.

From the main road it is about a half-hour walk to the main site.

Grotta de Su Mannau Fans of stalactites and stalagmites may want to join a 50-minute tour of these **caves** *(☎ 0781 58 01 89; admission €4.50; open 9.30am-6.30pm)*. Over the millennia two streams have carved out this series of caves, about 8km long in all. The guided visit takes you in about half a kilometre. As you proceed, the walkway passes through several chambers and above small lakes until you reach the Pozzo Rodriguez (Rodriguez Well), marked off by an 8m column, at which point you turn back.

You can also join beginners' speleological tours of the remainder of the caves. These excursions (equipment provided) need to be organised in advance. Costs vary according to duration and number of participants.

IGLESIENTE COAST
Gonnesa

Just a few kilometres south of Iglesias, this middling town has nothing much of interest but a place to stay if you have no luck in Iglesias itself.

Hotel Frau *(☎ 0781 4 51 04; Via della Pace 99; singles/doubles €18/28.40)* has half a dozen simple rooms – loos and showers are down the corridor.

Funtanamare

This long stretch of fine golden sands facing the Golfo di Gonnesa is the main beach for the people of Iglesias. It is popular but rarely gets too crowded, if only because it is so big. Behind it lies fertile farming country.

Up to 10 FMS buses run the 8km down to the beach (€0.88, 20 minutes) and there is plenty of parking if you want to drive. Other buses head to a point further south along the same strand known as **Plage Mesu**.

Nebida

Swing north from Funtanamare along the coast road, which quickly climbs the rocky walls of the Iglesiente coast to give you spectacular views northwards. Even before you reach the former mining settlement of Nebida, 5.5km away, three *faraglioni* (craggy outcrops jutting out of the sea) and the bizarre **Scoglio Pan di Zucchero** (Sugarloaf Rock) islet come into view against a majestic backdrop of sheer rugged cliffs.

Nebida itself is a sprawling place that stretches for a kilometre or so along the coast road. Shortly after entering the town stop at the **Belvedere** for the mesmerising views. This fenced-off walkway around the cliff face affords prime views of the Scoglio Pan di Zucchero and you can sit down for coffee at the **Caffè del Operaio** half way around. From here you can also see the **Laveria Lamarmora**, ruins of a building used for the washing and separation of minerals back in Nebida's mining days. A dirt track also winds down from the main road to the site.

About 500m further north, a side road leads down to **Portu Banda**, with a small pebble beach.

Hotel Pan di Zucchero (*☎/fax 0781 4 71 14; Via Centrale 366; singles/doubles €36/46*) is another reason for stopping by. The rooms are functional but clean and comfortable and some have balconies with stunning coastal views. The restaurant serves up copious helpings from a limited menu of mostly seafood pasta dishes (try the fish-stuffed *ravioli al pomodoro*). The *bistecca di cavallo* is more tender than you might expect horsemeat to be.

Up to 11 FMS buses run between Iglesias and Masua, just up from Nebida (€1.19, 30 minutes).

Masua

A few kilometres further north is another former mining centre, Masua, right by the Scoglio Pan di Zucchero. A side road leads down past a small snack-bar restaurant and the rather ugly mining complex to a reasonable beach whose main attraction is its position facing the massive islet.

If you're into mining, an interesting tour takes you through an original 'port'. Until the 1920s, much of the ore mined around the Iglesiente was transported to sailing vessels which were hauled up onto the beaches (a labour-intensive business – you can still see pictures of workers carrying loads of ore on their backs to the vessels). They then sailed down to Carloforte (Isola di San Pietro) to transfer the load to cargo vessels.

In 1924 a 600m twin tunnel was dug into the cliff here towards the open sea. An ingenious mobile 'arm' shoved the raw minerals from a conveyor belt to ships moored directly below. **Porto Flavia** (*☎ 348 661 51 92; adult/child €8/4.50*) can be visited daily for one-hour tours (they provide the hard hats!) in July and August (four or five visits a day depending on demand). In other months it is generally only possible for groups by calling ahead. To find it, head down to the beach. A dirt road leads back uphill and then around the coast for 2.5km to the entrance.

The same road leads to a shady lookout point to the **Scoglio Pan di Zucchero**, a 133m-high natural rocky fortress that soars out of the water just off the limestone walls of the mainland.

Cala Domestica

From Masua the road rises quickly in a series of tight turns as it works its way around Monte Guardianu. After reaching the top, it drops down again towards Buggerru. Beachlovers should take the Cala Domestica turnoff (signposted), 5km short of Buggerru. This narrow but broad sandy beach lies at the end of a deep natural inlet, walled on either side by craggy cliffs. The water is beautiful and sometimes curls up in decent sets of waves. A walk along the rocky path to the right of the beach brings you to a smaller, more sheltered side strand.

There is a parking area for camper vans. Parking a car close to the beach costs €2 for the morning or afternoon and €4 for the day. A snack stand behind the beach helps keep body and soul together.

Buggerru & Portixeddu

Another former mining town (note the ruins of the Planu Sartu mines to the west of the road just before you reach the town), and long accessible only by sea, Buggerru has become a modest holiday centre and yacht harbour. Next door to the line-up of pleasure craft is a perfectly acceptable little **beach**, although the options to the south and north are far superior.

Mining enthusiasts have another potential appointment here at the **Galleria Henry** (*☎ 339 484 66 40; adult/child €8/4.50*). The rail tunnels here allowed the transport of minerals from the rock face to filtering and washing centres. What makes this 1km tour (about an hour) are the views straight down the cliff side to the sea. As with Porto Flavia in Nebida (see earlier in this chapter) you can just turn up (follow the signs on the south side of Buggerru) in July and August and join a tour. Otherwise it's by appointment only.

The road out of Buggerru again climbs high along the cliff-face, providing stunning views for a couple of kilometres before you hit the long sandy stretches of **Spiaggia Portixeddu**. The beach extends 3km up the coast to the Rio Mannu river, which marks the end of the Iglesiente coast. Some parking is paid (up to €4 a day) but there are plenty of free spaces too.

You can stay at **Camping Ortus de Mari** (*☎/fax 0781 5 49 64; per person/tent space €7.75/10.33; open late May–Sept*), a little way northeast of the beach, about 1km from the Capo Pecora turn-off. The only other option in the area is **Hotel Golfo del Leone** (*☎ 0781 5 49 23, fax 0781 5 49 52; Località Caburu de Figu; singles/doubles €44/65*), on a back trail, a few hundred metres to the right of the Capo Pecora turn-off.

COSTA VERDE & AROUND

Capo Pecora, a low rocky promontory jutting out into the Mediterranean about 4km northwest of Portixeddu, marks the southern tip of the Costa Verde, so named for the splotches of green *macchia* (scrub) that unevenly carpet much of its length.

The coast is a splendid mix of soaring cliffs and fine sandy beaches, some backed by towering dunes, others by soft greenery.

Southern Beaches

From Capo Pecora head back via Portixeddu and northeast along the SS126 until you reach the turn-off for **Bau**, **Gennamari** and **Spiaggia Scivu**. If coming from Arbus, you'll see the signs on the right after 13km. Take this narrow mountain route into the windswept, *macchia*-covered southern heights to around 450m. When the sea comes into view the road drops down in a series of curves and finally flattens out. Five kilometres short of the beach, Spiaggia Scivu is signposted to the left. Going straight ahead would take you to the local penitentiary, something probably best avoided.

You arrive at a parking area (€4 a day in summer), where there's a kiosk and freshwater showers (€0.50) in summer only. As you walk towards the beach you find yourself atop 70m dunes. An enormous length of beach stretches before you. Some locals say it's called Spiaggia Narucci, and that the real Spiaggia Scivu is an hour's walk south along the coast. Whatever, you have before you kilometres of some of the best beach on the whole island. Even in August few people make the effort to get here. How long this state of affairs can last is anyone's guess.

A couple of hours' walk north would take you to **Spiaggia Piscinas**, another legendary beach of the Costa Verde with crystal clear deep water. Less time consuming is the drive. Some 3.7km northeast of the Spiaggia Scivu turn-off along the SS126 take the **Ingurtosu** exit. This is a worthwhile exercise in its own right, as the road drops down into a valley lined by the abandoned buildings, housing and machinery of a crumbling 19th-century mining settlement.

After 9km of dirt track you'll hit a fork. Take the left one for Spiaggia Piscinas. Back from the broad strand rise 30m dunes, some speckled with *macchia*. They call this, somewhat optimistically, Sardinia's desert. But the dunes are impressive enough.

In summer a couple of kiosk-cafés and even freshwater showers are set up on the beach. People park their camper vans here or stay in the nearby stylish **Hotel Le Dune** (*☎ 070 97 71 30; e ledune.ingurtosu@tiscalinet.it; rooms up to €160*), carved out of mining buildings that were at the head of a mini-railway used to ferry ore to the coast for transport.

Backtrack to the fork and turn left (north) to keep following the Costa Verde – a dirt trail for several kilometres with views back to dunes of Spiaggia Piscinas. A few kilometres after the asphalt begins you hit the raggedy looking holiday resort of **Portu Maga**, with a small beach, market, restaurants and uninspired holiday homes.

Four kilometres further north, **Marina di Arbus** is little more than a cluster of houses and the strangely terraced **Camping Costa Verde** (*☎/fax 070 97 70 09; per person/tent space €9.30/15; open mid-July–Aug*).

From here the road cuts inland for a few kilometres. When you reach the T-junction you could head right (south) for Montevecchio or left (north) to continue along the Costa Verde. Assuming you make the latter choice, you could elect to go straight ahead at the next intersection for **Spiaggia Funtanazza**, a reasonable sandy beach backed by pine stands with rocky headlands and the incredible, abandoned hulk of a 1950s holiday residence (plans have long been on the table to renovate it).

The road north runs too far inland to see the coast. After a few kilometres you arrive at the scruffy **Torre dei Corsari** resort and its fabulous broad beach, backed by dunes and named after the inevitable ruined watchtower at its southern end. The top end of this beach is known as **Pistis** – a good long walk or an 8km drive via **Sant'Antonio di Santadi** away. The water is incredibly limpid – a deep emerald green. There is paid parking at both ends (€2) and a couple of kiosks.

You could stay in Torre dei Corsari at **Ostello della Torre** (*☎/fax 070 97 71 55; Viale della Torre; singles/doubles €20/41, half board per person €35)*, perched up on a high point behind the southern headland that seals off the beach. Rooms are nicely arranged and amazingly good value. You can sit on terraces with sea views or in the garden. It also has a restaurant and the place remains open all year.

Hotel Caletta (*☎ 070 97 71 33, fax 070 97 71 73; w www.lacaletta.it; doubles €90, half board per person €77; open July-Aug)* is a classier option situated right on a rocky point (occupied by its boomerang-shaped swimming pool). Rooms have all mod-cons and the place is equipped with a restaurant (with sea views), a bar and even a little disco.

Capo della Frascas marks the northern end of the Costa Verde. Around it a couple of beaches are accessible only by sea in July and August when the military base here allows it. You could try organising a boat with fishermen in Marceddi, across **Stagno di Marceddi** (see the Oristano & the West chapter).

Montevecchio

Continuing the mining theme from Ingurtosu, the narrow and scenic road northeast of Ingurtosu leads to Montevecchio, a leafy hill town with still more spectacular ruins from its mining past. The impressive remains of mining structures and machinery lie outside the town in the valley to the east. The mountains around here are peppered with abandoned mine shafts.

It's possible to get onto tours (usually conducted in Italian) of the mines with the **Centro Escursioni Minerarie Naturalistiche** (*☎ 335 531 41 98; w www.guspini.net)*. General tourist information, including help with finding B&Bs or other rooms in the area, can be had (it is promised in various languages) by calling ☎ 368 53 89 97. Given that these are mobile phone numbers, you should also consider contacting the **Comune di Guspini** (*☎ 070 97 25 37)*.

The deeply wooded country around **Monte Arcuenta** (785m) to the north of Montevecchio is one of the last preserves of the *cervo sardo* or Sardinian deer.

The occasional bus runs up from Guspini, linked to Iglesias by up to four daily FMS bus runs (one hour 20 minutes).

Arbus
postcode 09031 • pop 7338 • elev 311m
If you are interested in Sardinian knives, you should head for Arbus, about 6km along a winding high-country road west of Montevecchio. The town is not particularly striking but visit the **Museo del Coltello** (*☎ 070 975 92 20; w www.coltelleria-arburesa.com; Via Roma 15; admission free; open 9am-noon & 4pm-8pm Mon-Fri, 9am-noon Sat)*, founded by Paolo Pusceddu, whose *arburesi* are among the most prized of Sardinian knives. Downstairs Mr Pusceddu has arranged his historic collection, with obsidian flint, Bronze-Age blades, knives, sword blades and the like from the 14th to the 19th centuries. In an adjacent room is an assortment of some of Pusceddu's finest creations, true masterpieces. Behind you walk into an old-style workshop while upstairs is a collection of knives from around the island. You can also watch a 30-minute video on the making of knives. Pusceddu works in his workshop next door. This would be a good place to consider a purchase – they don't come any better. To find the museum, head down Via Roma from the central Piazza Mercato.

The **Pro Loco** (*Piazza dell'Immacolata; open July-Aug)* has a tourist information booth further uphill.

Hotel Meridiana (*☎ 070 975 82 83, fax 070 975 64 47; Via della Repubblica 172; B&B singles/doubles €39/72.30)*, at the eastern entrance into town, is the only hotel choice. Rooms are spotless and well equipped and some have views out the back over the town.

Ristorante Sa Lolla (*☎ 070 975 40 04; Via Libertà 225; meals €25; open Mon-Sat)*, on the SS126 heading out southwest towards Fluminimaggiore, is one of the town's best eating options. It dishes up good pasta and pizzas.

FMS buses stop here en route to Guspini from Iglesias. There are up to four runs a day and the trip takes about an hour.

Villacidro
postcode 09039 • pop 14,819 • elev 267m
About 9km southeast of Arbus a minor road takes you to Gonnosfanadiga, worth popping into just to say you have been to this Tolkien-esque sounding place. Another 6km east on the SS196 brings you to the first of two turn-offs for Villacidro, to the south. Follow this winding country road and about 2.5km short of Villacidro you will see a signpost to the west for the **Cascata Su Spendula** (waterfall). Some 500m on you reach a parking area with a small snack bar. All around rise imposing rock walls and a thick curtain of trees. A short trail leads to the waterfall, or should do. In mid-summer you could easily find it has dried up. The Italian nationalist poet Gabriele d'Annunzio, judging by his effusive verse on the subject, visited in winter!

CARBONIA & AROUND
The SS126 road unfolds rapidly in flat territory south of Iglesias and soon runs into another of Mussolini's big ideas, Carbonia. This grand industrial town never really worked out and it holds little of interest for visitors today, save a couple of modest museums and an excursion into the island's ancient past just outside on Monte Sirai.

To the west is a more successful industrial exercise, Portoscuso, and the embarkation point for ferries to Isola di San Pietro.

To the east and southeast lie a handful of curious spots easily reached by those with their own wheels.

Carbonia
postcode 09013 • pop 32,650 • elev 111m
In the days when Fascists were in control and many a Sardinian sheep was nervous, Rome imperiously decreed that low-grade Sardinian coal would help make the nation self-sufficient in this essential raw material. A suitable city was needed to concentrate minds and effort, and so the unutterably depressing and imaginatively named Carbonia

(*carbone* means coal) was born. Work on its grid plan centre started in 1936 and two years later the city was open for business.

The whole blustering show was little more than a propaganda effort but the second-rate coal was mined until 1972, at which point Carbonia, whose grid-tentacles had spread, was left out on a limb. The city has since trundled along in the doldrums but managing to stay afloat with small business.

The focal point of town is Piazza Roma, dominated by the red trachyte belltower of the **Chiesa di San Ponziano**, modelled we are told on the cathedral of Aquilea in northern Italy and built in the 'third year of the Empire'. A plaque left over from Benito's time exhorts the workers *(O Lavoratore...!)* to give their best.

The square is also the town's bus station, which is handy because the only vague points of interest, two museums, are just down the road (signposted). If you intend to visit these and the Monte Sirai site, you should invest in the €3.60 *biglietto cumulativo* (group ticket) to all three.

The **Museu Archeologico Villa Sulcis** (☎ 0781 6 40 44; Via Napoli; admission €2.10; open 9am-1pm & 4pm-8pm Tues-Sun May-Sept, 9am-1pm & 3pm-7pm Tues-Sun Oct-Apr) has a very modest, musty collection of archaeological finds, the bulk of them from the nearby Phoenician-Carthaginian site on Monte Sirai.

Wander behind the museum; through the gate and across the road you arrive at the **Museo di Paleontologia e Speleologia** (☎ 0781 6 43 82; Piazza Garibaldi; admission €1.50; open 9am-1pm & 4pm-8pm Tues-Sun May-Sept, 9am-1pm & 3pm-7pm Tues-Sun Oct-Apr), dedicated to caves, caving and what you can occasionally turn up in them in an ancient place like Sardinia. It was founded in 1978.

Of more interest than either of these is the site of **Monte Sirai** (admission €2.60; open 9am-5pm daily Oct-Apr, 9am-1pm & 4pm-8pm daily May-Sept), about 4km northwest of Carbonia on the other side of the SS126 road.

The high flat-top plateau was a natural spot for a fort, commanding views over much of the mining areas of the southwest and down to the coast. Nowadays you can enjoy the visual pleasure of the industrial complex of Portoscuso. The Phoenicians of

Sulci (modern Sant'Antioco) ventured here to raise their fortress in 650 BC. Sardinian tribes took a disliking to it and prised the Phoenicians out of their eyrie, to be replaced a century later by the Carthaginians. Although not a great deal remains to be seen, you can make out the placement of the Carthaginian acropolis and defensive tower, a necropolis and *tophet* (sacred ground where it is thought the Carthaginians cremated the bodies of young children who died prematurely).

There's nowhere to stay and nowhere handy or worthwhile to eat so you'll be wanting a bus out of Carbonia pretty fast. Piazza Roma is the terminus and for tickets go to the unnamed bar at Viale Gramsci 4, after the first set of traffic lights about 70m off Piazza Roma. Buses run to Iglesias, Portoscuso, Sant'Antioco and other destinations around the southwest.

Local buses also run from Piazza Roma to the train station to coincide with trains from Cagliari (€3.35).

Portoscuso & Portovesme
postcode 09010 • pop 5496

The approach roads presage the worst. The enormous chimney stacks of the huffing, puffing thermo-electric industrial complex of Portoscuso are, however, a couple of kilometres east of the actual town, a small port capped by a Spanish-era tower with a tiny warren of agreeable lanes.

You may well find yourself around here on the way to or from Carloforte (with the ferry) on Isola di San Pietro and you can resolve accommodation and nutrition issues satisfactorily in Portoscuso.

Two hotels face the fishing and yacht port, well out of sight of its distant industrial neighbour. **Hotel Panorama** *(☎ 0781 50 80 77; Via G Cesare 40/42; singles/doubles €45/63)* has good if characterless rooms, many with balcony overlooking the port and equipped with TV, phone and air-con. About 50m away, **Hotel Don Pedro** *(☎ 0781 51 02 19, fax 0781 51 00 39; Via Vespucci 19; singles/doubles €68/83)* has similar rooms, although only a few have port views.

The best place and one of those rare Sardinian hotels with some charm is **Hotel La Ginghetta** *(☎ 0781 50 81 43, fax 0781 50 81 44; Via Cavour 26, Sa Caletta; singles/doubles €110/127, half board €116-145)*, an ivy- and bougainvillea-covered haven on a rocky cove. Rooms have a nautical bent (with ship steering wheels for bed heads and the like) but are comfortable and cosy. The restaurant is reputedly one of the island's best. Non-guests can eat here too – set menus, which tend to concentrate on seafood, start at €49 and are worth every cent.

La Tavernetta *(☎ 0781 50 99 16; Lungomare Colombo 35; meals €25; open lunch only)*, just by the Hotel Panorama, is a good spot for a filling home-cooked midday meal. The catch of the day is the main element and the pasta dishes in particular are generous.

FMS buses run to Portoscuso and neighbouring Portovesme from Cagliari (via Iglesias) up to three times a day (€4.44, two hours). Otherwise as many as 11 run from Iglesias (€1.45, 32 minutes) and 14 from Carbonia (€1.19, 35 minutes).

Saremar *(☎ 199 12 31 99, 0781 50 90 65)* has up to 17 sailings from Portovesme to Carloforte (Isola di San Pietro). The trip takes about 30 minutes and costs €2.43/7.22 per person/car. Be prepared for long queues in summer. The port is next door (east) to the industrial complex of Portoscuso.

Tratalias

When Sant'Antioco was abandoned in the 13th century, the archdiocese for the whole Sulcis area was transferred to this inland hamlet and the **Chiesa di Santa Maria** was built. A curious Romanesque construction, it presides over what little remains of the *vecchio borgo* (old town), abandoned since water from the nearby artificial Monte Pranu lake started seeping into the subsoil in the 1950s.

At the top of the facade you'll notice a curious external stairway leading nowhere in particular (strutting your stuff there would surely induce a severe case of vertigo). It continues on the inside of the church, which you enter by pushing open a side door. Rough hewn pillars separate the nave from the two aisles in what is otherwise a fairly bare interior.

The easiest way here is by car. Tratalias is 4km east of the SS126 and the church is right by the road.

Montessu

Lying 2.5km north of Villaperuccio, the site of Montessu *(admission €5; open 9am-1pm & 3pm-7pm)* makes for some nice strolling and avid archaeology buffs may get a kick out of it too. The site is peppered with *domus de janas* tombs carved out of the living stone. For the uninitiated these holes in the wall can become a trifle noisome as there really isn't much to see but wandering around up on this high ground and transporting yourself back through the millennia is a pleasant enough exercise of the imagination.

From the ticket booth you have a 500m walk up to what appears as a natural amphitheatre. When you first arrive up the stairs from the roadway to your immediate right is a *tomba santuario*, a rectangular foyer followed by three openings into a semicircular tomb area behind. Follow the trail to its right for a cluster of tombs and then the *tomba delle spirali*, which has curious spiral reliefs. Beyond that you can clamber about the site to your heart's content.

Santadi

A few kilometres down the road east of Villaperuccio, Santadi is a busy agricultural centre but in itself has little to hold you up for long. Once a year, on the first Sunday of August, it comes to surprising life for the **Matrimonio Maureddino**, a colourful ceremony in which a local couple is married in the main square in full traditional rural costume. For more details on this festival, see the special section 'Viva la Festa!'.

Le Grotte Is Zuddas

Five kilometres south of Santadi, these caves (☎ 0781 95 57 41; adult/child €6.50/3.62; open 9.30am-noon & 2.30pm-6pm daily Apr-Sept; noon-4pm Mon-Sat, 9.30am-noon & 2.30pm-7pm Sun & holidays Oct-Mar) are one of the island's many spectacular natural sculpture museums. The largely limestone rock lends the stalactites and stalagmites a particularly translucent quality. A singular attraction are the helictites in the main hall. No-one really knows how these weirdly shaped formations are created, although one theory suggests wind in the cave may have acted on drops dripping off stalactites.

From here the high winding road wends its way 13km to Teulada, at some points affording great views across the south to the coast.

Teulada

Possibly the inland medieval successor to a coastal Roman settlement known as Tegula,

this sleepy town on the slow dribble of a stream known as Rio Mannu attempts to attract a little attention by holding annual sculpture competitions. The contestants leave their works, which come in all shapes and sizes, scattered about the town's streets.

Hotel Sebera (☎ 070 927 08 76, fax 070 927 00 20; Via San Francesco 8; rooms up to €41.30) offers a simple place to rest up if you should get stuck here – oddly they have 10 single rooms. There is also a restaurant here. Otherwise a handful of *pizzerie* and small restaurants are dotted about.

The occasional bus runs down to Porto di Teulada (see later in this chapter). To the east a curly ribbon of a road negotiates the hilly 14km to the farming hamlet of Domus de Maria, from where it's another 4.5km to Chia on the coast (see Costa del Sud later).

ISOLA DI SAN PIETRO

San Pietro, while known to the ancients, was never seriously occupied by anyone until the 18th century. In 1736, Carlo Emanuele III granted this 51-sq-km island of St Peter (they say the saint was marooned here during a storm while en route to Karalis, present-day Cagliari) to a group of Ligurians (from Peglia) whose ancestors had been sent to the Tunisian islet of Tabarqa in 1540 to fish for coral. Abandoned to their already discomfited fate by the Genoese Lomellini family that had the islet in concession, the fishermen's descendants entered into slavery for the Bey of Tunis in the early 18th century. Then the Savoy monarch agreed to allow 140 of them to move to San Pietro. Pretending to have misunderstood, the fishermen embarked 140 *families* and so escaped their North-African imprisonment. In the following 15 years still more Pegliesi came. Almost out of spite, North-African pirates lobbed up in 1798 and made off with 1000 of these unfortunates. It took five years for the Savoys to ransom them. These fishing folk have until this day retained their ancient northern dialect (called *tabarkino* by some) and customs.

Carloforte

This pretty port town (population 6530) is reminiscent of La Maddalena at the northern extremity of Sardinia, with its pastel-coloured houses along tightly packed, orderly cobbled lanes rising up in serried ranks from the seaside. There's not a great deal to visit but a slow wander makes a pleasant prelude to a seaside aperitif and a fine meal at one of the town's several good restaurants.

The **Pro Loco** (☎ 0781 85 40 09; Piazza Carlo Emanuele III 19; open 9.30am-12.30pm & 5pm-8pm Mon-Sat, 10am-noon Sun) can help with any queries. Another information service, **Isola Verde** (☎ 0781 85 67 12; w www.carloforte.net), opens a summer (July to August) booth down by the ferries. You can change money at the **Banca Comerciale Italiana** (Via Garibaldi 5) on the waterfront.

The town's modest **Museo Civico** (adult/child €2/1; open 5pm-9pm Tues-Wed, 9am-1pm & 5pm-9pm Thur-Sun), housed in the little Carlo Emanuele III fort that was one of the first buildings to go up in the nascent Carloforte, deals with the history of the town and the nearby tonnare (tuna-fishing stations), as well as a collection of Mediterranean sea shells. Follow the signs uphill (eg, along Via Genova) from the town centre.

Carloforte Sail Charter (☎ 347 273 32 68; w www.carlofortesailcharter.it, Italian only; Via Danero 52) is one of several operators that organise trips around the island. Since roads around it are limited, the only way to visit many little coves and inlets is by boat. **Cartur Trasporti Marittimi** (☎ 0781 85 43 31) offers three-hour trips in highspeed maxi-dinghies around the island and up to the Scoglio Pan di Zucchero. You will find several booths along the central waterfront proposing various nautical diversions.

Diving is also possible. Contact **Isla Diving** (☎ 0781 85 56 34; Corso Battellieri 21), also on the waterfront.

Places to Stay You have a choice of several places to stay in Carloforte itself.

Hotel California (☎ 0781 85 44 70, fax 0781 85 55 39; Via Cavallera 15; singles/doubles €42/78) is the most awkwardly placed (inland from the Saline saltpans) and cheapest deal in town.

Hotel Riviera (☎ 0781 85 40 04, fax 0781 85 65 62; Corso Battellieri 26; singles/doubles €56.80/113.60), at the southern end of the town's main waterfront drag, is an anonymous building that jars with much of its surroundings. Rooms are perfectly comfortable but lacking in style.

Hotel Hieracon (☎ 0781 85 40 28; singles/doubles €54/93) is Carloforte's (faded) jewel,

a grey Liberty-Style mansion at the northern end of the waterfront. It has all sorts of rooms with up to four beds that can work out quite well.

Places to Eat Carloforte seems unjustly equipped with fine dining options but who's complaining – dig in!

Tonno di Corsa (☎ 0781 85 51 06; Via Marconi 47; meals €35-40; open Tues-Sun), up a few blocks from the seaside along Via Caprera (then turn right), is the paradise of tuna dishes. One of the best is the delicious ventresca di tonno, a sublime cut of the best tuna meat.

Da Nicolò (☎ 0781 85 40 48; Via Dante 46; meals €50-60; open Tues-Sun) is one of the island's gourmet bastions, and Sardinians come from far and wide to eat in the elegant restaurant or (in summer) the palm-fronted seaside terrace. The pasta dishes include such Ligurian items as trofie (a small, dense style of pasta) with various tempting toppings. Fish and lobster are house specialities and you can even get a T-bone steak.

Dau Bobba (☎ 0781 85 40 37; Lungocanale delle Saline; meals €45-50; open Wed-Mon), half a kilometre south of the main waterfront, is another charming den of gastronomic delights. The little courtyard garden inside makes an inviting shelter to taste anything from a great pesto to fresh catch of the day. It has an impressive local wine list too.

Entertainment For your evening drinks start at a couple of bars along the waterfront. A little noisier are **Barone Rosso** (Via XX Settembre 26), with a few tables in the side street, and the nameless bar across the road at No 17, where you can even find a Fosters! North of Piazza Repubblica another option in a similar vein is **L'Obló** (Via Garibaldi 23), where you can also get a decent snack.

In summer the island's only real club is **Disco Marlin** (☎ 0781 85 01 21; open Sat & Sun July, nightly Aug), shortly before the tonnara on the way to Punta. The popular La Caletta beach is also the scene of dancing fun, with summer beach parties pounding on until dawn on some busy July and August nights.

Getting There & Away

There's a **Saremar** (☎ 199 12 31 99, 0781 85 40 05; Piazza Carlo Emanuele III 29) ticket office here which has regular daytime and early-evening departures for Portovesme on the mainland (€2.43 per person) and Calasetta on the neighbouring island of Sant'Antioco.

Delcomar (☎ 0781 85 71 23) also runs up to 11 services to/from Calasetta, mostly late-night runs into the wee hours of the morning. It operates a ticket booth just in front of where the ferries dock. The crossing costs €2.50 per person each way.

In summer FMS buses run from Carloforte to La Punta (12 minutes, three a day), La Caletta (15 minutes, eight a day) and Capo Sandalo (18 minutes, three a day). Tickets cost €0.67.

Around the Island

Four roads radiate out of Carloforte across the island, sparsely inhabited and dotted only with the occasional cluster of houses.

A quick drive leads you north 5.5km to **La Punta**, a low point from where you can gaze across to the offshore islet **Isola Piana** and the billowing chimney stacks of Portoscuso. In May and June witness the frenzy of the tuna catch or *mattanza* in front of the old *tonnara*.

Shortly before you arrive at La Punta you'll see **Hotel Paola** (☎ 0781 85 00 98, fax 0781 85 01 04; W www.carloforte.net/hotel paola, Italian only; singles/doubles €44/83), a little way from the coast but with modest rates and good rooms.

An interesting excursion takes you west across some of the most dramatic of the island's inland scenery to reach the coast at **Capo Sandalo**, for splendid views of the cliffs that stretch away to the south.

On the southwest coast is the island's most popular beach, **La Caletta** (also known as Spiaggia Spalmatore), a relatively modest arc of fine sand closed off to the south by cliffs and often lapped by waves. **Camping Solaria** (☎ 0781 85 21 12; per person/tent space €8/10) is just back from the beach.

A couple of average beaches are sited in the southeast of the island. At the bottom of the island two great stone *colonne* (columns) rise out of the sea. Not surprisingly this point is known as Punta delle Colonne.

ISOLA DI SANT'ANTIOCO
postcode 09017 (Sant'Antioco)
• pop 14,544

Italy's fourth-largest island (after Sicily, Sardinia and Elba), Sant'Antioco really ceased to be such when the ever industrious Romans built a causeway across the Golfo di Palmas to link it with the mainland.

There are two ways of approaching the 108-sq-km island. The simplest clearly is to follow the SS126 highway south from Iglesias and Carbonia and cross the bridge to the town of Sant'Antioco. People have been doing it this way since the Romans came along, as remnants of the Roman bridge left forlornly to the right of the modern causeway attest. Clunkier and more romantic is the car ferry between the northwestern settlement of Calasetta and Carloforte in San Pietro.

Sant'Antioco

Preceded by a nuraghic settlement, the Phoenician town of Sulcis was founded in the 8th century BC. It became an important

---

Mad About the Mattanza

Lovers of tuna meat around the world, but especially the Japanese (the best-paying export market), watch anxiously each spring for the results of one of Sardinia's age-old fishing rituals, the *mattanza* (slaughter).

Since ancient times fishermen have awaited the arrival of schools of tuna that stream by along the same routes at about the same time for the annual mating season.

The *tonnara*, which refers to the buildings on land (in this case at La Punta and Portoscuso) where the tuna is brought ashore and prepared for sale, is also the name given to the complex net system deployed by the fishermen across the straits through which the fish pass. Tuna enter this underwater labyrinth and wind up in the last of six net chambers, called the *camera della morte* (death chamber). When several tuna (which can easily weigh in excess of 100kg each) are caught, the fishermen haul them aboard their vessels and bludgeon them to death.

In recent years fishermen have had a bonanza, fulfilling their quotas and so helping keep Japan's sushi-lovers content.

Carthaginian centre and its populace watched on aghast as a Roman naval squadron defeated the home side in 258 BC. A couple of centuries later the by-now Roman centre made the unfortunate mistake of siding with Pompey in his struggle with Caesar, who was not overly understanding with the losers. The city, which by now had adopted its present name, was finally abandoned by its Byzantine rulers, tired of repeated raids by North African corsairs, in the early Middle Ages. People would not return to live here until the 18th century.

Orientation & Information The place is surprisingly big. On wheels you will approach the centre from the bridge along Via Nazionale. It converges with another main road, Via Trieste, at Piazza Repubblica, which is where FMS buses stop (tickets at the pharmacy). The **Pro Loco tourist office** (☎ 0781 8 20 31; Piazza Repubblica 31a; open 9am-noon & 5.30pm-9pm Mon-Fri) can help with information. Shortly after, the main road enters the broad Piazza Italia (the site of a Roman spring) and becomes Corso Vittorio Emanuele, whose lines of trees form a cool leafy tunnel. This is the central boulevard and the focus of the town's summer nighttime shenanigans, lined with bars and eateries. It ends at Piazza Umberto I (where you can change money at two banks – the Banca di Sassari offers the Western Union money wiring service) into which Via Garibaldi also runs from the waterfront. From Piazza Umberto I, Via Regina Margherita climbs away to the heart of the old town.

Things to See & Do Via Regina Margherita spills into Piazza De Gasperi, the site of the **Chiesa di Sant'Antioco**. You can't always judge a church by its facade. The main baroque frontage on the square tells you little, and the side entrance, camouflaged by a bizarre neoclassical structure that makes it seem part of the library next door, reveals even less.

Walk inside and you are cast back to the 5th century AD. Originally the site of subterranean Punic tombs, Christian catacombs were later added and then the church raised. The original Paleochristian church was built on the Greek cross plan and covered with precious marble decoration, but many changes were in store. In the 12th century the

nave was extended to create a Latin cross church, the marble was replaced by frescoes (a few bits of the marble are preserved in the catacombs), which in turn were later simply painted over. What you see today is a mix of the medieval church and remnants of the original 5th-century structure.

To the right of the altar stands a wooden effigy of St Antioch. The dark complexion reflects the tale of his origins. The story goes that, refusing to renounce his religion, Antioch was deported from his native northern Africa (along with many others) as slave labour for the lead mines of the Iglesiente. Antioch (who died, according to tradition, in AD 127) managed to escape and was taken in by a small underground Christian group. They say he lived in one of the larger underground chambers in the **Catacombe** (admission €2.50; open 9am-12.30pm & 3pm-8pm Mon-Sat), to the right of the altar. You must wait for a guide to appear and take you around the chambers. What you see is a succession of burial rooms. Contrary to popular belief, the catacombs were not built as secret places of worship under the Romans, although the chambers may have been used to that effect. The Christians buried their dead here. The richest went into elaborate, frescoed family niches in the walls (up to six spaces). A few fragments of the frescos remain. Middle-class corpses wound up in unadorned niches and commoners in common ditches in the floor. For space reasons, bodies were wrapped tight in linen, dumped in their graves and covered in lime. Every so often the bones (rich and poor) were removed to make room for the more recently deceased. A few skeletons lying in situ render the idea a little more colourfully.

Since the 1970s archaeologists have penetrated further into the underground labyrinth and revealed a series of burial chambers dating to Punic times.

A few metres down Via Regina Margherita from the church is the modest **Museo Archeologico** (☎ 0781 8 35 90; adult/child €5.16/2.58; open 9am-1pm & 3.30pm-7pm Tues-Sun June-Sept, til 6pm Oct-May), which holds a small selection of the artefacts that were discovered at the nearby Carthaginian acropolis, necropolis and tophet. Visits to the museum and the remaining sites are guided; admission also includes entry to the sites listed following.

Walking away uphill from Piazza De Gasperi, you end up at what remains of the **Forte Su Pisu**, a fort built by the Piedmontese in 1812 and severely tested three years later when its garrison was massacred by North African corsairs.

Just over the hill and behind the fort lies the **Zona Archeologico**. To the left of the street are the truncated columns and rubble remaining from the Carthaginian **acropolis**. You can't enter but all is visible from the road. Across the road and spreading down the slope of the hill are the tombs of the **necropolis** *(closed at the time of writing)*. Another 500m downhill is the Punic **tophet**.

Lastly, get along to Via Necropoli (so-named because there was another Punic necropolis here) by following the signs from Via De Gasperi to the **Museo Etnografico** *(Via Necropoli 24a; included on the Museo Archeologico ticket; open 9am-1pm & 3.30pm-7pm Tues-Sun June-Sept, til 6pm Oct-May)*. For centuries locals have recycled elaborate Punic tombs here as houses and storage rooms. Some of these have been fixed up and together are known as the **Villaggio Ipogeo**. The museum itself is housed in a typical one-time warehouse with *lolla* (porticoed courtyard) and it contains an assortment of traditional farm and household implements.

Special Events Celebrated over four days around the second Sunday after Easter, the **Festa di Sant'Antioco** celebrates the city's patron saint with processions, traditional music and dancing, fireworks and concerts. It is one of the oldest documented saint's festivities on the island, dating to 1519.

Places to Stay & Eat For a straightforward sleeping stop, try **Hotel Moderno** *(☎ 0781 8 31 05, fax 0781 84 02 52; Via Nazionale 82; singles/doubles €41.30/62)*. The rooms are unimaginative but have all the basics, from en-suite loo to TV and air-con.

Hotel Eden *(☎ 0781 84 07 68; Piazza Parrocchia 15; singles/doubles €46.50/72.30)* is a more charming option, set in a modest mansion opposite the Chiesa di Sant'Antioco. Rooms are not particularly big but furnished with a touch of charm.

Hotel del Corso *(☎ 0781 80 02 65, fax 0781 8 23 78; Corso Vittorio Emanuele 32; B&B singles/doubles €57/93)* is the classiest place in town, right on the leafy central boulevard.

Along with well-appointed rooms, the hotel offers the handy extra of parking.

Various restaurants, *pizzerie* and snack spots are dotted about the town but none really shine.

Ristorante Caligula *(Via Garibaldi 15; pizza €5-9)* is not a bad spot for pizzas with various imperial Roman names.

Ristorante Sette Nani *(☎ 0781 84 09 00; Via Garibaldi 139; meals €25-30)* spreads out over several floors and boasts a garden dining area too. Dishes lean to the sea and are good without being magnificent. You will be offered a selection of Sardinian sweets and a glass of *mirto* (myrtle liqueur) to finish.

Entertainment People hang around in the several bars and eateries along Corso Vittorio Emanuele until well into the night. The oddly named **Fox Hunter Pierre Pub** *(☎ 0781 80 04 55; Corso Vittorio Emanuele 86)* does a lively business. In summer, keep an eye out for **Bar Colombo** *(Lungomare Colombo)*. The live music can be a little kitsch but it is fun for late-night drinkies.

In summer frequent free **concerts** are staged in Piazza Umberto I, ranging from local pop to traditional Sardinian tunes.

Around the Island

The island's better beaches start 8km south of the town. After 5km you take a turn-off for **Maladroxia**, a small tourist haven with a couple of hotels and a pleasant beach and port. You could do worse than stay at **Hotel Scala Longa** *(☎ 0781 81 72 02; singles/doubles €39/49, full board per person €51.65)*, a pleasing place back off the main road that leads down to the port. Rooms are simple but the all-in deal is good value. About 50m down the road **Hotel Maladroxia** *(☎/fax 0781 81 70 12; singles/doubles €59.40/72.30, half board per person €59.40)* is in much the same class, despite the added expense. Both are shut from October to April.

Back on the main road, you pass inland before hitting a big roundabout. Head left (east) to reach **Spiaggia Coa Quaddus**, a wild and woolly beach about 3km short of **Capo Sperone**, the southern point of the island. A few houses are clustered here, among them the cheery **Hotel Capo Sperone** *(☎ 0781 80 90 00, fax 0781 80 90 15; singles/doubles €59.40/92.95, half board*

€87.80), with its own swimming pool and tennis court.

A turn right (west) before you reach the Spiaggia Coa Quaddus takes you over to the southwest coast of the island and a few beaches. The best of them is **Cala Lunga**, where the road peters out. Before you reach the beach you'll pass a handy camping ground, the **Campeggio Tonnara** *(☎ 0781 80 90 58; Località Cala Saboni; per person/tent space €8.80/14.20; open Apr-Sept).*

Calasetta, the island's second town, lies 10km northwest of Sant'Antioco. It was originally founded by Ligurian families from Tabarqa in 1769, following the example of their brothers in Carloforte 40 years earlier. The town, dominated by the late Spanish-era watchtower that originally stood here quite alone, will be your first taste of the island if you arrive by ferry from Isola di San Pietro (see earlier in this chapter). The grid system of streets hides little else of interest, but there are several beaches a few kilometres south along the northwestern coast.

Camping Le Saline *(☎/fax 0781 8 86 15; per person/tent space €8.80/12, 4-person bungalows up to €129)* is located just back from **Spiaggia Le Saline**, 2.5km south of Calasetta. Of the four hotels in town, one of the best deals is **Hotel Bellavista** *(☎/fax 0781 8 82 11; Via Panoramica; singles/doubles €46.50/62)*, in a privileged position on the southwestern exit from town. The rooms are simple enough but some have wonderful views.

Getting There & Away

FMS buses reach Sant'Antioco from Iglesias and Carbonia regularly, while as many as four a day come in from Cagliari. Some go on to Calasetta.

Ferries run between Calasetta and Carloforte on Isola di San Pietro (see earlier in this chapter).

SOUTH COAST

If heading from the southwest to Cagliari, or the opposite, make every effort to follow the coast road. Its central stretch, known as the Costa del Sud, is a wonderful 20km spectacle of twisting, turning road above rugged cliffs that plunge into the deep blue sea. It is one of the prettiest coastal drives on the island.

Porto Botte to Porto di Teulada

Firmly back on the mainland after crossing the bridge from Sant'Antioco, head east (right) at San Giovanni Suergiu and follow the SS126 southeast. You could be on a beach after just 10km if you make directly for **Porto Botte**. Although long, mostly sandy and rarely crowded, it is not one of Sardinia's best and you're better off proceeding another 13km south for **Porto Pino**, host to a couple of beaches. The best of them requires a little foot work. Assuming you have your own transport and can park near **Spiaggia Porto Pino**, leave your metallic coach there and continue on foot south until you reach the next beach, **Spiaggia Sabbie Bianche** (White Sands). You are only allowed here in July and August, as it is on military land.

Back in Porto Pino, there is a busy, slightly tacky seaside ambience, with a makeshift amusement park and one or two disco attempts.

Camping Sardegna *(☎/fax 0781 96 70 13; per person/tent space €5.68/9.30, bungalows up to €56.80; open May-Sept)* is a fairly basic camping ground behind the beach. A couple of expensive hotels lurk some way from the beach as well, but you might want to try the more straightforward but recently renovated **Albergo Il Veliero** *(☎ 0781 96 70 12; singles/doubles €26/52, half board per person €44)*. The restaurant downstairs has a garden and they offer set meals (with main course of meat or fish, as you choose) including wine for €23.

From Porto Pino you have no choice but to head inland, turning right at Sant'Anna Arresi. After 10km, branch south (away from the signs to Teulada) towards Porto di Teulada. The hilly area between Porto Pino and Porto di Teulada, bordered by the road to the north, is military land, making Sardinia's southernmost point, **Capo Teulada**, inaccessible.

There are several beaches along this part of the coast, including **Cala Piombo**, **Porto Zafferano** and **Portu Piratsu**. They are only accessible in July and August by boat, which could be a reason for heading down to **Porto di Teulada**. This small fishing and pleasure port is just that (plus one kiosk-bar), but in summer you can organise to get on a sailboat for a tour of the Capo Teulada coast. Ask around the port or call ☎ 070 927 03 68.

The nearest beach is **Porto Tramatzu**, around on the other side of Porto di Teulada. Head back up the road a short way and turn left down a dirt road. After about 500m, and just past an entrance to the military base, you arrive at **Camping Porto Tramatzu** (☎ 070 928 30 27, fax 070 928 30 28; per person/tent space €7.50/10.35, bungalows €59.40), a pleasant, leafy location on the other side of which you will find the beach.

Costa del Sud

The Costa del Sud begins east of Porto di Teulada. The first stretch is just a prelude, passing several coves and gradually rising towards the high point of Capo Malfatano. As you wind your way around towards the cape, wonderful views of the coast to the east repeatedly spring into view and just about every point is capped by a watchtower dating to Spanish times.

Along the way, **Spiaggia Piscinni** is not the greatest strand in terms of sand (you have to deal with a fair amount of sun-dried algae) but the water is an incredible colour – it's like swimming in crystal.

Stop at the lookout point high above **Capo Malfatano**. A side track leads down off the coast route along the bay here, although there is not much in the line of beaches. Once around the bay and the next point, you could stop at **Cala Teuradda**, a popular spot (you can tell in summer by all the parked cars) that happens to be right at an ARST bus stop. In summer you'll find snack bars too.

From here the road climbs up inland away from the coast. You can get a look at the coast here too, if you take a narrow side road to the south at **Porto Campana** – it quickly turns to dust but does allow you to reach the lighthouse at **Capo Spartivento**. A series of beaches runs from the cape up to the next watchtower at **Chia** – watch out for signposted side roads leading off to **Cala Cipolla**, **Spiaggia Su Giudeu** and **Porto Campana**. At Chia itself there are two options, the long **Spiaggia Sa Colonia** to the west of the tower and the smaller arc of **Spiaggia Su Portu** to the east. You can walk up to the tower for views up and down the coast. In summer it is opened for little **exhibitions** (admission €1; open 9.30am-12.30pm & 3pm-7pm daily). The tower was a relative newcomer to these parts, as the

discovery of the remnants of Phoenician Bythia, at the foot of the tower, shows. Unfortunately, there is nothing to see of the site now.

Campeggio Torre Chia (☎ 070 923 00 54, fax 070 923 00 55; W www.campeggiotorrechia.it; per person/tent space €7.50/9, 4-person villas up to €130) is a few hundred metres back from Spiaggia Su Portu and often full in August.

Two reasonable hotel options exist around here too, just by the tower end of Spiaggia Sa Colonia. **Il Gabbiano** (☎ 070 923 01 60; doubles up to €124), with good rooms and a reputable restaurant, is run by the same people as the more subtle **Sa Colonia** (☎ 070 923 00 01; doubles €100), set in large house with gardens and restaurant.

ARST buses to/from Chia run along the Costa del Sud a couple of times daily in summer. Up to eight buses run between Cagliari and Chia daily (1¼ hours).

Santa Margherita

The Santa Margherita coastline is largely set aside for the guests of expensive hotel complexes and holiday residences. Most of the many side roads leading off the highway to the beach are in fact barred to outsiders (reserved for the residents). You may slip through one or two and get down to the white sandy beaches backed by pine stands. Otherwise you could head northeast of all this and make for the two camping grounds.

If coming from the southwest, ignore the first turn-off for the camping grounds and head on to a turn-off marked **Camping Flumendosa** (☎ 070 920 83 64, fax 070 924 92 82; per person/tent space €6.70/10.30; open year-round), a shady spot that stretches down to the beach. Another 1½ km along the beach road leads to **Camping Cala d'Ostia** (☎/fax 070 92 14 70; per person/tent space €7/8; open Apr-Sept). Opposite the first of these grounds you could opt for **Hotel Mare Pineta** (☎ 070 920 83 61, fax 070 920 83 59; doubles up to €127), part of the more expensive Hotel Flamingo complex and, you may be surprised to know, one of the cheapest possibilities around here. The whole area shuts down from about October to March.

Local orange buses run regularly (up to 10 a day in summer) out to Santa Margherita from Pula and Nora.

Nora

In AD 303, the disgraced Roman commander Ephysius was hauled down to the beach behind the port city of Nora, having been transported here from Karalis (Cagliari), condemned for his conversion to Christianity and executed.

In those days Nora was one of the most important urban settlements on the island. Linked to Karalis in the east and Bythia in the west by coast road, Nora's position on a long tongue of land made it an ideal port, as ships could approach from either side and so largely ignore adverse wind conditions.

It appears Phoenicians from Spain founded Nora. Indeed, semitic inscriptions mentioning it date to as early as the 11th century BC. They were in due course succeeded by the Carthaginians and Romans and under Byzantine rule it lingered on as a fortified emplacement. It had been abandoned by the time of the Giudicati.

You will arrive in Pula from the main road. From there follow the signs to the classical site of Nora (adult/child including Civico Museo Archeologico in Pula €5.50/2.50; open 9am-7pm daily).

Most of what you see dates to Roman times. Upon entry you pass by a single standing column of a former temple and then the small theatre now used for summer evening concerts. Towards the west are the substantial remains of the **Terme al Mare** (Baths by the Sea). Four columns (a tetrastyle) stand at the heart of what was a patrician villa whose surrounding rooms retain their mosaic floor decoration.

More remnants of mosaics can be seen at a temple complex towards the tip of the promontory.

In summer you can join night tours of the site, known as **Nora Sotto le Stelle** (Nora Under the Stars). Ask at the ticket office or call ☎ 070 920 91 38.

The summer concerts in the theatre generally cost €15/8 a performance per adult/child. Ask at the ticket desk or call ☎ 070 27 05 77 for programme details.

Just before the entrance to the ancient site of Nora is the pleasant **Spiaggia di Nora** (you won't be permitted into the site in bathing costume by the way), and a little further around the bigger **Spiaggia Su Guventeddu**.

A little way back from the beach stands the lonely little **Chiesa di Sant'Efisio**, a Romanesque job done by the Vittorini monks from Marseille and the supposed resting place of St Ephysius. Each year the procession in honour of the saint from Cagliari terminates at this church. Behind lie the remains of a Carthaginian *tophet* of Nora.

On the west side of the Nora promontory stretches the **Laguna di Nora** (☎ 070 920 95 44), where a didactic centre organises activities aimed mostly at kids. Apart from the aquarium, they offer little snorkelling and canoe excursions in the lagoon. A visit to the aquarium costs €4, while combining this with canoeing (€16) or snorkelling (€21) is a rather more expensive business. The activity takes place from June to September.

The best sleeping option here is **Hotel Su Guventuddu** (☎ 070 920 90 92, fax 070 920 94 68; singles/doubles €52/78), 2km from the Nora site on the road leading around to Su Guventeddu beach. It is a comfortable country house with pleasant rooms and a decent restaurant.

Up to 16 local shuttle buses circulate between Pula and Nora.

Pula

postcode 09010 • pop 6454

The rather busy town through which you must pass in order to reach Nora is a bustling, chaotic sort of place. You will probably want to call in to look the museum over but that will be about all.

There is a **Pro Loco** tourist office but far more useful is the private **Cooperative Le Torri** (☎ 070 920 83 73; Via Corinaldi), which has tons of information on Pula, Nora and around. It also rents out bicycles from €10 a day, scooters from €25 a day and Opel Corsas for €320 a week.

The **Civico Museo Archeologico** (☎ 070 920 96 10; Corso Vittorio Emanuele 67; adult/child including Nora site €5.50/2.50; open 9am-8pm daily Sept-July, 9am-midnight Aug), near the central Piazza Municipio, consists of one room of carefully selected finds from Nora, mostly ceramics found in Punic and Roman tombs, a few bits of gold and bone jewellery, Roman glassware and the like. Explanations are in Italian and English and there is even a small hands-on section in Braille. A series of sculptures from the Nora *tophet* decorated with symbols representing various divinities completes the picture.

If you get stuck here your choices are limited. **Hotel Quattro Mori** *(☎ 070 920 91 24; Via Cagliari 10; singles/doubles €23.30/ 33.60)* offers basic rooms, mostly without own bathroom.

Hotel Sandalyon *(☎ 070 920 91 51; Via Cagliari 30; singles/doubles €50/75)* has rather more comfortable rooms with en-suite bath, TV and heating in winter.

Zio Dino *(☎ 070 920 91 59; Viale Segni 14; meal €30; open Mon-Sat)* is one of central Pula's best eateries, with a tempting mix of seafood and meat dishes on the menu. Meals are best begun with the *spaghetti alla Zio Dino*, a seafood special.

Corte Noa *(☎ 070 924 55 55; SS195, km32.3; meals €25)*, outside the town centre on the main coast highway, is another well-established name. Try the *ravioli alla mentuccia selvaticca* (ravioli with wild mint). On weekends from May to September it also hosts a popular open-air disco.

Pula to Cagliari

There aren't too many reasons for making a halt between Pula and Cagliari. Drive by **Sarroch** at night and you'll think you've landed outside a sci-fi film set. The smoking, heaving industrial complex is eerily laced with nocturnal fairy lights that don't kid anyone but do strangely fascinate the passer-by. And pass by is about all you will want to do.

Closer to Cagliari, an inland turn-off leads 5km to **Capoterra**, beyond which is a small natural park around **Monte Arcosu** (948m). The park is one of three remaining habitats on the island of the once common *cervo sardo* (Sardinian deer).

The final run takes you across the **Stagno di Cagliari**, the immense lagoon that marks off the western limits of the capital city.

CAMPIDANO

Heading north out of Cagliari along the SS131, you enter a broad flat corridor known as the Campidano. While it represents a capital source of agricultural wealth for the island, it can be a little dispiriting for the visitor. On high summer days, when temperatures soar and the southern half of the island is often enveloped in a thick, grey heat haze, it all just looks so damn dusty and yellow. The dual-carriage highway means you can hurry northward through the plains but a few spots are worth a detour for those with time.

Uta, San Sperate & Castello di Acquafredda

Barely 20km northwest of Cagliari, at the eastern edge of the dispiriting, sprawling farm town of **Uta**, is one of the finer examples of Romanesque church-building in Sardinia and one of the few in the south of the island.

The **Chiesa di Santa Maria** (follow the brown signs for the Santuario di Santa Maria), built around 1140 by Vittorini monks from Marseille, is remarkable above all for the variegated statuary that runs around the top of the church's exterior. Busts of people and various animals (real and imaginary) mix in with floral and geometric patterns.

The church, for lovers of Romanesque architecture at any rate, is worth the effort of getting here from Cagliari but if you come by bus it will try your patience as it's a good half-hour walk from central Uta, a town that offers precious little else in the way of entertainment.

If you head west from here (a dual carriage road roars across the plains to Iglesias), consider a quick southward diversion at the Siliqua crossroads, 14km west of Uta. About 5km to the south you can see the fairy-tale image of castle ruins atop an extraordinary craggy mount that bursts forth from the plains. As you get closer you come to realise that little more than the crumbling walls of Castello di Acquafredda remain, and there is nowhere much to leave a car should you wish to make the steep rocky climb for a closer look (and panoramic views). The castle served as a temporary hiding place for Guelfo della Gherardesca when his father Ugolino was imprisoned in Pisa and the family banished.

Another minor diversion is San Sperate, situated 19km northwest of Cagliari. A self-proclaimed 'museum town', it is known for its murals. All over the place, much as in Orgosolo (see the Nuoro & the East chapter earlier in the book), you will sometimes see fine murals depicting anything from everyday life to surreal images almost reminiscent of Salvador Dalí. The town's best-known son, sculptor Pinuccio Sciola (born 1942), has also contributed a few open-air statues.

ARST buses from Cagliari make day trips possible, with up to 10 a day to Uta and San Sperate on weekdays (only one on Sundays). The trip (€1.19) takes 30 to 40 minutes in each case. For Castello di Acquafredda you need your own steam.

Sanluri
postcode 09025 • pop 8604

A busy rural centre some 45km north of Cagliari on the SS131, Sanluri has ancient roots of which it displays, however, virtually nothing. Just nearby the Catalano-Aragonese defeated the Sardinian forces in the Battle of Sanluri in 1409, thus extinguishing what was left of Sardinian independence.

As you penetrate the town's centre from the south you cannot help but run into the largely 18th-century **Chiesa della Madonne delle Grazie**. Little of the Gothic original remains and what stands out from afar is the rococo belltower.

Further up the main road, Via Carlo Felice, you emerge in Piazza Castello, which takes its name from the squat, brooding 14th-century bastion that seems to have gone into reclusion behind its high grill fences and thick greenery. The castle is a unique beast in Sardinia, built on a vague rise in the plains rather than atop an impossibly difficult hill, and subsequently completely enveloped by the town that grew up around it. Nowadays it houses the private **Museo Risorgimentale Duca d'Aosta** (☎ 070 930 71 05; open 4.30pm-8pm Tues-Fri July-Sept, 9.30am-1pm & 3pm-sunset Sun year-round). Modern artillery pieces greet you in the garden and inside you can see an extraordinary array of objects from period furniture to military mementos. The latter include photos, maps, arms and other oddments and cover conflicts ranging from Garibaldi's battles against the Austrians, WWI and Fascist Italy's escapades, particularly in Ethiopia (then known as Abyssinia).

Cross Via Carlo Felice and follow Via San Rocco a few hundred metres east, then take a left towards the Franciscan monastery at the top of the rise. Here you will find the rather bizarre and eclectic collection of the **Museo Etnografico Cappuccino** (☎ 070 930 79 19; admission €3; open 9am-noon & 4pm-6pm daily), the result of the limitless curiosity of one of the friars, Fra Fedele. Entry times (and fee) are completely hit and miss.

If you turn up and Fra Fedele is around, you may find yourself being led around for a good hour or two. One room contains ancient artefacts, from obsidian arrowheads to Roman era coins. Another is devoted to farm tools, with all sorts of objects on display, from ploughshares to horseshoes. Other rooms are devoted to old watches, cameras, wirelesses, gas lamps and other household items. Finally, the last room contains a collection of religious art and objects.

You are unlikely to want to hang around Sanluri overnight but if obliged to do so, you can stay in the drab **Hotel Mirage** (☎ 070 930 71 00, fax 070 930 79 02; Via Carlo Felice; singles/doubles €28/39) at the northern exit from town onto the SS131.

A plethora of buses and trains reach Sanluri from Cagliari. Proceeding from there to other destinations is possible but markedly more difficult, with rarely more than a couple of departures for any given destination. The train station is 5km out of town and linked to the centre by local buses.

Sardara
postcode 09030 • pop 4370

An 8km sprint northwest of Sanluri along the SS131 brings you to Sardara. The centre of the village is dominated by the Gothic **Chiesa di San Gregorio**, a nice example of transitional architecture from Romanesque to Gothic. Hints of the latter are the soaring facade, rose window and Gothic window in the apse.

Further uphill is the fine **Civico Museo Archeologico Villa Abbas** (☎ 070 938 61 83; Piazza Libertà 7; admission €4.13; open 9am-1pm & 5pm-8pm Tues-Sun). Several tombs from the Terr'e Cresia necropolis excavations have been recreated with skeletons and all. You can admire 3rd-century ceramics, glassware and other bits and bobs.

Among the finest pieces on display are two bronze nuraghic statuettes of archers with strong Assyrian features, found on the edge of Sardara in 1913 and dating to the 8th century BC. Outside, excavations have been carried out on the Sa Costa site that forms the museum's back yard.

A few hundred metres off is the **Chiesa di Sant'Anastasia** (Piazza Sant'Anastasia; admission free; open 9am-1pm & 5pm-8pm Tues-Sun), a little Gothic church planted right in the middle of what is now an archaeological dig, the site of a nuraghic well temple. You can wander into the simple church and downstairs into the well temple, to your left as you face the church entrance.

A few kilometres west of town (on the other side of the SS131) is **Santa Maria de Is Acquas**, the site of thermal baths since Roman times and nowadays home to a couple of thermal spa hotels. The low, speckled walls of the late-Gothic **Chiesa di Santa Maria** give the area its name. About 4km to the south a dirt road leads to the empty walls of the **Castello Monreale**, built by the Giudicato di Arborea and used as a temporary refuge by the defeated troops of Brancaleone Doria after the Battle of Sanluri. The Catalano-Aragonese garrisoned it for a time in 1478 but thereafter it soon fell into disuse. You can see some of the colourful medieval ceramics and other material dug up in the castle in Sardara's museum.

Hotel Sardara (☎ 070 938 78 11; Via Cedrino 5; singles/doubles €24/39) is a no-nonsense hotel with eight rooms in the new part of town. Those in need of thermal water treatment could try their luck at the two hotels in Santa Maria de Is Acquas.

LA MARMILLA

The land directly north of Sardara changes aspect radically from the flat plains of the Campidano, which continue to accompany the SS131 on its northwestern drive towards Oristano.

La Marmilla is an oddly bumpy territory, although it too is interspersed with tracts of broad plains, especially in the shadows of the Giara high plateau that closes off the northern limits of Cagliari province.

Villanovaforru & Genna Maria
postcode 09020 • pop 707 • elev 324m

Villanovaforru could win a tidy town award, although apart from its museum it has little to hold your interest for long. Just outside to the west is the important nuraghic settlement of Genna Maria, which with Su Nuraxi (see Barumini & Nuraghe Su Nuraxi later in this chapter) is a must on the ancient history buff's travels through this part of the island.

The **Museo Archeologico** (☎ 070 930 00 50; Piazza Costituzione; admission €2.50; open 9.30am-1pm & 3.30pm-6pm Tues-Sun) is a well set-out museum displaying a broad collection of material found mostly in the Marmilla region, including items from Su Nuraxi and Genna Maria. Spread over two floors in a restored mansion, items range from enormous amphorae and other pots to oil lamps, jewellery, coins and the like. The range runs from pre-nuraghic to Roman times. Upstairs among the Punic items is a good example of a *kermophoroi*, an ancient perfume burner. The oil was placed in the dish-like part that sits on the head of a bust of Demetra. In Carthaginian festivals dedicated to this deity, women paraded with offerings placed on their heads, thus providing the model for the perfume burner.

The **Sala delle Mostre** (☎ 070 930 00 50; admission €1.50; open 9.30am-1pm & 3.30pm-6pm Tues-Sun) is adjacent to the archaeological museum and often hosts temporary exhibitions on local life and history.

The **Nuraghe di Genna Maria** (☎ 070 930 00 50; admission €1.50; open 9.30am-1pm & 3.30pm-6pm Tues-Sun) is about 1km out on the road west to Collinas; turn south at the sign. The oldest part of the *nuraghe* is the central tower, around which was later raised the three-cornered bastion. Much later an encircling wall was also raised, but little of it remains here today. Between the bastion and the wall huddled the villagers' houses and workshops, which appear to date back to the Iron Age, while the fortifications date to the Middle Bronze Age. The site was abandoned in the 8th century BC but later used by the Carthaginians as a place of worship.

Places to Stay & Eat The nicest option here is **Residence Funtana Noa** (☎/fax 070 933 10 19; W www.residencefuntananoa.it; Via Vittorio Emanuele III 66-68; singles/doubles €40/62), a tasteful new hotel with 30 rooms, all spacious and decorated with timber furniture in a crisp unfussy style. Rooms are gathered around a courtyard and most have views over the surrounding countryside. Upstairs is a reading room and they have their own restaurant.

Otherwise, a couple of hotels are located just outside town off the Collinas road.

Three ARST buses run here from Cagliari on weekdays (€3.72, 1½ hours). Up to four run to/from Sardara (€0.67, 15 minutes) and Sanluri (€1.19, 25 minutes). The occasional service proceeds to Tuili.

Las Plassas

Zig-zagging northeast from Villanovaforru you find yourself heading in the direction of Barumini. Long before you hit this town you will see the ruined walls of the 12th-century **Castello di Marmilla** atop an impossibly conical hill beside the hamlet of Las Plassas. It was part of the defensive line built on the frontier with the Giudicato di Cagliari by the rulers of Arborea.

To approach you can take the left fork at the beginning of Las Plassas (for Tuili) and you will see on your a left a winding footpath to the top of this hill. If approaching *from* Barumini, make for the yellow **Chiesa di Maria Maddalena**, cross the above mentioned road and start hiking.

Barumini & Nuraghe Su Nuraxi

postcode 09021 • pop 1418 • elev 202m

From Las Plassas you speed up the road past odd humps of hill to Barumini. The tiny **Chiesa di Santa Tecla** marks the crossroads in the centre of town. Make a pit stop here to admire the curvaceous rose window of the church and enter for a small multimedia show and **museum** *(admission €1.03; open 10am-1pm & 3.30pm-7pm Thur-Sun)* dedicated to the Nuraghe Su Nuraxi.

The Nuraghe Su Nuraxi *(over/under 25s €4.20/3.10; open 9am-8pm daily)* itself is barely half a kilometre to the west on the road to Tuili. The hulk of the central tower of the complex makes a prominent landmark but what makes it impressive to the profane is not so much the central tower but the extent of the village ruins around it, a veritable beehive of circular buildings, mostly not more than a metre high now. The Bronze-Age central three-storey (only the base remains of the top floor) tower is made of heavy basalt blocks and was raised in the 13th century BC. Around it a rectangular defensive wall with four towers was later constructed, beyond which a village began to grow. Then a more complex defensive wall with up to nine towers was built around the core of the village. In the 7th century BC the site was partly destroyed but not abandoned. In fact it grew and was still inhabited in Roman times. Elements of basic sewage and canalisation have been identified in this, one of the most important nuraghic sites on the entire island.

There are frequently queues (in summer at least) and if you are too impatient to hang about you can get an idea of the place by peering in through the fence. Entry is by guided tours which run every half hour and consist of no more than 20 people.

Albergo Sa Lolla *(☎ 070 936 84 19, fax 070 936 11 07; Via Cavour 49; singles/doubles €42/62; open July-Aug)* is a lovely renovated mansion with seven rooms in Barumini. It also has a restaurant. To find it head east from the Chiesa di Santa Tecla and follow the signs – it's only a few hundred metres from the church.

La Giara di Gesturi

Wild *cavallini* ('mini-horses' or ponies), as many as 500 or so at last count, roam free (or freeish since local farmers claim them as their own) on the extraordinary **Altopiano della Giara** plateau that closes off this part of the northern limits of Cagliari province. The number of these extraordinary midget ponies dropped to 150 in the 1960s but efforts to protect them have borne fruit.

This strange high plain, splashed with *macchia* and small cork oaks, is also home to cattle (including the red long-horned bulls peculiar to the island) and a sprinkling of broken-down nuraghes and ancient tombs. You can also see the occasional *pinedda* (old-style thatched shepherds hut), such as the one on the left if you start following the trail from the Setzu approach road.

The best places to find the horses, in the early morning or late afternoon, are the seasonal lakes, called *paulis* (such as Pauli Maiori). In winter they usually have a shallow patina of surface water but in the warmer months most of it evaporates. At some, such as Pauli S'Ala de Mengianu, the water trapped in underground basalt sources bubbles to the surface around the *paulis*, and that is where the horses will be slaking their thirst.

A few dirt tracks (one linking approach roads from Setzu and Tuili) make it possible to get around part of the Giara in a vehicle, although they are a little rough.

For the approach road from **Setzu**, turn right just north of the town. The road winds up 3km (at the 2km mark you'll see the Sa Domu de S'Orcu *tomba dei giganti* to the left) high above the stark plains. The asphalt peters out at the entrance to Parco della Giara but you can follow the rough dirt track (slowly) in a normal car east to the Gesturi exit.

One place to find guides for the plateau is **Sa Jara Manna** (☎ *070 936 81 70;* W *www.sa jaramanna.it, SS197, km44)* outside Barumini.

There is another approach road from the hamlet of **Tuili**, from which locals set out in August for the annual round-up and branding of the *cavallini*. In the town's **Chiesa di San Pietro** are some fine works of art, including a grand retablo done in 1500 by the Maestro di Castelsardo.

Finally, you can also enter the Giara at its eastern end from **Gesturi**. The town itself is dominated by the big 17th-century baroque **Chiesa di Santa Teresa d'Ávila** and is a centre of pilgrimage for the faithful who flock here to celebrate Gesturi's greatest son, Fra Nicola 'Silenzio' (1882–1958), a Franciscan friar known for his particular religious devotion, wisdom and simplicity of life. His beatification in 1999 was a source of great pride to the good citizens of Gesturi, who have decorated the place with murals and grand portraits of the man they also knew as Brother Silence.

Cagliari & the Southeast

To the ancients southern Sardinia was of far greater interest than the unruly interior or even the north. The Phoenicians and their successors founded and maintained several bases along the southern coast, well placed to exploit the Campidano plains and mines in the southwest. Of these settlements, the port town of Cagliari proved the longest lasting, and for centuries has been the senior Sardinian city. With its hilltop defensive core, bustling harbour and busy beaches, Cagliari exerts an urban magnetism and even sophistication largely absent elsewhere in Sardinia. As for the unsightly swathe of industry that blights the coast to its southwest, the less said the better.

The coast road southeast to Villasimius, although developed in parts, takes you past some fine beaches and on to the glittering turquoise Costa Rei. Inland lies one of the least inhabited domains of the island, which is eerily silent.

If you want to combine some beach time with the gritty flavour of a real city, make the effort to get to Cagliari.

Cagliari

postcode 09100 • pop 174,180
Landing at Cagliari's docks is a singular experience. The proud and busy Via Roma presents the unmistakable hallmarks of a Mediterranean port city. Portentous civic buildings, a grand department store, hotels and the buzz of timeless waterfront cafés let you know you have arrived in *the* city. Behind it, alleys wind north and upwards to the sandy-coloured Castello district, its medieval walls and churches rising like the upper layers of some weighty birthday cake. As many guides are at pains to stress, DH Lawrence found it all rather fetching.

Even a brief exploration of the island's capital and largest city reveals it as a cosmopolitan enclave quite apart from the rest of the island. Most Sardinians regard it with diffidence, which the Cagliaritani dismiss as dull provincialism.

The hilly labyrinth of Castello, the bright pastel colours of the restored facades and the taverns and restaurants jostle for your

Highlights

- Seek out the many great eateries huddled in the lanes of Cagliari's Marina quarter
- Admire the best collection of archaeological finds on the island in the capital's Museo Archeologico Nazionale
- Explore the high-walled Castello district, the core of the old city, and the lively lanes and cluster of churches in nearby Stampace
- Join in the festivities of Cagliari's May Festa di Sant'Efisio
- Take a slow train through mountains from Mandas to Arbatax
- Choose your spot along the great white beaches of the Costa Rei

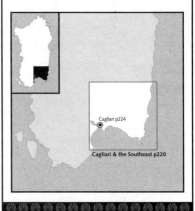

Cagliari p224

Cagliari & the Southeast p220

attention (especially in the Marina district). Several fine monuments and the essential archaeology museum, with its priceless nuraghic collections (Bronze-Age stone artefacts), will keep you well occupied for a day or two. And the city's long Poetto beach, while hardly Sardinia's finest, is not bad for a city-side splash.

HISTORY

The Phoenicians first established themselves around here in the 8th century BC. They were probably preceded by nuraghic settlers (perhaps as early as 2000 BC) but it was not until the Carthaginians took control of what they called Karel or Karalis around 520 BC that a town structure began to emerge. The Romans attached particular importance to Karalis and Julius Caesar declared it a Roman municipality in 46 BC. For centuries it remained a prosperous port at the head of the grain trade with mainland Italy and capital of the province taking in Sardinia and Corsica, but with the eclipse of Rome's power came more turbulent times.

Vandals, operating out of North Africa, waltzed into the city in AD 455 only to be unseated by a resurgent Byzantine Empire in 533. Cagliari thus became capital of one of four districts, which later became the medieval provinces called *giudicati*. By the 11th century, weakening Byzantine influence (accentuated by repeated Arab raids) led

Cagliari and the other districts to become virtually autonomous.

The emerging rival sea powers of Genoa and Pisa were soon poking their noses around and in 1258 the Pisans took the town, fortified the Castello area and replaced the local population with Pisans. A similar fate awaited them as the Catalano-Aragonese took over in 1326. In the ensuing years of conflict around the island, the Catalano-Aragonese managed always to keep Cagliari. The Black Death swept through, as in most of Europe, in 1348, followed by frequent repeat episodes of the plague in the succeeding decades.

With Spain unified at the end of the 15th century, the Catalans themselves were subordinated to the Spaniards. Cagliari fared better than most of the island under Spanish

CAGLIARI & THE SOUTHEAST

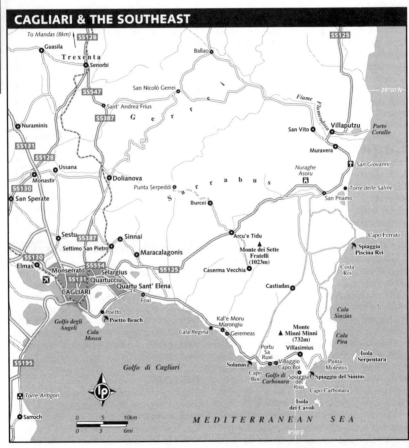

inertia and mismanagement, and in 1620 the city's university opened its doors.

The dukes of Savoy (who in 1720 became kings of Sardinia) followed the Spanish precedent in keeping Cagliari as the vice-regal seat and it endured several anxious events (such as the 1794 anti-Savoy riots). From 1799 to 1814 the royal family, forced out of Piedmont by Napoleon, spent much time in Cagliari protected by the British Royal Navy.

The first street lighting appeared in 1811 and a regular postal service with Genoa was established in 1835. Meanwhile King Carlo Felice had built a modern highway to Sassari that still bears his name today. Cagliari continued to develop slowly throughout the 19th century. Parts of the city walls were destroyed and the city expanded as the population grew. Cagliari, like the rest of Sardinia, got through WWI unscathed and until 1943 it looked like this might be the case again in WWII. But the city was subjected to heavy Allied bombing in February and May, events that led Rome to decorate the entire city with a medal for bravery.

Reconstruction commenced shortly after the end of the war and was partly complete by the time Cagliari was declared capital of the semi-autonomous region of Sardinia in the new Italian republic in 1949. A good deal of Sardinia's modern industry, especially petrochemicals, has since developed around the lagoons and along the coast southwest as far as Sarroch. Recent projects to expand its commercial port have been mired in controversy, with many predicting failure.

ORIENTATION

The part of town that will interest visitors is compact but can be a little confusing. The main port, bus and train stations are located on or near Piazza Matteotti, where you will also find the useful city tourist office. Running through that square is the broad Via Roma, part of the principal route to Poetto and Villasimius in the east, and Pula and the south coast to the west.

The warren of lanes just inland from Via Roma is known as Marina. Clustered here is about a third of the city's hotels and a plethora of eateries, from cheap and cheerful trattorias to a handful of gourmet options. Marina is bounded to the west by Largo Carlo Felice, which runs up to Piazza Yenne, where the island's north–south route, the SS131, officially begins.

A walk up the Scalette di Santa Chiara north of Piazza Yenne takes you high into the old medieval core of the city, the Castello district, signalled by the tall Pisan watchtowers from which you have great views. The city's main museums are up here.

Downhill to the left (west of the city) are the busy, working class lanes of Stampace, while to the right (east) is the more modern Villanova district.

Beyond, the city spreads east to the Saline (salt pans) and Poetto beach, while in the west the housing creeps around the north shore of the immense Stagno di Santa Gilla lagoon.

Maps

The tourist office handout map is adequate for getting about, although not a grand work of cartography. Some bookshops sell the Litografia Artistica Cartografica city map of Cagliari, the best available.

INFORMATION
Tourist Offices

The main city tourist office is the **Azienda Autonoma di Soggiorno e Turismo** *(AAST; ☎ 070 66 92 55; Piazza Matteotti; open 8am-8pm Mon-Sat Apr-Sept, 8am-2pm Sun July-Aug, 9am-2pm & 3pm-6pm Mon-Fri, 9am-2pm Sat Oct-Mar • ☎ 070 66 83 52; Stazione Marittima; open 8.30am-1.30pm & 3pm-7pm daily)*. The branch office has a good deal less information.

The regional tourism body, **ESIT** *(☎ 070 60 42 41; Via Mameli 97)*, is an administrative unit, although you might be able to get hotel lists for the rest of the island here.

The tourist office at Elmas airport was closed at the time of writing.

Foreign Consulates

Several countries are represented by honorary consuls in Cagliari. They include:

Denmark (☎ 070 66 82 08) Via Roma 121
France (☎ 070 66 42 72) Piazza Deffennu 9
Germany (☎ 070 30 72 29) Via Rafa Garzia 9
Holland (☎ 070 30 38 73) Viale Diaz 76
Norway (☎ 070 66 82 08) Via Roma 121
Spain (☎ 070 66 82 08) Via Roma 121
Sweden (☎ 070 67 08 30) Via Roma 101
UK (☎ 070 82 86 28) Viale Colombo 160, Quartu Sant'Elena

Money

Handy banks include the **Banco di San Paolo**, next to the main train station (ATMs inside the station) and **Banco di Sardegna** *(Piazza del Carmine 28)*. ·

If you need to send or receive money by Western Union, you can do so at **Mail Boxes Etc** *(☎ 070 67 37 04; Viale Trieste 65/b)*.

Post & Communications

The main **post office** *(Piazza del Carmine; open 8.15am-6.40pm Mon-Fri, 8.15am-1.20pm Sat)* has a fax service and *fermo posta* (poste restante). For the latter, exit the main building and head for a side entrance to the left. Take ID to pick up mail.

Email & Internet Access Access the Internet at **Internet Cafe** *(Via San Domenico 28; open 8am-9am Mon-Sat)*. It has a handful of clunky computers and charges €2.60 an hour.

Intermedia Point *(Via Eleonora d'Arborea 4; open 10am-1pm & 4pm-9pm Mon-Fri, 11am-1pm & 5pm-9pm Sat)* also charges €2.60 an hour.

Travel Agencies

The national youth travel agent, **CTS** *(☎ 070 48 82 60; Via Cesare Balbo 12)*, has a branch in town.

Bookshops & CD Stores

Libreria Dattena *(☎ 070 67 02 20; Via Garibaldi 175)* has a small section of novels and foreign-language books.

The people at **Grand Wazoo** *(☎ 070 66 60 39; Via Garibaldi 143)* can give guidance on Sardinian and international music.

Libraries

The **Biblioteca dell'Università** *(☎ 070 66 00 17; Via Università 32)* is part of the city's university buildings in Castello.

Laundry

Self-service laundrettes are virtually non-existent in Sardinia, but in Cagliari there is a soap suds paradise for the great unwashed. **Lavanderia Ghilbi** *(Via Sicilia 20; open 8am-10pm daily)*. A 6kg load costs €3 to wash. Washing and drying takes about an hour.

Left Luggage

Those with a boat ticket (arriving or departing) you can leave luggage at the *deposito* *(open 7am-7pm daily)* in the Stazione Marittima for free.

Medical Services

The city's **Ospedale Civile Brotzu** *(☎ 070 54 32 66; Via Peretti)* is out to the northwest of the city centre. Take bus No 1 from Via Roma if you need to make a non-emergency visit. For a night-time emergency callout doctor, call the **Guardia Medica** *(☎ 070 50 29 31)*.

Farmacia Centrale *(Via Sardegna 10)* is handy for any medicine you might need.

Emergency

The main police station, or **Questura** *(☎ 070 49 21 69; Via Amat 9)*, is behind the imposing law courts.

Dangers & Annoyances

At night some spots around town are not so appealing. The steps leading up to the Bastione San Remy and the little park at the bottom of Viale Regina Margherita, for instance, attract a crowd of drunks and drug-takers. Petty theft is always a risk for tourists. Take the usual precautions, which include leaving nothing in vehicles – if you must, at least keep things hidden.

THINGS TO SEE & DO

A nice touch is the informative notice boards placed outside most sights. They are written, happily, in Italian and English and provide a quick insight into each location as you wander about.

Castello

The precipitous white stone walls of medieval Cagliari, with two of the grand Pisan towers still standing, watch over the hubbub below, enclosing what has always been known as Il Castello (the Castle). The Sardinians call it Su Casteddu, by which they also refer to the whole city. The city's defenders enjoyed vast views over land and sea from a fortress that was virtually impregnable. The walls are best admired from afar – one good spot is the Roman amphitheatre across the valley to the west.

You can reach this citadel from various approaches. The most impressive introduction is from the busy intersection of Piazza Costituzione. After a pleasant breakfast at Antico Caffè (see Places to Eat, later) you could approach the monumental stairway entrance to the **Bastione San Remy**. The grand flights of steps, part of an early-20th-century remodelling of the entire bastion, are now dripping with hideous graffiti and serve as a hang-out for drunks and drug abusers. Once a strong point in the fortifications, the bastion is now a stately belvedere offering views across the city and its lagoons. For decades a flea market has set up here on Sundays, perhaps the successor to the 1948 fair, which was held as the city tried to pull itself out of the post-war mire.

Standing at the bastion walls and staring down into Piazza Costituzione is not recommended for vertigo sufferers!

Cattedrale di Santa Maria & Around

A brisk march north brings you into Piazza Duomo and face to face with the new Pisan-Romanesque facade (built in 1938) of the Cattedrale di Santa Maria (☎ 070 66 38 37; Piazza Palazzo 4; open 8am-12.30pm & 4.30pm-8pm), also known as the Duomo. Little remains of the original 13th-century church, buried in a heavy baroque remake in the 17th century. Then in 1933–38 they tried to turn the clock back with the neo-classical facade. Purists are horrified by this gimmick but actually, with its bright mosaics and geometric patterns, it is not such a displeasing imitation. The lions on the other side of the square are another typical Tuscan touch. To the left the square-based belltower is one of the few bits of the church largely left in peace since it was raised in the 13th century.

Inside, the once-Gothic church has largely disappeared beneath the rich icing of baroque excess. Bright frescoes adorn the ceilings, the three narrow chapels at either side of the aisles spill over with florid sculptural whirls and the effect is at once cheering and sickening. The third chapel to the right is perhaps the pinnacle of the genre. A serene St Michael, who appears in typically baroque fashion to be in the eye of a swirling storm (or perhaps a washing machine's spin cycle), casts devils into hell.

Still, there are some less gaudy bits and pieces. The two magnificently intricate stone pulpits on either side of the central door as you enter the church, sculpted by Guglielmo da Pisa and donated by that city to Cagliari in 1312, actually formed a single pulpit until split in two in the 16th century.

The original rested on the four stone lions now fronting the altar. Each of the lions dominates another animal (a typical scene from the northern Tuscan tradition).

To the right of the altar is the worn looking *Trittico di Clemente VII*, attributed by some to the school of Rogier van der Weyden. The left transept is capped by the baroque tomb of Martí II of Aragon.

For more tombs, head down into the crypt, underneath the altar. You find yourself in a central vault, at the end of which doors lead to two lateral chambers. The back end of these is occupied by the tombs of (to the left) Carlo Emanuele and (to the right) Giuseppina Maria Luisa, two of the Savoy family. The crypt, hewn out of stone and tamed by the sculptor's chisel, is a riot of decoration – not a centimetre has been left bare.

Next door to the cathedral is the **Palazzo Arcivescovile** (archbishop's residence) followed by the pale lime facade of the **Palazzo Viceregio** (Palazzo Regio; ☎ 070 409 23 72; Piazza Palazzo; open 8.30am-1.30pm Mon-Fri), which was once home to the Spanish and Savoy viceroys and today serves as the provincial assembly. Above the entrance, a memorial recalls King Carlo Emanuele of Savoy. It is closed for restoration.

Torre di San Pancrazio A further stroll northwards brings you into the pleasant Piazza Indipendenza. The grand white tower (admission free; open 9am-1pm & 3.30pm-7.30pm Tues-Sun Apr-Oct, 9am-5pm Nov-Mar) that stands to the right of the city gate is one of the two great medieval Pisan defensive towers still standing. The 'missing' back wall has been variously interpreted, some attributing it to Pisan stinginess. One can only surmise that they and their successors thought it pointless fortifying the inside of the walls – if any enemies made it that far, the game was probably up anyway.

This tower was built on the city's highest point and gave its guardians a sweeping view of the Cagliari coast as far west as Pula and east to Villasimius. Under the Catalano-Aragonese it became an office block with a view for public servants and in the 17th century it was downgraded into a prison (perhaps it felt that way to the public servants too).

Citadella dei Musei Once beyond the city gate you are in Piazza dell'Arsenale, a

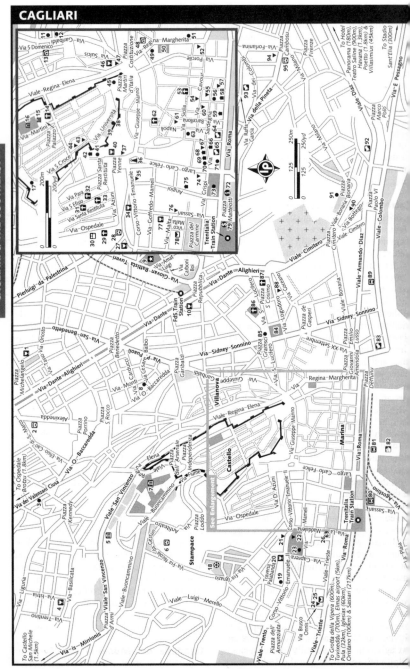

CAGLIARI

PLACES TO STAY
42 Hotel Aurora
50 Hotel Regina Margherita
58 Hotel Miramare
59 Hotel A&R Bundes Jack &
     Pensione Vittoria
66 Hotel Italia
68 Albergo La Perla
69 Albergo Palmas
75 Hotel Quattro Mori

PLACES TO EAT
21 Crackers
22 San Crispino
24 Parsifal
35 Ristorante Quattro Mori
37 Isola del Gelato
43 Sotto La Torre
44 Caffè Libarium Nostrum
47 Antico Caffè
52 Dal Corsaro
54 Trattoria Dal Conte
55 Lillicu
57 Il Buongustaio
60 Antica Hostaria
61 Caffè Barcellona
67 Ristorante Italia
74 Caffè Svizzero
76 Ristorante Flora
88 Ristorante Del Monte
90 Ristorante Royal
94 Pepe Rosa

ENTERTAINMENT
 1 Pub Ribot
 4 Nautilus

10 Cork Irish Pub
20 Break Net Café
27 Al Merlo Parlante
34 Oblomow
40 Forum Caffè
46 Brasserie Vecchia Bruxelles
77 Sax By Marcella

OTHER
 2 Teatro Comunale
 3 Isola
 5 Galleria Comunale d'Arte
 6 Anfiteatro Romano
 7 Citadella dei Musei
 8 CTS
 9 Questura
11 Libreria Dattena
12 Grand Wazoo
13 Internet Cafe
14 Cattedrale di Santa Maria
15 Palazzo Arcivescovile
16 Palazzo Viceregio
17 Ghetto degli Ebrei
18 Orto Botanico
19 Villa di Tigellio
23 ESIT Tourist Office
25 Mail Boxes Etc
26 Banco di Sardegna
28 Teatro dell' Arco
29 Chiesa di San Michele
30 Cine Namaste
31 Chiesa di Sant'Efisio
32 Chiesa di Sant'Anna
33 Chiesa di Santa Restituta
36 Statue of Carlo Felice
38 Biblioteca dell'Università

39 Università di Cagliari
41 Torre dell'Elefante
45 Bastione San Remy
48 Intermedia Point
49 Bastione di Nostra Signora di
     Monserrato
51 BoxOffice Tickets
53 Chiesa di Sant'Eulalia & Museo
     del Tesoro e Area Archeologica
     di Sant'Eulalia
56 Ruvioli Rentacar
62 Chiesa di San Sepolcro
63 Lavanderia Ghilbi
64 Swedish Consulate
65 Danish, Norwegian & Spanish
     Consulate
70 Farmacia Centrale
71 La Rinascente
72 AAST Tourist Office
73 Municipio
78 Main Post Office
79 Banco di San Paolo
80 ARST Bus Station
81 PANI Bus Terminal
82 Stazione Marittima
83 French Consulate
84 Exma
85 Parco delle Rimembranze
86 Chiesa di San Lucifero
87 Basilica di San Saturno
89 FMS Bus Terminal
91 Santuario & Basilica di Nostra
     Signora di Bonaria
92 Dutch Consulate
93 German Consulate
95 Teatro Alfieri

CAGLIARI & THE SOUTHEAST

kind of antechamber with four entrances – south into Piazza Indipendenza, east and west downhill into the rest of the city and north into what was once the city's arsenal (Regio Arsenale).

Four museums, including the island's most important archaeological and art collections, are crammed into the modern buildings, cleverly incorporated into the remains of the old arsenal and city walls, bits of which you will observe as you explore the museums. Disabled-friendly ramps have also been installed, so getting around should present few problems.

As you enter there is a snack stand on your left. To the right is a curiously ghoulish collection, the **Raccolta di Cere Anatomiche** (admission €1.50; open 9am-1pm & 4pm-7pm Tues-Sun), 23 anatomical cross-section wax models done by the Florentine Clemente Susini from 1802 to 1805. They include

bisected heads and even a cutaway of the torso of a fully pregnant woman. Should you be into this sort of thing and planning a trip to Florence one day, you can see much more of Susini's handiwork in that city's Museo Zoologico La Specola.

You could turn immediately right out of this museum and head up to the **Museo d'Arte Siamese** (☎ 070 65 18 88; admission €2; open 9am-1pm & 4pm-8pm Tues-Sun June-Sept, 9am-1pm & 3.30pm-7.30pm Oct-May). A local engineer, Stefano Cardu, spent many years in Thailand (formerly Siam) and, judging by this museum, had a lot of time on his hands. He collected all sorts of local arts and crafts, ranging from silk paintings to weapons and porcelain. Some of it comes from elsewhere in Asia, including China and Japan.

Now for the serious stuff. If you want to get a grip on the ancient past of this island you should not pass up the **Museo Archeo-logico Nazionale** (☎ 070 68 40 00; admission €4, with Pinacoteca Nazionale €5; open 9am-8pm Tues-Sun). In some years the summer closing time (June to September) has been known to be extended to 11pm.

On the three floors of this museum are collections dating from pre-nuraghic to late-Roman times, found at sites across Sardinia. Without doubt the single most impressive part of the collection are the *bronzetti*, astonishing bronze figurines that (in the absence of any written record) form one of the few precious clues to nuraghic culture. There are two separate displays of the statuettes on the ground and 2nd floors. Throughout the museum most explanations are in Italian, although some general material is in English.

The exposition on the ground floor is chronological, starting with explanatory panels on various aspects of Stone Age societies and followed by a series of 25 window cases.

The first few contain stone and marble statuettes of female divinities typical of Stone Age societies, obsidian and flint tools, arrowheads, ceramics and the like. You then move into the Bronze Age, with examples of axeheads, swords and spears. The perfection of the moulds used for some of these tools and weapons is breathtaking. Window case 10 is a star, containing *bronzetti* depicting soldiers, archers, people praying, tribal leaders and so on. More Bronze Age implements and votive vessels follow, along with Iron Age ceramics. The stone statues, and especially the stone model *nuraghe* in window cases 14 to 16, are also remarkable. It is thought that at some point there may have been a cult of the nuraghes themselves. Finally, the last six displays cover a range of Phoenician, Carthaginian and especially Roman ceramics, jewellery, gold and other objects. There is also a limited collection of Carthaginian and Roman bronze coins.

The 1st and 2nd floors contain more of the same but are divided by region and important sites rather than chronologically. Among the highlights on the 1st floor are some Roman-era mosaics, a collection of Roman statues, busts and tombstones from Cagliari, and displays of more coins.

On the 2nd floor the single most engaging display is the extraordinary array of nuraghic *bronzetti*, more numerous and engaging than the ground floor display. Of all the fine figures here, the 'chieftain' stands out above them all. He is depicted with a flowing mantle, staff and sword attached to his belt. A great variety of other figures is represented. One interesting scene shows two men wrestling – one is clearly coming off second best. Otherwise, you will also come across some material from classical sites such as the Antas temple, Nora and Bythia. Among the jewellery, coins and household items are some captivating Roman miniature figurines.

Above and behind the archaeological museum is the **Pinacoteca Nazionale** (☎ 070 68 40 00; admission €2, with Museu Archeo-logico Nazionale €5; open 9am-8pm Tues-Sun). If you are interested in the art history of Sardinia, this is a good place to get an idea of the kind of work being produced from the 15th to 17th centuries. The collection is not particularly large and many of the works, mostly *retablos* (grand altarpieces of the kind commonly found in Spain), are by unknown artists. Of the known painters, some were Catalans who put in time on the island. The four works by Pietro Cavaro, father of the so-called Stampace school and possibly Sardinia's most important artist, are outstanding. They include a moving *Deposizione* (Deposition) and portraits of Saints Peter, Paul and Augustine. Also represented are his father Lorenzo and son Michele. Another of the few Sardinian artists of note was Francesco Pinna, whose *Pala di Sant'Orsola* hangs here.

On the ground floor is a brief line-up of 19th- and early-20th-century painters active in Sardinia, such as Giovanni Marghinotti and Giuseppe Sciuti.

Ghetto degli Ebrei (Jewish Ghetto) The area around Via Santa Croce was at the heart of Cagliari's small Jewish community until the order came from the Spanish Monarchs in 1492 to expel all Jews who did not convert to Christianity. Nothing much remains today but the name, applied to a restored former barracks at No 18 (☎ 070 640 21 15) that is now used for temporary exhibits. In 2002–03 these ranged from photos by Robert Cappa through to medieval illuminated bibles. Opening times and admission vary according to the exposition.

Torre dell'Elefante Fully saturated by art and artefacts, you will probably be reeling. One way of dealing with this situation is to return to Piazza Indipendenza and then make your way along Castello's canyon-like streets to the other great defensive tower, the Torre dell'Elefante *(Via Università; admission free; open 9am-1pm & 3.30pm-7.30pm Tues-Sun Apr-Oct, 9am-5pm Nov-Mar)*, which takes its name from a small sculpted elephant at the tower's base as you enter from Via Università.

During the Spanish period of control of Cagliari, the heads of executed prisoners were strung in cages above the tower's portcullis. In 1852 a crenellated storey was added to the top of the tower, which was converted into a prison for political detainees.

You could climb the tower for the views or head directly for a drink or snack at Sotto La Torre (see Places to Eat, later).

From there you could follow Via Università, flanked by the noble facade of one of Sardinia's oldest centres of learning, back to Bastione San Remy. Or head out past the tower and down the Scalette di Santa Chiara into buzzy, café-lined Piazza Yenne.

Marina

Just south of Piazza Costituzione, an untidy jumble of lanes leads you to the Cagliari waterfront, called Marina. It bursts with all sorts of eateries and a handful of hotels, and it is loaded up with churches.

Of these, the most interesting is the **Chiesa di Sant'Eulalia**, not so much for the church (which can't be visited) but it's attached **Museo del Tesoro e Area Archeologica di Sant'Eulalia** *(☎ 070 66 37 24; Vico del Collegio 2; admission €2.50; open 10am-1pm & 5pm-11pm daily July-Sept, 10am-1pm & 5pm-8pm Tues-Sun Oct-June)*. In the underground area you can see evidence of Roman roads discovered when restoration work began on the church. Upstairs is the church's treasury, a particularly rich collection of religious art, ranging from exquisite priests' vestments and silverware through to medieval codices and other precious documents. Fine wooden sculptures abound, along with an Ecce Homo, depicting Christ front and back after his flagellation. The painting has been attributed to a 17th-century Flemish artist.

A quick stroll to the northwest is the **Chiesa di Santo Sepolcro** *(☎ 070 65 51 35;*

Piazza del Santo Sepolcro; open 10am-1pm & 5pm-8pm daily), whose most astonishing feature is an enormous 17th-century gilded wooden altarpiece housing a figure of the Virgin Mary.

Just beyond the limits of the Marina quarter stands the grand pile that is the town hall, or **Municipio** *(☎ 800 01 60 58; Via Roma; closed at the time of writing)*. A capricious neogothic affair, it was built in 1899–1913 and faithfully reconstructed after bombing in 1943.

Stampace & Around

From the Municipio, head up Largo Carlo Felice to Piazza Yenne. A bronze **statue** of King Carlo Felice in Roman garb marks the beginning of the project for which he is best remembered, the Carlo Felice (SS131) highway to Sassari and Porto Torres. At night (in summer at least) Piazza Yenne heaves as the city's young and restless come out to play in its various bars and cafés.

North of the square you could head up the Scalette di Santa Chiara and make for the Torre dell'Elefante in Castello (see earlier) or left into Via Azuni (which until well into the 19th century was the stage for popular but unruly horse races). Via Azuni leads you directly into the medieval working-class district of Stampace, with housing piled high and washing strung across the narrow lanes.

Chiesa di Sant'Anna *(Piazza Santa Restituta; admission free; open 10am-1pm & 5pm-7pm daily)* pops out at you as if from nowhere and its imposing sand-coloured facade rises high above the little square it dominates. Largely destroyed in WWII and painstakingly rebuilt afterwards, it is basically baroque but the Ionic columns melded into the undulating facade give it a slightly severe neoclassical edge.

Virtually next door is the **Chiesa di Santa Restituta** *(Via Sant'Efisio; admission free; open 9am-1pm & 3.30pm-7.30pm Tues-Sun)*, whose crypt has been in use since pre-Christian times. Orthodox (Eastern Rite) Christians took it over until the 13th century (remnants of their frescoes remain), when it was abandoned. In WWII it was used as an air-raid shelter, a task it was not up to, since many died while holed up here during a raid in February 1943.

A pretty orange facade marks out the **Chiesa di Sant'Efisio** *(Via Sant'Efisio; admission*

CAGLIARI & THE SOUTHEAST

free; open 9am-1pm & 3.30pm-7.30pm Tues-Sun), supposedly built on the site of the martyr's prison. The side-street entrance to the prison where St Ephisius was supposedly held before being executed in Nora is marked in stone: Carcer Sancti Ephysii M (Prison of the Martyr St Ephisius). More information on Sardinia's unofficial patron saint and the festivals held in his honour can be found under Special Events, later.

Where Via Azuni runs into the little square of the same name you run up against the ebullient baroque facade of the **Chiesa di San Michele** *(Via Ospedale 2; admission free; 7am-11am & 6pm-8.30pm daily)*. It's unusual in that as you pass the facade you enter a vast atrium and more stairs lead into the church proper to the right. Directly in front of you in the atrium is a grand pulpit named after Habsburg Emperor Carlos V (who is said to have delivered a stirring speech there before setting off on a fruitless campaign against Arab corsairs in Tunisia). The majesty of the octagonal interior, with chapels radiating from the centre and topped by a grand dome, reflects the power of its Jesuit builders. The heady decor, all marble, stucco and bright frescoes, dates to the first half of the 18th century and is one of the best examples of rococo in Sardinia.

From the church head south under the grand medieval archway and head up Via Fra Ignazio to the **Orto Botanico** *(Viale Fra Ignazio 11; admission €0.50; open 8am-1.30pm & 3pm-8pm daily May-Aug, 8am-1.30pm & 3pm-6.30pm April & Sept–mid-Oct, 8am-1.30pm mid-Oct–Mar)*. You can enter only a section of the gardens, parts of which are a little worse for wear. Specimens from as far afield as Asia, Australia, Africa and the Americas sidle up next to trees and plants from closer to home. A few minor ancient relics, including the odd Roman well, have also been found here. You can join guided visits of a much greater part of the gardens at 11am on the second and fourth Sundays of the month.

Around the corner is more evidence of the Roman presence here. Known as the **Villa di Tigellio** *(Via Tigellio; open 9am-1pm Mon-Fri)*, the site appears to have been three contiguous houses and baths in a suburb of Roman Karalis. What you see (and you can do so quite easily from the street) is a higgledy piggledy jumble of truncated columns and masonry.

The next Roman relic is more spectacular. Head north up Via Fra Ignazio and into Via Nicola da Gesturi and to your left spreads out the **Anfiteatro Romano** *(open 10am-1pm & 3pm-6pm Tues-Sun Apr-Oct, 10am-4pm Nov-Mar)*. It's a bit of a climb to this marvellous 2nd-century outdoor theatre carved largely out of the hillside rock. Much of the original theatre was cannibalised for other construction over the centuries but enough has survived for us to imagine a good Roman afternoon out. Crowds of up to 10,000 could watch their favourite gladiators doing battle with wild beasts while munching on nuts and looking out over the big blue Mediterranean (the sea views are now partially obscured by apartment blocks). In summer it recovers something of its vocation, hosting summer concerts – you may find it closed during concert seasons.

From here you can head further north and back downhill for a dose of contemporary culture at the **Galleria Comunale d'Arte** *(☎ 070 49 07 27; Viale Regina Elena – Giardini Pubblici; adult/child €3.10/1.03; open 9am-1pm & 5pm-9pm Wed-Mon)* dedicated to the Collezione Ingrao, which displays more than 650 works of Italian art from mid-19th century to the late-20th century. The donation of the collection to Cagliari by Francesco Ingrao, after his death in 1999, resulted in the gallery's former modest group of 20th-century Sardinian artworks being placed into storage.

Villanova

The 'new town' of Villanova spreads away to the north and east of the old traditional quarters of Castello, Marina and Stampace. Most of it is fairly nondescript residential stuff but a few sights are buried amid the humdrum apartment buildings.

The **Basilica di San Saturno** *(Piazza San Cosimo; open 9am-1pm Mon-Sat)* may look like a wreck, but it is a fascinating one. According to legend the Christian martyr Saturninus, another of those unfortunates who fell foul of Diocletian's anti-Christian campaign, was executed on this spot in AD 304. Excavation has revealed that there may have been a place of Christian worship here as early as the 4th century, and certainly there was in the 6th century, making it one of the oldest churches in Sardinia. Identifying it is a little difficult as the Vittorini monks from Marseille were at work in the 11th century converting the original into a grander Romanesque church. And then in 1662 it was partly demolished to provide building material for the Cattedrale di Santa Maria.

Directly across the leafy modern square towers a rather awful apartment block, while to one side of the same square is another church, the baroque **Chiesa di San Lucifero**. Below the church is a 6th-century crypt where the tomb of the early Archbishop of Cagliari, St Lucifer, rests. In earlier times the area had been part of a Roman burial ground.

The former abattoir (or *ex-mattatoio*) was cleverly revamped as a cultural centre and opened in 1990 as **Exma** (☎ 070 66 63 99; *Via San Lucifero 11; around €3 depending on exhibitions; open 10am-2pm & 5pm-midnight Tues-Sun June-Sept, 9am-8pm Oct-May*). It hosts temporary art shows, such as one dedicated to Andy Warhol in 2002.

Across the road, the **Parco delle Rimembranze** is a Fascist war memorial erected in 1935 to honour the dead from WWI and other battles fought since Italian Unification.

Santuario & Basilica di Nostra Signora di Bonaria Of the original fortress and church complex built by the Catalano-Aragonese to defeat the Pisans in 1323, little remains today. The truncated belltower served as a watchtower. Below it is the Santuario di Nostra Signora di Bonaria *(Viale Bonaria; open 6.30am-midday & 4.30pm-7.30pm daily Apr-Oct, 6.30am-midday & 4pm-6.30pm Nov-Mar)*, of which only the Catalan Gothic apse dates from the 14th century. In a niche behind the altar stands the statue of the Virgin Mary and Christ that caused such a kerfuffle when it washed ashore in the 14th century (see the 'Fresh Airs & Graces' boxed text), or at least it's a nice 15th-century replacement. In keeping with the generally miraculous atmosphere of the place, the tiny ivory boat hanging from the ceiling above the altar supposedly moves mysteriously to indicate the wind direction in the Golfo degli Angeli.

Among the collection of model boats and other *ex voto* offerings in the museum off the cloister is a golden crown from Carlo Emanuele I. Also in there are four mummified Catalano-Aragonese nobles exhumed from the church. Finding the museum open is a hit-or-miss affair.

The sanctuary is dwarfed by the basilica to its right. Begun in 1704, money ran out and it was not finished until 1926. Then the Allies bombed it in 1943. Restoration work was completed only in 1998.

Beyond the Centre

Grotta della Vipera As you head west out of town along Via Sant'Avendrace you may

Fresh Airs & Graces

When the Catalano-Aragonese landed on the coast to take Cagliari in 1323, it became clear it would be no easy task. They set up camp east of the centre of Cagliari in a spot that came to be known as Bonaria (*buon'aria*, or 'good air') – no doubt it was fresher here than in besieged Cagliari. In the three years of the siege the camp became a fortress with its own church.

With the Pisans ejected, the city's new masters invited Mercedari monks from Barcelona to set up a monastery at the Bonaria church in 1335. The order has remained ever since. Created to ransom Christian slaves from Muslim pirates, the order's Bonaria branch was kept well employed in this task for centuries. But what makes this a place of international pilgrimage (Pope John Paul II came by in 1985) is a simple wooden statue of the Virgin Mary and Christ child.

Legend says the statue was washed up after being cast aside at sea by Spanish seamen caught in a storm in the 14th century. Monks found the Madonna not only in perfect shape on the beach in front of their sanctuary but with a candle alight in her hand. 'It's a miracle!' they cried, as one routinely did in such circumstances, and the statue was placed in a niche behind the altar in the church.

Over the years, Christian seamen became especially devoted to Nostra Signora di Bonaria, attributing all manner of close shaves on the high seas (ie, more miracles) to her intervention. In her honour the Spanish conquistadores later named a future capital city (Buenos Aires in Argentina). And as a result of all the devotion a collection of the most curious *ex voto* offerings, in the form of model ships, paintings and the like, has slowly accumulated in the church and is now held in its museum.

notice on your right a rather bulbous rock formation (shortly after passing through Piazza Trento). The grotto earned its nickname from the image of two snakes that adorns what is in fact the decrepit resting place of a Roman noblewoman, Attilia Pompilia. She offered herself to the gods if only they would spare her beloved and ill husband, Cassius Philippus – it would appear they complied.

Tuvixeddu A little further along and on the same side of the road, a stairway leads up to this weed-infested Punic necropolis. The place is a beehive of tombs cut into the rock and was used for centuries by Carthaginians and Romans alike. Many of the objects found here are now in the Museo Archeologico Nazionale but you can't go scouting for more as the area has been fenced off to keep vandals out.

Castello di San Michele This stout three-tower Spanish fortress *(admission €5; open 10am-1pm & 6pm-10pm Tues-Sun)*, also known as Castillo de San Miguel, remains in a commanding position at the rear end of the city. From here you can see across the entire city, out to Poetto and the coast beyond, inland far across the Campidano plain, east to the Sarrabus (inland mountainous terrain), and west to the industrial inferno of Sarroch.

The castle is used for temporary exhibitions, so the times and entry prices can change. It is quite a hike, even by bus. You'll need to take the No 8 to Piazza d'Armi and change to the No 20 or No 21.

Monte Irpinu Spreading out to the northeast of the city centre, this is the city's green lung. You can drive (or take a long walk) up here for views over the city and the Saline (saltpans).

Beaches
The nearest beach to the city is the small **Calamosca**, which is all right for a quick dip. If you are using public transport it's easier and more worthwhile to head a few kilometres farther east to **Poetto**, about 5km of decent strand. Locals complain it's not what it used to be since the city council attempted to replace the badly eroded, original, fine white sand with less-appealing, darker stuff

in 2002. Catch the PF or PQ buses from the terminus in Piazza Matteotti. Both run the full length of the beach.

The southern end, marked off by Marina Piccola, a small harbour for pleasure craft, tends to be the most crowded. You can hire pedalos (€7 for an hour), umbrellas and sun loungers (€6). Windsurfing is another popular option.

Bars, snack stands, pizzerias and restaurants are spread out at regular intervals along the whole beach.

The hilly promontory that separates Calamosca and Poetto is known as the Sella del Diavolo (Devil's Saddle) and it's easy enough to see why, looking at the clear saddle-like dip in the rocky ridge.

SPECIAL EVENTS
The **Festa di Sant'Efisio**, for the patron saint of Sardinia, is one of the most important on the island. Cagliaritani pour into the streets on 1 May to greet the effigy of the saint Ephisius as it is paraded around on a baroque bullock-drawn carriage starting from the Chiesa di Sant'Efisio (see that section, earlier). For more information on various festivals, see the special section.

Cagliari is also known for a lively **Carnevale** in February.

PLACES TO STAY
There are no camping grounds in Cagliari. The nearest one (see later) is 22km east of town.

Albergo Palmas *(☎/fax 070 6516769; Via Sardegna 14; singles/doubles €21/36)* is about the cheapest deal in town. Rooms do not have their own bathroom and some are quite gloomy, but they are clean and quiet.

Albergo La Perla *(☎ 070 66 94 46; Via Sardegna 18; singles/doubles €30/38)*, a few paces up, is in much the same league. Again, bathrooms are in the corridor and don't expect a view of anything much more than a shaft.

Hotel A&R Bundes Jack *(☎/fax 070 66 79 70; Via Roma 75; singles/doubles €40/60, with private bathroom €45/65)* is the pick of the crop in Marina. The high-ceilinged rooms are spotless and comfortable, even furnished with a muted elegance. Pay extra for the en suite bathrooms. The same people run the slightly barer **Pensione Vittoria** *(☎ 070 65 79 70, fax 070 66 79 70; Via Roma*

75; singles/doubles €37/54, with private bathroom €43/62) in the building. Check out in both hotels is a slightly cheeky 10.30am.

Hotel Miramare *(☎/fax 070 66 40 21; Via Roma 59; singles/doubles €31/33.50, with private bathroom €44/46.50)* is also a reasonable deal. Rooms are not as spick and span as those at A&R Bundes Jack, but they do have air-con; some have TV too.

Hotel Aurora *(☎ 070 65 86 25; Salita Santa Chiara 19; singles/doubles €23/38, with private bathroom €29/49)* is in a cheerful spot just off busy Piazza Yenne. Most of the clean but basic rooms have a view of the Torre dell'Elefante.

Hotel Italia *(☎ 070 66 04 10, fax 070 65 02 40; Via Sardegna 31; singles/doubles €61/85)* guarantees a reasonable level of comfort and almost always has a room or two spare. They are fairly run-of-the-mill but offer the usual basic comforts of air-con, heating and TV.

Hotel Quattro Mori *(☎ 070 66 85 35, fax 070 66 60 87; W www.hotel4mori.it, Italian only; Via GM Angioi 27; singles/doubles €52/73)* has a mix of rooms, some of them nicely placed looking onto the street.

Hotel Regina Margherita *(☎ 070 67 03 42, fax 070 66 83 25; W www.hotelreginamargherita.com; Viale Regina Margherita 44; singles/doubles €120/155)* is in another bracket altogether. Comfortable rooms are hidden behind tinted glass in a rather ugly sprawling block, but from the inside you don't have to look at it! It's the handiest choice for the centre in this range.

Hotel Panorama *(☎ 070 30 76 91, fax 070 30 54 13; e info@hotelpanorama.it; Viale Diaz 231; singles/doubles €95/145)* is a nicer option on much the same scale, with its own swimming pool, but it's quite a hike to the east of the centre.

Hotel Calamosca *(☎ 070 37 16 28, fax 070 37 03 46; W www.hotelcalamosca.it; Viale Calamosca 50; singles/doubles €57/73)* is a great option right by the sea at the nearest beach to Cagliari's city centre. Rooms have heating in winter, TV and views of the cove.

PLACES TO EAT

You won't go hungry in Cagliari. From McDonald's in the main bus station and several home-grown fast-food joints the gamut proceeds through a forest of little eateries and finer restaurants in the centre of town and beyond.

Many restaurants shut for at least part of August.

Restaurants

Marina The lanes of Marina are riddled with cheap trattoria, some of them excellent, where you can get a set lunch, including house wine, for less than €10.

Ristorante Italia *(☎ 070 65 79 87; Via Sardegna 30; meals €20-35; open Mon-Sat)* is divided into two parts. The so-called bistro section serves up pretty cheap meals while the other half likes to think of itself as more posh. Try the *cassita de pisci* (fish soup).

Antica Hostaria *(☎ 070 66 58 60; Via Cavour 60; meals €45; closed Aug)* is one of the strongholds of fine dining in Cagliari. Antique furnishings in a warm ambience set the scene for classic, simple Italian cooking as well as more refined items *al tartufo* (with truffles). Local VIPs frequent this place.

Trattoria Dal Conte *(☎ 070 66 33 36; Via Cavour 83; meals €25-30; open Tues-Sun)* is a less exalted alternative up the road and a good choice. They do a fine version of *culurgiones* (type of ravioli), good risottos and a great homemade tiramisù for dessert.

Lillicu *(☎ 070 65 29 70; Via Sardegna 78; meals €25; open daily except Sun Aug)* is a down-to-earth trattoria that has been going for decades in the heart of Marina and is frequently packed to the rafters. Fish and meat dishes are available and punters rarely leave dissatisfied.

Il Buongustaio *(☎ 070 66 81 24; Via Concezione 7; meals €25-30; open Wed-Sun & lunch Mon)* is a more foodie-oriented place but still concentrates largely on good home cooking, which it has been doing since 1955. Again, land and sea critters get a fairly even run, and the homemade pasta options are especially tasty.

Dal Corsaro *(☎ 070 66 43 18; Viale Regina Margherita 28; meals €40-50; open Mon-Sat)* is a classic of Cagliari's fine dining scene. Apart from à la carte dining they offer a range of set meal options starting at €45. The dining room is elegant and the service close to impeccable.

Around Corso Vittorio Emanuele Quite a few notable eateries are gathered around this boulevard.

Ristorante Flora *(☎ 070 66 47 35; Via Sassari 45; meals €30-35; open Mon-Sat)* offers good home cooking in elegant surroundings. In winter try some of the hearty vegetable soups.

Ristorante Quattro Mori (☎ 070 65 02 69; Via GM Angioi 93; meals €40; open Tues-Sat & lunch Sun) purveys fine Sardinian dishes in one of the city's long-standing cuisine bastions.

Crackers (☎ 070 65 39 12; Corso Vittorio Emanuele 193; meals €25; open Thur-Tues) has a big cream-coloured vault beneath it where you can sit down to northern Italian specialities, including a variety of risottos and dishes garnished with truffles.

San Crispino (☎ 070 65 18 53; Corso Vittorio Emanuele 190; meals €30; open Mon-Sat), just across the road, brings you firmly back to Sardinia with a range of classical island dishes. The *mallodoreddus* (sea shell–shaped pasta) are good.

Out of the Centre A handful of worthy options are tucked away in seemingly unlikely locations away from the city centre.

Ristorante Royal (☎ 070 34 13 13; Via Bottego 24; meals €25-30; open daily) is a window on Tuscany. Here you can tuck into a succulent Florentine steak or choose from a range of other meat and vegetable dishes. Fish lovers should stay away.

Ristorante Del Monte (☎ 070 66 77 44; Via Goceano 10; meals €30; open Mon-Sat & lunch Sun) is not far from the Royal and in an equally unpromising looking street. It is a pleasant, unpretentious eatery that tends more to Roman cooking with such dishes as *saltimbocca* (rolled veal with ham and herbs).

Pepe Rosa (☎ 070 30 33١13; Via della Pineta 108; meals €25-30; open Mon-Sat) is a hike from the centre but has become a fave with locals. Try the *pennette allo zafferano con gamberi* (saffron pennette with prawns). They have a nice garden for summer dining.

Poetto Cagliari's beach is lined with summertime bars, snack joints and restaurants. They are all perfectly cheerful.

Spinnaker del Corsaro di Marina Piccola (☎ 070 37 02 95; Località Marina Piccola; meals €30-35; open Tues-Sun) is the place of choice if you are more demanding about your seaside munching. The pizzas are popular but you could be more adventurous with, say, the vegetable and prawn couscous.

Gelato

Isola del Gelato (☎ 070 65 98 24; Piazza Yenne 35; open 9am-2am Tues-Sun) offers an incredible 280 variations on the ice cream theme, including several soya-based concoctions.

Cafés

Antico Caffè (☎ 070 65 82 06; Piazza Costituzione; open daily) is the city's most elegant and strategically located café. If the traffic puts you off its cute terrace, head for the charming interior with its marble-top tables. A splurge on breakfast will set you back €8.20, while in the evening you can splash out on cocktails at around €4 to €5.

Caffè Barcellona (☎ 070 65 97 12; Via Barcellona 84; open Mon-Sat) has been offering coffee, snacks and mixed drinks to its clients since the late 1940s – it makes a nice backstreet alternative to the line of more obvious cafés on Via Roma.

Sotto La Torre (Piazza San Giuseppe 2; open 8am-3am Thur-Tues) takes you on a trip through the centuries as you sip anything from coffee to *cuba libres*. The decor is 17th century and you can peer into a couple of cisterns dating to Roman and Punic times. In between, try the teas or, if it's that time of night, the grappa.

Caffè Libarium Nostrum (☎ 070 65 09 43; Via Santa Croce 33; open Tues-Sun), a few metres up the road from Sotto La Torre, is another charming spot, with dark timber tables in cosy rooms separated by thick stone arches. In summer they set up tables across the road by the city walls. The *panini* are great for those pangs of hunger.

Caffè Svizzero (☎ 070 65 37 84; Largo Carlo Felice 6; open Tues-Sun) has been a classic of the Cagliari café scene since the early 20th century. Anything from English tea to cocktails are on offer in this elegantly frescoed locale, founded by a group of Swiss almost 100 years ago.

Parsifal (☎ 070 65 57 56; Via Bruscu Onnis 7; open Mon-Sat) is a pleasant space for breakfast but is even better for bar snacks during the day.

ENTERTAINMENT

A handy spot for buying tickets to most shows in Cagliari (and beyond) is **BoxOffice Tickets** (Viale Regina Margherita 43; open 9am-1pm & 5pm-8pm Mon-Fri, 9am-1pm Sat).

If you are staying in Cagliari for a while, you might want to get a hold of *Cagliarintasca* (€7.70), a guide to hotels, cafés and bars in town and around the province. It is not strong on eateries but the bar tips can come in handy. Most central newsstands have it.

Bars

Al Merlo Parlante (☎ 070 65 39 81; Via Portoscalas 69; open Tues-Sun) is a big rollicking beer scene for a mostly young clientele. Anyone for Amsterdam Maximator (11.9% proof)?

Oblomow (☎ 070 413 75 40; Corso Vittorio Emanuele 73; open Mon-Sat) is a quieter, modern spot a short stumble away. You can get snacks here or proceed straight to a cocktail as you wind up for an out-of-town summer club.

Forum Caffè (Piazza Yenne; open Tues-Sun) is a popular bar on this busy square. It has a distinctly blue hue and hip sounds filter into the streets. This square is the nerve centre of Cagliari's pre-club doings, with young night owls firmly in control of the entire square until the wee hours.

Brasserie Vecchia Bruxelles (☎ 070 68 20 37; Via Sulcis 4; open Mon-Sat) is an elegant spot to have a beer, snack or one of a dozen whiskies. With long sofas beneath stone vaulting, it's definitely for a more refined crowd.

Cork Irish Pub (Via Dante 58; open until 4am daily) is not only a popular pseudo-Irish locale, it happens to open after most other joints except discos have closed the shutters – plenty of time to get in a Guinness.

Break Net Café (☎ 070 65 52 62; Corso Vittorio Emanuele II 313; open Mon-Sat) is an Internet café with cocktails and various mixed drinks. It is an earnest affair during the week but livens up on a Saturday night, when it opens until 2am.

Sax By Marcella (☎ 070 66 61 74; Via Sassari 98; open Mon-Sat) is a New York–style cocktail bar that attracts local showbiz types. Try the frozen cocktails.

Havana (☎ 070 37 30 96; Via del Pozzetto 9; open Thurs-Sat) is a long march from the centre of town, but people come to waft away from the Med towards the Caribbean. Music is exclusively Latin American and keeps going until 3am.

Pub Ribot (☎ 070 40 29 82; Piazza Michelangelo 15; open Mon-Sat & evenings Sun) is worth keeping in mind if only for one key fact: it opens 24 hours a day (except Sunday morning)! You can even get snacks and light meals until 5am.

Clubs (Discoteche)

The summer and winter club scenes in Cagliari are quite different. For nine months of the year, the bulk of the action takes place in half a dozen locales in Assemini, 16km northwest of Cagliari, although there are also a few spots around the city itself. A couple of clubs are on Via Venturi, north of the city centre just off Viale Marconi as it heads around the *stagno* (lagoon) to Quarto Sant'Elena.

Most of these shut down in summer as the seaside takes over. Cagliaritani and holiday-makers alike head for clubs, many of them open air, along the coast as far east as Villasimius and west to Pula and Santa Margherita.

In the city, **Garden Abbey Road** (Via Dolcetta) is, as is often the case in Italy, a bit of a mix, part pizzeria and part disco. In summer they often have live music (frequently of indifferent quality) but it can be a fun, lively spot. Otherwise look in the *Unione Sarda* newspaper for tips on clubs in Pula, Santa Margherita, Nora and around. A couple of recurrent names include **Pirata**, along the SS195 in Pula (at Km 29.5) and **Corte Noa**, 3km farther along.

Gay & Lesbian Venues

There is not much of an open gay scene in Cagliari and as a consequence the nightlife options are severely limited.

Nautilus (☎ 070 45 41 99; Via Basilicata 33) is one quiet possibility a good way out of the town centre.

Nirvana (☎ 0360 531 89 23; Centro Commerciale Bellavista Località Foxi, Quartu Santa Elena), still farther out, is a club popular with the modest Cagliari gay crowd.

Live Concerts

Live-music concerts, sometimes on a big scale, occur mainly in summer. Many are staged over July and August in the Anfiteatro Romano (see Stampace and Around, earlier). Major rock concerts by the occasional international act and big Italian bands like Ligabue and Jovanotti are often staged at the Fiera Campionaria fairgrounds in the east of the city. Tickets for good seats at such concerts can easily cost around €20.

Cinemas

Several cinemas are scattered across town but films are almost always dubbed into Italian. You may, however, get lucky at the little art-house cinema **Cine Namaste** (☎ 070 68 36 38; Via Ospedale 4).

Theatre & Classical Music

Cagliari is the epicentre of theatre in Sardinia, and from October to June there is a fair amount of activity. Pretty much everything is done in Italian.

Teatro Alfieri (☎ 070 30 13 78; Via della Pineta 29) hosts much of the grand classic theatre in Cagliari, from Shakespeare to Goldoni. The occasional modern piece slips through too.

Teatro Saline (☎ 070 34 13 22; Via La Palma) puts on all sorts of things, from children's theatre to popular modern pieces.

Teatro dell'Arco (☎ 070 66 32 88; Via Portoscalas 47) is worth keeping an eye on for more alternative theatre.

Teatro Comunale (☎ 070 408 22 30; Via Sant'Alexinedda) is the main stage for classical music concerts and opera. The season gets under way in autumn and continues until spring.

Football

Cagliari football team is the island's main soccer representative. The team is one of the top clubs in the Serie B (2nd Division) competition and started the 2002–03 season well enough to be a contender for promotion to Serie A (1st Division). At home they play at the **Stadio Sant'Elia** (☎ 070 37 14 22; Via Vespucci). Tickets cost from €10 to €30 and can be bought from **Cagliari Point** (☎ 070 604 20 50; Viale La Playa 15) or the **Centro Coordinamento Cagliari Club** (☎ 070 48 51 71; Via Ariosto 26).

SHOPPING

For Sardinian crafts your best first stop is the regional crafts body, **Isola** (☎ 070 49 27 56; Via Bacaredda 176-8), where you can look at a range of quality products. Even if you don't buy anything it's useful to get an idea of products and prices.

Cagliari is the only real chance you'll get in Sardinia to go shopping in the big-city

sense of the word. Italy's quality chain store, **La Rinascente** (Via Roma 141; open 9am-8.30pm Mon-Sat, 10am-1.30pm & 5.30pm-9pm Sun), has a branch in Cagliari – several floors of shopping paradise.

If you're looking for clothes, shoes and accessories, head also for Via Manno and its extension on the other side of Piazza Costituzione, Via Garibaldi – a curving boulevard crammed with boutiques of all sorts.

A handful of antique shops and artists' dens lurks along Via San Domenico.

Sunday is market day in Cagliari, but the locations and themes move around. On the first Sunday of the month **Piazza Giovanni XXIII** (open 9am to 8pm) hosts an antiques and collectors' market. The following week the antiques move to **Piazza Carlo Alberto** (open 5pm-11pm summer; 8.30am-2pm winter). On the third Sunday **Piazza Galilei** (open 6pm-11pm) hosts a similar market, while on the last Sunday of the month an organic farm produce market, with various other odds and ends on display, takes place in **Piazza San Sepolcro**. Second-hand goods markets are held every Sunday at **Bastione San Remy** and **Piazza Trento**.

GETTING THERE & AWAY
Air

Cagliari's **Elmas airport** is 6km northwest of the centre and easily accessible by bus.

For information on flights and airfares, see the Air section in the Getting There & Away chapter.

Bus

The main ARST intercity bus station is on Piazza Matteotti. Local and intercity ARST buses use the station, and curiously you'll find the ticket counters in the attached McDonald's.

PANI buses to Oristano (€5.84, one hour 35 minutes), Nuoro (€5.84, 3½ hours), Sassari (€13.43 nonstop, 3¼ hours) leave from outside the Stazione Marittima port. The ticket office is in the port building itself. Four services run from Nuoro via Oristano while seven connect Cagliari with Sassari (the four all-stops journeys cost a little less and take about half an hour longer). Two connect to Porto Torres.

For Iglesias (€2.89, one to 1½ hours), Carbonia, Portovesme (€4.44, two hours) and the Sulcis area, FMS buses leave from

Via Colombo 24. You buy tickets at the bar here. Some FdS buses leave from FdS railway station (see next).

Train
The main Trenitalia station is on Piazza Matteotti. Trains serve Iglesias (€2.56) and Carbonia (€3.35) in the southwest, while the main line proceeds north to Sassari (€12.10, 4¼ hours) and Porto Torres via Oristano (€4.55, one to two hours) and Macomer. A branch line from Chilivani heads for Olbia (€12.95, four hours) and Golfo Aranci.

The FdS railway station for trains north to Dolianova, Mandas and Isili is on Piazza Repubblica. In summer, a *trenino verde* scenic service runs between Mandas and Arbatax on the east coast – a slow ride through some wild country, mostly in the province of Nuoro. Another similar line runs north from Isili to Sorgono.

Car & Motorcycle
The SS131 Carlo Felice highway, first laid in 1820, links the capital with Porto Torres via Oristano and Sassari. It is the island's main dual-carriage artery. Another, the SS-130, leads east to Iglesias.

The coast roads approaching from the east and west can get highly congested in peak times such as the midsummer holiday season.

Boat
Boats run to Cagliari from Civitavecchia, Livorno and Naples on the Italian mainland, as well as Palermo and Trapani in Sicily. In addition there's a weekly service to/from Tunisia. For details of fares and schedules, see the Getting There & Away chapter.

GETTING AROUND
Moving around on foot, although a little tiring at times in the hilly tracts around Castello, is generally the best option. The city is looking into the feasibility of installing lifts and escalators in strategic spots around the centre but this isn't likely to happen in the near future.

To/From the Airport
Up to 24 daily buses connect the city centre (ARST station in Piazza Matteotti) with Elmas airport. The trip normally takes 10 to 15 minutes and costs €0.67.

A taxi will cost up to €10, depending on where you are going. To park in the airport's parking area you pay €0.80 an hour or up to €4.80 for each 24-hour period.

Bus
CTM (*Consorzio Trasporti e Mobilità;* ☎ 070 209 12 10) buses run on routes across the city and surrounding area. You might use them to reach a handful of out-of-the-way sights and they come in handy for the Calamosca and Poetto beaches. A normal ticket costs €0.77 and is valid for 90 minutes. There are all sorts of combinations of day, weekly and monthly passes.

Car & Motorcycle
Parking in the city centre generally means paying. Parking in blue zones costs €0.52 for the first hour and €1.03 for each hour thereafter. Either buy special tickets to leave on the dash from newsstands or pay one of the attendants who should be milling around.

All the big international car-rental agencies are represented at the airport and several at the port. You'll also find a few local outfits. **Ruvioli Rentacar** (☎ 070 65 89 55; W *www.ruvioli.it; Via dei Mille 9*) is in the heart of the Marina district. They charge €166 for a Fiat Panda for three days.

Taxi
There are taxi ranks at Piazza Matteotti, Piazza della Repubblica and on Largo Carlo Felice. You can call for one on ☎ 070 40 01 01 from 5.30am to 2am. Outside those times you might have difficulty. Other numbers include ☎ 070 28 82 04, ☎ 070 65 06 20 and ☎ 070 66 79 34.

The Southeast

Once past the Poetto beach, the road east pretty much hugs the coast all the way around to Villasimius and then north along the Costa Rei.

The landscape is bare and hilly and the more distance you put between yourself and Cagliari the more enticing the beaches become. Numerous anonymous hotels along here can put you up, but you are better off pushing on to Villasimius and the Costa Rei. A couple of exceptions might detain you along the way.

Camping Pini e Mare *(☎/fax 070 80 31 03; person/tent space €8/9, 4-person bungalows up to €103; open mid-June–mid-Sept)* is the only camping option on the south coast this side of Cagliari. The camping ground is across the road from a beach and 22km east of central Cagliari. You can get here by city transport – catch a local bus (circle lines Nos 30 and 31 from Piazza Matteotti) to Quartu Sant'Elena (Piazza Marconi) and change there for the 1Q bus to Terramala. There is a stop right outside the ground.

You might want to stop for a dip at the pebbly **Cala Regina**, 27km east of central Cagliari or **Kala e Moru**, a long, decent sandy strip 3km farther on. The water here is of an almost eerie translucence. The bay preceding it also presents incredibly turquoise water, although the beach itself is little more than a narrow, stony strip.

Between the two and stretching back to the SP17 main road is a colony of holiday residences, but across the main coast road and 300m down a dirt track is a gem of a hotel in Località Geremeas. **Hotel Monastero** *(☎ 070 80 22 00, fax 070 80 22 01; w www .welcometoitaly.it, Italian only; doubles €75)* is a tastefully restored, rambling, 16th-century monastery with a large courtyard, around which are 10 guest rooms in former monks' cells. The rooms are spacious and have their own bath and antique furniture. The huge dining area turns out good food at reasonable prices and the complex also boasts its own pool and horse riding. They even run **Fantasilandia**, a water-slides park. The only downside for those wanting a good sleep is the disco, which on some (but by no means all) summer nights turns up the decibels.

The road continues to rise and fall with the caprice of the coast, with the multi-hued sea ever present, along with the occasional good beach. **Solanas**, 10km west of Villasimius, holds a good stretch of sand between two headlands and is backed by a modest huddle of holiday homes.

Beyond **Capo Boi** stretches the **Golfo di Carbonara**, which combines a few stretches of mediocre beach, such as **Portu Sa Ruxi** with holiday homes – ranks of them camouflaged by stands of trees and what remains of the *macchia* (scrub) here.

A few kilometres short of Villasimius, the heart of the tourist coast around here, a road

veers off to the south along the peninsula that leads to **Capo Carbonara**, the most southeasterly point of Sardinia. On the way are a camping ground, pleasure-boat marina and what remains of a square Spanish tower, signposted as the **Fortezza Vecchia**. South of the fort are a few sections of beach, although the main beach on this side of the peninsula is **Spiaggia del Riso**. The eastern side is dominated by the **Stagno Notteri** lagoon, often host to flamingos in winter. On its seaward side is a nice long beach, **Spiaggia del Simius**. You can't go to the tip of the cape as it's military land but you can easily see the offshore **Isola dei Cavoli** from various points.

Villasimius
postcode 09049 • pop 2930
Villasimius is a cheerful enough summer resort centre, although it dies completely out of season. On the central Piazza Gramsci there is a **tourist office** *(☎ 070 793 02 08; Piazza Gramsci 8; open 10am-1pm & 9pm-midnight Mon-Sat)*. You can change money at the **Banco di Sardegna** *(11 Piazza Gramsci)*.

The **Festa della Madonna del Naufrago**, held on the second Sunday of July, is a striking seaborne procession to a spot off the coast where a statue of the Virgin Mary lies on the seabed in honour of shipwrecked sailors.

Places to Stay The only nearby camping ground is **Campeggio Spiaggia del Riso** *(☎ 070 79 10 52, fax 070 79 71 50; per person €7.30-26.90; open May-Oct)*, on the beach of the same name about halfway down the west side of the Capo Carbonara peninsula. It gets hellishly crowded in midsummer.

Albergo Stella d'Oro *(☎ 070 79 12 55, fax 070 79 26 32; Via Vittorio Emanuele 25; singles/doubles €36.50/67.50)* is a simple but pleasant enough deal about 50m east of Piazza Gramsci. Rooms are of a reasonable size and all have own bathroom.

Albergo Sa Tankitta *(☎ 070 79 13 38; Via Umberto I 240; doubles €40)* is a restaurant bar situated at the northern exit from town and they also have five straightforward double rooms.

Hotel Blu Marlin *(☎/fax 070 79 03 57; Via Giotto 7; doubles €140)*, right off Via Umberto I about 300m north of Piazza Gramsci, is the only other option in the town itself.

Otherwise holiday hotels in the three- to five-star range and starting at close to €200 a double are scattered all over the area.

Places to Eat One quality eating option is **Ristorante La Lanterna** (☎ 070 79 16 59; Via Roma 62; meals €30). You enter through a little garden (where you can eat in summer) which leads into the dining area proper. The seafood risotto is a classic. It is north along a side road from Piazza Gramsci, about 150m away.

Ristorante Carbonara (☎ 070 79 12 70; Via Umberto I 60; meals €30) is a cheerful pale blue place for fish meals. The watery critters are on display for you to choose your main course.

Entertainment Just before the turn-off for Capo Carbonara on the road into Villasimius from the west, **Peyote** and **Fortesa** are right next to one another. Acting as maxidiscos in summer, the former also dishes up a little Tex-Mex cooking.

Getting There & Around ARST buses from Cagliari (€2.58, 1½ hours) run up to nine times a day in summer. In summer, Autolinee Vacca runs local buses between Villasimius down to Capo Carbonara and around other nearby beaches.

Costa Rei

To take the wonderful high coast road west and then north towards Costa Rei, head *south* out of Villasimius and follow the signs. The road gains height on an inland stretch and hits the coast at **Punta Molentis**, the nearest beach to Villasimius on this side. The beach is marked by a strange tall rock formation. The road then tracks north at high altitude, affording breathtaking views down to the sea and across to the **Isola Serpentara**.

About 15km out of Villasimius the road descends and eagle eyes will notice a dirt trail leading off to the east – it takes you to the fine beach of **Cala Pira**. Another 10km and you reach the signposted **Cala Sinzias**, a lovely sandy beach that has the services of two camping grounds next door to one another. **Camping Garden Cala Sinzias** (☎ 070 99 50 37, fax 070 99 50 82; person/tent space €7.75/11.50) is slightly cheaper than its neighbour, **Camping Limone Beach** (☎ 070 99 50 06, fax 070 99 50 26; person/tent space

€9.30/13.95) but they are fairly similar. Both have bungalows. Check them both out before deciding.

ARST buses on the coastal route from Cagliari to Muravera stop on the main road turn-off to Cala Sinzias.

About 7km inland to the northwest lies the strange, mostly deserted former 19th-century penitentiary of **Castiadas**. There is little to do but admire the one-time penal colony's crumbling rose-tinged walls and have a pizza at the nearby pizzeria/bar. Just before you enter the town roads peel off south to the **Foresta Minni Minni**, which spreads out around Monte Minni Minni (732m).

Back on the coast, you come to a turn-off for **Costa Rei** and the **Hotel Sant'Elmo Beach**. This marks the beginning of a line of wonderful white-sand beaches. The road runs a couple of hundred metres inland from the beaches (including Playa di Santa Giusta). Just park on the side of the road and wander down one of the dirt trails. Crystal clear waters and the occasional snack-cum-cocktail beach bar await.

A few more kilometres north and you enter the Costa Rei resort proper. Uniform but not unpleasant holiday villas lead the way into the core, where you will find shops, bars, one or two summer clubs and a handful of indifferent eateries. **Spiaggia Costa Rei** is, like those to its south and north, a dazzling white beach lapped by remarkably clear blue-green water.

Camping Capo Ferrato (☎/fax 070 99 10 12; person/tent space €6.60/12.50, 4-person bungalows up to €70) is a good-value camping ground at the southern entrance to the Costa Rei resort. The only hotel option is **Hotel Alba Ruja** (☎ 070 99 15 57, fax 070 99 14 59; Via Colombo; rooms with up to 3 beds €176), a set of villa-style residences at the northern end of the core Costa Rei complex. Otherwise you could inquire at apartment rental outlets.

From the beaches of Costa Rei you can take various **boat excursions** (up to 12 people). One stand (☎ 070 99 13 45) on the beach reached from the southern end of Via Colombo offers various trips, including one to Isola Serpentara (€30 per person).

North of the resort scene, **Spiaggia Piscina Rei** is a continuation of the blinding white sand and turquoise water theme with a camping ground fenced in just behind it.

CAGLIARI & THE SOUTHEAST

A couple more beaches fill the remaining length of coast up to **Capo Ferrato**, beyond which drivable dirt trails lead north.

The same ARST buses from Cagliari to Villasimius continue around to Costa Rei, taking about half an hour.

North of Costa Rei

If driving, it's easier on your vehicle to head back to the entrance of the Costa Rei resort and get on to the main northbound road. Follow the road heading for **San Priamo**, a tiny hamlet on the SS125 inland route where it reaches the coast.

If you want to see a *nuraghe*, this is one of your best chances in southeastern Sardinia, which is virtually devoid of seriously interesting specimens. About 5km west of San Priamo, the **Nuraghe Asoru** stands just on the northern side of the SS125 highway. Its central *tholos* tower is in reasonable nick, but if you have already seen some of the truly important nuraghes this one is not likely to excite too much.

North out of San Priamo to the coast you quickly hit a turn-off for **Torre delle Saline**, a good beach capped at its southern end by a promontory with the mandatory Spanish-era watchtower. You have two accommodation options here too. **Camping Torre Salinas** (☎ 070 99 90 32, fax 070 99 90 01; person/tent space €9/11; open Apr–mid-Oct) is a few hundred metres back from the seaside.

Hotel Torre Salina (☎ 070 99 91 22; singles/doubles €24/42.35; open June-Sept) is a basic red-brick building just a few metres short of the sand. It is something akin to camping within four walls, but it's handy and cheap. It also has a restaurant.

The **Spiaggia Torre delle Saline** is just the first in a line of the almost predictable stretch of white beach and near-perfect water that continues north up the coast to the mouth of the Fiume Flumendosa.

Muravera & Around

Muravera, along with two neighbouring villages, San Vito and Villaputzu, is at the heart of one of the island's most important citrus growing districts. These market towns can make a curious stop if you want a change from the beach scene but none is likely to hold your attention for long.

You can stick around if you need to, but there's no real point. **Hotel Sa Ferula** (☎ 070 993 02 37; Piazza Libertà 3; singles/doubles €31/51.65) is just off Via Roma at the eastern end of Muravera and is visible as you enter the town. It's a little worn around the edges and rooms contain only what is strictly necessary.

Hotel Corallo (☎ 070 993 05 02, fax 070 993 02 98; w www.albergocorallo.it; Via Roma 31; singles/doubles €62/90), about 100m away, is a classier job although you might not know it judging from the outside. Rooms have a TV and phone.

Several restaurants, pizzerias and bars line Via Roma, Muravera's seemingly endless main drag.

Four of the ARST buses from Cagliari to Villasimius and Costa Rei run to Muravera (€4.91, three hours from Cagliari) but none operates on Sunday. A few others take the quicker inland route. The same buses proceed to Villaputzu and San Vito.

The SS387 winds northwest into some of the most remote territory in the northern Cagliari province. The branch through Villaputzu leads you back to the coast, with a turn-off almost immediately for **Porto Corallo**, a small pleasure-craft port that sits at the northern end of a pleasant beach of the same name, just north of the Rio Flumendosa. A camping ground and a couple of beach bar/restaurants keep people lodged and fed.

THE INTERIOR

Much of the stark inland mountainous territory known as the Sarrabus, to the north and east of Cagliari, is uninhabited and far removed from the cheerful summer bustle of the coast.

The FdS train line leads north out of Cagliari to Mandas and on to Isili in Nuoro province (see that chapter). From Isili you could take the scenic FdS *trenino verde* train on up to Sorgono, while from Mandas another slow train winds through the mountains east to Arbatax.

There is not a great deal to hold you up along the way north from Cagliari, although you could get off at **Dolianova**. The town is not without a few pleasing buildings but the only real reason to visit is to see the **Chiesa di San Pantaleo**, a unique mix of Pisan Romanesque, early Gothic and some original external decoration of a clearly Islamic inspiration. If you're driving and have a taste for the wild and woolly, you could take the minor road out of Dolianova northeast for **San Nicolò Gerrei**, in the heart of the Gerrei district north of the Sarrabus. It is pretty barren land but that is part of its charm. From San Nicolò you could swing east to Muravera and the coast (see that section earlier) or north for Ballao and points beyond. Of particular interest are the Pranu Mutteddu necropolis and Nuraghe Arrubiu (see the Nuoro & the East chapter for both of these).

East of Cagliari, the SS125 highway passes to the north of the saw-like profile of **Monte dei Sette Fratelli** (Mount of the Seven Brothers, 1023m), one of only three remaining redoubts of the *cervo sardo* or Sardinian deer (the others are Monte Arcosu, just west of Cagliari and Monte Arcuentu, inland from the Costa Verde on the southwestern coast). It is possible to walk through surprisingly dense, green woodland to the rocky roller-coaster summit from the **Caserma Vecchia**, an old Forestry Corps station down a 6km trail south off the Burcei turn-off along the SS125. North of the highway, a lonely hill road crawls 6km to **Burcei** and another 8km northwest to **Punta Serpeddi** (1067m), from where you can gaze out across the lonely land of the Sarrabus to Cagliari and the sea.

CAGLIARI & THE SOUTHEAST

Language

Sardinians with a fluent command of foreign languages are not all that thick on the ground, but this is perhaps to be expected on an island with a long history of introspection.

Many Sardinians are bilingual, speaking Sardinian and Italian with equal ease, although a growing proportion of people, especially those in the cities and bigger towns, are losing command of the island tongue (which itself divides into several dialects). A 16th century version of Catalan is still spoken in Alghero, although locals differ in opinion on how widely it is used.

Tourism to the island has been, at least until recently, predominantly Italian (more than 80% even now), so locals haven't felt a pressing need to devote too much time to other tongues. This will no doubt change with time, but if you bother to learn a little Italian, you'll find it both useful (especially in the interior) and culturally rewarding.

ITALIAN

Italian is a Romance language related to French, Spanish, Portuguese and Romanian, all of which are directly descended from Latin. The Romance languages belong to the Indo-European group of languages, which includes English. Indeed, as English and Italian share common roots in Latin, you will recognise many Italian words.

Although it's commonly accepted that modern standard Italian developed from the Tuscan dialect, history shows that Tuscany's status as the political, cultural and financial power base of the nation ensured that the region's dialect would ultimately be installed as the national tongue.

The Italian of today is something of a composite. What you hear on the radio and TV, in educated discourse and indeed in the everyday language of many people is the result of centuries of cross-fertilisation between the dialects, greatly accelerated in the postwar decades by the modern media.

If you have more than the most fundamental grasp of the Italian language, you need to be aware that many Sardinians still expect to be addressed in the third person formal (*lei* instead of *tu*). Also, it isn't polite

to use the greeting *ciao* when addressing strangers unless they use it first; it's better to say *buongiorno* (or *buona sera*, as the case may be) and *arrivederci* (or the more polite form, *arrivederla*). This is true of most of Italy, but in Sardinia use of the informal can be considered gravely impolite – and in some cases downright insulting – especially when talking to an older person.

We've used the formal mode of address for most of the phrases in this guide. Use of the informal address is indicated by 'inf' in brackets. Italian also has both masculine and feminine forms (usually ending in 'o' and 'a' respectively). Where both forms are given in this guide, they are separated by a slash, the masculine form first.

If you'd like a more comprehensive guide to the language, get a copy of Lonely Planet's *Italian phrasebook*.

Pronunciation

Sardinian's pronunciation of standard Italian is refreshingly clear and easy to understand, even if you have only a limited command of the language.

Italian isn't difficult to pronounce once you learn a few easy rules. Although some of the more clipped vowels, and stress on double letters, require careful practice for English-speakers, it's easy enough to make yourself understood.

Vowels

a	as in 'art', eg, *caro* (dear); sometimes short, eg, *amico/a* (friend m/f)
e	as in 'tell', eg, *mettere* (to put)
i	as in 'inn', eg, *inizio* (start)
o	as in 'dot', eg, *donna* (woman); as in 'port', eg, *dormire* (to sleep)
u	as the 'oo' in 'book', eg, *puro* (pure)

Consonants

The pronunciation of many Italian consonants is similar to that of their English counterparts. Pronunciation of some consonants depends on certain rules:

c	as 'k' before **a**, **o** and **u**; as the 'ch' in 'choose' before **e** and **i**
ch	hard 'k' sound

Sardinian – a Latin Language & its Dialects

Speakers of Italian will not be long in noticing the oddness of Sardinian. Signs, family and place names and traditional menus will soon have you wondering about all the 'uddus' and other strange sounds and suffixes. Another giveaway are the definite articles, *su, sa, sus, sos, sas* etc, in place of the Italian *il, lo, la, i, gli* and *le*.

Sardinia has seen colonists, occupiers, pirates, foreign viceroys and kings come and go since Rome managed to occupy the island more than 2000 years ago. Many Sardinians reacted by retreating into themselves and their island and it is probably largely due to this passive defiance that they've managed to preserve a key to their own identity – their language.

Sardinians will tell you with a sort of contrary pride that their language is much closer to its mother tongue, Latin, than any of its other offshoots, Italian and all its dialects included. Simple words confirm the claim – while in Italian the word for house is *casa*, the Sardinians have stuck with the Latin *domus* (the Italian equivalent, *duomo* has come to mean cathedral).

The 'purest' form of Sardinian is supposedly *logudorese*, the dialect of the Logudoro area in the north, although it is probably more a question of quantity (of speakers) than quality. Also considered important is the southern *campidanese*. Other dialectal variants thrive across the island.

Nowadays, Sardinian (*sardo*) is experiencing the same problems other minority regional languages face in the fight for survival against imposed national tongues. Since Italian unity in the 19th century, the erosion of Sardinian in the cities and towns has accelerated. While many Sardinians still understand the language, city folk tend not to speak it. You're more likely to hear it in the small towns and villages of the interior.

No language is impermeable and the centuries of Catalan and Spanish rule inevitably had an effect on Sardinian. In particular, Catalan words managed to slip through. In Catalonia and Sardinia a river is generally called a *riu* (often rendered in the Spanish *rio* in Sardinia now), while glasses are *ulleres* in the former and *oglieras* in the latter. The spelling may be different but the pronunciation is virtually the same.

On the subject of Catalan, some residents of Alghero, long an independent Catalan settlement, even today speak a dated version of Catalan, snubbing both Sardinian and Italian.

---

g   as the 'g' in 'get' before **a**, **o** and **u**; as the 'j' in 'job' before **e** and **i**

gh hard, as in 'get'

gli as the 'lli' in 'million'

gn as the 'ny' in 'canyon'

h   always silent

r   a rolled 'rr' sound

sc as the 'sh' in 'sheep' before **e** and **i**; as 'sk' before **h**, **a**, **o** and **u**

sch hard 'sk' sound

z   as the 'ts' in 'lights', except at the beginning of a word, when it's as the 'ds' in 'beds'

Note that when **ci**, **gi** and **sci** are followed by **a**, **o** or **u**, the 'i' is not pronounced unless the accent falls on the 'i'. Thus the name 'Giovanni' is pronounced 'joh-**vahn**-nee'.

Word Stress

A double consonant is pronounced as a longer, often more forceful sound than a single consonant.

Stress often falls on the second-last syllable, as in *spa-**ghet**-ti*. When a word has an accent, the stress is on that syllable, as in *cit-**tà*** (city).

Greetings & Civilities

Hello.	*Buongiorno.*
	Ciao. (inf)
Goodbye.	*Arrivederci.*
	Ciao. (inf)
Yes.	*Sì.*
No.	*No.*
Please.	*Per favore/*
	Per piacere.
Thank you.	*Grazie.*
That's fine/	*Prego.*
You're welcome.	
Excuse me.	*Mi scusi.*
	Scusam. (inf)
Sorry (forgive me).	*Mi scusi/Mi perdoni.*

Small Talk

| What's your name? | *Come si chiama?* |
| | *Come ti chiami?* (inf) |

My name is ...	*Mi chiamo ...*
Where are you from?	*Di dov'è?*
	Di dove sei? (inf)
I'm from ...	*Sono di ...*
How old are you?	*Quanti anni ha?*
	Quanti anni hai? (inf)
I'm ... years old.	*Ho ... anni.*
I (don't) like ...	*(Non) Mi piace ...*
Just a minute.	*Un momento.*

Language Difficulties

I (don't) understand.	*(Non) Capisco.*
Please write it down.	*Può scriverlo, per favore?*
Can you show me (on the map)?	*Può mostrarmelo (sulla carta/pianta)?*
Do you speak English?	*Parla inglese?*
	Parli inglese? (inf)
Does anyone here speak English?	*C'è qualcuno che parla inglese?*
How do you say ... in Italian?	*Come si dice ... in italiano?*
What does ... mean?	*Che vuole dire ...?*

Paperwork

name	*nome*
nationality	*nazionalità*
date of birth	*data di nascita*
place of birth	*luogo di nascita*
sex (gender)	*sesso*
passport	*passaporto*
visa	*visto*

Getting Around

What time does ... leave/arrive?	*A che ora parte/ arriva ...?*
the (city) bus	*l'autobus*
the (intercity) bus	*il pullman/corriere*
the ferry	*il traghetto*
the plane	*l'aereo*
the ship	*la nave*
the train	*il treno*

| I want to go to ... | *Voglio andare a ...* |

I'd like a ... ticket.	*Vorrei un biglietto ...*
one-way	*di solo andata*
return	*di andata e ritorno*
1st-class	*prima classe*
2nd-class	*seconda classe*

| The train has been cancelled/ delayed. | *Il treno è soppresso/ in ritardo.* |

Signs

Ingresso/Entrata	Entrance
Uscita	Exit
Informazione	Information
Aperto	Open
Chiuso	Closed
Proibitio/Vietato	Prohibited
Polizia/Carabinieri	Police
Questura	Police Station
Camere Libere	Rooms Available
Completo	Full/No Vacancies
Gabinetti/Bagni	Toilets
Uomini	Men
Donne	Women

the first	*il primo*
the last	*l'ultimo*
platform number	*binario numero*
station	*stazione*
ticket office	*biglietteria*
timetable	*orario*

I'd like to hire ...	*Vorrei noleggiare ...*
a bicycle	*una bicicletta*
a boat	*una barca*
a car	*una macchina*
a motorcycle	*una moto(cicletta)*

Directions

Where is ...?	*Dov'è ...?*
Go straight ahead.	*Si va sempre diritto.*
	Vai sempre diritto (inf).
Turn left.	*Gira a sinistra.*
Turn right.	*Gira a destra.*
at the next corner	*al prossimo angolo*
at the traffic lights	*al semaforo*
behind	*dietro*
in front of	*davanti*
far	*lontano*
near	*vicino*
opposite	*di fronte a*

Around Town

I'm looking for ...	*Cerco ...*
an ATM	*un bancomat*
a bank	*un banco*
the church	*la chiesa*
the city centre	*il centro (città)*
my hotel	*mio albergo*
the market	*il mercato*
the museum	*il museo*
the post office	*la posta*
a public toilet	*un gabinetto/ bagno pubblico*

| the telephone centre | *il centro telefonico* |
| the tourist office | *l'ufficio di turismo/ d'informazione* |

I want to change ...	*Voglio cambiare ...*
money	*denaro*
travellers cheques	*degli assegni per viaggiatori*

beach	*la spiaggia*
bridge	*il ponte*
castle	*il castello*
cathedral	*il duomo/la cattedrale*
island	*l'isola*
main square	*la piazza principale*
market	*il mercato*
old city	*il centro storico*
palace	*il palazzo*
ruins	*le rovine*
square	*la piazza*
tower	*la torre*

Accommodation

I'm looking for ...	*Cerco ...*
a guesthouse	*una pensione*
a hotel	*un albergo*
a youth hostel	*un ostello per la gioventù*
a room in a private house	*una camera in una casa privata*

Where is a cheap hotel?	*Dov'è un albergo che costa poco?*
What is the address?	*Cos'è l'indirizzo?*
Could you write the address, please?	*Può scrivere l'indirizzo, per favore?*
Do you have any rooms available?	*Ha camere libere/C'è una camera libera?*

I'd like ...	*Vorrei ...*
a bed	*un letto*
a single room	*una camera singola*
a double room	*una camera matrimoniale*
a room with two beds	*una camera doppia*
a room with a bathroom	*una camera con bagno*
to share a dorm	*un letto in dormitorio*

How much is it ...?	*Quanto costa ...?*
per night	*per la notte*
per person	*per ciascuno?*

May I see it?	*Posso vederla?*
Where is the bathroom?	*Dov'è il bagno?*
I'm/We're leaving today.	*Parto/Partiamo oggi.*

Shopping

I'd like to buy ...	*Vorrei comprare ...*
How much is it?	*Quanto costa?*
I (don't) like it.	*(Non) Mi piace.*
May I look at it?	*Posso dare un'occhiata?*
I'm just looking.	*Sto solo guardando.*
It's cheap.	*Non è caro/a.*
It's too expensive.	*È troppo caro/a.*
I'll take it.	*Lo/La prendo.*

Do you accept ...	*Accettate ...?*
credit cards	*carte di credito*
travellers cheques	*assegni per viaggiatori?*

more	*più*
less	*meno*
smaller	*più piccolo/a*
bigger	*più grande*

Time & Dates

What time is it?	*Che ora è?*
	Che ore sono?
It's (8 o'clock).	*Sono (le otto).*
in the morning	*di mattina*
in the afternoon	*di pomeriggio*
in the evening	*di sera*
When?	*Quando?*
today	*oggi*
tomorrow	*domani*
yesterday	*ieri*

Monday	*lunedì*
Tuesday	*martedì*
Wednesday	*mercoledì*
Thursday	*giovedì*
Friday	*venerdì*
Saturday	*sabato*
Sunday	*domenica*

January	*gennaio*
February	*febbraio*
March	*marzo*
April	*aprile*
May	*maggio*
June	*giugno*
July	*luglio*
August	*agosto*
September	*settembre*

Emergencies

Help!	Aiuto!
Call ... !	Chiami ... !
	Chiama ... ! (inf)
a doctor	un dottore/
	un medico
the police	la polizia
There's been an	C'è stato un
accident	incidente!
I'm lost.	Mi sono perso/a.
Go away!	Lasciami in pace!
	Vai via! (inf)

October	ottobre
November	novembre
December	dicembre

Numbers

0	zero
1	uno
2	due
3	tre
4	quattro
5	cinque
6	sei
7	sette
8	otto
9	nove
10	dieci
11	undici
12	dodici
13	tredici
14	quattordici
15	quindici
16	sedici
17	diciassette
18	diciotto
19	diciannove
20	venti
21	ventuno
22	ventidue
30	trenta
31	trentuna
40	quaranta
50	cinquanta
60	sessanta
70	settanta
80	ottanta
90	novanta
100	cento
1000	mille
2000	due mila

one million	un milione

Health

I'm ill.	Mi sento male.
It hurts here.	Mi fa male qui.
I'm ...	Sono ...
asthmatic	asmatico/a
diabetic	diabetico/a
epileptic	epilettico/a
I'm allergic ...	Sono allergico/a ...
to antibiotics	agli antibiotici
to penicillin	alla penicillina
antiseptic	antisettico
aspirin	aspirina
condoms	preservativi
contraceptive	anticoncezionale
diarrhoea	diarrea
medicine	medicina
sunblock cream	crema/latte solare
	(per protezione)
tampons	tamponi

FOOD

This glossary is intended as a brief guide to some of the basics and by no means covers all of the dishes you're likely to encounter in Sardinia. For information on Sardinian food and drink specialities, see the special section 'Out to Lunch in Sardinia'.

Most travellers to the region will already be well acquainted with the various Italian pastas, which include spaghetti, fettuccine, penne, rigatoni, gnocchi, lasagne, tortellini and ravioli. The names are the same throughout Italy and no further definitions are given here.

Basics

breakfast	(prima) colazione
lunch	pranzo
dinner	cena
restaurant	ristorante
grocery shop	alimentari
What is this?	(Che) cos'è?
I would like the set menu.	Vorrei il menù turistico
Is service included in the bill?	È compreso il servizio?
I'm a vegetarian	Sono vegetariano/a

Useful Words

affumicato	smoked
al dente	firm (as all good pasta should be)

alla brace	cooked over hot coals
alla griglia	grilled
arrosto	roasted
ben cotto	well done (cooked)
bollito	boiled
cameriere/a	waiter/waitress
coltello	knife
conto	bill/cheque
cotto	cooked
crudo	raw
cucchiaino	teaspoon
cucchiaio	spoon
forchetta	fork
fritto	fried
menù	menu
piatto	plate

Staples & Condiments

aceto	vinegar
burro	butter
formaggio	cheese
limone	lemon
marmellata	jam
miele	honey
olio	oil
olive	olives
pane	bread
panna	cream
pepe	pepper
peperoncino	chilli
polenta	cooked cornmeal
riso	rice
risotto	rice cooked with wine and stock
sale	salt
uovo/uova	egg/eggs
zucchero	sugar

Meat & Fish

acciughe	anchovies
agnello	lamb
aragosta	lobster
bistecca	steak
calamari	squid
coniglio	rabbit
cotoletta	cutlet or thin cut of meat, usually crumbed and fried
cozze	mussels
dentice	dentex (type of fish)
fegato	liver
gamberi	prawns
granchio	crab
manzo	beef
ostriche	oysters
pesce spada	swordfish

pollo	chicken
polpo	octopus
salsiccia	sausage
sarde	sardines
sgombro	mackerel
sogliola	sole
tonno	tuna
trippa	tripe
vitello	veal
vongole	clams

Vegetables

asparagi	asparagus
carciofi	artichokes
carote	carrots
cavolo/verza	cabbage
cicoria	chicory
cipolla	onion
fagiolini	string beans
melanzane	aubergines
patate	potatoes
peperoni	capsicum, peppers
piselli	peas
spinaci	spinach

Fruit

arance	oranges
banane	bananas
ciliegie	cherries
fragole	strawberries
mele	apples
pere	pears
pesche	peaches
uva	grapes

Soups & Antipasti

brodo – broth
carpaccio – very fine slices of raw meat
caponata – sweet-and-sour dish of tomatoes aubergines, anchovies and olives
insalata caprese – sliced tomatoes with mozzarella and basil
insalata di mare – seafood, generally crustaceans
minestrina in brodo – pasta in broth
minestrone – vegetable soup
olive ascolane – stuffed, deep-fried olives
prosciutto e melone – cured ham with melon
ripieni – stuffed, oven-baked vegetables
stracciatella – egg in broth

Pasta Sauces

alla matriciana – tomato and bacon
al ragù – meat sauce (bolognese)
all'arrabbiata – tomato and chilli
alla carbonara – egg, bacon and pepper

napoletana – tomato and basil

con panna – cream, prosciutto and sometimes peas

pesto – basil, garlic and oil; often with pine nuts

alle vongole – clams, garlic and oil; sometimes with tomato

Pizzas

All pizzas listed have a tomato (and sometimes mozzarella) base.

capricciosa – olives, prosciutto, mushrooms and artichokes

frutti di mare – seafood

funghi – mushrooms

margherita – oregano

napoletana – anchovies

pugliese – tomato, mozzarella and onions

quattro formaggi – with four types of cheese

quattro stagioni – like a capricciosa, but sometimes with egg

verdura – mixed vegetables

Glossary

AAST – Azienda Autonoma di Soggiorno e Turismo (tourist office)
ACI – Automobile Club Italiano, the Italian automobile club
aereo – aeroplane
affittacamere – rooms for rent in a private house
affresco – fresco; the painting method in which watercolour paint is applied to wet plaster
agriturismo – tourist accommodation on farms
AIG – Associazione Italiana Alberghi per la Gioventù, Italy's youth hostel association
albergo – hotel (up to five stars)
alimentari – grocery shop
alto – high
ambulanza – ambulance
anfiteatro – amphitheatre
appartamento – apartment, flat
apse – domed or arched semicircular recess at the altar end of a church
arco – arch
assicurato/a – insured
atrium – forecourt of a Roman house or a Christian basilica
autobus – local bus
autostazione – bus station/terminal
autostop – hitchhiking
autostrada – freeway, motorway

bagno – bathroom; also toilet
baldacchino – canopy supported by columns over the altar in a church
basilica – in ancient Rome, a building used for public administration, with a rectangular hall flanked by aisles and an apse at the end; later, a Christian church built in the same style
battistero – baptistry
benzina – petrol
bicicletta – bicycle
biglietteria – ticket office
biglietto – ticket
binario – platform
borgo – ancient town or village
busta – envelope

camera – room
camera doppia – double room with twin beds

camera matrimoniale – double room with a double bed
camera singola – single room
campanile – bell tower
cappella – chapel
carabinieri – military police (see *polizia*)
carta telefonica – phonecard
cartoleria – paper-goods shop
cartolina (postale) – postcard
castello – castle
cattedrale – cathedral
cena – evening meal
centro – centre
centro storico – (literally, historical centre) old town
chiesa – church
chiostro – cloister; covered walkway, enclosed by columns, around a quadrangle
cin cin – cheers (a drinking toast)
Cinquecento – 16th century
circo – oval or circular arena
CIT – Compagnia Italiana di Turismo, the Italian national tourist/travel agency
codice fiscale – tax number
colazione – breakfast
colonna – column
comune – equivalent to a municipality or county; town or city council; historically, a *commune* (self-governing town or city)
coperto – cover charge
corso – main street, avenue
cortile – courtyard
CTS – Centro Turistico Studentesco e Giovanile, the student/youth travel agency
cumbessias – simple pilgrims' lodgings found in courtyards around certain country churches traditionally the scene of annual religious festivities (of up to nine days' duration) in honour of a particular saint
cupola – dome

deposito bagagli – left luggage
digestivo – after-dinner liqueur
distributore di benzina – petrol pump (see *stazione di servizio*)
domus de janas – 'fairy house', actually ancient tombs cut into the rock
duomo – cathedral

ENIT – Ente Nazionale Italiano per il Turismo, the Italian state tourist office

espresso – express mail; express train; short black coffee

farmacia – pharmacy
farmacia di turno – late-night pharmacy
fassois – traditional rush fishing vessels from Oristano province
ferrovia – railway
festa – festival
fiume – (main) river
fontana – fountain
foro – forum
francobollo – postage stamp
fresco – see *affresco*
funicolare – funicular railway
funivia – cable car

gabinetto – toilet
golfo – gulf
grotta – cave

isola – island

lago – lake
largo – (small) square
lavanderia – laundrette
lavasecco – dry-cleaning
lettera – letter
lettera raccomandata – registered letter
lungomare – seafront road; promenade

macchia – Mediterranean scrub
mare – sea
mercato – market
monte – mountain, mount
motorino – moped
municipio – town hall
muristenes – see *cumbessias*
murra – a popular game in the Barbagia region, in which participants try to guess what numbers their opponents will form with their fingers

navata centrale – nave; central part of a church
navata laterale – aisle of a church
nave – ship
necropolis – (ancient) cemetery, burial site
nuraghe – Bronze-Age stone towers and fortified settlements

oggetti smarriti – lost property
ospedale – hospital
ostello – hostel
osteria – snack bar/cheap restaurant

pacco – package, parcel
palazzo – palace; a large building of any type, including an apartment block
panino – bread roll with filling
parco – park
passaggio ponte – deck class
passeggiata – traditional evening stroll
pasta – the widely known (and loved) staple made from a mix of flour, water and sometimes egg; also a cake, pastry or dough
pasticceria – shop selling cakes, pastries and biscuits
pensione – small hotel, often with board
permesso di soggiorno – residence permit
piazza – square
piazzale – (large) open square
pietà – (literally, pity or compassion) sculpture, drawing or painting of the dead Christ supported by the Madonna
polizia – police
poltrona – (literally, armchair) airline-type chair on a ferry
polyptych – altarpiece consisting of more than three panels (see *triptych*)
ponte – bridge
portico – portico; covered walkway, usually attached to the outside of buildings
porto – port
posta aerea – air mail
presepio – nativity scene
pronto soccorso – first aid, casualty ward
pullman – long-distance bus
Punic – adjective often used to mean Carthaginian (ie, the Punic Wars were those fought between Rome and Carthage)

Quattrocento – 15th century
questura – police station

rio – secondary river
rocca – fortress

sagra – festival (usually dedicated to one culinary item, such as *funghi* (mushrooms), wine etc)
salumeria – delicatessen that sells mainly cheeses and sausage meats
santuario – sanctuary, often with a country chapel
scalette – 'little stairs' (as in Scalette di Santa Chiara, a rather steep stairway up into Cagliari's Castello district)
scavi – excavations
scheda telefonica – see *carta telefonica*
Seicento – 17th century

servizio – service fee
S'Istrumpa – Sardinian wrestling
spiaggia – beach
stagno – lagoon
stazione – station
stazione di servizio – service/petrol station
stazione marittima – ferry terminal
stazzo/u – farmstead in the Gallura region of Sardinia
strada – street, road
superstrada – expressway; highway with divided lanes (but no tolls)

teatro – theatre
telegramma – telegram
tempio – temple
terme – thermal baths
tesoro – treasury
tetrastyle – four columns forming a square
tholos – name used to describe the conical shape of many nuraghes.
tomba di giganti – 'giants' tomb', ancient mass grave

tophet – sacred ground where it is thought the Carthaginians cremated the bodies of young children who died prematurely
torre – tower
torrente – stream
traghetto – ferry
tramezzini – sandwiches
trattoria – restaurant
treno – train
triptych – painting or carving on three panels, hinged so that the outer panels fold over the middle one, often used as an altarpiece (see *polyptych*)
trompe l'oeil – painting or other illustration designed to 'deceive the eye', creating the impression that the image is real

ufficio stranieri – (police) foreigners' bureau

via – street, road
via aerea – air mail
villa – townhouse or country house; also the park surrounding the house

LONELY PLANET

You already know that Lonely Planet produces more than this one guidebook, but you might not be aware of the other products we have on this region. Here is a selection of titles that you may want to check out as well:

Rome Condensed
ISBN 1 74104 150 3
US$11.99 • UK£6.99

Italian Phrasebook
ISBN 1 86450 317 3
US$7.99 • UK£3.99

Italy
ISBN 1 86450 352 1
US$24.99 • UK£14.99

Rome
ISBN 1 86450 311 4
US$15.99 • UK£9.99

World Food Italy
ISBN 1 86450 022 0
US$12.95 • UK£7.99

Europe on a Shoestring
ISBN 1 74059 314 6
US$24.99 • UK£14.99

Tuscany
ISBN 1 86450 357 2
US$17.99 • UK£10.99

Florence
ISBN 1 74059 030 9
US$17.99 • UK£8.99

Sicily
ISBN 1 74059 031 7
US$16.99 • UK£10.99

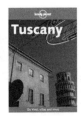

Venice
ISBN 1 86450 321 1
US$15.99 • UK£8.99

Walking in Italy
ISBN 1 74059 244 1
US$19.99 • UK£12.99

Available wherever books are sold

Index

Text

Bold indicates maps.

Boxed Text

MAP LEGEND

CITY ROUTES

Freeway	Freeway
Highway	Primary Road
Road	Secondary Road
Street	Street
Lane	Lane
	On/Off Ramp

Unsealed Road	
One-Way Street	
Pedestrian Street	
Stepped Street	
Tunnel	
Footbridge	

REGIONAL ROUTES

Tollway; Freeway	
Primary Road	
Secondary Road	
Minor Road	

BOUNDARIES

International	
State	
Cliff	
Fortified Wall	

HYDROGRAPHY

River; Creek	
Canal	
Lake	

Dry Lake; Salt Lake	
Spring; Rapids	
Waterfalls	

TRANSPORT ROUTES & STATIONS

Train	Ferry/Jetty
Underground Train	Walking Trail
Metro	Walking Tour
Tramway	Bicycle Track
Cable Car; Chairlift	Pier or Jetty

AREA FEATURES

Building	Market
Park; Gardens	Sports Ground

Beach	Campus
Cemetery	Plaza

POPULATION SYMBOLS

○ **CAPITAL**	National Capital	● **CITY**	City	● Village	Village
◉ **CAPITAL**	State Capital	● **Town**	Town		Urban Area

MAP SYMBOLS

■	Place to Stay	▼ Place to Eat	● Point of Interest

Airfield		Castle		Internet Café	Ruins
Airport		Cave		Monument	Spring
Bank		Church; Cathedral		Mountain	Stately Building
Bar		Cinema		Museum	Taxi Rank
Bus Stop		Embassy; Consulate		National Park	Theatre
Bus Terminal		Garden		Police Station	Tourist Information
Camping Ground		Hospital; Clinic		Post Office	Tomb

Note: not all symbols displayed above appear in this book

LONELY PLANET OFFICES

Australia
Locked Bag 1, Footscray, Victoria 3011
☎ 03 8379 8000 fax 03 8379 8111
email: talk2us@lonelyplanet.com.au

UK
72-82 Rosebery Ave, London, EC1R 4RW
☎ 44 20 7841 9000 fax 44 20 7841 9001
email: go@lonelyplanet.co.uk

USA
150 Linden St, Oakland, CA 94607
☎ 510 893 8555 TOLL FREE: 800 275 8555
fax 510 893 8572
email: info@lonelyplanet.com

France
1 rue du Dahomey, 75011 Paris
☎ 01 55 25 33 00 fax 01 55 25 33 01
email: bip@lonelyplanet.fr
www.lonelyplanet.fr

World Wide Web: www.lonelyplanet.com *or* AOL keyword: lp
Lonely Planet Images: www.lonelyplanetimages.com